The Future of Finance with ChatGPT and Power BI

Transform your trading, investing, and financial reporting with ChatGPT and Power BI

James Bryant

Aloke Mukherjee

BIRMINGHAM—MUMBAI

The Future of Finance with ChatGPT and Power BI

Group Product Manager: Niranjan Naikwadi
Publishing Product Manager: Nitin Nainani
Senior Editor: Aamir Ahmed, Nathanya Dias
Book Project Manager: Aishwarya Mohan
Technical Editor: K Bimala Singha
Copy Editor: Safis Editing
Proofreader: Safis Editing
Indexer: Manju Arasan
Production Designer: Aparna Bhagat
DevRel Marketing Coordinator: Nivedita Pandey, Anamika Singh

First published: December 2023

Production reference: 1011223

Published by Packt Publishing Ltd.
Grosvenor House
11 St Paul's Square
Birmingham
B3 1RB, UK

ISBN 978-1-80512-334-7

www.packtpub.com

To my wife, Kathy – thank you for being the rock on which I could always lean. To my daughter, Avery – you inspire me daily with your curiosity and zest for life; keep seeking, and you will find wonderful adventures await you.

To my sister, Jennifer, and my parents, Joe and Judy – thank you for instilling in me the values of hard work and perseverance, and for always being there with words of wisdom and guidance.

– James Bryant

This book would not have been possible without the patience and understanding of my partner, Sangita Patel, and my mother, Ila Mukherjee. Thanks for all the support.

– Aloke Mukherjee

Contributors

About the authors

James Bryant stands at the intersection of finance and technology, a seasoned expert with a track record that spans finance automation, risk management, investments, trading, and banking. He's not just known for his expertise but also his knack for staying ahead of trends, consistently embracing innovations that redefine the financial landscape at companies such as Salesforce, Cisco WebEx, Verizon, and Stanford Health Care.

His crowning achievements include building corporate treasuries for giants such as Salesforce from scratch and pioneering digital transformation at Stanford Health Care. Notably, during the COVID-19 market disruption, James pivoted from declining investments and executed trades that garnered significant gains.

"Ask, and it will be given you; Seek, and you will find; Knock, and the door will be opened to you."

– Matthew 7:7

This verse has been the driving force behind my incessant pursuit of knowledge and understanding in the intricate worlds of finance and technology. It has guided me to keep seeking, keep questioning, and keep knocking on the doors of opportunity.

Thanks to Packt Publishing for nurturing this vision into a powerful narrative.

Aloke Mukherjee is a seasoned technologist boasting over a decade of hands-on experience in bridging the gap between business and technology. Specializing in business architecture, digital transformation, and solutions design, he has a proven track record of driving measurable results across various industry verticals.

After distinguished tenures at EMC Corp and Genentech, Aloke has transitioned into a pivotal role at Stanford Health Care. As a key player in the finance business intelligence initiative, he is tasked with steering the organization toward a unified, data-centric platform. His leadership and expertise are instrumental in transforming the way data drives decision-making processes across financial sectors within the healthcare environment.

I'd like to extend my heartfelt thanks to everyone who contributed to the success of this book. The journey of writing it has been both challenging and rewarding, made easier by the collaborative spirit and collective intelligence of the team. I would like to thank Matt Potts for reading through the chapters and providing a great critique.

Special thanks to our senior editor, Aamir Ahmed, and the staff at Packt Publishing for their professionalism and commitment.

About the reviewers

Mubeen Bhatti stands out in the finance industry, with almost 20 years of leadership in project and product management. Adept at steering key initiatives in risk management and strategic planning, he skillfully navigates complex scenarios, driving innovation and growth. His leadership has enhanced team efficiency and client relationships, underpinned by his expertise in Python, R, and various financial models. A Wharton-certified leader, Mubeen excels in fostering collaborative and high-performing teams.

Divit Gupta is a seasoned IT professional with 20 years of industry expertise, who excels in driving strategic architecture initiatives and providing leadership in multi-pillar sales cycles. With a global impact, he spearheads technical partnerships, defines team vision, and champions new strategic endeavors.

As the host of popular podcasts such as *Tech Talk with Divit*, *Live Labs with Divit*, and *Cloud Bites with Divit*, he showcases Oracle's technological initiatives and leadership. In 2022–2023, he served as Oracle TV's correspondent for *CloudWorld*. His passion for knowledge sharing extends to international conference talks, technical blogs, and multiple books on emerging technologies.

A recognized expert, Divit presented on the subject of Oracle database technology at Oracle CloudWorld FY 2023. Holding over 40 certifications from Microsoft, Oracle, AWS, and Databricks, he remains at the forefront of technology.

Table of Contents

Part 1: From Financial Fundamentals to Frontier Tech: Navigating the New Paradigms of Data, EVs, and AgTech

1

Financial Mastery with ChatGPT: From Basics to AI Insights   3

2

Creating Financial Narratives with Power BI and ChatGPT   33

3

Tesla's Financial Journey: AI Analysis and Bias Unveiled   59

4

John Deere's AgTech Revolution – AI Insights and Challenges   109

Part 2: Pioneers and Protectors: AI Transformations in Software, Finance, Biotech, and Cybersecurity

5

Salesforce Reimagined: Navigating Software and LLMs   167

6

SVB's Downfall and Ethical AI: Smart AI Regulation   213

7

Moderna and OpenAI – Biotech and AGI Breakthroughs   267

8

CrowdStrike: Cybersecurity in the Era of Deepfakes   327

Preface

The world of finance is undergoing a radical transformation, driven by the rapid advances in artificial intelligence and data analytics. The emergence of large language models, such as ChatGPT, has opened up new possibilities to generate insights, narratives, and predictions from massive amounts of financial data. The integration of these models with powerful visualization tools, such as Power BI, has enabled the creation of compelling financial stories that can inform, persuade, and inspire audiences across various domains and industries.

This book is designed to help you master the skills and knowledge needed to harness the power of ChatGPT and Power BI for your financial endeavors. Whether you are a trader, an investor, a financial analyst, a journalist, or a student, you will find this book to be a valuable resource to enhance your financial literacy and acumen. You will learn how to use ChatGPT and Power BI to analyze financial data, generate insights, craft narratives, and communicate effectively with your stakeholders. You will also learn how to evaluate the quality, reliability, and ethics of AI-generated output, and how to avoid potential pitfalls and biases that may arise from using large language models.

Who this book is for

The best audience for this book is anyone who is interested in learning how to use artificial intelligence and data visualization to enhance their financial skills and knowledge. The book is suitable for both beginners and experts, as it covers a wide range of topics and applications, from the basics of ChatGPT and Power BI to the advanced challenges and opportunities of AI in finance. The book is also relevant for anyone who wants to explore the fascinating stories and insights behind various industries and sectors, such as electric vehicles, agriculture, software, banking, biotechnology, and cybersecurity. The book is written in an engaging and accessible style, with plenty of examples, exercises, and tips to help you master the concepts and techniques. The book is a must-read for anyone who wants to transform their financial analysis, reporting, and decision-making with ChatGPT and Power BI.

What this book covers

The book is divided into two parts, each consisting of four chapters that cover different aspects of finance and technology.

In *Part 1*, you will explore the fundamentals of ChatGPT and Power BI, and how they can be used to create financial mastery. You will also dive into the exciting domains of the electric vehicle industry and the agricultural technology revolution, learning how ChatGPT and Power BI can help you uncover the stories behind the numbers.

This section contains the following chapters.

Chapter 1, Financial Mastery with ChatGPT: From Basics to AI Insights: is your gateway from fundamental concepts to revolutionary AI insights.

Chapter 1 serves as your comprehensive gateway into the world of finance and investment, equipped for both novices and seasoned investors. Dive into essential financial concepts, demystify financial statements, and grasp the critical metrics that matter. Discover how cutting-edge technology such as ChatGPT revolutionizes traditional financial analysis, offering a more efficient and insightful approach to making smart investment choices.

Chapter 2, Creating Financial Narratives with Power BI and ChatGPT: unveils stories through Power BI and ChatGPT insights.

Chapter 2 allows you to unlock the power of data-driven decision-making in finance, providing a focused guide on leveraging Microsoft Power BI and ChatGPT insights. Discover how to create compelling financial dashboards, optimize data modeling, and integrate ChatGPT's predictive capabilities to illuminate trends, spot opportunities, and drive growth. Learn how to merge the visual strengths of Power BI with the analytical acumen of ChatGPT, and explore the best practices to elevate your financial analyses to new heights.

Chapter 3, Tesla's Financial Journey: AI Analysis and Bias Unveiled: we see Tesla's financial saga through the lens of AI and unraveling the maze of AI Bias.

Chapter 3 dives into the transformative impact of ChatGPT and AI on financial analysis, focusing on Tesla and the EV industry. We explore unconventional data sources and redefine performance metrics, while also leveraging AI to dissect news sentiment and earnings call transcripts for predictive insights. Through a blend of traditional and AI-driven tools, we offer a comprehensive guide to trading strategies, bias mitigation in AI models, and vivid Power BI visualizations that dissect Tesla's growth and market positioning.

Chapter 4, John Deere's AgTech Revolution – AI Insights and Challenges: pioneering technology in the fields and unveiling the mysteries of large language model hallucinations.

Chapter 4 takes you on a technological journey through the world of agriculture, spotlighting John Deere as a case in point for digital transformation and investment potential. We dive deep into AgTech, AI-driven financial analysis, and innovative trading strategies, all brought to life through vivid Power BI visualizations. We harness the power of autonomous AI and weather-based trading, and we provide a cutting-edge playbook to invest in the agri-business sector.

In *Part 2*, you will discover how ChatGPT and Power BI can be applied to various industry giants in the software, banking, biotechnology, and cybersecurity sectors. You will also learn how to navigate the challenges and opportunities that arise from the intersection of AI and finance, such as ethical AI, artificial general intelligence, deepfakes, and indirect prompt injection.

This section contains the following chapters.

Chapter 5, Salesforce Reimagined: Navigating Software and LLMs: we navigate the software industry while deciphering open source and proprietary Large Language Models (LLMs). It highlights Salesforce's extraordinary turnaround, examining each pivotal moment, from detecting the initial downtrend to ultimately igniting a new era powered by artificial intelligence. You will gain an expansive view, exploring topics such as market sentiment analysis, option trading strategies, and the impact of AI. The chapter culminates in a comprehensive discussion on the future of open-source and proprietary **Large Language Models (LLMs)**, offering actionable insights for finance professionals looking to navigate this evolving landscape.

Chapter 6, SVB's Downfall and Ethical AI: Smart AI Regulation: steering smart regulation in the new financial era. It takes an analytical deep-dive into the downfall of Silicon Valley Bank and explores broader themes of data-driven trading strategies and AI's role in financial oversight. You'll be guided through AI-driven bank regulation with the persona `BankRegulatorGPT`, all visualized compellingly through Power BI dashboards. The chapter concludes by laying down the urgent need for smart AI regulation, presenting both a comprehensive timeline and a call for global cooperation to safeguard the future of finance.

Chapter 7, Moderna and OpenAI – Biotech and AGI Breakthroughs: pioneering biotech innovations and unveiling AGI's potential. It embarks on a robust investment guide through Moderna Momentum, a sentiment-sensitive stock strategy, presented visually using Power BI and ChatGPT insights. As the narrative unfolds, you'll encounter AI personas such as `FoodandDrugAdminGPT` and cutting-edge AGI initiatives from OpenAI, wrapping up with an eye-opening discussion on the future alignment and principles of AGI in finance.

Chapter 8, CrowdStrike: Cybersecurity in the Era of Deepfakes: AI literacy in an era of deepfakes and indirect prompt injection. It takes you on a journey through the cutting-edge intersection of finance and cybersecurity, spotlighting the game-changing implications of GPT-4 and deepfakes. Navigate the ethical maze of indirect prompt injections in LLMs, and arm yourself with AI literacy tailored for finance pros and enthusiasts alike. From CrowdStrike's revolutionary threat management to the transformative power of HackerGPT, the chapter offers both cautionary tales and empowering insights into today's digital financial landscape.

By the end of this book, you will have gained a comprehensive understanding of how ChatGPT and Power BI can transform your financial analysis, reporting, and decision-making. You will also have developed a critical mindset that can help you evaluate the strengths and limitations of AI in finance. You will be equipped with the tools and techniques to create your own financial stories that can captivate and influence your audience. You will be ready to embrace the future of finance with ChatGPT and Power BI.

To get the most out of this book

To get the most value from this book, read through the introductory material and then follow on with the use cases listed. We recommend copying the code and running it on your own. This provides valuable hands-on experience.

Throughout this book, we use ChatGPT, Python, and Power BI, so it is a good idea to have these available for the code examples.

Here are a few recommended steps to set up ChatGPT, Python, and Power BI:

Install Python and enable Python in Power BI:

1. First, install Python, if you have not done so already. Visit the official website (`https://www.python.org/downloads/`) for your download. We recommend versions 3.9 or 3.10.

2. After Python has installed, enable Python scripting in Power BI. Open the Power BI desktop. Click **File | Options and settings | Options | Python scripting**. Select the checkbox and **OK**.

3. Then, set the Python path in Power BI. Go to **File | Options and settings | Options | Python scripting**, and then click on **Detect**. This selects the Python installation path automatically. You can also do this manually by clicking on the ellipsis (**...**) and selecting the Python executable file.

4. Restart the Power BI desktop for the changes you made to take effect.

Setting up ChatGPT using ChatGPT API:

1. First, you will need to obtain an API key from OpenAI. Navigate to the OpenAI website (`https://openai.com`) and create a (personal) account.

2. Then, request and get an API key. Use this in all your integration projects.

> **Tip**
> These API keys are not free. When you sign up with OpenAI, you get about $18 worth of tokens for use with your API key. After that, it is billed (pay as you go). The details are available on the OpenAI site under **Pricing** (`https://openai.com/pricing`).

3. The ChatGPT API has SDKs and libraries available in several programming languages. Select Python. We use Python extensively in this book and recommend it.

4. Install the SDK with a package manager such as `pip`.

We assume you are running Windows 10 or any version after on your device. Although the code has been tested, the installations might be slightly different for Linux, Chrome, and macOS. There are no known issues with installations. You will also need a stable robust browser (MS Edge or similar is recommended).

If you are using the digital version of this book, we advise you to type the code yourself or access the code from the book's GitHub repository (a link is available in the next section). Doing so will help you avoid any potential errors related to the copying and pasting of code.

Download the example code files

You can download the example code files for this book from GitHub at `https://github.com/PacktPublishing/The-Future-of-Finance-with-ChatGPT-and-PowerBI`. If there's an update to the code, it will be updated in the GitHub repository.

We also have other code bundles from our rich catalog of books and videos available at `https://github.com/PacktPublishing/`. Check them out!

Conventions used

There are a number of text conventions used throughout this book.

`Code in text`: Indicates code words in text, database table names, folder names, filenames, file extensions, pathnames, dummy URLs, user input, and Twitter (now X) handles. Here is an example: "The `fetch_data` function will print all the entries in the database."

A block of code is set as follows:

```
from sklearn.model_selection import train_test_split

X = df['article']
y = df['sentiment']

X_train, X_test, y_train, y_test = train_test_split(X, y, test_
size=0.2, random_state=42)
```

Any command-line input or output is written as follows:

```
$ mkdir AutoGPT
$ cd AutoGPT
```

Bold: Indicates a new term, an important word, or words that you see on screen. For instance, words in menus or dialog boxes appear in **bold**. Here is an example: "Open the Power BI desktop and click on **Home** in the ribbon at the top."

> Tips or important notes
> Appear like this.

Get in touch

Feedback from our readers is always welcome.

General feedback: If you have questions about any aspect of this book, email us at `customercare@packtpub.com` and mention the book title in the subject of your message.

Share Your Thoughts

Once you've read *The Future of Finance with ChatGPT and Power BI*, we'd love to hear your thoughts! Scan the QR code below to go straight to the Amazon review page for this book and share your feedback.

`https://packt.link/r/1-805-12109-X`

Your review is important to us and the tech community and will help us make sure we're delivering excellent quality content.

Download a free PDF copy of this book

Thanks for purchasing this book!

Do you like to read on the go but are unable to carry your print books everywhere? Is your eBook purchase not compatible with the device of your choice?

Don't worry, now with every Packt book you get a DRM-free PDF version of that book at no cost.

Read anywhere, any place, on any device. Search, copy, and paste code from your favorite technical books directly into your application.

The perks don't stop there, you can get exclusive access to discounts, newsletters, and great free content in your inbox daily

Follow these simple steps to get the benefits:

1. Scan the QR code or visit the link below

https://packt.link/free-ebook/9781805123347

2. Submit your proof of purchase
3. That's it! We'll send your free PDF and other benefits to your email directly

Part 1:
From Financial Fundamentals to Frontier Tech: Navigating the New Paradigms of Data, EVs, and AgTech

In *Part 1*, prepare to embark on a groundbreaking journey through the modern landscapes of finance and technology. Beginning with a foundational exploration in *Chapter 1*, we lay the baseline for a deep understanding of ChatGPT's transformative role in financial analysis, setting the stage for a revolutionary shift from conventional approaches to AI-enhanced insights. The journey continues in *Chapter 2*, where you will learn the art of crafting compelling financial narratives through the synergy of Power BI and ChatGPT insights, offering a fresh perspective on financial storytelling. In *Chapter 3*, the spotlight shifts to the exhilarating world of the EV industry, offering a deep dive into Tesla's financial saga, discerned through the lens of AI, while also unraveling the critical nuances of AI bias. Lastly, *Chapter 4* takes you to the heart of the AgTech renaissance, pioneering the harmonization of technology and agriculture with a focus on John Deere's initiatives, coupled with an educational unraveling of the complexities surrounding large language model hallucinations. Equip yourself with the knowledge to navigate the dynamic intersection of finance and technology, as you forge your path toward financial mastery with perspectives enriched by ChatGPT.

This part contains the following chapters:

- *Chapter 1, Financial Mastery with ChatGPT: From Basics to AI Insights*
- *Chapter 2, Creating Financial Narratives with Power BI and ChatGPT*
- *Chapter 3, Tesla's Financial Journey: AI Analysis and Bias Unveiled*
- *Chapter 4, John Deere's AgTech Revolution – AI Insights and Challenges*

1

Financial Mastery with ChatGPT: From Basics to AI Insights

Everyone is looking for a competitive edge in finance, which demands a deep understanding of financial concepts and the ability to harness cutting-edge tools. This book's journey begins by establishing a strong foundation in investing, trading, and financial analysis while introducing the groundbreaking potential of **artificial intelligence (AI)**, particularly ChatGPT, to revolutionize the way we approach financial decision-making.

The traditional methods of financial analysis have long been the cornerstone of investment and trading strategies. However, with the advent of AI and **large language models (LLMs)** such as ChatGPT, we now have the opportunity to harness the power of technology to enhance these traditional techniques, providing deeper insights and greater precision in our assessments.

In this first chapter, we will lay the groundwork for our exploration of finance by covering key financial concepts, investment principles, and types of financial assets. We will also dive into the basics of financial statements, ratios, and metrics, and explore the complementary roles of fundamental and technical analysis. This will set the stage for our exciting journey into the world of ChatGPT and its potential to transform the financial landscape. Readers will be introduced to the foundations of financial analysis and the role of AI, specifically ChatGPT, in modern financial analysis techniques. The chapter will begin by discussing the basics of financial analysis, including its purpose, importance, and the key financial statements used for analysis. You will gain an understanding of how to read and interpret balance sheets, income statements, and cash flow statements.

As the chapter progresses, the focus will shift to the potential of AI and ChatGPT in financial analysis, exploring their capabilities and benefits. You will learn how AI-driven tools such as ChatGPT can streamline and enhance financial analysis by automating tasks, providing valuable insights, and reducing human error. The chapter will also cover how to integrate ChatGPT into your financial analysis workflow and effectively use it to analyze financial data and reports.

As we embark on this journey together, you will discover how ChatGPT can quickly analyze and summarize financial information, highlight key trends and insights, and provide valuable context to help you make more informed decisions. This chapter will not only equip you with the essential knowledge to navigate the world of finance but also open the door to the limitless possibilities that AI and ChatGPT offer, in revolutionizing financial analysis and decision-making.

In this chapter, we will cover the following topics:

- An introduction to key financial concepts and investment principles
- Introducing financial statements
- Understanding financial ratios and metrics
- The fundamentals of technical analysis
- Understanding the power of ChatGPT in financial analysis
- Getting started with ChatGPT for finance
- ChatGPT for financial analysis – analyzing earnings reports for Palo Alto Networks
- Combining ChatGPT with fundamental analysis

After completing this chapter, you will be able to do the following:

- Grasp the basics of financial analysis, including its purpose, importance, and key financial statements, equipping you with the essential knowledge to effectively evaluate companies for investment and trading opportunities
- Understand how to read and interpret balance sheets, income statements, and cash flow statements, providing a solid foundation to analyze a company's financial health and make well-informed investment decisions
- Discover the transformative potential of AI and ChatGPT in financial analysis, enabling you to streamline processes, enhance accuracy, and uncover valuable insights not easily accessible through traditional analysis methods
- Learn how to integrate ChatGPT into your financial analysis workflow, empowering you to harness AI-driven insights for improved decision-making and a competitive edge in the world of investing and trading
- Delve into the capabilities and benefits of ChatGPT, exploring how AI-driven tools can automate tasks, reduce human error, and provide a deeper understanding of financial data, ultimately leading to better investment choices and increased profits
- Learn how ChatGPT can reveal hidden trends and insights in financial data, helping investors and traders make informed decisions and maximize profits while staying ahead of the competition
- Get excited about combining advanced financial analysis techniques with AI-driven tools such as ChatGPT for a competitive advantage in investing and trading, optimizing investment strategies, and anticipating market movements

By the end of this chapter, you will have a solid foundation in financial analysis and an understanding of how AI and ChatGPT can transform traditional analysis methods. Armed with this knowledge, you will be well prepared to delve deeper into more advanced financial analysis techniques and further explore the integration of AI and ChatGPT in subsequent chapters.

Technical requirements

Here are the hardware requirements for this chapter:

- A computer with at least 4 GB of RAM (8 GB or more is recommended)
- A stable internet connection to access financial data, news sources, and APIs
- A processor with a minimum of two cores (four cores or more is recommended for efficient computations)

Here are the software requirements for this chapter:

- Python (version 3.11.3 or newer) installed on your computer
- Python libraries such as Requests, Beautiful Soup, and pandas for data analysis, manipulation, and visualization

Here are the APIs and data sources for this chapter:

- An OpenAI API key to access GPT-based models for natural language processing and AI-driven insights
- Financial data APIs, such as Quandl, Alpha Vantage, Intrinio, and Yahoo Finance, to fetch historical stock prices, financial statements, and other relevant data

These technical requirements should provide a solid foundation to perform the tasks outlined in this chapter, including financial analysis and working with Python and the OpenAI API.

An introduction to key financial concepts and investment principles

Welcome to the beginning of your journey into the future of finance, where the power of AI and ChatGPT is at your fingertips. Let's get started!

The learning objectives for this section are as follows:

- Mastering the essential building blocks of finance, such as risk and return, asset allocation, diversification, and the time value of money to confidently evaluate investments and make informed decisions

- Discovering the various investment types, including stocks, bonds, cash, real estate, and commodities, to diversify your portfolio and optimize returns

- Exploring a range of investment strategies, from passive and active investing to value and growth investing, to align with your financial goals, risk tolerance, and investment horizon

- Leveraging your newfound understanding of key financial concepts and principles to build a strong foundation for a successful investment journey and financial future

In the world of finance, several key concepts and principles form the foundation for understanding how to evaluate investments and make informed decisions. In this section, we will introduce you to these essential building blocks, which include concepts such as risk and return, asset allocation, diversification, and the time value of money:

- **Risk and return**: Risk refers to the potential for an investment to lose value, while return represents the potential gain an investor can realize from an investment. Typically, investments with greater risk potential have the opportunity for increased returns, and those with lower risk profiles usually yield comparatively modest returns. Understanding the risk-return trade-off is crucial for investors when making decisions about their investment portfolios.

- **Asset allocation**: This refers to the method of distributing investments among different asset categories (such as equities, fixed income, and cash) to balance risk and reward in line with an investor's objectives, risk appetite, and investment time horizon. A well-structured asset allocation strategy can help investors achieve their financial objectives while managing their exposure to risk.

- **Diversification and the time value of money**:

  - **Diversification**: This investment principle involves spreading investments across multiple assets, industries, or geographical regions to reduce risk. Through diversification, investors can lessen the effects of underperforming assets on their total portfolio, as potential losses from a single investment may be counterbalanced by gains from other investments. Diversification is a vital strategy for long-term investment success.

  - **The time value of money**: The time value of money represents a core principle in finance, recognizing that a dollar obtained today holds greater value than the same dollar received in the future. This is due to factors such as inflation, opportunity cost, and the potential for investments to grow over time. Understanding the time value of money is essential to make informed investment decisions, as it helps investors evaluate the present and future value of investments and compare different investment opportunities.

As we move forward in our exploration of finance, we will dive deeper into the various investment types and strategies, each offering unique opportunities and challenges for investors. In the upcoming section, we will examine the distinct characteristics of common financial assets, such as stocks, bonds, cash and cash equivalents, real estate, and commodities. Furthermore, we will discuss the diverse investment strategies that cater to investors with different financial goals, risk tolerance, and investment horizons, including passive investing, active investing, value investing, and growth investing. By gaining a deeper understanding of these investment types and strategies, you will be better equipped to make informed financial decisions and optimize your investment portfolio.

Basic investment types and investment strategies

Financial assets come in various forms, each with its own risk and return characteristics. Some common investment types include the following:

- **Stocks**: Ownership shares in a company that provide the potential for capital gains and dividend income.

- **Bonds**: These are debt instruments issued by governments or companies that provide periodic interest payments and repay the principal upon reaching the maturity date.

- **Cash and cash equivalents**: These represent safe, liquid, short-term assets, which are cash or similar to cash. These could include savings accounts, certificates of deposit, and money market funds.

- **Real estate**: Investments in physical property, either directly or through vehicles such as **Real Estate Investment Trusts (REITs)**.

- **Commodities**: Investments in raw materials or primary agricultural products, such as gold, oil, or wheat.

Investors can choose from various strategies depending on their financial goals, risk tolerance, and investment horizon. Some common strategies include the following:

- **Passive investing**: An approach that seeks to replicate the performance of a market index or benchmark through low-cost index funds or **Exchange-Traded Funds (ETFs)**

- **Active investing**: A strategy that involves actively selecting and managing individual investments, aiming to outperform the market or a specific benchmark

- **Value investing**: Focuses on identifying undervalued assets that have the potential for long-term growth

- **Growth investing**: Concentrates on investments with high growth potential, even if they are currently overvalued

Understanding these key financial concepts, investment principles, and investment types will help you build a solid foundation to make well-informed financial decisions. In the next section, we will discuss different types of financial assets and their characteristics.

Introducing financial statements

The learning objectives for this section are as follows:

- **Mastering the essentials of financial statements**: Acquire a strong grasp of the three main financial statements – balance sheet, income statement, and cash flow statement – and their vital function in assessing a company's financial well-being and performance

- **Unleashing the potential of balance sheets**: Discover how to examine a company's assets, liabilities, and shareholders' equity to evaluate its financial standing at a particular moment in time

- **Diving deep into income statements**: Discover how to evaluate a company's revenues, expenses, and net income to understand its profitability over a specific period

- **Unraveling the mysteries of cash flow statements**: Develop the skills to analyze cash inflows and outflows from operating, investing, and financing activities to gain insights into a company's liquidity and financial flexibility

Financial statements are essential tools to evaluate the financial health and performance of a company. These documents provide a snapshot of a company's financial position, profitability, and cash flow. There are three primary financial statements:

- **Balance sheet**: This financial document offers a detailed view of a company's assets, liabilities, and shareholders' equity at a particular point in time, illustrating its financial standing. Assets are items of value owned by the company, such as cash, inventory, and property. Liabilities represent the company's obligations, such as loans and accounts payable. Shareholders' equity reflects the residual interest in the company's assets after liabilities have been deducted.

- **Income statement**: Often referred to as the **Profit and Loss (P&L)** statement, this financial document displays a company's revenue, costs, and net income during a specified time frame. Revenue is the income generated through the company's core business operations, while expenses represent the costs associated with generating that income. The net income is calculated as the difference between the revenue and expenses.

- **Cash flow statement**: This financial document monitors the movement of cash into and out of a company over a defined period. It is divided into three sections – operating activities (cash generated or used by the company's core business), investing activities (cash spent or received from investments), and financing activities (cash transactions related to debt and equity).

As we move on to the next section, we will delve into understanding financial ratios and metrics, crucial tools to analyze and interpret a company's financial statements. By examining liquidity, profitability, solvency, and efficiency ratios, we can gain insights into a company's financial performance and stability. Furthermore, we will explore the importance of comparing these ratios against industry benchmarks, historical performance, and competitors, allowing us to make well-informed investment decisions. Stay tuned as we explore the world of financial analysis and unveil the secrets behind successful investing.

Understanding financial ratios and metrics

Financial ratios and metrics are used to analyze and interpret financial statements, providing insights into a company's performance, liquidity, solvency, and efficiency. Some key financial ratios and metrics include the following:

- **Liquidity ratios**: These calculations evaluate a company's capacity to fulfill its short-term financial commitments. Widely used liquidity ratios consist of the current ratio (current assets/current liabilities) and the quick ratio (current assets – inventory/current liabilities).

- **Profitability ratios**: These metrics evaluate a business's capacity to earn profits. Some examples are the gross profit margin (gross profit/revenue), operating margin (operating income/revenue), and net profit margin (net income/revenue).

- **Solvency ratios**: These metrics analyze a firm's capacity to handle long-term commitments and maintain financial stability. Key solvency metrics include the debt-to-equity ratio (total debt/shareholder equity) and the equity ratio (shareholder equity/total assets).

- **Efficiency ratios**: These metrics evaluate the effectiveness of a company's asset utilization and operational management. Some examples are the turnover of the inventory ratio (cost of goods sold/average inventory) and the accounts receivable turnover ratio (net credit sales/average accounts receivable). In the upcoming section, we will interpret financial ratios and metrics, which play a critical role in evaluating a company's financial health and making well-informed investment decisions. We will explore various techniques, such as trend analysis and industry benchmarking, to assess a company's performance within its market and against its competitors. Furthermore, we will examine the limitations of ratio analysis and how they can be addressed.

Following that, we will introduce the principles of fundamental analysis, a method aimed at determining a company's intrinsic value by evaluating its financial statements, management team, competitive landscape, and industry trends. Through financial statement analysis, earnings analysis, management analysis, and industry and competitive analysis, we will learn how to identify stocks that are overvalued or undervalued, ultimately guiding your investment decisions.

Interpreting financial ratios and metrics

When analyzing financial ratios and metrics, it's essential to compare them against historical performance, industry benchmarks, and competitors. This context helps investors identify trends and assess a company's relative performance. It's also important to consider the limitations of financial ratios, as they are based on historical data and may not always accurately predict future performance.

Here are some tips to interpret financial ratios and metrics:

- **Trend analysis**: Compare a company's ratios over several periods to identify trends and changes in performance. This can help investors spot potential areas of strength or weakness.

- **Industry benchmarking**: Compare a company's ratios to industry averages or specific competitors to evaluate its relative performance within the market.

- **Ratio analysis limitations**: Keep in mind that financial ratios are based on historical data and may not always accurately predict future performance. Additionally, ratio analysis may be less informative for companies with unique business models or operating in niche industries.

Fundamental analysis is a method of evaluating a company's intrinsic value by examining its financial statements, management team, competitive landscape, and overall industry trends. The goal of fundamental analysis is to determine whether a stock is overvalued or undervalued, based on the company's underlying financial health and future growth prospects. Key components of fundamental analysis include the following:

- **Financial statement analysis**: Reviewing a company's balance sheet, income statement, and cash flow statement to assess its financial health, profitability, and solvency

- **Earnings analysis**: Evaluating a company's earnings growth, **earnings per share** (EPS), and **price-to-earnings** (P/E) ratio to assess its profitability and valuation

- **Management analysis**: Assessing the quality and effectiveness of a company's management team, including their experience, track record, and decision-making abilities

- **Industry and competitive analysis**: Examining the overall industry trends and a company's position within its market, including its competitive advantages and barriers to entry

Understanding and interpreting financial statements, ratios, and metrics are crucial for evaluating a company's financial health and making informed investment decisions. We will look at this in detail in the following section, *The fundamentals of technical analysis*.

The fundamentals of technical analysis

Technical analysis is an investment analysis method that focuses on historical price and volume data to predict future price movements. Technical analysts, or chartists, believe that price patterns and trends can provide valuable insights into a stock's future performance. Key components of technical analysis include the following:

- **Price charts**: Visual representations of historical price data, such as line charts, bar charts, and candlestick charts, which help identify trends and patterns.

- **Trend analysis**: Evaluating the direction and strength of price movements, including uptrends, downtrends, and sideways trends.

- **Technical indicators**: Mathematical calculations based on price and volume data that provide insights into market sentiment, momentum, and volatility. Examples include moving averages, the **relative strength index** (RSI), and **moving average convergence divergence** (MACD).

- **Support and resistance levels**: Key price levels at which buying or selling pressure tends to prevent further price movement, acting as a floor (support) or ceiling (resistance) for the stock price.

As we move forward, the next section will explore the advantages of combining both fundamental and technical analysis in the investment process. By merging the strengths of each approach, investors can gain a more comprehensive understanding of a stock's potential, allowing for more informed decisions and better optimization of investment strategies. We will discuss how fundamental analysis can be used to pinpoint promising investment opportunities, while technical analysis can be employed to identify the best entry and exit points for those investments. This harmonious blend of techniques paves the way for a more holistic approach to investing.

Combining fundamental and technical analysis

Both fundamental and technical analysis provide valuable insights into the investment process. While fundamental analysis helps determine the intrinsic value of a stock and its growth potential, technical analysis focuses on identifying trends and price patterns that may signal future price movements.

Investors can benefit from combining these two approaches, using fundamental analysis to identify attractive investment opportunities and technical analysis to determine optimal entry and exit points. This integrated approach can help investors make more informed decisions and optimize their investment strategies.

In the next section, we will explore how the transformative power of ChatGPT and AI can enhance traditional financial analysis methods and provide a competitive edge in the world of finance.

Understanding the power of ChatGPT in financial analysis

As the world of finance grows increasingly complex, the need for cutting-edge tools that can help investors make informed decisions has never been more apparent. Enter ChatGPT, a powerful AI language model that can revolutionize the way we approach financial analysis.

ChatGPT has the ability to quickly and accurately process vast amounts of data, making it an invaluable resource for investors looking to gain insights into financial trends, risks, and opportunities. With its natural language processing capabilities, ChatGPT can analyze and summarize complex financial documents, identify key metrics and trends, and even generate forecasts and predictions.

Imagine having a personal AI-powered financial analyst at your fingertips, ready to help you dissect financial statements, identify investment opportunities, and uncover hidden risks. With ChatGPT, this becomes a reality. By integrating ChatGPT into your financial analysis process, you can do the following:

- Save time and effort by automating repetitive tasks, such as data collection, processing, and analysis
- Access deeper insights and uncover hidden patterns within financial data
- Enhance your decision-making process with AI-generated recommendations and predictions

As we delve into the next section, we'll discuss the various ways to effectively integrate ChatGPT into your financial analysis workflow. By combining the capabilities of AI with traditional financial analysis techniques, you can create a more robust and efficient decision-making process for your investments.

We will explore how ChatGPT can be utilized to do the following:

- Summarize financial statements efficiently
- Compare the performance of companies and industries
- Analyze market sentiment by processing various sources of information
- Generate investment ideas tailored to your specific criteria

Embracing the power of AI and ChatGPT offers a competitive advantage in the ever-evolving world of finance, enhancing your financial analysis skills and leading to more informed investment decisions. Stay tuned as we explore these exciting possibilities in the upcoming section.

Integrating ChatGPT into Your Financial Analysis Workflow

Incorporating ChatGPT into your financial analysis workflow is easier than you might think. The key is to seamlessly blend the power of AI with traditional financial analysis methods, creating a comprehensive and efficient approach to investment decision-making.

Here are some ways you can integrate ChatGPT into your financial analysis process:

- **Summarizing financial statements**: Use ChatGPT to quickly analyze and summarize a company's financial statements, highlighting key metrics and trends that can inform your investment decisions
- **Comparing companies and industries**: Leverage ChatGPT to compare the financial performance of multiple companies within the same industry, identifying potential outperformers or underperformers
- **Analyzing market sentiment**: Utilize ChatGPT to gauge market sentiment by processing news articles, analyst reports, and social media data, providing you with valuable insights into investor sentiment and potential market movements
- **Generating investment ideas**: Ask ChatGPT for investment ideas based on specific criteria, such as industry, market capitalization, or growth potential, and receive a list of potential investment opportunities tailored to your preferences

The power of ChatGPT in financial analysis lies in its ability to complement and enhance traditional financial analysis methods, providing you with a competitive edge in today's fast-paced and ever-changing financial landscape. By harnessing the power of AI and ChatGPT, you can elevate your financial analysis capabilities and make more informed investment decisions.

In the previous section, we discussed the various ways to integrate ChatGPT into your financial analysis workflow, emphasizing the importance of combining AI with traditional methods to create a comprehensive and efficient approach to investment decision-making. We explored how ChatGPT could be used to summarize financial statements, compare companies and industries, analyze market sentiment, and generate investment ideas tailored to your preferences. By harnessing the power of AI and ChatGPT, you can elevate your financial analysis capabilities and make more informed investment decisions.

In the next section, *Getting started with ChatGPT for finance*, we'll guide you through the process of incorporating ChatGPT into your financial analysis routine. We'll cover essential steps such as accessing ChatGPT through an API or web-based interface, understanding its capabilities, and learning how to make the most of this versatile tool to revolutionize your approach to financial analysis. Stay tuned for valuable insights and tips on how to get started with ChatGPT for finance.

Getting started with ChatGPT for finance

Embarking on your journey with ChatGPT for finance is an exciting step towards revolutionizing your approach to financial analysis. As you begin to explore the potential of AI-driven insights, it's essential to understand how to effectively leverage ChatGPT to maximize its benefits. In this section, we'll guide you through the initial steps of getting started with ChatGPT for finance:

Step 1 – access ChatGPT:

To begin using ChatGPT, you'll need to access the platform through an API or a web-based interface. There are several options available, with some requiring a subscription or usage fees. Choose the one that best suits your needs and budget, and familiarize yourself with the user interface and available features.

Step 2 – understand ChatGPT's capabilities:

ChatGPT is an incredibly versatile tool that can perform a wide range of tasks related to financial analysis. Take some time to explore its capabilities, such as summarizing financial reports, generating investment ideas, or analyzing market sentiment. Knowing what ChatGPT can do will help you make the most of its potential in your financial analysis process.

As we transition to the next section, we will continue exploring ways to further enhance your experience with ChatGPT in finance. We'll discuss the best practices, potential challenges, and strategies to overcome these obstacles, ensuring that you're making the most of this powerful AI tool in your financial analysis process. By consistently refining your interactions with ChatGPT and staying up to date on new features and capabilities, you'll be well equipped to harness AI-driven insights for more informed investing and financial decision-making.

Refining your interactions with ChatGPT

As you become more comfortable with ChatGPT's capabilities, you'll want to fine-tune your interactions to generate more targeted and accurate insights. Here are a few tips to refine your communication with ChatGPT:

- **Be specific**: When posing questions or requests to ChatGPT, be as specific as possible. Providing clear instructions and detailed criteria will help the AI generate more accurate and relevant results.

- **Break down complex queries**: If you have a multi-layered question or request, consider breaking it down into smaller, more manageable components. This can help ChatGPT process your query more effectively and provide you with more accurate results.

- **Iterate and refine**: ChatGPT is an iterative tool, meaning you may need to refine your queries or requests to get the desired output. Don't be afraid to experiment with different phrasings or approaches to find the optimal way of communicating with ChatGPT.

- **Leverage examples**: Sometimes, providing examples can help ChatGPT better understand your request and deliver more accurate results. If you're looking for a specific type of information or analysis, consider providing an example to guide ChatGPT's response.

> Key takeaway
>
> Keep in mind that the GPT-4 only includes data up to September 2021. The recently released GPT-4 Turbo has a cut-off date of April 2023. GPT-4 Turbo is also integrated with Bing AI which allows real-time updates.

To incorporate current information, you can follow these steps:

1. **Gather information**: Manually, collect the latest information on the topic or data you want to analyze from reliable sources. This may involve visiting news websites, financial portals, or official company reports.

2. **Summarize and structure the data**: Organize the information you've collected into a structured and concise format. This will make it easier for you to provide the data to ChatGPT for analysis.

3. **Input the data into ChatGPT**: Feed the summarized and structured information to ChatGPT as context or prompts, specifying the kind of analysis or output you expect.

4. **Analyze the output**: Review the output generated by ChatGPT, and combine it with your knowledge and understanding of the subject matter to make informed decisions or derive insights.

Ensure that you verify the accuracy and reliability of the information you gather before using it in your analysis.

With these tips in mind, you're well on your way to unlocking the full potential of ChatGPT in your financial analysis process. As you continue to explore its capabilities and refine your interactions, you'll discover how AI-driven insights can complement and enhance your approach to investing and financial decision-making. Remember, practice makes perfect – the more you work with ChatGPT, the more adept you'll become at harnessing its power for finance.

In this section, we discussed refining your interactions with ChatGPT, offering tips such as being specific, breaking down complex queries, iterating and refining, and leveraging examples to improve the AI's accuracy and relevance. We also covered the importance of incorporating real-time data into ChatGPT and suggested a workaround, to manually include current information.

In the next section, we will focus on a practical application of ChatGPT for financial analysis – analyzing earnings reports, specifically for Palo Alto Networks. We'll demonstrate how to extract key data points from earnings reports and leverage ChatGPT's capabilities, identifying trends and potential issues that could impact a company's stock price or investment potential. By following these steps and incorporating the tips from the previous section, you'll be better equipped to harness the power of ChatGPT for insightful financial analysis.

ChatGPT for financial analysis – analyzing earnings reports for Palo Alto Networks

In this section, we will explore an interesting example of how ChatGPT can be used to analyze and summarize earnings reports, enabling you to identify key insights and trends quickly. With the vast amount of information available in earnings reports, it can be challenging to sift through data and identify the most critical elements. Let's see how ChatGPT can help.

Here's the scenario – Palo Alto Networks has just released its quarterly earnings report. You want to understand the company's financial performance and identify any trends or potential issues that may impact the stock price or investment potential:

Step 1 – extract key data points:

To get started, provide ChatGPT with the relevant earnings report data, such as revenue, net income, EPS, and any other important metrics. Be sure to include both current and historical data for comparison purposes. You can either input this data manually or automate the process using an API or web scraper. Let's explore the automated process to add Palo Alto Networks' financial information from September 2021 to March 2023 to ChatGPT.

Step 1.1 – automating data collection with Python and API/web scraping:

1. Choose a financial API or web scraping library in Python:

    -   If using an API, explore options such as Alpha Vantage (`alphavantage.co`):

        -   Obtain an API key from the Alpha Vantage website (free and paid versions).

        -   Choose a method – Python requests.

        -   Make a request.

    -   If web scraping, use libraries such as Requests and Beautiful Soup

        -   For web scraping, identify the URLs of the company's financial statements or earnings reports from websites such as Yahoo Finance (`finance.yahoo.com`), Nasdaq (`nasdaq.com`), or the company's investor relations page.

2. Set up your Python script for data collection:

    -   For APIs: a. Import the necessary libraries (e.g., requests or pandas) – for example, `import requests import pandas as pd`. b. Define the API key, endpoint URL, and required parameters. c. Make a request to the API to fetch data using the requests library. d. Parse the response data and convert it into a pandas `DataFrame`.

    -   For web scraping: a. Import the necessary libraries (e.g., requests, BeautifulSoup, or pandas) – for example, `import requests from bs4 import BeautifulSoup import pandas as pd`. b. Define the URL(s) containing the financial data. c. Use the requests library to fetch the HTML content of the web page. d. Parse the HTML content using `BeautifulSoup` to extract the required financial data. e. Convert the extracted data into a pandas `DataFrame`.

3. Collect historical data from September 2021 to March 2023 for the relevant financial metrics:

    -   Adjust the parameters in your API request or web scraping script to target the specified date range.

4. Save the collected data in a structured format, such as a CSV file or a pandas `DataFrame`, for further processing and analysis:

    -   Use pandas' `DataFrame.to_csv()` method to save the collected data as a CSV file

    -   Alternatively, keep the data in a pandas `DataFrame` for further analysis within the Python script.

With these additions, you should have a better understanding of where to obtain financial data and the necessary Python libraries to import for their data collection scripts.

We will now provide a step-by-step guide using Python code for Palo Alto Networks' financial data.

Extract Palo Alto Networks' quarterly financial data (revenue, net income, and EPS) for the time period September 2021–March 2023, and save it in a CSV file as text input, using the Alpha Vantage API key (finance website):

1. Install the necessary Python package and pandas library in Command Prompt:

```
pip install requests
pip install pandas
```

2. Create a new Python script file in Notepad, Notepad++, PyCharm, or Visual Studio code. It is important that you add your Alpha Vantage API key in the following `api_key` line. Copy and paste the following code into your Python script file, and name it `PANW.py`:

```
import requests
import pandas as pd
api_key = "YOUR_API_KEY"
symbol = "PANW"
url = f"https://www.alphavantage.co/
query?function=EARNINGS&symbol={symbol}&apikey={api_key}"
try:

  response = requests.get(url)
    response.raise_for_status()  # Raise HTTPError for bad
responses
    data = response.json()
    if 'quarterlyEarnings' in data:
        quarterly_data = data['quarterlyEarnings']
        df = pd.DataFrame(quarterly_data)

        df_filtered = df[(df['reportedDate'] >= '2021-09-01') &
(df['reportedDate'] <= '2023-03-31')]

        df_filtered.to_csv("palo_alto_financial_data.csv",
index=False)

        input_text = "Analyze the earnings data of Palo Alto
Networks from September 2021 to March 2023.\n\n"
        for idx, row in df_filtered.iterrows():
            quarter = idx + 1
            revenue = row.get('revenue', 'N/A')
            net_income = row.get('netIncome', 'N/A')
            eps = row.get('earningsPerShare', 'N/A')
            input_text += f"Quarter {quarter}:\n"
            input_text += f"Revenue: ${revenue}\n"
```

```
            input_text += f"Net Income: ${net_income}\n"
            input_text += f"Earnings Per Share: ${eps}\n\n"

        with open("palo_alto_financial_summary.txt", "w") as f:
            f.write(input_text)
    else:
        print("Data not available.")

except requests.RequestException as e:
    print(f"An error occurred: {e}")
```

3. Run the Python script file:

    `Python PANW.py`

4. A separate text file, `palo_alto_financial_summary.txt`, and a CSV file, `palo_alto_financial_data.csv`, will be created once the Python script has been executed:

    -   When the Python script, `PANW.py`, is executed, it performs several tasks to fetch and analyze the earnings data of Palo Alto Networks (the symbol `PANW`). First, it imports two essential libraries – `requests` to make API calls and `pandas` for data manipulation.

    -   The script starts by defining a few key variables – the API key to access financial data, the stock symbol of the company, and the URL to the Alpha Vantage API where the data can be retrieved. Then, a `try` block is initiated to safely execute the following operations.

    -   The script uses the `requests.get()` method to query the Alpha Vantage API. If the request is successful, the response is parsed as JSON and stored in a variable named `data`. It then checks whether `data` contains a key called `quarterlyEarnings`.

    -   If this key exists, the script proceeds to convert the quarterly earnings data into a pandas DataFrame. It filters this DataFrame to include only the entries between September 2021 and March 2023. The filtered data is then saved as a CSV file named `palo_alto_financial_data.csv`:

        -   The CSV file contains raw financial data in tabular form

        -   The CSV file can be imported into Excel, Google Sheets, or other specialized data analysis tools

    -   The script also constructs a text-based summary of the filtered earnings data, including revenue, net income, and EPS for each quarter within the specified date range. This summary is saved as a text file named `palo_alto_financial_summary.txt`:

        -   The TXT file provides a human-readable summary of the financial data for Palo Alto Networks for the specified data range

        -   TXT files can be used for quick overviews and presentations

- If any errors occur during this process, such as a failed API request, the script will catch these exceptions and print an error message, thanks to the `except` block. This ensures that the script fails gracefully, providing useful feedback instead of crashing.

You can upload the CSV file (`palo_alto_financial_data.csv`) to ChatGPT directly if you are a ChatGPT Plus user by following these steps:

Uploading a CSV file directly into ChatGPT is supported through the Advanced Data Analysis option for ChatGPT Plus users. You can access the OpenAI website at `https://openai.com/`, and then log in using your login credentials. Once logged in, access your Settings and Beta options by clicking on the three dots near your email address in the bottom-left corner of the screen. Go to Beta features and activate the Advanced data analysis function by moving the slider to the right to activate (the option will turn green). You can click on the plus sign in the dialog box to upload the CSV file to ChatGPT:

- **GPT-4 CSV file size limitations**: 500 MB

- **GPT-4 CSV file retention**: Files are retained while a conversation is active and for three hours after the conversation is paused

If you are not a ChatGPT Plus user, follow the following instructions using the OpenAI API to upload the CSV file (`palo_alto_financial_data.csv`) into ChatGPT, and analyze the data using the GPT 3.5 turbo model:

1. Create a new Python script file in Notepad, Notepad++, PyCharm, or Visual Studio Code. It is important that you add your OpenAI API key to the following `api_key` line. Copy and paste the following code into your Python script file and name it `OPENAIAPI.py`:

```
import openai
import pandas as pd
df = pd.read_csv("palo_alto_financial_data.csv")
csv_string = df.to_string(index=False)

api_key = "your_openai_api_key_here"
openai.api_key = api_key

input_text = f"Here is the financial data for Palo Alto
Networks:\n\n{csv_string}\n\nPlease analyze the data and provide
insights."

response = openai.Completion.create(
    engine="gpt-3.5-turbo",   # Specifying GPT-3.5-turbo engine
    prompt=input_text,
```

```
        max_tokens=200  # Limiting the length of the generated text
    )
    generated_text = response.choices[0].text.strip()
    print("GPT-3.5-turbo PANW Analysis:", generated_text)
```

2. Run the Python script file:

    Python OPENAIAPI.py

This Python code snippet is responsible for interacting with the OpenAI API to send the formatted text input (the financial data prompt) to ChatGPT and receive the generated response. Here's a breakdown of each part:

- The Python code snippet starts by importing two essential Python libraries – `openai` for interacting with the OpenAI API, and `pandas` for data manipulation.

- The script reads financial data from a CSV file named `palo_alto_financial_data.csv` using `pandas`, converting this data into a formatted string. It then sets up the OpenAI API by initializing it with a user-provided API key.

- Following this, the script prepares a prompt for GPT-3.5-turbo, consisting of the loaded financial data and a request for analysis. This prompt is sent to the GPT-3.5-turbo engine via the OpenAI API, which returns a text-based analysis, limited to 200 tokens.

- The generated analysis is then extracted from the API's response and printed to the console with the label "GPT-3.5-turbo PANW Analysis." The script essentially automates the process of sending financial data to the GPT-3.5-turbo engine for insightful analysis, making it easy to obtain quick, AI-generated insights on Palo Alto Networks' financial performance.

In the next section, we will provide an alternative, more detailed method to extract SEC 10-Q filings for Palo Alto Networks between September 2021 and March 2023, directly from the SEC website. If you have already successfully obtained the 10-Q information for the specified period, feel free to skip this section. However, if you're interested in learning another approach, please continue reading.

Instructions to access and store Palo Alto Networks' 10-Q reports using sec-api (September 2021–March 2023)

In this section, we'll present an alternative, more detailed method to load Palo Alto Networks' 10-Q filings into ChatGPT, should you prefer not to use the high-level instructions provided on page 16. This approach is designed to help you extract 10-Q information for the period between September 2021 and March 2023. We've included this method as we'll refer to it in later chapters when updating ChatGPT with more recent financial information, which is necessary for our examples and case studies. This alternative ensures you have a choice in how you prefer to access and load the SEC data.

The SEC reports for instructions on how to access and store the 10-Q reports using `sec-api` and Python for Palo Alto Networks (non-technical user step-by-step instructions) are required, since the ChatGPT model only includes information up to September 2021. Follow these steps:

1. Open a command prompt or terminal window on your computer for GPT-4. GPT-4 Turbo includes information through April 2023 but you can still follow the steps below and change your date range to be more current.

2. Install the `sec-api` package by running the following command:

   pip install sec-api==1.0.16

3. Open a code editor or IDE of your choice, and create a new file named `sec_api_example.py`.

4. Copy and paste the following code into the new Python file that we just created:

```python
import requests
import json
import re
from xbrl import XBRLParser
url = "https://api.sec-api.io"
query = {
    "query": {
        "query_string": {
            "query": "ticker:PANW AND formType:10-Q AND
filedAt:{2021-09-01 TO 2023-03-31}"
        }
    },
    "from": "0",
    "size": "10",
    "sort": [{"filedAt": {"order": "desc"}}]
}
api_key = "YOUR_API_KEY"
response = requests.post(url, json=query,
headers={"Authorization": api_key})
filings = json.loads(response.content)
with open("panw_10q_filings.json", "w") as outfile:
    json.dump(filings, outfile)

print("10-Q filings for Palo Alto Networks have been saved to
panw_10q_filings.json")

revenue_xbrl = []
net_income_xbrl = []
eps_xbrl = []

for xbrl_file in xbrl_files:
```

```
    xbrl_parser = XBRLParser()
    xbrl = xbrl_parser.parse(open(xbrl_file))
    revenue_xbrl.append(xbrl_parser.extract_value(xbrl,
'us-gaap:Revenues'))
    net_income_xbrl.append(xbrl_parser.extract_value(xbrl,
'us-gaap:NetIncomeLoss'))
    eps_xbrl.append(xbrl_parser.extract_value(xbrl,
'us-gaap:EarningsPerShare'))

revenue_text = []
net_income_text = []
eps_text = []

for text_file in text_files:
    with open(text_file, 'r') as f:
        content = f.read()
    revenue_text.append(re.search('Revenue\s+(\d+)', content).
group(1))
    net_income_text.append(re.search('Net Income\s+(\d+)',
content).group(1))
    eps_text.append(re.search('Earnings Per Share\s+(\d+.\d+)',
content).group(1))

data = {
    'revenue_xbrl': revenue_xbrl,
    'net_income_xbrl': net_income_xbrl,
    'eps_xbrl': eps_xbrl,
    'revenue_text': revenue_text,
    'net_income_text': net_income_text,
    'eps_text': eps_text
}

with open('financial_metrics.json', 'w') as f:
    json.dump(data, f)

print("Extracted financial metrics have been saved to financial_
metrics.json")
```

5. Run the Python script file:

```
python sec_api_example.py
```

The Python code provided here is used to fetch Palo Alto Networks' 10-Q filings between September 1, 2021 and March 31, 2023 from the SEC API, with the results saved as a JSON file. Here's a step-by-step explanation of the code:

Fetch 10-Q filings:

1. Import the `requests` library to make HTTP requests and the `json` library to handle JSON data.

2. Define the API endpoint URL and the query parameters. The `query` dictionary specifies the search criteria.

3. Define your SEC API key by replacing `"YOUR_API_KEY"` with your actual API key.

4. Make a `POST` request to the SEC API using `requests.post()`, with the specified URL, query parameters, and API key as headers.

5. Parse the response content using `json.loads()`, and store it in the `filings` variable.

6. Save the filings data to a JSON file named `"panw_10q_filings.json"` using `json.dump()`.

7. Print a confirmation message.

Extract the metrics from XBRL files:

1. Import the `XBRLParser` class from the `xbrl` library.

2. Initialize empty lists to store revenue, net income, and EPS metrics.

3. Loop through each XBRL file (assumed to be in a list named `xbrl_files`).

4. Use the `XBRLParser` to parse the XBRL file and extract the required financial metrics.

5. Append the extracted metrics to the lists initialized earlier.

Extract the metrics from the text files:

1. Import the `re` (regular expressions) library.

2. Initialize empty lists to store revenue, net income, and EPS metrics.

3. Loop through each text file (assumed to be in a list named `text_files`).

4. Use regular expressions to extract the required financial metrics from the text content.

5. Append the extracted metrics to the lists initialized earlier.

Save the extracted metrics to a JSON file:

1. Create a dictionary to store all the extracted metrics.

2. Save this dictionary as a JSON file named `'financial_metrics.json'`, using `json.dump()`.

3. Print a confirmation message.

In the next section, we'll provide additional instructions for the alternative method to import Palo Alto Networks' 10-Q filings into ChatGPT, via the sec-api. As this method will be referenced in future chapters when updating ChatGPT with recent financial information, it allows you to choose your preferred way of accessing and loading SEC data. This is the final step required to load the extracted data from the SEC website via the sec-api into ChatGPT, ensuring a seamless integration of financial information.

Instructions for analyzing 10-Q reports with ChatGPT

In these final steps of the alternative method, you will use Python code to access the SEC data for Palo Alto Networks via the sec-api. You'll make API requests to retrieve the relevant 10-Q filings for the specified date range, parse the response data, and then save it as a JSON file. Ultimately, this process allows you to efficiently load the extracted financial information from the SEC website into ChatGPT, setting the stage for further analysis and application in the examples and case studies throughout the book.

Follow the following steps to insert the Palo Alto Networks financial data into ChatGPT for further analysis:

1. Open the `financial_metrics.json` file that we generated in the previous section.
2. Review the contents of the JSON file to locate the specific information you want to analyze.
3. Copy the relevant information from the JSON file.
4. Open ChatGPT in your web browser, and paste the copied information into the ChatGPT interface if you are not a ChatGPT Plus user. If you are a ChatGPT Plus user, you can upload the file through the Advanced Data Analysis feature in, GPT-4 using the instructions provided.
5. Ask ChatGPT specific questions, or request insights based on the information you provided.

Once you have loaded more current SEC information into ChatGPT, you can ask various interesting questions to gain insights into a company's financial performance, trends, and potential opportunities.

Here are a few examples of such questions:

A. How has the revenue growth of Company X changed in the last three quarters compared to the previous year?
B. What were the major expense categories for Company Y in their latest 10-Q filing, and how do they compare to the same period last year?
C. Has Company Z reported any significant changes in its cash flow from operations in the most recent filing, compared to the previous quarter?
D. What were the key risks and uncertainties mentioned by Company X in their latest 10-K filing, and how do they compare to those mentioned in the previous year's filing?
E. How has the debt-to-equity ratio of Company Y evolved over the past year, and what factors have contributed to this change?

Note that these instructions are intended to provide a general overview of how to access and analyze 10-Q reports using the `sec-api` package and ChatGPT. The process may vary depending on the specific version of Python, the `sec-api` package, and the ChatGPT interface you use. Additionally, the instructions assume that you have Python and pip (the package installer for Python) already installed on your computer.

> **Important note**
>
> Note that the `sec-api` package requires an API key, which you can obtain by signing up on the `sec-api` website. Make sure to replace "`YOUR_API_KEY`" in the code with your actual API key.

In the following section, we will explore ChatGPT's ability to generate insightful analyses and uncover trends in financial data. We will demonstrate how to frame specific questions for ChatGPT to obtain targeted insights, such as drivers of revenue increase, reasons for net income decline, EPS performance, and trends in research and development investment. Additionally, we will discuss further exploration with ChatGPT, including comparisons to industry benchmarks, analysis of the impact on stock prices, and evaluation of a company's financial health based on key financial ratios. By the end of this section, you will know how to effectively utilize ChatGPT for comprehensive financial analysis and make informed decisions, based on the generated insights.

ChatGPT's analysis and insights

Once you've provided ChatGPT with the necessary data, it will quickly analyze the earnings report and generate a summary, highlighting the key findings, trends, and comparisons to previous quarters. For instance, ChatGPT might provide insights like:

To get specific insights from ChatGPT, you can frame your questions by providing a clear and concise context, along with the data you have loaded. Here's an example of how to frame your questions for ChatGPT:

1. Revenue increase and its drivers:

    ```
    input_text = f"{input_text}What is the percentage increase in
    revenue compared to the previous quarter, and what are the main
    drivers of this increase?"
    ```

2. Net income decline and its reasons:

    ```
    input_text = f"{input_text}What is the percentage decline in net
    income compared to the previous quarter, and what are the main
    reasons for this decline?"
    ```

3. EPS performance compared to analysts' expectations:

    ```
    input_text = f"{input_text}How does the earnings per share (EPS)
    performance compare to analysts' expectations, and has the
    company consistently outperformed these expectations in recent
    quarters?"
    ```

4. Trends in research and development investment:

```
input_text = f"{input_text}Are there any notable trends in
the company's research and development investment, and what
does this signal about their focus on innovation and long-term
growth?"
```

This Python code demonstrates how to append specific questions to the `input_text` variable, which will be sent to ChatGPT for analysis. The questions focus on four key aspects of the company's financial performance:

1. **Revenue increase and its drivers**: This line of code appends a question to `input_text`, asking ChatGPT to calculate the percentage increase in revenue compared to the previous quarter and identify the main drivers of this increase.

2. **Net income decline and its reasons**: Similarly, this line appends a question asking ChatGPT to calculate the percentage decline in net income compared to the previous quarter, determining the main reasons for this decline.

3. **EPS performance compared to analysts' expectations**: Here, the question appended to `input_text` asks ChatGPT to compare the EPS performance to analysts' expectations, assessing whether the company has consistently outperformed these expectations in recent quarters.

4. **Trends in research and development investment**: This line adds a question asking ChatGPT to identify any notable trends in the company's research and development investment, explaining what these trends might signal about the company's focus on innovation and long-term growth.

By appending these questions to `input_text`, the user is able to direct ChatGPT's focus to specific areas of interest within the financial data, allowing for a more targeted and detailed analysis.

After framing your questions, you can send `input_text` to ChatGPT using the OpenAI API, as shown in the previous response. ChatGPT will then analyze the data and provide the requested insights.

Remember to keep your questions clear, specific, and focused on the data you've provided to ChatGPT. This will help the model understand your context and provide relevant and accurate insights.

Further exploration with ChatGPT

With the initial analysis provided by ChatGPT, you can now dive deeper into specific aspects of the earnings report or request further information. For example, you might ask ChatGPT to answer the following:

1. **Comparing financial performance to industry benchmarks or competitors**:

```
input_text = f"{input_text}How does Palo Alto Networks'
financial performance compare to industry benchmarks and key
competitors in the cybersecurity sector?"
```

2. **Analyzing the impact of the earnings report on the stock price and potential trading opportunities**:

    ```
    input_text = f"{input_text}What is the impact of the latest
    earnings report on Palo Alto Networks' stock price, and
    are there any potential trading opportunities based on this
    information?"
    ```

3. **Evaluating the company's financial health based on key financial ratios**:

    ```
    input_text = f"{input_text}Can you evaluate the financial health
    of Palo Alto Networks based on key financial ratios such as
    debt-to-equity, current ratio, and price-to-earnings ratio?
    What do these ratios indicate about the company's financial
    position?"
    ```

After framing your questions, you can send `input_text` to ChatGPT using the OpenAI API. ChatGPT will then analyze the data provided and generate the requested insights.

In this section, we discussed how to use ChatGPT to quickly analyze a company's earnings report by appending specific questions related to revenue, net income, EPS, and research and development investment to the `input_text` variable. This allows for a more targeted and detailed analysis of the company's financial performance. Furthermore, we explored how to dive deeper into specific aspects of the earnings report and request additional insights from ChatGPT, on topics such as financial performance comparisons, stock price impact, and financial health evaluation.

In the next section, *Combining ChatGPT with fundamental analysis*, we will explore how to integrate ChatGPT's AI-driven insights with traditional analysis methods to make more informed investment decisions. We will discuss additional questions you can ask ChatGPT to gain insights on dividend analysis, revenue and earnings growth trends, stock price momentum, analysts' recommendations, and potential risks and opportunities in the industry. By leveraging both AI-driven analysis and conventional methods, you can save time while obtaining a deeper understanding of a company's financial performance and potential investment opportunities.

Combining ChatGPT with fundamental analysis

While ChatGPT provides valuable insights and helps streamline the financial analysis process, it's essential to combine these AI-driven findings with your own research and fundamental analysis methods. By integrating ChatGPT's insights with a comprehensive understanding of the company, industry, and market context, you can make more informed decisions about your investments. If you are a ChatGPT Plus user, you can **Browse with Bing**, and copy the following questions into ChatGPT to get answers based on the latest information available. If you are not a ChatGPT Plus user, your answers will reflect information up to January 2022, which is the cut-off date for training GPT-GPT-3.5 Turbo.

Here are some additional questions to consider:

1. **Dividend analysis:**

   ```
   input_text = f"{input_text}Does Palo Alto Networks pay
   dividends? If so, how has the dividend payout evolved over time,
   and what is the current dividend yield?"
   ```

2. **Revenue and earnings growth trends:**

   ```
   input_text = f"{input_text}What are the revenue and earnings
   growth trends for Palo Alto Networks, and how do these trends
   compare to the industry average and competitors? Do these trends
   suggest any potential trading opportunities?"
   ```

3. **Stock price momentum and technical indicators:**

   ```
   input_text = f"{input_text}Based on recent stock price momentum
   and technical indicators, are there any bullish or bearish
   signals for Palo Alto Networks stock? What do these signals
   imply about potential trading opportunities?"
   ```

4. **Analysts' recommendations and price targets:**

   ```
   input_text = f"{input_text}What are the recent analysts'
   recommendations and price targets for Palo Alto Networks stock?
   How do these recommendations align with the current stock price,
   and what trading opportunities might they suggest?"
   ```

5. **Potential risks and opportunities in the industry or sector:**

   ```
   input_text = f"{input_text}What are the potential risks and
   opportunities in the cybersecurity industry or sector that
   could impact Palo Alto Networks stock? How can these risks and
   opportunities inform potential trading strategies?"
   ```

Remember to send the `input_text` containing your questions to ChatGPT, using the OpenAI API. ChatGPT will then process the data and generate the requested insights.

In summary, ChatGPT can be a powerful tool for analyzing earnings reports and extracting key insights quickly and efficiently. By leveraging AI-driven analysis alongside traditional methods, you can save time and gain a deeper understanding of a company's financial performance and potential investment opportunities.

To maintain a competitive edge in the dynamic world of finance, it's essential to effectively merge traditional financial analysis techniques with the power of AI-driven insights. ChatGPT has emerged as a game-changing tool that can be seamlessly integrated with conventional methods to provide more comprehensive and actionable intelligence.

Here, we will discuss some best practices to combine traditional analysis and AI insights using ChatGPT, along with interesting examples:

- **Start with a strong foundation**: Before diving into AI-enhanced analysis, make sure you have a solid understanding of traditional financial analysis methods, such as fundamental and technical analysis. ChatGPT can augment your existing knowledge, but it should not be considered a replacement for foundational skills.

- **Use ChatGPT to enhance, not replace, your analysis**: ChatGPT can provide valuable insights into a company's financial health, such as highlighting key metrics or trends in a company's balance sheet. However, it's essential to use it as a complementary tool alongside conventional techniques, such as assessing the company's competitive position within its industry.

- **Verify the accuracy of AI-generated insights**: ChatGPT Plus users have the ability to get answers based on the latest information available, while those who are not ChatGPT Plus users rely on historical data up until September 2021. We recommend that you cross-check all information provided by ChatGPT with Palo Alto Network's SEC reports, stock analyst reports, and financial news. For example, if ChatGPT suggests that a company has strong revenue growth, verify this with the most recent financial statements.

- **Ask targeted questions**: To get the most out of ChatGPT, frame your queries or prompts in a clear and specific manner. For instance, instead of asking, *"What do you think of Company X's financials?"*, ask, *"What is the trend in Company X's net income over the past five years?"*

- **Refine inputs based on AI feedback**: As you interact with ChatGPT, use its feedback to refine your inputs or ask follow-up questions. For example, if ChatGPT identifies a significant increase in a company's operating expenses, you can inquire about the possible reasons behind this increase.

- **Use AI to identify trends and patterns**: ChatGPT's ability to process large amounts of data quickly makes it an excellent tool for spotting trends and patterns. For instance, ChatGPT can help you uncover hidden correlations between financial ratios and stock prices, which might be difficult to identify through traditional analysis alone.

- **Leverage ChatGPT for natural language explanations**: ChatGPT can generate human-like, easy-to-understand explanations for complex financial concepts or data. For example, use ChatGPT to break down the implications of a high debt-to-equity ratio and how it might affect a company's overall financial health.

- **Continuously learn and adapt**: Both traditional financial analysis and AI technologies are continuously evolving. Stay up-to-date with the latest developments, tools, and techniques to ensure you are always equipped with the most advanced knowledge and skills in the field.

By incorporating these best practices, you can successfully combine traditional financial analysis with the power of ChatGPT to gain a competitive edge in the world of finance, making more informed investment and trading decisions.

In this practice use case, we will walk you through an example of evaluating the investment potential of a company, using a combination of traditional financial analysis techniques and the insights provided by ChatGPT. This process will help you gain a more comprehensive understanding of the company's financial health, making more informed investment decisions.

Imagine that you are considering investing in Company *XYZ*, a technology firm that has recently caught your attention due to its innovative products and strong market presence. To evaluate its investment potential, you would typically begin by conducting a fundamental analysis, examining the company's financial statements, and calculating key financial ratios. With the help of ChatGPT, you can enhance your analysis and gain a more in-depth understanding of the company's performance and prospects:

- **Step 1: Gather financial data to start**: Gather the company's financial statements, such as the balance sheet, income statement, and cash flow statement, for the past five years. This information will serve as the basis for your fundamental analysis and provide the necessary context for ChatGPT to deliver meaningful insights.

- **Step 2: Calculate the key financial ratios using the financial data**: Calculate the essential financial ratios such as the **price-to-earnings (P/E)** ratio, the debt-to-equity ratio, the **return on equity (ROE)**, and operating margin. These ratios will help you assess the company's profitability, financial stability, and overall performance.

- **Step 3: Engage with ChatGPT now that you have the key financial ratios**: Engage with ChatGPT to obtain insights and explanations for each ratio. For instance, you could ask ChatGPT, "*What does a P/E ratio of 25 mean for Company XYZ, and how does it compare to the industry average?*" ChatGPT may respond with an explanation of the P/E ratio, its implications for the company, and its relative standing within the industry.

- **Step 4: Perform technical analysis in addition to fundamental analysis**: You may also want to perform technical analysis to identify trends, patterns, and potential entry or exit points for the stock. Examine the stock's historical price and volume data, and use technical indicators such as moving averages, the **relative strength index (RSI)**, and Bollinger Bands. ChatGPT can assist in identifying potential price patterns and interpreting technical indicators. For example, you could ask, "*What does an RSI of 30 for Company XYZ indicate?*"

- **Step 5: Combine insights from fundamental and technical analysis**: After conducting both fundamental and technical analysis, combine your findings with the insights provided by ChatGPT to gain a more comprehensive understanding of Company XYZ's investment potential. Take note of any strengths, weaknesses, opportunities, or risks that have emerged during your analysis, and consider how they may impact the company's future performance and stock price.

- **Step 6: Make an informed investment decision with the information and insights gathered**: You can now make a more informed investment decision about *Company XYZ*. If your analysis suggests that the company has strong financials, a promising outlook, and a stock price that presents a good entry point, you may decide to invest in the company. Conversely, if you identify significant risks or concerns, you may choose to hold off on investing or explore alternative investment opportunities.

This practice use case demonstrates how combining traditional financial analysis techniques with the power of ChatGPT can help you gain a deeper understanding of a company's investment potential. By leveraging the capabilities of AI-driven tools such as ChatGPT, you can enhance your analysis, uncover hidden trends and patterns, and make more informed investment decisions in today's dynamic financial landscape.

Summary

As we conclude *Chapter 1*, let's recap the key skills and concepts you have learned, which will serve as a foundation for the rest of the book. This chapter has provided you with an overview of essential financial concepts, investment principles, and various types of financial assets, along with an introduction to fundamental and technical analysis methods in finance. Additionally, you have been introduced to the transformative power of ChatGPT in financial analysis, learning how to harness its capabilities for a more comprehensive understanding of financial trends, risks, and opportunities.

Skills development: When we refer to "skills development," we are emphasizing the various techniques and competencies that you will acquire throughout the book. By working through the chapter, you will learn the following:

- **Understanding basic financial concepts**: Familiarize yourself with the fundamental principles of finance, including concepts such as the time value of money, risk and return, and diversification

- **Investment principles**: Learn the different types of financial assets, such as stocks, bonds, and derivatives, and understand the underlying principles of investing, including risk management and portfolio construction

- **Reading and interpreting financial statements**: Develop the ability to analyze a company's balance sheet, income statement, and cash flow statement to gain insight into its financial health and performance

- **Calculating and analyzing financial ratios and metrics**: Enhance your skills in calculating key financial ratios, such as the P/E ratio, debt-to-equity ratio, and ROE, and learn to interpret these metrics in the context of evaluating investment opportunities

- **Differentiating between fundamental and technical analysis**: Understand the distinctions between these two approaches to financial analysis, and learn how they can complement each other in the investment decision-making process

- **Integrating ChatGPT into financial analysis**: Learn how to effectively engage with ChatGPT to obtain AI-driven insights that enhance your financial analysis, including interpreting financial ratios, identifying trends, and evaluating investment potential

- **Practicing use cases**: Apply the skills you have learned in practical examples, such as evaluating the investment potential of a company, using a combination of fundamental and technical analysis and ChatGPT insights

As you progress through the book, you will continue to develop and refine these skills, gaining a deeper understanding of financial analysis techniques and learning how to effectively incorporate ChatGPT and Power BI into your financial decision-making process. By building on this foundation, you will become a more proficient and confident investor, able to navigate the complex world of finance and make more informed investment decisions.

As we conclude the first chapter on the remarkable capabilities of ChatGPT in financial analysis, we're excited to introduce *Chapter 2*, which will dive into an indispensable tool for the financial world – *Creating Financial Narratives with Power BI and ChatGPT*. In the upcoming chapter, you will discover how Power BI can help you visualize and analyze financial data with unparalleled ease and efficiency, as well as how to effectively integrate ChatGPT's AI-driven insights into your Power BI workflows.

Chapter 2 will guide you through the process of leveraging Power BI to create visually stunning dashboards, explore key financial metrics, and identify trends and patterns in financial data. We'll also explore captivating real-life examples and scenarios to demonstrate how Power BI can transform the way you approach financial analysis, making it more dynamic and insightful when combined with the intelligence of ChatGPT.

Whether you're a seasoned financial professional or a curious newcomer, *Chapter 2* will equip you with the knowledge and skills to harness the power of Power BI in your financial analysis, as well as integrate ChatGPT's advanced capabilities for a comprehensive understanding of financial data. Prepare to embark on an engaging journey through the world of financial data visualization and AI-powered insights, as we unlock the true potential of Power BI and ChatGPT in revolutionizing the way we analyze and understand financial information. Don't miss out on this opportunity to elevate your financial analysis skills with Power BI and ChatGPT!

Creating Financial Narratives with Power BI and ChatGPT

This chapter provides a brief overview of Microsoft Power BI and its applications in finance. We will also cover a list of the benefits of Power BI and its uses in finance. Then, we will consider the importance of data modeling in financial analysis and provide tips for creating effective financial visualizations. Finally, we will cover best practices for data modeling, visualization, and ChatGPT integration.

In this chapter, we will cover the following topics:

- A brief overview of Power BI and its applications in finance
- The importance of structuring data in financial analysis
- Visualization techniques in Power BI
- Creating financial dashboards with Power BI
- Best practices for data modeling, visualization, and ChatGPT integration
- Walk-through use case – analyzing financial data using Power BI
- Walk-through use case – analyzing financial ratios using Power BI and ChatGPT

By the end of this chapter, you should have a good understanding of what Microsoft Power BI can do in terms of visualizing financial information and how we can leverage ChatGPT and AI to enhance these with powerful insights.

Technical requirements

There are a few technical issues that you will need to address if you are to follow along and understand/try the examples yourself. You will require the following:

- Access to a stable and reasonably fast internet connection.
- A newer version of Microsoft Power BI on your desktop. Microsoft sells one of its Office versions with Power BI included. Pricing varies.

- Python 3.5 or above installed on your desktop. Look for the latest stable version.
- A basic understanding of visualizations using Power BI – simple reports and charts.
- A basic understanding of Python scripting and the use of packages in Python.
- An account with Open AI. You must also understand what "API" means.
- A basic understanding of finance. You must be acquainted with company balance sheets and income statements and understand the difference between the two.

With this set of knowledge and tools, we are confident that you will understand the chapters to follow.

A brief overview of Power BI and its applications in finance

This section is an introduction to Power BI and its applications in finance.

Power BI is a powerful data analytics and visualization tool developed by Microsoft. It has gained popularity in recent years due to its ease of use, versatility, and ability to handle substantial amounts of data.

In finance, Power BI can be used to analyze and visualize financial data to provide deeper insights into a company's financial performance. Finance professionals can connect to a wide range of data sources, including spreadsheets, databases, and cloud-based applications, to create dynamic and visual reports that can be shared across the organization.

One key application of Power BI in finance is creating financial dashboards. Power BI enables finance professionals to create interactive dashboards that provide a real-time view of a company's financial performance. Dashboards can include **key performance indicators** (**KPIs**) such as revenue, gross margin, and operating expenses, as well as visualizations such as line charts, bar charts, and pie charts. These dashboards provide a quick and easy way for decision-makers to understand the financial health of the organization and make informed decisions.

Another application of Power BI is analyzing financial statements. Power BI can be used to analyze financial statements such as income statements, balance sheets, and cash flow statements. By visualizing financial data in this way, finance professionals can identify trends and patterns that might otherwise be difficult to spot. For example, they can analyze revenue and expenses by department or location or identify changes in working capital over time.

Power BI can also be used for forecasting and budgeting. Finance professionals can create predictive models that forecast financial outcomes, such as revenue and expenses, based on historical data. This can help finance professionals make more accurate predictions and create better budgets. By identifying trends and patterns in the data, they can also adjust budgets in real time, making more informed decisions about resource allocation.

Power BI is also useful for identifying opportunities for cost savings. By analyzing financial data in Power BI, finance professionals can identify areas where costs can be reduced or eliminated. For example, they can identify inefficiencies in the supply chain or reduce excess inventory. By reducing costs, they can help increase profitability and drive business growth.

Finally, Power BI enables finance professionals to collaborate with other departments. By sharing interactive dashboards and reports, teams can make data-driven decisions that align around common goals and drive business growth.

Overall, Power BI is a valuable tool for finance professionals that can help them gain insights from complex financial data and make data-driven decisions that drive business growth. By visualizing and analyzing financial data in this way, finance professionals can identify trends, spot opportunities, and make informed decisions that help their organizations succeed.

In the next section, we'll review the benefits of combining Power BI with ChatGPT insights.

The benefits of combining Power BI with ChatGPT insights

In this section, we will review the benefits of combining Power BI with ChatGPT insights.

A big advantage of using Power BI in financial analysis is improved data accuracy. Power BI enables finance professionals to connect to various data sources and analyze data in real time. This means that the data is always up-to-date and accurate, which improves the accuracy of financial analysis.

Power BI also provides a range of visualization options that allow finance professionals to present complex financial data in a clear and consumable way. By visualizing data in this way, decision-makers can quickly understand trends, patterns, and relationships between different financial metrics.

Furthermore, Power BI enables teams to work together on financial analysis by sharing reports and dashboards. This means that multiple stakeholders can collaborate on financial analysis, share insights, and make better-informed decisions. This can help finance professionals break down silos and work more effectively with other parts of the organization.

Since Power BI can handle substantial amounts of data, it makes it ideal for financial analysis. As companies grow and generate more financial data, Power BI can scale to meet the needs of the organization.

It can be a time-saving tool because, with Power BI, finance professionals can quickly create reports and dashboards that provide insights into financial performance. Compare this to traditional methods of financial analysis, such as manual data entry and spreadsheet analysis.

Power BI enables the creation of interactive dashboards. They provide a real-time view of financial performance. Dashboards can include KPIs, visualizations, and other data that provide a quick and easy way for decision-makers to understand the financial health of the organization. By visualizing financial data in this way, finance professionals can identify trends and patterns that might otherwise be difficult to spot. For example, they can identify areas where costs can be reduced or identify growth opportunities. By making data-driven decisions, organizations can better align around common goals and drive business success.

Power BI can be used to create predictive models that forecast financial outcomes. By identifying trends and patterns in the data, finance professionals can make more accurate predictions and create better budgets.

Power BI can be a cost-effective solution for financial analysis as it is part of Microsoft Power Platform, which includes Power Apps and Power Automate, and is available as a cloud-based service or as an on-premises solution. This means that organizations can choose the deployment option that best meets their needs and budget.

ChatGPT, and its **large language model** (**LLM**) base, extend the already excellent capabilities of Power BI. There are multiple areas of potential synergy between Power BI and ChatGPT.

ChatGPT insights can be used to predict future trends and patterns based on past financial data. Power BI can then be used to visualize these insights and provide a more in-depth understanding of financial performance quickly.

Using ChatGPT's **natural language processing** (**NLP**) capabilities, the insights it provides can be used to process unstructured data such as customer feedback, social media posts, and emails. Power BI can then be used to visualize this data in a way that provides insights into customer behavior and preferences.

ChatGPT insights can be used to provide insights into customer behavior and preferences, which can then be used to inform financial decision-making. Power BI can then be used to visualize this data in a way that makes it easy for decision-makers to understand.

Power BI can be used to connect to various data sources, including ChatGPT insights. This enables finance professionals to combine insights from multiple sources and create a more comprehensive view of financial performance. Furthermore, by combining these tools, teams can work together on financial analysis, share insights, and make better-informed decisions. Another use of combining ChatGPT and Power BI is in automating many of the tasks associated with financial analysis. This can include tasks such as data preparation, data cleansing, and report creation. By automating these tasks, finance professionals can spend more time on analysis and decision-making.

Overall, the combination of Power BI and ChatGPT insights provides finance professionals with a powerful set of tools that can be used to gain insights into financial performance. By visualizing and analyzing financial data in this way, decision-makers can identify trends, spot opportunities, and make informed decisions that help their organizations succeed.

In the next section, we'll talk about the importance of structuring data in financial analysis.

The importance of structuring data in financial analysis

In this section, we will look at the importance of structuring data when performing financial analysis.

Power BI offers several techniques for structuring financial data, including data modeling, data shaping, and data transformation:

- **Data modeling**: As we stated previously, data modeling is the process of creating a data model or schema that defines the relationships between different data points. In Power BI, data modeling involves creating a model using the Power Pivot data modeling engine. This allows finance professionals to define relationships between tables, create calculated columns and measures, and create hierarchies. A well-designed data model can make it easier to analyze financial data and gain insights. Data modeling forms a critical aspect of financial analysis. It enables finance professionals to transform raw data into useful insights that can inform financial decisions.

- **Data shaping**: Data shaping is the process of filtering, sorting, and aggregating data to make it more useful for analysis. In Power BI, data shaping is accomplished using Power Query Editor, which provides a graphical interface for shaping data, including filtering data, removing columns, and merging tables. By shaping the data, finance professionals can eliminate irrelevant data and focus on the data that is most relevant to their analysis.

- **Data transformation**: Data transformation is the process of converting data from one form into another. In Power BI, data transformation can be accomplished using Power Query Editor, which provides a wide range of transformation options, including splitting columns, merging tables, and pivoting data. By transforming data, finance professionals can create new insights and visualizations that were not previously possible.

- **Time intelligence**: Time intelligence is a technique that allows finance professionals to analyze financial data over time. In Power BI, time intelligence is accomplished using functions that calculate values based on dates and time periods. These functions include `DATESYTD`, `TOTALYTD`, and `SAMEPERIODLASTYEAR`. Time intelligence can be used to analyze trends, identify seasonality, and forecast future performance.

- **Custom visuals**: Power BI provides a wide range of custom visuals that can be used to create more engaging and informative visualizations. Custom visuals include charts, gauges, and maps, as well as more specialized visuals such as bullet charts and Gantt charts. By using custom visuals, finance professionals can create visualizations that are tailored to their specific needs and requirements.

So, Power BI offers a range of techniques for structuring financial data, including data modeling, data shaping, and data transformation. These techniques can be used to create a well-designed data model, eliminate irrelevant data, analyze trends over time, and create more engaging and informative visualizations. By using these techniques, finance professionals can gain a more comprehensive understanding of financial performance and make more informed decisions.

To effectively use Power BI for financial analysis, it is essential to understand how to connect data sources and create relationships between tables. This process allows users to create powerful reports and visualizations that provide valuable insights into financial performance.

The first step in using Power BI for financial analysis is to connect to the data sources that contain the financial data. When connecting to a data source in Power BI, there are several options available, including importing data, connecting directly to a database, or using a custom data connector. Power BI can connect to a large number of data sources, including Excel files, CSV files, SQL databases, and cloud-based sources such as Azure and Salesforce. Once the data sources are connected, the next step is to import the data into Power BI.

Importing data into Power BI

Importing data into Power BI is a straightforward process. Users can select the tables they want to import and then click on the **Load** button. Power BI will import the data and create a table for each source. Once the data has been imported, the next step is to create relationships between tables.

Creating relationships between tables is a crucial step in using Power BI for financial analysis. Relationships allow users to create reports and visualizations that show the relationship between different sets of data. To create relationships between tables, users need to understand the concept of a relationship key.

A relationship key is a unique identifier that is used to link two tables together. For example, if we are analyzing sales data and inventory data, we might use the product ID as the relationship key. The product ID is a unique identifier that is assigned to each product, and it can be used to link the sales table and the inventory table together.

Power BI provides several tools to establish relationships, including the diagram view, which allows for a visual representation of the data model and relationships. In this view, tables can be dragged and dropped to create relationships, and fields can be selected as keys for establishing relationships.

To create a relationship between two tables in Power BI, users need to select the **Manage Relationships** option from the **Home** tab. They can then select the tables they want to link together and choose the columns they want to use as the relationship key. Once the relationship has been created, users can use it to create powerful reports and visualizations that show the relationship between different sets of data.

In addition to the diagram view, Power BI also provides the relationship view, which allows for more advanced management of relationships. In this view, users can define relationship properties, such as cardinality and cross-filtering, to ensure that the relationships are properly defined and functioning as intended.

Let's look at an example to understand how to create relationships between tables in Power BI. Suppose we are analyzing the financial performance of a retail company, and we have data from two sources: sales data and inventory data. The sales data is in an Excel file, and the inventory data is in a SQL database. We want to create a report that shows the relationship between sales and inventory levels.

In this case, we would start by connecting to the Excel file and the SQL database in Power BI. We would then import the sales data and the inventory data into Power BI. Once the data has been imported, we can create a relationship between the sales table and the inventory table by selecting the **Manage Relationships** option and choosing the product ID column as the relationship key.

Once the relationship has been created, we can create a report that shows the relationship between sales and inventory levels. For example, we could create a report that shows sales by product category, with a visual that shows inventory levels for each category. We could then use the relationship between the sales table and the inventory table to show how changes in inventory levels affect sales.

In conclusion, connecting data sources and creating relationships between tables is a crucial step in using Power BI for financial analysis. By connecting data sources and creating relationships, finance professionals can create powerful reports and visualizations that provide valuable insights into financial performance. By using the Power BI data modeling engine, finance professionals can easily create relationships between tables and analyze complex financial data.

This leads us to the next section, where we'll look at visualization techniques in Power BI.

Visualization techniques in Power BI

As we noted earlier, Power BI offers a wide range of visualization techniques to help users effectively communicate insights from their data. These include standard charts such as bar charts, line charts, and scatterplots, as well as more advanced visuals such as heat maps, tree maps, and gauges. Power BI also allows for custom visualizations to be created using JavaScript or R. In addition to these visuals, Power BI provides options for interactivity, such as drill-down and filtering, to enable users to explore their data and gain deeper insights. Overall, Power BI's visualization capabilities allow for clear and impactful communication of data-driven insights.

Selecting appropriate visualizations for financial data

Selecting appropriate visualizations is an important aspect of creating effective financial dashboards and reports in Power BI. Here are five considerations to keep in mind when choosing visualizations for financial data:

- **Determine the purpose of the visualization**: What story are you trying to tell with your data? Are you looking to compare values, show trends over time, or display proportions? The purpose of the visualization will dictate the type of chart or graph that is most appropriate.

- **Consider the nature of the data**: The type of data being visualized is also important. For example, a stacked bar chart may be appropriate for comparing revenue from different product lines, but not for displaying a time series of revenue growth over multiple years.

- **Focus on simplicity**: While it can be tempting to use complex visualizations to show off your data analysis skills, simplicity is often more effective. Choose visuals that are easy to understand and communicate the intended message.

- **Use color effectively**: Color can be a powerful tool in visualizing financial data, but it can also be overwhelming if not used appropriately. Use color sparingly and intentionally to draw attention to key data points or highlight trends.

- **Utilize interactivity**: Power BI allows for interactivity, such as drill-down and filtering, which can be particularly useful for financial data. Consider how users will want to interact with the data and provide appropriate options.

Here is a list of some common visualizations for financial data:

- **Bar charts**: Used for comparing values across categories
- **Line charts**: Used for showing trends over time
- **Pie charts**: Used for showing proportions or percentages
- **Area charts**: Like line charts but with shaded areas to represent the magnitude of the values
- **Heat maps**: Used for displaying large amounts of data in a visual format, with color coding indicating the magnitude of the values

Ultimately, the appropriate visualization will depend on the specific financial data being analyzed and the story you are trying to tell with that data. By considering the purpose of the visualization, the nature of the data, and other factors such as simplicity and interactivity, you can create impactful and informative financial dashboards and reports in Power BI.

Tips for creating effective financial visualizations

Here are a few tips for creating effective financial visualizations with Power BI:

- **Understand your audience**: Before creating any visualizations, it's important to understand who your audience is and what information they need. Consider what questions they may have and what insights they are looking for.

- **Keep it simple**: Avoid cluttering visualizations with unnecessary information. Focus on the key data points that will provide the most valuable insights.

- **Use the right chart types**: Different chart types are suited for different types of data. It's important to choose the appropriate chart type to effectively communicate the data. For example, line charts are ideal for showing trends over time, while bar charts are better suited for comparing different categories of data.

- **Utilize color**: Color can be a powerful tool in visualizations to highlight key data points or trends. However, it's important to use color effectively and not overdo it, as too many colors can be overwhelming.

- **Use data labels**: Data labels can provide additional context and clarity to visualizations. Use them to highlight important data points or provide additional information.

- **Provide context**: Visualizations should provide context to the data being displayed. This can be achieved through the use of axis labels, titles, and annotations.

- **Consider interactivity**: Power BI offers a range of interactive features, such as drill-down and filtering. Consider how these features can be used to provide deeper insights into the data.

- **Utilize branding**: Branding can be used to make visualizations more professional and cohesive. Use company colors, logos, and fonts to help tie visualizations into the overall brand.

- **Test and iterate**: Visualizations should be tested and iterated upon to ensure they effectively communicate the desired insights. Solicit feedback from stakeholders and make adjustments as needed.

- **Keep it up to date**: Visualizations should be updated regularly to ensure they reflect the most current data and insights.

By following these tips, you can create effective and impactful financial visualizations with Power BI that provide valuable insights to your audience.

Let's look at an example of how Power BI can be used in analyzing sales data for a company's products, using the information detailed in the previous sections. Let's say you're analyzing sales data for a company's products. You've pulled in data from multiple sources, cleaned and transformed it using Power BI's data modeling capabilities, and now you want to create a visualization to help you better understand the data.

You have decided to create a bar chart to compare the sales performance of each product. You choose to color code the bars based on the product category to help differentiate them. You also add data labels to each bar to show the exact sales amount for each product.

To provide context, you add axis labels for the sales amount and the product names. You also add a title to the chart to give a clear indication of what it represents.

As you review the chart, you notice that one product category is significantly outperforming the others. To investigate further, you use Power BI's interactive features to drill down into the data for that category and discover that a particular product is responsible for the majority of the sales.

By creating this visualization, you were able to quickly identify which products were performing well and which needed improvement, and easily drill down into the data to gain deeper insights.

This is just one example of how Power BI can be used to create effective financial visualizations that provide valuable insights.

In this section, we learned about visualization techniques in Power BI and how these visuals can provide a graphic and understandable view of financial data. In the next section, we'll talk a bit more about the process of creating financial dashboards with Power BI.

Creating financial dashboards with Power BI

Planning and designing a financial dashboard in Power BI involves a few key steps to ensure that the dashboard meets the needs of its users.

The first step is to determine the purpose of the dashboard and what key metrics and KPIs should be included. This will depend on the specific needs of the organization or business unit.

The second step is to gather the necessary data and organize it in a way that makes sense for the dashboard. This may involve connecting to multiple data sources and transforming the data into a format that is suitable for analysis.

Once the data has been organized, the next step is to select appropriate visualizations to display the data. This involves considering the types of data being displayed and choosing visualizations that are both visually appealing and easy to interpret.

The next step is to design the layout of the dashboard. This involves determining which visualizations should be placed where, and how they should be arranged to create an effective and visually appealing dashboard.

For a dashboard to be a self-service visualization, it is necessary to make the dashboard more interactive and user-friendly. Consider adding interactive elements such as drilldowns, filters, and slicers. These elements allow users to explore the data in more detail and customize the dashboard to meet their specific needs.

Once the dashboard has been designed, it is important to test it thoroughly and refine it as necessary. This may involve gathering feedback from users and making adjustments to the layout, visualizations, and interactive elements to ensure that the dashboard meets the needs of its users.

When planning and designing a financial dashboard in Power BI, it is important to keep the end user in mind and design the dashboard to meet their specific needs. By following these key steps, it is possible to create an effective and visually appealing dashboard that provides users with the insights they need to make informed decisions.

In the next section, we'll focus on arranging financial information for visual clarity using Power BI.

Arranging financial visuals for clarity in Power BI

When designing financial dashboards in Power BI, arranging visuals for clarity is crucial to effectively communicate insights to users. Here are some key considerations for arranging financial visuals to enhance clarity:

- **Group related visuals**: Grouping related visuals together helps users understand the relationships between different elements of the financial analysis. For example, you can place visuals related to revenue and expenses side by side, or group visuals that show different aspects of the same financial metric. This grouping allows users to easily compare and analyze related data.

- **Prioritize important visuals**: Place the most critical visuals prominently within the dashboard layout. Important metrics or KPIs should be positioned in a way that catches users' attention immediately. Consider placing these visuals at the top or center of the dashboard to ensure they are easily visible and accessible.

- **Use clear and concise titles**: Provide clear and concise titles for each visual to convey its purpose and context. The title should effectively describe the data being presented and enable users to quickly understand the information that's displayed. Use descriptive titles that align with the overall objective of the financial analysis.

- **Align visuals for consistency**: Align visuals within the dashboard to create a sense of consistency and order. Aligning visuals along a common axis or grid helps create a visually pleasing and organized layout. Consider aligning visual elements such as legends, data labels, and axis titles for a more cohesive appearance.

- **Utilize white space**: Don't overcrowd the dashboard with visuals and information. Incorporate sufficient white space between visuals to improve readability and prevent visual clutter. White space helps users focus on important information without feeling overwhelmed. It also enhances the overall aesthetic appeal of the dashboard.

- **Provide clear data labels**: Data labels play a critical role in conveying precise information. Ensure that data labels are legible and appropriately positioned to avoid any confusion. Use appropriate formatting options, such as font size and color, to make the labels stand out and improve readability.

- **Consider the flow of information**: Arrange visuals in a logical sequence that guides users through the story or analysis. Think about the natural flow of information, from top to bottom or left to right, to ensure that users can easily follow the narrative of the financial analysis.

- **Include relevant tooltips**: Tooltips can provide additional details or context to specific data points within a visual. By incorporating informative tooltips, you can offer users the ability to explore the finer details of the data without overwhelming the main visual.

By following these guidelines and arranging financial visuals for clarity in Power BI, you can create dashboards that effectively communicate insights, enable efficient data analysis, and provide a user-friendly experience. Remember to iterate and seek feedback from users to continuously improve the clarity and effectiveness of your financial visuals.

Now that we know a little bit more about data modeling and using Power BI, we can start looking at sharing visualizations and insights using Power BI.

In the next section, we will provide an illustration that pulls together what we have been talking about in the previous sections. We will take an example from the Microsoft Learn website. It looks at financial data related to sales and returns for a skateboard company.

Illustration – Power BI dashboard of finance data

The following is an example of an interactive Power BI dashboard. This example can be downloaded from the Microsoft site as an example. It is called **Sales & Return Sample v201912**.

You can download the sales and returns sample Power BI report (a `.pbix` file) from the Microsoft Learn website (*Get samples for Power BI – Power BI | Microsoft Learn*: `https://learn.microsoft.com/en-us/power-bi/create-reports/sample-datasets`). You can view it in the Data Stories Gallery, open and explore it in Power BI Desktop, or upload it to the Power BI service. Here are some more resources:

- *Store Sales sample for Power BI: Take a tour – Power BI* | Microsoft Learn: `https://learn.microsoft.com/en-us/power-bi/create-reports/sample-store-sales`

- *Sales and Marketing sample for Power BI: Take a tour*: `https://learn.microsoft.com/en-us/power-bi/create-reports/sample-sales-and-marketing`

- *Take a Tour of the New Sales & Returns Sample Report* | *Microsoft*: `https://powerbi.microsoft.com/en-us/blog/take_a_tour_of_the_new_sales_returns_sample_report/`

This dashboard of a skateboard company allows you to drill into the data and explore all the factors that impact sales and returns. It also analyzes what types of products are most popular in different regions and provides insights into areas to focus marketing efforts.

This report is loaded with Power BI features that will allow the user to understand a large amount of data with an easy-to-use interface. By integrating Power Apps within this Power BI report, the users can get from data to insights to action rapidly:

Figure 2.1 – Sales and returns dashboard for the skateboard company

The following figure shows the dashboard of the sales and returns of the company:

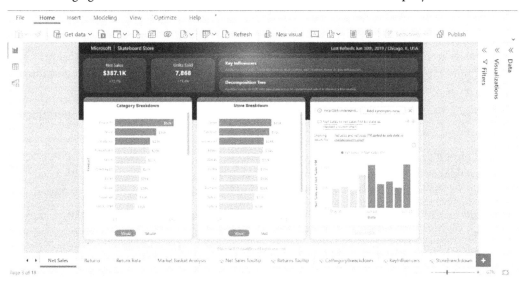

Figure 2.2 – Sales and returns dashboard for the skateboard company showing Net Sales and Units Sold

It is best to download this sample to your Power BI desktop and peruse the interactive features that come with it – utilizing a lot of what Power BI has to offer. As stated at the start of this section, you can download this example from https://learn.microsoft.com/en-us/power-bi/create-reports/sample-datasets.

In this section, we learned how to create a Power BI dashboard using sample resources from Microsoft Learn using the available visualization techniques and tools. Some best practices are worth following when using Power BI in financial analysis. We'll look at them in the next section.

Best practices for data modeling, visualization, and ChatGPT integration

Effective data modeling, visualization, and ChatGPT integration are critical aspects of leveraging Power BI for enhanced financial analysis. This section explores best practices to ensure clean and well-structured data modeling, choosing the right visualizations for effective communication, and leveraging ChatGPT insights to enhance financial analysis.

Ensuring clean and well-structured data modeling

- **Start with data cleansing**. Before modeling financial data in Power BI, ensure that the data is clean and free from errors, inconsistencies, and duplicates. This involves removing irrelevant or incomplete records, handling missing values, and standardizing data formats.

- Here's an example of how you may go about doing this:

- **Import data**: Import your financial data into Power BI. This could be from a CSV file, a database, or any other source.

- **Identify irrelevant records**: Look through your data and identify any records that are not relevant to your analysis. For example, if you're analyzing sales data, you might want to remove any records related to internal transactions.

- **Remove duplicates**: Check for duplicate records in your data and remove them. Power BI has a **Remove Duplicates** function that you can use for this.

- **Handle missing values**: Identify any missing values in your data. Depending on the nature of the data and the purpose of your analysis, you might choose to fill in missing values with a default value, interpolate between existing values, or exclude the records with missing values altogether.

- **Standardize data formats**: Ensure that all of your data is in a consistent format. For example, dates should all be in the same format (DD-MM-YYYY, MM-DD-YYYY, and so on), and monetary values should all have the same number of decimal places.

- **Check for inconsistencies**: Finally, look through your data for any inconsistencies. For example, if you have a column for "Sales Region" and another for "Sales Representative," make sure that each representative is correctly matched with their region.

- **Establish relationships**. Establish appropriate relationships between tables based on key fields such as customer ID, product ID, or transaction ID. This allows for seamless navigation and analysis of financial data across different dimensions. Here's an example of how you might establish between tables in Power BI:

- **Import tables**: Import your financial data tables into Power BI. This could be sales data, customer data, product data, and so on.

- **Identify key fields**: Identify the key fields that are common between your tables. These could be fields such as `Customer ID`, `Product ID` or `Transaction ID`

- **Create relationships**: In Power BI Desktop, go to the **Model** view. Here, you can see all your tables and fields. To create a relationship, simply click and drag the key field from one table to the corresponding field in another table. A line will appear connecting these two tables, indicating that a relationship has been established.

- **Set relationship properties**: Once you've created a relationship, you can set its properties. For example, you can specify the type of relationship (one-to-one, one-to-many, and so on) and the cross-filter direction.

- **Test your model**: After setting up your relationships, test your model by creating some visuals. You should be able to seamlessly analyze data across different tables.

For example, if you have a `Sales` table with `Transaction ID`, `Product ID` and `Sales Amount`, and a `Product` table with `Product ID`, `Product Name`, and `Product Category`, you can establish a relationship based on the `Product ID` field. This would allow you to analyze sales data by product name or category.

- **Implement data validation**. Apply data validation rules to ensure data integrity and accuracy. Validate data against predefined business rules, detect outliers, and flag potential errors for further investigation. Here's how you might implement data validation in Power BI:

- **Define business rules**: Define the business rules that your data must adhere to. For example, sales figures must be positive, customer IDs must be unique, and so on.

- **Create validation measures**: Create measures in Power BI to validate your data against these rules. For example, you could create a measure that counts the number of negative sales figures or duplicate customer IDs.

- **Detect outliers**: Use statistical functions to detect outliers in your data. For example, you could use the `STDEV.P` function to calculate the standard deviation of a dataset and flag any values that are more than three standard deviations away from the mean.

- **Flag errors**: Create calculated columns or measures to flag potential errors in your data. For example, you could create a calculated column that returns `ERROR` if a sales figure is negative or a customer ID is duplicated.

- **Investigate errors**: Use Power BI's data exploration features to investigate any potential errors flagged by your validation measures. This might involve filtering or drilling down into your data to identify the cause of the error.

- **Implement calculated columns and measures**. Utilize calculated columns and measures to perform necessary calculations, aggregations, and financial metrics. This helps derive meaningful insights and simplifies analysis within Power BI. Here's an example of how you might implement calculated columns and measures in Power BI:

- **Calculated column**: Let's say you have a sales data table with `Quantity Sold` and `Price Per Unit` for each transaction. You can create a calculated column named `Total Sales` using the *Total Sales = [Quantity Sold] * [Price Per Unit]* formula. This will calculate the total sales for each transaction.

- **Measure**: Now, if you want to calculate the total sales across all transactions, you can create a measure, such as *Total Sales = SUM('Sales'[Total Sales])*. This measure will dynamically calculate the total sales based on the current filter context of your report.

Choosing the right visualizations for effective communication

- **Understand data characteristics**. Gain a deep understanding of the characteristics of financial data, such as trends, comparisons, distributions, and correlations. This understanding will guide the selection of appropriate visualizations.

- **Use simple and clear visuals**. Avoid clutter and complexity in financial visualizations. Opt for clean and intuitive visualizations that effectively communicate the intended message without overwhelming the audience.

Leverage key visualizations:

- **Line charts**: Use line charts to depict trends over time, such as revenue growth or expense fluctuations

- **Bar charts**: Utilize bar charts to compare financial data, such as the sales performance of assorted products or regions

- **Pie charts**: Employ pie charts to showcase proportions, such as the composition of expenses or revenue sources

- **Tables**: Use tables to present detailed financial data, such as transactional information or financial statements

Leveraging ChatGPT insights to enhance financial analysis

- **Contextual conversations**: Integrate ChatGPT within Power BI to enable users to have interactive conversations and seek insights related to financial data. Contextual conversations provide a natural language interface for querying financial information and gaining additional insights.

- **Interpret user queries**: Develop ChatGPT models that can understand and interpret user queries related to financial analysis. Train the models to recognize common financial terms, metrics, and context to provide accurate responses.

- **Generate actionable insights**: Leverage ChatGPT to generate insightful responses based on user queries. The model can provide recommendations, predictions, or explanations that enhance the understanding and analysis of financial data.

- **Continuous improvement**: Collect user feedback and iterate on the ChatGPT integration to improve the quality of generated insights. Refine the model's training data, incorporate user suggestions, and update the responses based on the evolving needs of financial analysis.

Ensuring data security and privacy

- **Data anonymization**: Prioritize data privacy and confidentiality by anonymizing sensitive financial data. Ensure that **personally identifiable information** (**PII**) or sensitive financial details are masked or encrypted to protect user privacy.

- **Access control**: Implement robust access control mechanisms within Power BI to restrict data access based on user roles and responsibilities. Ensure that only authorized individuals can access and interact with sensitive financial information.

In conclusion, by adhering to best practices for data modeling, visualization, and ChatGPT integration, financial analysts can unlock the full potential of Power BI for enhanced financial analysis. Clean and well-structured data modeling enables accurate insights while selecting the right visualizations facilitates effective communication. Integrating ChatGPT brings the power of natural language understanding to financial analysis, enabling interactive conversations and generating valuable insights. Embracing these best practices empowers financial professionals to make informed decisions, uncover hidden patterns, and drive better business outcomes. The next section provides a walkthrough of using Power BI in financial analysis.

Walk-through use case – analyzing financial data using Power BI

In the world of investing, it's crucial to understand not just a company's standalone performance, but also its performance relative to its peers. That's where our Power BI visualization comes in. Let's walk through pulling a dataset and creating a Power BI visual that compares Apple with its main competitors in the tech industry.

We'll take available financial data and transform it into visual narratives that give you an at-a-glance understanding of how Apple measures up against its competitors. We'll examine historical stock data for Apple, Google, and Microsoft and use this to create Power BI visualizations that bring the data to life.

In the following steps, we will show how to install the necessary packages in Python, pull data from different locations, extract relevant information, and build a Power BI dashboard.

1. **Step 1 – installing the necessary Python libraries**

    In this step, we must set up the necessary Python libraries:

> **Tip**
>
> Libraries in Python are collections of modules that provide specific functionalities, making our programming tasks easier. We'll be using `pandas` for data manipulation and analysis, `yfinance` to download Yahoo! Finance data, `requests` to send HTTP requests, and `BeautifulSoup` to extract data from HTML and XML files. By installing these libraries, we can prepare our Python environment for the subsequent data extraction and analysis tasks.

```
pip install pandas
pip install yfinance
```

Here's a Python code snippet that uses the yfinance library to download historical stock data for Apple, Google, and Microsoft. The `yfinance` library is a convenient tool that allows you to access Yahoo! Finance's historical stock price data. You can use the following code to download the data:

```
import yfinance as yf
import pandas as pd

# Define the ticker symbols
tickers = ['AAPL', 'GOOG', 'MSFT']

# Define the start and end dates
start_date = '2020-01-01'
end_date = '2022-12-31'

# Create an empty DataFrame to store the data
data = pd.DataFrame()

# Download the data
for ticker in tickers:
 df = yf.download(ticker, start=start_date, end=end_date,
interval='1mo')
 df['Ticker'] = ticker # Add a column with the ticker symbol
```

```
    data = pd.concat([data, df])

  # Reset the index
  data.reset_index(inplace=True)

  # Save the data to a CSV file
  data.to_csv('stock_data.csv', index=False)
```

Here's a step-by-step breakdown:

- **Import the necessary libraries**: The script starts by importing the necessary Python libraries – yfinance for downloading stock data from Yahoo! Finance and pandas for data manipulation.

- **Define ticker symbols**: The ticker symbols for the stocks of interest are defined in a list – AAPL for Apple, GOOG for Google, and MSFT for Microsoft.

- **Define the date range**: The start and end dates for the historical data are defined as 2020-01-01 and 2022-12-31, respectively.

- **Create an empty DataFrame**: An empty pandas DataFrame is created to store the downloaded data.

- **Download the data**: The script then loops over each ticker symbol in the list, downloads the monthly stock data for the defined date range using the yf.download() function, adds a new column to the downloaded data to store the ticker symbol, and appends this data to the main DataFrame.

- **Reset the index**: The index of the main DataFrame is reset using the reset_index() function. This is done because when new DataFrames are concatenated, pandas keeps the original indices. Resetting the index ensures that we have a continuous index in the final DataFrame.

- **Save the data to a CSV file**: Finally, the consolidated stock data is saved to a CSV file named stock_data.csv using the to_csv() function. The index=False argument is used to prevent pandas from saving the index as a separate column in the CSV file.

Now, we will take this data and create visualizations with Power BI.

With the stock data you have, you can create several types of charts in Power BI. Here are a few examples:

- **Candlestick chart**: This chart is used to show price movement for the securities in the stock market. It contains information about the open, high, low, and closing prices of stock.

- **Stock chart**: A stock chart in a Power BI paginated report is specifically designed for financial or scientific data that uses up to four values per data point. These values align with the high, low, open, and close values that are used to plot financial stock data.

The following are some other custom visualizations available in Power BI:

- Mekko charts
- Hexbin scatterplot
- Word cloud
- Pulse charts
- Interactive chord diagrams

To create a candlestick chart in Power BI, follow these steps:

1. Open Power BI and connect to your dataset.
2. Select the candlestick chart visualization from the **Visualizations** pane.
3. Drag and drop the required fields onto the chart, such as date, high, low, open, and close prices.
4. The chart will automatically generate based on the data you have selected.

> **Tip**
>
> You might need to download the candlestick visualization from the web. Click on the ellipsis in the **Visualizations** pane (**Get more visuals**). Search for `candlestick`; it should show up as a free add-on. Please select it and add it to the **Visualizations** pane.

Remember, the candlestick chart is a powerful tool that can help you understand market trends and identify potential opportunities:

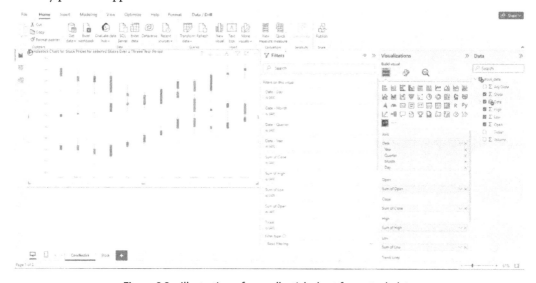

Figure 2.3 – Illustration of a candlestick chart from stock data

To create a stock chart in Power BI using the data you've downloaded from `yfinance`, you can follow these steps:

1. **Import the data**: Open Power BI and import the CSV file you created (`stock_data.csv`). You can do this by clicking on **Home** > **External Data** > **Get Data** > **Text/CSV**.

2. **Create a new chart**: Click on the **Report** view (the bar chart icon on the left), and then click on the line chart icon in the **Visualizations** pane.

3. **Add data to the chart**: In the **Fields** pane, drag and drop the required fields onto the chart. For a basic stock chart, you would typically use the following values:

   - **Date** for the axis

   - **Open**, **High**, **Low**, and **Close** as values

   - **Ticker** for the legend (optional)

4. **Customize the chart**: You can further customize your chart by clicking on the paint roller icon in the **Visualizations** pane. Here, you can change things such as colors, add a title, modify axis settings, and more.

5. **Save your report**: Once you're happy with your chart, don't forget to save your report by clicking on **File** > **Save**.

Remember, these are just basic steps to create a simple line chart for stock data. Power BI offers many other types of charts and advanced features that you can explore to create more complex and insightful visualizations:

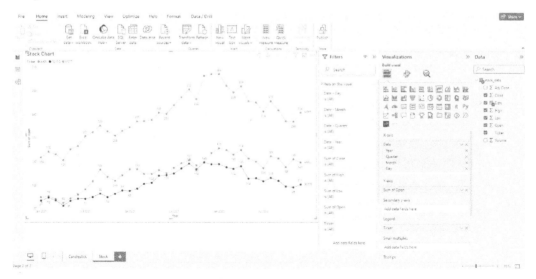

Figure 2.4 – Illustration of a stock chart in Power BI using the stock data

> **Tip**
>
> Remember to format and label your charts clearly to make them easy to understand. You can also add filters to allow viewers to drill down into specific periods or companies.

Finally, you can ask ChatGPT for insights and interpretations based on the visualizations you've created. For example, you might ask why there was a spike in patent filings in a particular year, or how a company's R&D spending compares to its competitors.

In the next section, we'll look at a different walkthrough, this time incorporating ChatGPT insights with Power BI.

Walk-through use case – analyzing financial ratios using Power BI and ChatGPT

The following is an example that you can try to emulate. It is a simple illustration of how you can integrate Power BI and ChatGPT. (Note: this example is courtesy of Amer Mahmood, who posted this article on medium.com).

In this example, we will create a report in Power BI and feed the data to ChatGPT, asking for insights. Some steps need to be completed before we start:

1. Install Python and enable Python in Power BI:

   I.   First, install Python, if you have not done so already. Please visit the official website (`https://www.python.org/downloads/`) to download it. We recommend versions 3.9 and 3.10.

   II.   Once Python has been installed, enable Python scripting in Power BI. To do so, open Power BI Desktop. Then, click **File** > **Options** and go to **Settings** > **Options** > **Python scripting**. Select the checkbox and click **OK**.

   III. Next, set the Python path in Power BI. Go to **File** > **Options** and then to **Settings** > **Options** > **Python scripting**. Here, click **Detect**. This selects the Python installation path automatically. You can also do this manually by clicking on the ellipsis (…) and selecting the Python executable file.

   IV.   Restart Power BI Desktop for the changes you made to take effect.

2. Follow these steps to set up ChatGPT using the ChatGPT API:

   I.   First, you will need to obtain an API key from Open AI. Navigate to the Open AI website (`https://openai.com`) and create a (personal) account.

   II.   Next, ask for and get an API key. You will use this in all your integration projects.

> **Tip**
>
> These API keys are not free. When you sign up with Open AI, you get about $18 worth of tokens for use with your API Key. After that, you are billed (pay-as-you-go). The details are available on the Open AI site under **Pricing** (`https://openai.com/pricing`).

III.   The ChatGPT API has SDKs and libraries available in several programming languages. Select **Python**. We will use Python extensively in this book and recommend it.

IV.   Install the SDK with a package manager such as `pip`:

```
pip install openai
```

3.   Now, we need to create a dataset to analyze. Follow these steps:

I.   Use Excel to create a sample dataset similar to the following. Name it `Tech Stocks`:

Current Ratio	Debt to Equity	Gross Margin %	Price to Book	Price to Earnings	Return on Equity %
0.94	1.96	42.96	40.75	24.79	147.94
2.38	0.12	53.11	4.63	20.5	23.62
0.89	2.45	58.65	5.81	73.28	8.73
2.2	0.22	78.63	3.63	20.33	18.52
1.93	0.43	66.85	10.21	27.92	39.31
3.52	0.54	63.34	26.01	133.88	17.93

II.   Create a simple report in Power BI Desktop by connecting this dataset to Power BI. Go to the **Modeling** tab via the left column. This is what should appear:

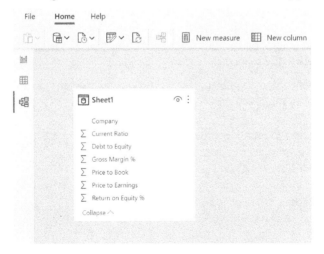

Figure 2.5 – A view of the Modeling tab in Power BI

III.   Select the third icon from the left in the ribbon to **Transform** the data.

IV.   Add **Run Python script** to the **Applied Steps** section.

V.   Now, we can put the code in the next section directly into Power BI and run it.

4.   Now, we must call the ChatGPT API from Power BI. Here, we will integrate ChatGPT with Power BI using the Power Query Editor in Power BI and writing an executable Python code. The code is as follows:

I.   To start, import the necessary Python libraries:

```
# 'dataset' holds the input data for this script
# Import Libraries
import openai
import os
```

II.   Next, add your Open AI key to the code:

```
# Get Open AI API from windows environment
openai.api_key = "Your Open AI API Key"
```

III.   To pass data to the API, loop through each row of the dataset and create a single string:

```
# Loop through each row in dataset & concatenate the data
into a single string. Pass resulting string to the API
for index,row in dataset.iterrows():
messages="I am going to give you a set of company information
in the following order Company,Price to Earnings,Price to
Book,Return on Equity %,Debt to Equity,Current Ratio,Gross
Margin %,analyze the ratios for each company, refer to the
company by its name and write a concise response"
message = ''.join ([str(col) for col in row])
```

IV.   Now, build the API request so tha–t it includes the row-level data and makes a chat completion request for the API. Once we've done this, we can process the response and write it back to the report:

```
#Build the API request to include row level data from source
    messages += " " + str(message)

    #Make a chat completion Request for the API
    chat = openai.ChatCompletion.create(
    model = "gpt-3.5-turbo",
    messages = [{"role":"user","content":messages}],
    temperature = 0.9,
    max_tokens = 500,
    top_p = 1,
```

```
    frequency_penalty = 0,
    presence_penalty = 0.6
    )

#Process the response from API
reply = chat.choices[0].message.content

#Write the response Back to the Report
dataset.at[index, "reslt"] = reply
```

When we run this script, the Python code loops through each row of the Power BI table and uses the report data to construct the prompt for ChatGPT. This prompt is passed to ChatGPT with the API response being written back to the Power BI DataFrame and table one row (company) at a time.

Keep in mind that the dataset is a built-in pandas DataFrame-like structure that allows the Power BI developer to access and manipulate data from the Power BI table using Python.

The result of the ChatGPT response can be rendered as a visual in the Power BI report you've created. It should look like this:

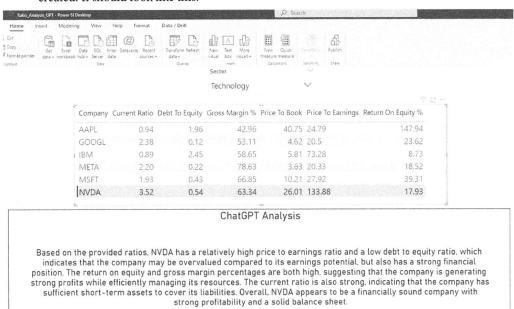

Figure 2.6 – Power BI dashboard showing ChatGPT insights

You can use this format to pass through any number of datasets and leverage insights using ChatGPT. Try using this with existing reports in Power BI.

Next, we'll summarize the key takeaways from this chapter.

Summary

In this chapter, we learned about Power BI in finance and that it is a powerful tool for financial analysis, offering features such as data modeling, visualization, and integration with ChatGPT for enhanced insights.

We followed this up with a section on data modeling and visualization techniques. We explained why clean and well-structured data modeling is essential for effective financial analysis in Power BI. This involves data cleansing, establishing relationships, implementing validation, and utilizing calculated columns and measures. We detailed how choosing the right visualizations is crucial for communicating financial information effectively, understanding the characteristics of the data, and leveraging visuals such as line charts, bar charts, pie charts, and tables for clear and concise representation.

Then, we learned about ChatGPT integration with Power BI. Integrating ChatGPT with Power BI allows users to have contextual conversations and seek insights related to financial data. We also learned how to develop ChatGPT models that interpret user queries and generate actionable insights for improved financial analysis.

Next, we listed some best practices, which included the following:

- Ensuring data security and privacy by anonymizing sensitive information and implementing access control

- Continuously refining and improving data models, visualizations, and ChatGPT integration based on user feedback and evolving needs

- Planning and designing financial dashboards with a focus on clarity, interactivity, and relevant KPIs

Finally, we listed the benefits of Power BI – how Power BI provides real-time, interactive, and visually appealing dashboards that enable stakeholders to gain valuable insights into financial performance, analyze trends, identify opportunities, and make data-driven decisions.

Get ready to shift gears in *Chapter 3* as we delve deep into the electrifying intersection of ChatGPT, AI, and the financial world, all through the lens of Tesla. We'll kickstart your journey by unveiling how ChatGPT can decode intricate data and transform it into actionable investment insights. Ready to disrupt conventional wisdom? We'll reveal Tesla's unique data sources and KPIs, offering you an edge in your financial decisions. Take a spin through the world of sentiment analysis as we dissect news articles and earnings call transcripts to gauge market sentiment like never before. Whether you're an investor or a planner, our AI-driven trading strategies will have something tailored just for you. We'll dazzle you with Power BI visualizations that make complex financial metrics as easy to read as your car's dashboard. And because fairness matters, we'll guide you on how to ensure your AI models are unbiased.

3

Tesla's Financial Journey: AI Analysis and Bias Unveiled

In the previous chapter, we delved into the essentials of using Power BI for financial analysis. By taking you through a comprehensive guide to this powerful tool, we showed you how to integrate ChatGPT insights to augment your decision-making process. You learned the ins and outs of data modeling, visualization techniques, and dashboard creation in Power BI. The chapter emphasized the value of blending AI technology, such as ChatGPT, with traditional financial analytics tools. We walked you through examples demonstrating how to use Power BI for visualizing a company's financial performance over time, supplemented by ChatGPT insights to identify potential trends, risks, or opportunities. We emphasized the best practices for data modeling, creating visualizations, and integrating ChatGPT insights to ensure a comprehensive understanding of financial trends, risks, and opportunities.

In this chapter, we will explore the fascinating world of AI in financial analysis, specifically focusing on ChatGPT's role. This chapter will provide an overview of both fundamental and technical analysis, demonstrating how AI and ChatGPT can enhance these traditional finance methods. You will witness the power of AI and ChatGPT through real-world examples and case studies, observing how they generate insights, identify trends, and assess risks. We will delve into how ChatGPT can be utilized for predicting financial performance, market trends, and economic indicators, along with its role in risk assessment.

One of the highlights of this chapter will be a practical use case where we will employ AI-generated insights and ChatGPT to evaluate a company's financial performance, thereby identifying potential investment opportunities and assessing risks. This chapter will also address the best practices and ethical considerations for using AI-driven tools in financial analysis, discussing potential challenges such as data privacy and algorithm bias.

In this chapter, we will cover the following topics:

- **Unveiling the power of AI in finance**: Step into the exciting intersection of finance and artificial intelligence. Discover how AI can redefine traditional financial analysis methods and create transformative solutions in financial markets.

- **ChatGPT-enhanced fundamental and technical analysis**: See how ChatGPT can bring a novel depth and perspective to the fundamental and technical aspects of financial analysis. Through practical exercises and real-world examples, experience the enhancements AI can provide to these foundational methodologies.

- **Predicting stock prices and risks using AI**: Acquire practical skills in predicting stock prices and risks using AI. With our hands-on approach, you'll grasp AI-driven techniques to stay ahead in the fast-paced financial world.

- **In-depth Tesla analysis with ChatGPT**: Discover how ChatGPT can interpret and present comprehensive insights into a leading company such as Tesla. Understand their performance and market position and get a peek into future trends.

- **Power BI for data visualization**: Learn to transform complex financial data into compelling visual narratives using Power BI. Create dynamic and insightful visualizations that amplify your data storytelling abilities.

- **ChatGPT-informed Tesla competitive analysis**: Apply your newfound skills to analyze Tesla in comparison to its competitors. Use Power BI to create dynamic visualizations and metrics, guided by insights from ChatGPT, for a clearer understanding of the automotive market dynamics.

- **Trading examples for Tesla**: We'll illustrate examples of aggressive and passive trading strategies using Tesla's options and stock, helping you gain practical knowledge for real-world trading.

- **Understanding AI ethics in finance**: Explore the ethical implications and best practices of using AI in financial analysis. We'll guide you through responsibly navigating the AI landscape and ensuring optimal security, fairness, and efficacy.

This chapter promises a thrilling exploration into the world of AI-driven financial analysis. Brace yourself for a captivating journey that marries traditional finance with cutting-edge AI, enriching your understanding and skills in this innovative field.

By the end of this chapter, you will have gained a solid foundation in applying AI, specifically ChatGPT, to financial analysis, opening up a new dimension to your finance analytics toolkit.

Introduction to ChatGPT and AI in financial analysis

In this section, we will dive deep into Tesla, using it as a primary example for our exploration of AI in investing, trading, and financial analysis. We selected Tesla as a case study because it perfectly exemplifies the intersections of AI technology and finance while providing Power BI visualizations that help the reader understand the data. Tesla's unique position as a leading innovator in the electric vehicle and renewable energy sectors provides us with a rich, real-world context of the concepts we will explore, showcasing how they apply in a highly disruptive and fast-paced industry.

Each of these subsections provides a unique lens through which we can examine Tesla:

- **Data sources—Tesla's data universe**: Join us as we explore the rich and varied data landscape of Tesla, diving into financial reports, SEC filings, earnings call transcripts, and market data **application programming interfaces (APIs)**. We're not just looking at numbers; we're going under the hood of Tesla's groundbreaking electric vehicle technology, its innovative strides in battery enhancements, its race toward full self-driving capabilities, and its ambitious ventures into solar power and energy storage.

- **Risk assessments—Tesla's wild ride**: Strap in for an electrifying journey into the world of Tesla's stock performance. Using the power of AI, we will navigate the twists and turns of Tesla's high-growth yet volatile journey in the EV and renewable energy markets.

- **Visualizations—painting Tesla's future with Power BI**: We're taking you on a visual journey with Power BI, turning Tesla's financials and market performance into vivid, insightful visuals. Witness Tesla's breathtaking revenue growth, ambitious R&D commitments, and unpredictable net income unfold.

- **Trading examples—steering through Tesla's market with ChatGPT**: Hold on tight as we switch to autopilot and let AI and ChatGPT guide you through Tesla's thrilling trading landscape. We'll predict market trends, forecast potential obstacles, and navigate investment strategies as if we're behind the wheel of a Tesla Model S. Whether you're a day trader on the lookout for short-term gains or a long-term investor aiming for a stake in the EV revolution, we have you covered. Before we dive into the specifics of AI-driven financial analysis, let's briefly recap the concepts of fundamental and technical analysis. These two methods form the foundation of traditional financial analysis, but when combined with the power of AI and ChatGPT, they become even more potent.

Fundamental analysis focuses on evaluating a company's intrinsic value by examining its financial statements, industry trends, and economic indicators. Technical analysis, on the other hand, relies on historical price data and trading volume to identify patterns and trends that can inform future price movements.

AI and ChatGPT can significantly enhance both types of analysis by providing data-driven insights, automating complex calculations, and identifying trends and patterns that might not be readily apparent to the human eye. By integrating AI insights with traditional analysis methods, financial professionals can make better-informed decisions and stay ahead of the competition. Let's take a quick look at Tesla's unconventional data trove and determine what we can incorporate into our case study analysis of this unconventional company.

Venturing beyond convention—exploring Tesla's unconventional data sources

Tesla, being a multi-dimensional innovator, defies traditional boundaries of assessment. To capture its comprehensive value, we need to examine unconventional yet crucial data sources that the conventional financial world may not heavily weigh. Although we won't examine each area in detail, we will expose you to a breadth of topics and equip you with the mindset and tools to independently explore these exciting realms:

- **Elon Musk—unconventional leader and visionary**: Musk's unique style of leadership and public communication often influences market sentiment, providing insights into Tesla's potential trajectory. Our AI, ChatGPT, will aid us in sifting through his dynamic commentary, assisting us in separating his characteristic bold vision from the practical business forecasts.

- **Tesla—the multi-domain innovator**: Tesla's transcendence from a car company to a technology and energy powerhouse necessitates a broad lens of evaluation. Areas such as electric vehicle technology, self-driving AI, and energy storage form part of this complex puzzle.

- **Navigating the future—full self-driving (FSD) and AI**: Tesla's autopilot and future FSD technologies hold revolutionary potential. While challenging to quantify, these aspects can't be overlooked when assessing Tesla's long-term prospects.

- **Tesla's charge into energy**: Tesla's strides into the energy sector, particularly solar power and battery storage, reflect a strategic diversification. This segment holds potential for substantial growth, warranting a keen eye.

- **Competitor landscape**: Tesla competes not only with traditional automakers but also tech behemoths venturing into the auto space. This unique competitive set impacts Tesla's strategic and financial outcomes.

- **The Tesla ecosystem**: Tesla, akin to Apple, is crafting an ecosystem of interconnected products and services. The ensuing network effect could bolster Tesla's growth and profitability.

- **The cool factor—Tesla's cultural impact**: Tesla's cultural impact and brand recognition, translating to customer loyalty and free advertising, is a valuable, albeit intangible, asset. Its quantification may pose a challenge, but its influence on Tesla's success is undeniable.

By presenting these areas, we encourage you to think outside the traditional analytical box, exploring less conventional yet impactful data sources. Harnessing these can offer you a nuanced and comprehensive understanding of Tesla's stock, positioning you a step above conventional market participants. We need to think about what metrics and **key performance indicators** (**KPIs**) we should include in our evaluation of this EV company, which pushed the norms of how a car maker should operate. Let's take a look at our options in the next section.

Shifting gears—rethinking metrics and KPIs for Tesla

Tesla's revolutionary approach to transportation, energy, and technology challenges us to reconsider conventional financial metrics and KPIs. As investors, we need to venture beyond traditional financial analysis and explore a range of metrics and KPIs uniquely suited to Tesla's multifaceted business model.

While we will delve into a few key metrics in detail, we also present a broader set of metrics and KPIs that can provide a more comprehensive understanding of Tesla's potential:

- **Revenue breakdown by segment**: Assessing the growth rates and potential of Tesla's diverse revenue streams, such as automotive sales, regulatory credits, energy storage, and services, offers us a more nuanced understanding.

- **Autopilot and FSD metrics**: As FSD technology matures, tracking metrics such as miles driven on Autopilot, human intervention frequency, and FSD package sales could be crucial indicators of progress.

- **Energy storage deployments**: Monitoring the megawatt-hours of energy storage deployed could provide insights into the growth and potential of Tesla's burgeoning energy business.

- **Vehicle software upgrades**: As a carmaker with a unique recurring revenue stream from over-the-air software updates and premium software offerings, tracking software sales as a percentage of total vehicle sales could be enlightening.

- **Supercharger network growth**: The growth of Tesla's Supercharger network, gauged by the number of stations or connectors, could reflect on its infrastructure investment and customer experience enhancement.

- **Battery production and cost**: Tesla's ability to produce batteries at scale and at decreasing costs is central to its mission. Metrics such as gigawatt hours of battery capacity produced and cost per kilowatt-hour of battery capacity can serve as KPIs.

- **Brand perception metrics**: Surveys or social media sentiment analysis could provide valuable insights into customer perception and loyalty to Tesla's influential brand.

- **Sustainability metrics**: Tracking metrics related to Tesla's sustainability efforts could offer a unique way to gauge its progress towards its mission.

- **Innovation and R&D metrics**: Tracing R&D spending as a percentage of revenue, patents filed, and progress toward key research goals could shed light on Tesla's capacity for innovation.

Remember, no single metric offers a complete snapshot of a complex and dynamic company such as Tesla. It's crucial to explore a broad spectrum of factors, both qualitative and quantitative, to understand their interconnected dynamics. In this chapter, we will delve into a selection of these metrics using Power BI, equipping you with the tools and insights to extend your analysis based on the preceding comprehensive list. There is no getting around the fact that Tesla is surrounded by controversy, so how do we capture that data and make sense of it? We can take a look at what is being said about the company and gauge sentiment through a number of sources and apply some creativity by including investor sentiment and considering how we might include it in our analysis in this upcoming section.

News and earnings call transcripts—unveiling the sentiment spectrum

Investor sentiment is a critical facet of stock market dynamics, and gauging it can offer valuable insights into stock price movements. Two particularly rich sources for decoding investor sentiment are news articles and earnings call transcripts. Each offers a different yet complementary perspective, and creatively tapping into them presents us with novel ways to gather additional market sentiment and insights:

- **News articles**: Major news outlets significantly influence public sentiment toward a company. The way they report on an organization can sway investor perception, leading to stock price fluctuations. However, the sentiment embedded within these articles isn't confined to the content alone; it extends to readers' comments. These comments are a treasure trove of investor sentiment, comprising diverse viewpoints, insights, and reactions. By harnessing AI and ChatGPT, we can sift through a multitude of articles and reader comments, turning the hidden sentiment into an actionable data stream. This innovative approach offers a fresh perspective on investor sentiment.

- **Earnings call transcripts**: Earnings calls are pivotal events with a direct impact on a company's stock price. They offer a unique platform where company executives share crucial financial updates, growth strategies, and future plans. Of particular interest is the Q&A segment, where Wall Street analysts pose probing questions. This exchange provides an unfiltered glimpse into the minds of those who actively shape the market's perception of the company. Using AI and ChatGPT to analyze these transcripts allows us to convert this raw, complex information into discernible sentiment patterns. This creative method can be used to anticipate potential market reactions to Tesla's strategies and performance.

However, parsing and categorizing comments can be a challenging task due to the nuances of human language, such as humor, sarcasm, and argumentative exchanges. Leveraging advanced **Natural Language Processing** (**NLP**) tools such as ChatGPT, which are trained to understand these nuances, can help in accurately classifying comments.

Despite the challenges, combining these diverse data sources—earnings call transcripts, news articles, Wall Street analyst Q&A, and reader comments—could provide a multi-dimensional view of the sentiment around Tesla. It's crucial to remember, though, that sentiment analysis is only one part of a comprehensive investment evaluation strategy and should be used in conjunction with fundamental and technical analysis. We should start our assessment of Tesla at a high level by looking at growth drivers, potential risks, benchmarking, and ratio analysis as a starting point. This next section will provide a starting point for us to review and think about in more detail.

Tesla: growth drivers and potential risks

The following are Tesla's growth drivers:

- **Vehicle deliveries**: You can analyze Tesla's growth trajectory through the lens of Model 3 and Model Y sales and the Gigafactory's production capacity

- **Gross margin improvements**: You can gauge efficiency and cost-effectiveness by evaluating manufacturing efficiencies and declining battery costs

- **Energy storage/solar deployments**: You can examine the expansion of Tesla's energy segment, focusing on Megapack and Solar Roof installations

The following are its risks and weaknesses:

- **Global chip shortage**: Assess the impact of the global chip shortage on Tesla's production capabilities

- **Competition**: Evaluate threats from established automakers such as Volkswagen and GM, as well as new entrants such as Rivian and Lucid

- **Regulatory challenges**: Consider the potential legal challenges related to autonomous driving features and other regulatory issues

As we shift our focus to a deeper financial analysis, let's equip ourselves with key tools to accurately assess Tesla's performance. Benchmarking and ratio analysis offer an insightful perspective, while different trading strategies cater to distinct risk preferences.

Benchmarking and ratio analysis: AI-driven insights

- **Benchmarking**: Compare Tesla's financial performance against industry benchmarks and key competitors, such as NIO, XPeng, Rivian, and Lucid, and traditional automakers, such as Ford and General Motors. Consider metrics such as revenue growth rate, profitability, and market share.

- **Ratio Analysis**: Leverage ratios such as **Price-to-Earnings (P/E)**, **Price-to-Sales (P/S)**, and debt-to-equity to evaluate Tesla's valuation and performance compared to other EV manufacturers or the broader automotive industry.

Trading strategies based on risk preference

- **Aggressive trading strategy**: Use options strategies such as buying call options for bullish moves in Tesla's stock price or put options for bearish moves.

- **Conservative trading strategy**: Engage in position trading based on fundamental analysis. For example, take long positions when Tesla shows strong revenue growth or expanding gross margins.

In the upcoming section, we will delve into a practical use case of applying this financial analysis approach to Tesla Inc., an American electric vehicle and clean energy company, and how ChatGPT can provide valuable assistance in evaluating investment opportunities.

Case study: Tesla Inc.

We will focus on evaluating Tesla's financial performance and identifying potential investment opportunities and risks using ChatGPT and AI-generated insights.

Using ChatGPT, we'll scrutinize key trends and growth drivers from financial statements and SEC filings and identify potential risks and weaknesses, such as global chip shortages or increased competition. We'll also benchmark Tesla's performance against key competitors and industry averages.

Lastly, we will discuss trading strategies that vary based on risk tolerance levels: aggressive and conservative. For each strategy, we will provide examples of how one might go about investing in Tesla.

Evaluating investment opportunities and risks with AI-driven insights

In this practical use case, let's explore how to use AI-generated insights and ChatGPT to evaluate Tesla's financial performance and identify potential investment opportunities and risks.

We'll be examining Tesla's key growth drivers that can consistently move the stock price:

- Vehicle deliveries: Tesla's ability to increase vehicle deliveries quarter over quarter is often seen as a critical measure of the company's growth and execution

- Gross margin: Tesla's gross margin can indicate the company's ability to control production costs, which is essential for maintaining profitability

- Energy storage and solar deployments: The growth in Tesla's energy storage and solar business segments may demonstrate the company's diversification beyond electric vehicles

Buckle up for a high-octane journey through the financial landscape of Tesla, propelled by the analytical prowess of ChatGPT. Our exhilarating tour will zoom into the key trends observed in Tesla's financial statements and SEC filings, spotlighting specifics such as contrasting revenue growth or changes in operating expenses over time. Prepare to dive into the high-stakes world of Tesla trading strategies in the next section. Trading isn't just about numbers; it's a game of strategy and patience where the players are as dynamic as the market they're navigating.

First off, we're plunging into the depths of aggressive trading strategies. Feel the rush as we leverage options, buying call options in anticipation of a bullish market and put options for the bears. And how are we predicting these market moves? Through sentiment analysis. That's right, we're unlocking the emotions behind the numbers, making sense of the buzz in news, social media, earnings call transcripts to help guide our trading decisions.

Next, we'll explore the realms of conservative trading strategies. This is a different beast entirely— a realm where patience and strategy are king. Here, we follow a simple long position strategy, buying shares of Tesla when certain fundamental conditions are met.

Tesla trading strategy (aggressive and conservative)

Kicking things off, we're delving into the realm of aggressive trading strategies. Here, we'll explore the intricate mechanics of options trading, specifically buying call options in anticipation of a bullish move, and conversely, put options for bearish moves. But these aren't mere gambles; these moves are rooted in careful observation and sharp analysis.

In this exciting intersection of finance and artificial intelligence, we'll harness the power of ChatGPT to sieve through the vast sea of news and earnings call transcripts. It will help us gauge public sentiment toward Tesla, which can often provide a hint or two about the company's stock movements.

In parallel to this, you'll have the Power BI dashboard at your disposal. This will serve as your cockpit, laying out the current and historical stock price of Tesla and the volume and price of the options you are trading. It can also display the sentiment analysis results, making it a comprehensive tool to aid your aggressive trading strategy.

How do you make sense of the data? This is where Python comes in. We'll be utilizing a broker with a Python API such as Alpaca, allowing you to turn raw data into actionable insights. You'll find that with the right code, even the most daunting data can be tamed. However, remember that each broker's API is unique, so the exact code will depend on your specific broker.

Aggressive trading strategy using options

Here, we'll use a simple options strategy: buying call options when anticipating a bullish move and put options for bearish moves. We will use sentiment analysis on news and social media to help predict these moves.

For simplicity, let's assume we are using a broker with a Python API such as Alpaca. Note that the exact code will depend on the specifics of your broker's API:

```
a. Install first
pip install alpaca-trade-api

b. Run Python code
import alpaca_trade_api as tradeapi


# Initialize the Alpaca API
api = tradeapi.REST('<APCA-API-KEY-ID>', '<APCA-API-SECRET-KEY>',
base_url='https://paper-api.alpaca.markets')

# Define the stock symbol
symbol = 'TSLA'
contract = api.get_option_contracts(symbol)

# Function to buy a call option
def buy_call(api, symbol, contract):
    order = api.submit_order(
        symbol=symbol,
```

```
        qty=1,
        side='buy',
        type='limit',
        time_in_force='gtc',
        limit_price=contract.ask_price
    )
    print(f"Call option order submitted. ID: {order.id}")

# Function to buy a put option
def buy_put(api, symbol, contract):
    order = api.submit_order(
        symbol=symbol,
        qty=1,
        side='buy',
        type='limit',
        time_in_force='gtc',
        limit_price=contract.bid_price
    )
    print(f"Put option order submitted. ID: {order.id}")

# Example usage
buy_call(api, symbol, contract)
buy_put(api, symbol, contract)
```

> **IMPORTANT**
> Replace `<APCA-API-KEY-ID>` and `<APCA-API-SECRET-KEY>` with your actual Alpaca API key and secret.

Let's look at what this code does:

- **Imports Alpaca trade API**: Alpaca is an online brokerage that offers a modern platform for trading and has its own Python library that allows you to interact with their platform programmatically. We start by importing this library, which is a collection of code that we can use to do things such as place trades.

- **Defines the Alpaca API**: Here, we are connecting to Alpaca's trading platform by using their API. This is like establishing a secure line of communication between our Python code and Alpaca's trading services.

- **Defines the option contract**: An option contract represents 100 shares of a stock. Defining the option contract involves specifying details such as the stock (Tesla, in our case), the price at which you have the right to buy or sell the stock (the strike price), and the date when the option expires.

- **Buys a call option**: A call option gives us the right (but not the obligation) to buy the stock at the strike price. This is what we do when we anticipate that Tesla's stock price will go up. We're effectively betting on a bullish market movement.

- **Buys a put option**: Conversely, a put option gives us the right (but not the obligation) to sell the stock at the strike price. We do this when we expect Tesla's stock price to go down or when we're anticipating a bearish market movement.

To decide whether we should buy a call or put option, we are using sentiment analysis on news and social media as well as earnings call transcripts. Sentiment analysis involves using algorithms to determine whether the sentiment toward Tesla in news articles and social media posts is positive or negative. If the sentiment is bullish (positive), we might buy a call option. If it's bearish (negative), we might buy a put option.

It's important to remember, though, that this is a simplified overview; actual trading involves more complexity and risk. Always ensure that you understand a strategy fully and consider consulting a financial advisor before implementing it.

Conservative trading strategy using position trading

For a more conservative strategy, we can use a simple long position strategy where we buy shares of Tesla when certain fundamental conditions are met. We will assume that the `alpaca-trade-api` package is not installed in the following example. If you have already installed it, please remove the first line in this Python code example:

```
pip install alpaca-trade-api
import alpaca_trade_api as tradeapi

# Initialize the Alpaca API
api = tradeapi.REST('<Your-API-Key>', '<Your-Secret-Key>', base_
url='https://paper-api.alpaca.markets')

# Define the stock symbol
symbol = 'TSLA'

try:
    # Place a buy order
    api.submit_order(
        symbol=symbol,
        qty=1,
        side='buy',
        type='market',
        time_in_force='day'
```

```
    )

    # Place a sell order
    api.submit_order(
        symbol=symbol,
        qty=1,
        side='sell',
        type='market',
        time_in_force='day'
    )

    # List current positions
    positions = api.list_positions()
    for position in positions:
        print(f"{position.symbol} {position.qty}")

except Exception as e:
    print(f"An error occurred: {e}")
```

- **API key and secret key**: Ensure you replace `<Your-API-Key>` and `<Your-Secret-Key>` with the actual Alpaca API key and secret key.

- **Market orders**: The code is currently placing market orders. Make sure the market is open when you run this code, or else the orders may not execute.

- **time-in-force**: You've set `time_in_force` to `gtc` (good-til-cancelled). This is fine for limit orders, but for market orders, you may consider using 'day' to specify that the order is only valid during the trading day.

- **Error handling**: The code does not include any error handling. You might want to add some try-except blocks.

The following is an explanation of this Python code snippet:

- **Imports Alpaca trade API**: This code will import Alpaca's library into your Python script.

- **Establishes Alpaca API connection**: This will set up a connection to Alpaca's API using your personal API keys.

- **Defines the stock**: This is where you specify the stock you're interested in trading (Tesla, in this case).

- **Buys Tesla shares**: When you're ready to buy shares, you can place an order using Alpaca's `submit_order` function. Here's how you could place a simple market order to buy one share of Tesla:

```
    api.submit_order(
        symbol=symbol,
```

```
        qty=1,
        side='buy',
        type='market',
        time_in_force='gtc'
    )
```

- **Sells Tesla shares**: Similarly, when you're ready to sell shares, you could use the same `submit_order` function:

```
api.submit_order(
    symbol=symbol,
    qty=1,
    side='sell',
    type='market',
    time_in_force='day'
)
```

- `print`: Lastly, the `print` statement is used to output the result of a particular action in your code. For instance, if you want to print the list of your current positions, you could use the `list_positions` function and print it as follows:

```
positions = api.list_positions()
for position in positions:
    print(f"{position.symbol} {position.qty}")
```

Keep in mind that this code is illustrative and assumes that you have API keys from Alpaca. Always remember to protect your API keys and don't share them with others.

In the next section, we will highlight how to pull in news and earnings call transcript data to help pull in data that can be reviewed by ChatGPT to determine sentiment (positive, neutral, or negative). This can signal whether or not we should buy, hold, or sell based on the sentiment indicators.

News and market sentiment integration for trading strategies: aggressive and conservative

In this section, we will delve into the pivotal role of news and market sentiment in shaping intelligent trading strategies and learning how to interpret and integrate real-time data and market indicators into investment decisions. You will master the art of leveraging cutting-edge tools and analytics to predict market trends, understand investor behaviors, and enhance your trading performance and financial acumen.

This section will provide a step-by-step process:

1. Install libraries `newsapi` and `Beautifulsoup4`.

2. Use an API from NewsAPI to fetch Tesla news articles and `BeautifulSoup` to pull the Tesla earnings transcripts.

3. Perform sentiment analysis with ChatGPT (including comments in articles and Q&A in earnings transcripts).

4. Save the data into a CSV file(s).

5. Import the data into Power BI.

6. Create visualizations to use for your Tesla aggressive and conservative trading decisions.

Using a Python library called NewsAPI to get news data and a library called TextBlob for simple sentiment analysis, NLTK library. or even pre-trained models from transformers library (such as BERT or GPT-3.5) to evaluate sentiment from news and social media. For the integration of the data into Power BI, we will outline a simple method using CSV files. Let's dive into these steps in detail:

1. Install the required libraries.

   In Python, you need to install the following libraries using pip:

   ```
   pip install newsapi-python
   pip install requests
   pip install textblob
   pip install pandas
   ```

2. Get Tesla news and earnings call data from Tesla articles and Tesla earnings call transcripts.

   To extract news articles about Tesla, use the following code:

   ```
   from newsapi import NewsApiClient

   # Initialize the News API client
   newsapi = NewsApiClient(api_key='your-newsapi-key')

   try:
       # Fetch news articles related to Tesla
       all_articles = newsapi.get_everything(q='Tesla',
                                             from_param='2022-10-
   01',

                                             to='2022-12-31',
                                             sort_by='relevancy')

       # Display articles
       for article in all_articles['articles']:
           print(article['title'], article['url'],
   article['content'])

   except Exception as e:
       print(f"An error occurred: {e}")
   ```

   IMPORTANT: Replace 'your-newsapi-key' with your actual News API key.

The date range above requires a paid membership to obtain all the Tesla news articles from 2022-10-01 to 2022-12-31. See the following instructions to access the paid membership at the News API website.

3. Navigate to the News API website. Go to News API and click on **Get API key**.

4. Sign up or log in. If you don't have an account, you'll need to create one. If you already have an account, log in.

5. Select a plan. News API offers multiple plans, including a free tier with limited access and paid memberships for more comprehensive access. In this case, a paid plan will be required to run the Python code shown previously.

6. If you've selected a paid plan, you'll be prompted to enter your payment information.

7. Once the account setup is complete, you'll be provided with an API key. This is what you'll use to access the service programmatically.

For earnings call transcripts, let's use the Financial Modeling Prep API as an example. First, we can use it to extract the page content and then parse the data:

1. Navigate to the Financial Modeling Prep website.

2. Register or log in. If you are new, you'll need to create an account. If you already have an account, log in.

3. Choose a plan. Go to the pricing section and choose Ultimate Plan. Follow the steps for payment to activate your subscription.

4. Once your account is set up and the subscription is active, go to your dashboard to generate an API key:

```
import requests
import json

# Initialize API endpoint and API key
api_key = "your_api_key_here"
api_endpoint = f"https://financialmodelingprep.com/api/v3/your_
endpoint_here?apikey={api_key}"

# Payload or parameters for date range (Modify as per actual API
documentation)
params = {
    "from": "2022-10-01",
    "to": "2022-12-31"
}

try:
    # Make the API request
```

```
response = requests.get(api_endpoint, params=params)
response.raise_for_status()

# Parse the JSON data
data = json.loads(response.text)

# Extract and print the data (Modify as per actual API
response)
# For demonstration, assuming data is a list of dictionaries
with a 'transcript' key
for item in data:
    print(item.get("transcript", "Transcript not
available"))

except Exception as e:
    print(f"An error occurred: {e}")
```

Replace `"your_api_key_here"` and `"your_endpoint_here"` with your actual API key and the API endpoint you're interested in. Also, adjust the `params` according to the API's actual documentation.

> **Important note**
>
> The provided Python code is a general template and may not work out of the box due to API-specific requirements and data structures. Always refer to the API documentation for accurate and up-to-date information.

As for parsing the Q&A part and comments, the structure of the HTML would dictate how to isolate that section. If it's consistently structured across transcripts, you could simply adjust your selectors to grab that specific part of the page.

Here's a Python code snippet that assumes you have the earnings call transcript in a string format. It looks for the line where Martin Viecha, VP of investor relations at Tesla, announces the start of the Q&A section in the earnings call. Then, it separates investor questions from the answers from the management team in the earnings call transcript:

```
def parse_transcript(transcript):
    lines = transcript.split('\n')  # Assume the transcript uses
newline characters to separate lines
    in_qa_section = False
    questions = []
    answers = []
    current_q = ""
    current_a = ""
```

```
    for line in lines:
        # Check if the Q&A section starts
        if "Martin Viecha" in line and "investor question" in
line.lower():
            in_qa_section = True
            continue  # Skip this line and move to the next line

        if in_qa_section:
            # Assume that a line starting with "Q:" signifies a
question
            if line.startswith("Q:"):
                # Save the previous Q&A pair before moving on to
the next question
                if current_q and current_a:
                    questions.append(current_q.strip())
                    answers.append(current_a.strip())
                current_q = line[2:].strip()  # Skip "Q:" and
save the rest
                current_a = ""  # Reset the answer string
            else:
                # Accumulate lines for the current answer
                current_a += " " + line.strip()

    # Save the last Q&A pair if it exists
    if current_q and current_a:
        questions.append(current_q.strip())
        answers.append(current_a.strip())

    return questions, answers

# Sample transcript (Replace this string with your actual
transcript data)
sample_transcript = """
Martin Viecha: We will now start the investor question part of
the earnings call.
Q: What is the outlook for next quarter?
Elon Musk: We expect to grow substantially.
Q: What about competition?
Elon Musk: Competition is always good for the market.
"""

questions, answers = parse_transcript(sample_transcript)
print("Questions:")
for q in questions:
```

```
        print(q)

    print("\nAnswers:")
    for a in answers:
        print(a)
```

This is a simple example and might not handle all the intricacies of real-world earnings call transcripts. For example, some earnings calls might have multiple people answering a single question, the VP of investor relations might be different in the future, or the Q&A format may vary on the earnings call.

Note that this assumes the transcript is well-formatted and follows the patterns coded into the function. You might need to adapt the code to fit the specific formatting and structure of the transcripts you're working with.

5. Save the data as a CVS file(s).

Now, you can save the news articles and earnings call transcripts data as a CSV file. You can easily save the data as a CSV file using the `pandas` library. Here's how you might modify the previous scripts to save the data into a CSV file:

For the `NewsAPI` data, use the following code:

```
import pandas as pd
from newsapi import NewsApiClient


newsapi = NewsApiClient(api_key='your-newsapi-key')


# You can adjust the dates and sort type as per your
requirements
all_articles = newsapi.get_everything(q='Tesla',
                                    from_param='2022-10-01',
                                    to='2022-12-31',
                                    sort_by='relevancy')


# Create a DataFrame to store the article data
df = pd.DataFrame(all_articles['articles'])


# Save the DataFrame to a CSV file
df.to_csv('newsapi_data.csv')
B). For the Earnings Call Transcript data from the Financial
Modeling Prep API:
import requests
import json
import pandas as pd
```

```
# Initialize API endpoint and API key
api_endpoint = "https://financialmodelingprep.com/api/v3/your_
earnings_call_endpoint_here"
api_key = "your_api_key_here"

# Payload or parameters for date range and Tesla's ticker symbol
params = {
    "from": "2022-10-01",
    "to": "2022-12-31",
    "ticker": "TSLA",
    "apikey": api_key
}

try:
    # Make the API request
    response = requests.get(api_endpoint, params=params)
    response.raise_for_status()

    # Parse the JSON data
    data = json.loads(response.text)

    # Extract the transcript, assuming it's in a key called
'transcript'
    # (Modify as per actual API response)
    transcript_data = data.get("transcript", [])

    # Convert the transcript data to a DataFrame
    df = pd.DataFrame(transcript_data, columns=['Transcript'])

    # Save the DataFrame to a CSV file
    df.to_csv('Tesla_earnings_call_transcript.csv', index=False)

except Exception as e:
    print(f"An error occurred: {e}")
```

Important note

In this code snippet, we included `"ticker"`: `"TSLA"` to the `params` dictionary to specify that we're interested in Tesla's earnings call transcripts. This assumes that the API uses a parameter named ticker to specify the company. You may need to consult Financial Modeling Prep's API documentation to confirm the exact parameter name and usage.

The reasons why we chose to save the raw data in the CSV files as opposed to saving it after the sentiment analysis was completed are as follows:

- **Reusability of raw data**: If you believe the raw data could be useful for other analyses in the future, it might be a good idea to save it as is. This way, you can always go back to the original data and perform different or additional analyses as required.

- **Computational resources**: If you're dealing with a large amount of data and limited computational resources, it might be more efficient to perform sentiment analysis on-the-fly as the data comes in and then save the results. This way, you don't need to store large amounts of raw data and then process it all at once.

- **Iterative improvement**: If you plan to improve or change your sentiment analysis method over time, saving the raw data would be beneficial. You can re-run your new and improved analysis on the original data at any time.

6. Perform sentiment analysis.

    Once you have the news and earnings call data, we can perform sentiment analysis on it using TextBlob.

    Here's an outline of the process using the TextBlob library in Python for Tesla news articles:

    ```
    from textblob import TextBlob# Function to calculate sentiment
    def calculate_sentiment(text: str):
        blob = TextBlob(text)
        return blob.sentiment.polarity


    # Let's assume you have a list of news articles
    news_articles = [...] # replace with your list of news articles


    # Calculate sentiment for each article
    sentiments = [calculate_sentiment(article) for article in news_
    articles]


    # You could then save these sentiments to a CSV file along with
    the articles:
    import pandas as pd

    df = pd.DataFrame({
        'Article': news_articles,
        'Sentiment': sentiments,
    })
    df.to_csv('article_sentiments.csv', index=False)
    ```

    This will create a CSV file named `article_sentiments.csv`, which contains each article along with its sentiment score.

    You can then import this CSV file into Power BI to create visualizations.

For the news articles, consider separating the text by speaker and then running sentiment analysis. This could provide insights into how different people commenting on the article are perceived or whether different individuals have different sentiment in their speech.

Here's an outline of the process using the `TextBlob` library in Python for Tesla earnings call transcripts:

```python
from textblob import TextBlob
import pandas as pd

# Function to calculate sentiment
def calculate_sentiment(text: str):
    blob = TextBlob(text)
    return blob.sentiment.polarity

# Assuming 'transcript' is a list of strings where each string
is an earnings call transcript
transcripts = [...]   # replace with your list of earnings call
transcripts

# Calculate sentiment for each transcript
sentiments = [calculate_sentiment(transcript) for transcript in
transcripts]

# Save these sentiments to a CSV file along with the
transcripts:
df = pd.DataFrame({
    'Transcript': transcripts,
    'Sentiment': sentiments,
})

df.to_csv('transcript_sentiments.csv', index=False)
```

This code will create a new CSV file named `transcript_sentiments.csv`, which includes each earnings call transcript along with its sentiment score. As with the news articles, you can then import this CSV file into Power BI to create visualizations.

For the earnings call transcript, consider separating the text by speaker and then running sentiment analysis. This could provide insights into how different people (e.g., CEO, CFO, investor relations, Wall Street analysts) are perceived or whether different individuals have different sentiments in their speech.

Again, it's important to note that `TextBlob` provides a simple form of sentiment analysis. For more nuanced analysis, consider using more sophisticated models from libraries such as transformers, i.e., GPT 3.5.

I.   Import the data into Power BI or GPT-4.

II.   Once you've saved your sentiment analysis data to a CSV file(s), you can import it into Power BI.

III. Open the Power BI desktop and select **Home > Get Data > Text/CSV**.

IV. In the file explorer window, navigate to the location of your CSV file, select it, and click **Open**.

V. Power BI will display a preview of your data. Check that it looks correct, then click **Load**.

VI. Now that your data is loaded into Power BI, you can start creating visualizations.

7. Create visualizations in Power BI.

For this dataset, it would be interesting to create a pie chart showing the distribution of sentiments (positive, neutral, negative) and a bar chart to show how the sentiment changes over time for the news articles and earnings call transcripts. You could show the datasets individually in Power BI using filters and then combine the two so you have a consolidated sentiment view.

- For individual visualizations, import the `news_article_sentiments.csv` and `transcript_sentiments.csv` files separately into Power BI. Then, for each data source, follow the steps provided to create a pie chart and a bar chart. You'll do this once for the news article data and once for the earnings call data.

- To consolidate these visualizations, you first need to consolidate the data. Power BI allows you to append queries, which essentially stacks one dataset on top of another. You would need to make sure the data columns align correctly. For instance, you could have a common structure such as `{Source, Text, Sentiment, PublishedAt}`, where `Source` would be either `News Article` or `Earnings Call`. Then, follow the same steps to create your pie chart and bar chart.

Here's how to append the data:

VII. In the Power BI desktop, go to the **Home** tab in the ribbon and click on **Edit Queries > Append**.

VIII. In the **Append Queries** dialog box, select the datasets you want to combine and click **OK**.

It's important to note that `publishedAt` might not be the right field for the earnings call data unless you have a specific timestamp for each portion of the transcript. For the consolidated bar chart over time, it might be more useful to focus on articles or ensure you have a suitable time-based field for the earnings calls.

This way, you can create individual visualizations for the sentiment from news articles and earnings call transcripts, as well as a consolidated view that shows the overall sentiment that takes into account both these data sources.

The following are Power BI visualization steps for news article and earnings call transcript sentiment data:

- Pie Chart: Click on the pie chart icon in the **Visualizations** pane. Then, in the **Fields** pane, drag the `sentiment` field into the **Values** area and again into the **Legend** area. Power BI will automatically count the number of each sentiment.

- Bar Chart: Click on the bar chart icon in the **Visualizations** pane. Then, in the **Fields** pane, drag the `publishedAt` field into the **Axis** area and the `sentiment` field into the **Values** area. Power BI will create a bar chart showing the sentiment over time.

8. Integrate the sentiment analysis with a trading strategy.

The sentiment analysis data can be used as a signal in a trading strategy. For instance, a significant increase in positive sentiment could be a signal to buy, while an increase in negative sentiment could be a signal to sell or short.

Please consider these as illustrative examples rather than ready-to-use code.

Let's assume you have two Python scripts, one for sentiment analysis (`sentiment_analysis.py`) and another for decision making and trade execution (`trade_execution.py`).

For the sentiment analysis script (`sentiment_analysis.py`), here's a simplified version of a script that performs sentiment analysis and saves the results:

```python
from newsapi import NewsApiClient
from textblob import TextBlob
import pandas as pd
import os

def get_sentiment(text):
    analysis = TextBlob(text)
    if analysis.sentiment.polarity > 0:
        return 'positive'
    elif analysis.sentiment.polarity == 0:
        return 'neutral'
    else:
        return 'negative'

newsapi = NewsApiClient(api_key='YOUR_API_KEY')
data = newsapi.get_everything(q='Tesla', language='en')

articles = data['articles']
sentiments = [get_sentiment(article['description']) for article
in articles]
df = pd.DataFrame({'Article': articles, 'Sentiment':
sentiments})

# Save to CSV
df.to_csv('sentiment_scores.csv', index=False)
```

For the decision making and trade execution script (`trade_execution.py`), here's a simplified version of a script that reads the sentiment scores, makes decisions, and executes trades:

```python
import pandas as pd
import alpaca_trade_api as tradeapi
import os


api = tradeapi.REST('APCA-API-KEY-ID', 'APCA-API-SECRET-KEY',
base_url='https://paper-api.alpaca.markets')


df = pd.read_csv('sentiment_scores.csv')


# Analyze the sentiment scores and make a decision
positive_articles = df[df['Sentiment'] == 'positive'].shape[0]
negative_articles = df[df['Sentiment'] == 'negative'].shape[0]


# Placeholder for your trading strategy
if positive_articles > negative_articles:
    decision = 'buy'
elif negative_articles > positive_articles:
    decision = 'sell'
else:
    decision = 'hold'


# Execute the decision
if decision == 'buy':
    api.submit_order(
        symbol='TSLA',
        qty=1,
        side='buy',
        type='market',
        time_in_force='gtc'
    )
elif decision == 'sell':
    api.submit_order(
        symbol='TSLA',
        qty=1,
        side='sell',
        type='market',
        time_in_force='gtc'
    )
```

To run these scripts at specific intervals, you might use a task scheduler. For example, on Unix-based systems, you might use `cron`. Here's a sample `cron` job that runs `sentiment_analysis.py` every day at 8 AM and `trade_execution.py` every day at 9 AM:

```
# Edit your crontab file with crontab -e and add the following
lines:
# Run sentiment_analysis.py at 8 AM every day
0 8 * * * cd /path/to/your/scripts && /usr/bin/python3
sentiment_analysis.py
# Run trade_execution.py at 9 AM every day
0 9 * * * cd /path/to/your/scripts && /usr/bin/python3 trade_
execution.py
```

In the Windows environment, you can use Task Scheduler to accomplish the same task. Remember to replace `/path/to/your/scripts` with the actual path to your scripts and `/usr/bin/python3` with the path to your Python interpreter.

9. Involve ChatGPT in the process.

Including ChatGPT in this process could provide an additional layer of analysis to support your trading strategy. Specifically, ChatGPT can be used to provide additional insights from the news articles or transcripts and help with decision-making.

For instance, instead of a simple positive, neutral, or negative sentiment analysis, you could use ChatGPT to generate a summary of each article or transcript. This summary could be analyzed for more nuanced sentiment, such as enthusiasm for a new Tesla product or concerns about supply chain issues.

To implement this, you would need to feed the text of each article or transcript into ChatGPT and then analyze the resulting output.

See the python code example below:

```
import openai
from textblob import TextBlob

openai.api_key = 'your-openai-key'

def get_summary(text):
    response = openai.Completion.create(
      engine="text-davinci-002",
      prompt=text,
      temperature=0.3,
      max_tokens=100
    )
    return response.choices[0].text.strip()
```

```
def get_sentiment(text):
    analysis = TextBlob(text)
    if analysis.sentiment.polarity > 0:
        return 'positive'
    elif analysis.sentiment.polarity == 0:
        return 'neutral'
    else:
        return 'negative'

# Let's assume we have a list of articles
articles = ["Article 1 text...", "Article 2 text...", "..."]

summaries = [get_summary(article) for article in articles]
sentiments = [get_sentiment(summary) for summary in summaries]

# You can now proceed to save the summaries and sentiments and
use them in your decision-making process
```

> **Important note**
> Remember that this is a simplified example and the actual implementation might require handling various edge cases and API limits.

Moreover, incorporating ChatGPT into your process might require an adjustment of the sentiment analysis, as you're moving from analyzing the entire articles to analyzing summaries generated by GPT-4. You'll also need to account for the costs associated with using the OpenAI API.

In the upcoming section, Power BI will be used to create several visualizations based on different aspects of Tesla's financial performance, market competition, and KPIs. Here's a summary of the visualizations:

- Financial visualizations: A pie or donut chart can illustrate the market share of Tesla and its competitors in the EV market.

  - Operating efficiency ratio: A bar chart comparing the operating efficiency ratios (**Cost of Good Sold (COGS)** + **Operating Expenses (OpEx)** / revenue) of Tesla and its competitors.

  - Revenue growth: A line or area chart tracking the growth in revenue over time for each automaker from EV sales.

  - Gross Margin: A bar chart comparing the gross margins of each automaker to identify cost efficiency and profitability.

  - Research and development (R&D) Investment: A stacked bar or line chart displaying R&D investments made by different automakers over multiple years if data is available.

- Geographic revenue distribution: A TreeMap to visualize revenue distribution by country or region for Tesla, and a line chart to display the revenue trends by country or region over time.

• Market competition visualizations:

- Vehicle Range and Performance: A scatter plot to visualize vehicle range against charging time for various automakers' models. Also, a bar chart to compare acceleration (0-60 mph time) for different EV models.

- Infrastructure: A map that visualizes the charging network infrastructure if geographical data for charging stations is available. A stacked bar chart can also be used to compare total charging infrastructure between different automakers.

• KPI visualizations:

- Vehicle Deliveries: A bar chart with a line chart overlay to show vehicle deliveries by quarter, and a stacked bar chart to breakdown vehicle deliveries by model (e.g., Model S, Model 3, Model X, Model Y).

- Energy Storage and Solar Deployments: A bar chart with a line chart overlay to display energy storage deployments and solar installations by quarter.

Power BI visualizations—Tesla

Visualizations are, in essence, a universal language of shapes, patterns, and colors that the human brain can quickly interpret. With the burgeoning availability of big data and AI, we are now able to process and understand more information than ever before. However, this information is often complex and multi-dimensional. This is where visualizations step in as a transformative tool.

Our brains are exceptionally well-adapted to interpret visual information. Research suggests that the human brain processes images 60,000 times faster than text, and 90% of the information transmitted to the brain is visual. As such, visualizations harness this power, translating intricate patterns within raw data into something digestible and intuitive.

Let's start this section by pulling in the required data for the following visualizations from Tesla's 10-K annual report(s) and 10-Q quarterly report(s) in detail.

Financial visualizations—data extraction to Power BI visualizations

Here are the steps to build the financial visualizations discussed in the previous section. We will take you through the process of extracting the data, saving it, and then extracting it to create each visualization.

Use Python to download the 10-Q and 10-K reports from the EDGAR database on the SEC's website. Here's a basic Python script using the `requests` library to download a single file:

```
import requests

def download_file(url, filename):
```

```
    response = requests.get(url)
    open(filename, 'wb').write(response.content)


# URL to the file (link you get from the SEC's EDGAR database)
url = 'https://www.sec.gov/Archives/edgar/
data/1318605/000156459021004599/0001564590-21-004599-index.htm'


# Path where you want to store the file
filename = 'tesla_10k.html'


download_file(url, filename)
```

This script simply downloads a file from a given URL and saves it to the specified location. You need to replace the `url` variable with the URL of the 10-K or 10-Q report that you want to download.

Keep in mind that you would need to repeat this process for each 10-K and 10-Q company report you want to include in the Power BI visualizations to compare to Tesla. We would recommend adding from the upcoming list to complete your comparison analysis through SEC filings.

Instructions

You will need to locate the **Central Index Key (CIK)** number for any company from which you want to find SEC filings, such as 10-K annual reports or 10-Q quarterly reports. The CIK number is a unique identifier assigned by the **US Securities and Exchange Commission (SEC)** to corporations who are obligated to disclose financial information with the SEC.

Here's a concise guide on how to obtain a CIK number for a public company.

SEC's EDGAR database:

1. Go to the SEC's EDGAR database: `https://www.sec.gov/edgar/searchedgar/companysearch.html`

2. In the **Company Name** field, type the name of the company you're interested in.

    The search results will display the company's CIK number alongside its name.

Google or Bing online search:

- You can obtain a CIK number by conducting a simple online search. Type the company's name followed by `CIK number` into the search engine of your choice (e.g., `Google CIK number`).

    Company's website or filings:

- Public companies often include their CIK number on their official website, especially in the investor relations section or in their SEC filings.

- General Motors (GM) SEC CIK Number: 0001467858

GM is a traditional automaker that's investing heavily in electrification and autonomous driving technologies. Its Chevrolet Bolt and upcoming GMC Hummer EV and Cadillac Lyriq are direct competitors to Tesla's models.

- Ford (F) SEC CIK Number: 0000037996

Ford's Mustang Mach-E and the upcoming all-electric F-150 Lightning show the company's commitment to electrification. Ford is a legacy car manufacturer similar to GM and is in the midst of a transition to the EV market.

- Rivian (RIVN) SEC CIK Number: 0001809779

A pure-play EV company, Rivian is a US-based EV manufacturer backed by Ford and Amazon, which recently went public and is a direct competitor to Tesla in the electric truck market.

- NIO Inc. (NIO) SEC CIK Number: 0001736541

While not US-based (it's a Chinese company), NIO is listed on the NYSE. NIO is a manufacturer of premium EVs and is often referred to as the "Tesla of China."

- XPeng Inc. (XPEV) SEC CIK Number: 0001821684

Another Chinese EV manufacturer listed on the NYSE, XPeng is focused on developing affordable EVs and advanced autonomous driving technologies.

- Lucid Group (LCID) SEC CIK Number: 0001736874

Lucid Motors is an American EV manufacturer that recently went public. Its first model, the Lucid Air, is a luxury electric sedan that competes with Tesla's Model S.

By comparing Tesla with both traditional automakers (GM, Ford) and pure-play EV companies (Rivian, NIO, XPeng, Lucid), the visualizations should provide a comprehensive view of Tesla's performance in the rapidly evolving EV market.

Automating this for multiple companies over multiple years would involve building a more sophisticated process that can navigate the SEC's EDGAR database, which is beyond the scope of this example. You can also reference the SEC API process provided in *Chapter 1*.

Once you have these files, you would then need to process them to extract the relevant financial data. This could be done using Python's built-in string methods or regular expressions for simple cases or with a library such as `BeautifulSoup` for more complex HTML processing.

As an alternative to *step 1* (CSV file option), you can extract data from a company's 10-K and 10-Q reports for analysis involves web scraping from SEC's EDGAR database, HTML/XML parsing, and handling CSV files for data storage. Here's a basic script that demonstrates these steps:

```
a. Install first
pip install beautifulsoup4

b. Run Python code
```

```python
import os

import requests
from bs4 import BeautifulSoup
import csv

# Set the URL for the company's filings page on EDGAR
company_url = "https://www.sec.gov/cgi-bin/browse-edgar?action=getcomp
any&CIK=0001318605&type=&dateb=&owner=exclude&count=40"

# Download the page
response = requests.get(company_url)
page_content = response.content

# Parse the page with BeautifulSoup
soup = BeautifulSoup(page_content, 'html.parser')

# Find all document links on the page
doc_links = soup.find_all('a', {'id': 'documentsbutton'})

# If no such id exists, find links by text (this assumes that the text
'Documents' is consistent)
if not doc_links:
    doc_links = soup.find_all('a', string='Documents')

# Loop through the document links
for doc_link in doc_links:
    # Get the URL of the document page
    doc_page_url = 'https://www.sec.gov' + doc_link.get('href')

    # Download the document page
    response = requests.get(doc_page_url)
    doc_page_content = response.content

    # Parse the document page
    soup = BeautifulSoup(doc_page_content, 'html.parser')

    # Find the link to the 10-K or 10-Q file
    filing_link = soup.find_all('a', {'href': lambda href: (href and
("10-K" in href or "10-Q" in href))})

    # If a filing link was found
    if filing_link:
        # Get the URL of the 10-K or 10-Q file
        filing_url = 'https://www.sec.gov' + filing_link[0].
get('href')
```

```
# Download the file
response = requests.get(filing_url)
filing_content = response.content

# Parse the file content (as text for simplicity)
soup = BeautifulSoup(filing_content, 'html.parser')

# Find all tables in the file
tables = soup.find_all('table')

# Loop through the tables and save each as a CSV file
for i, table in enumerate(tables):
    with open(f'{doc_link.text}_{i}.csv', 'w', newline='') as
f:
        writer = csv.writer(f)
        for row in table.find_all('tr'):
            writer.writerow([col.text for col in row.find_
all('td')])
```

1. Extract Power BI visualization data for each visualization.

    The next step is to identify which tables contain the data you need and to extract that data into
    CSV files. Here's a simple Python script to illustrate this process:

    ```
    import csv

    # List of tables parsed from the 10-K or 10-Q file
    tables = [...]

    # The indices of the tables containing the data we need
    market_share_table_index = ...
    operating_efficiency_ratio_table_index = ...
    revenue_growth_table_index = ...
    gross_margin_table_index = ...
    rd_investment_table_index = ...
    geographic_revenue_distribution_table_index = ...

    # List of the table indices
    table_indices = [
        market_share_table_index,
        operating_efficiency_ratio_table_index,
        revenue_growth_table_index,
        gross_margin_table_index,
        rd_investment_table_index,
        geographic_revenue_distribution_table_index
    ]
    ```

```
# List of names for the CSV files
csv_names = [
    "market_share.csv",
    "operating_efficiency_ratio.csv",
    "revenue_growth.csv",
    "gross_margin.csv",
    "rd_investment.csv",
    "geographic_revenue_distribution.csv"
]

# Loop through the table indices
for i in range(len(table_indices)):
    # Get the table
    table = tables[table_indices[i]]

    # Open a CSV file
    with open(csv_names[i], 'w', newline='') as f:
        writer = csv.writer(f)

        # Loop through the rows in the table
        for row in table.find_all('tr'):
            # Write the row to the CSV file
            writer.writerow([col.text for col in row.find_
all('td')])
```

You'll need to manually inspect the 10-K and 10-Q documents to determine which tables contain the data you need (market_share_table_index, operating_efficiency_ratio_table_index, etc., in the script). Once you've identified those tables, this script will extract the data from them and save it into separate CSV files.

However, this is still a simplified example. In practice, the data may need cleaning or reshaping before it can be used for visualizations. You may also need to extract data from other parts of the document besides tables. Furthermore, some of the data you're interested in, such as market share or operating efficiency ratio, might not be directly reported in the 10-K or 10-Q. In these cases, you would need to calculate these metrics from the available data or find alternative data sources.

Import the data.

Let's walk through the steps of importing the CSV files and creating the visualizations. We'll use market_share.csv as an example, but the same process applies to the other CSV files that will be used for the other visualizations listed in the upcoming financial visualization section.

- Open the Power BI desktop and click on **Home** in the ribbon at the top.

- In the **External Data** section, click on **Get Data**.

- In the drop-down menu, select **Text/CSV**.

- Navigate to the `market_share.csv` file, select it, and click **Open**. In the preview window, verify that the data is correct and click Load.

Create the Power BI visualizations for the financial visualizations:

- Compare Tesla's market share in the EV space with that of other automakers:

- **Visualization type**: Pie chart or donut chart.

- **Description**: Show the market share of each automaker, including Tesla. The pie chart segments will represent the proportion of market share each automaker holds.

- **Instructions**: Drag the `Company` field into the **Legend** or **Details** area of the visual and the Market Share field into the Values area.

- Operating efficiency ratio – COGS + OpEX / revenue for Tesla and its competitors

- **Visualization type**: Bar chart

- **Description**: Compare the operating efficiency ratios of Tesla and its competitors

- **Instructions**: Drag the Company field into the Axis area and the Operating Efficiency Ratio field into the Values area

Revenue growth: Compare the growth in revenue from EV sales across different automakers:

- **Visualization type**: Line chart or area chart

- **Description**: Track the growth in revenue over time for each automaker

- **Instructions**: Drag the `Year` field into the **Axis** area, the `Revenue Growth` field into the **Values** area, and the `Company` field into the **Legend** area

- Gross margin: Compare gross margins for EV sales to understand cost efficiency and profitability

- **Visualization type**: Bar chart

- **Description**: Compare the gross margins of each company to identify which are more cost efficient and profitable

- **Instructions**: Drag the `Company` field into the **Axis** area and the `Gross Margin` field into the **Values** area

R&D investment: Compare the R&D investments made by different automakers in the EV space

- **Visualization type**: Stacked bar chart or line chart.

- **Description**: Show R&D investments made by different automakers. This can be shown for multiple years, if data is available.

- **Instructions**: Drag the `Year` field into the **Axis** area, the `R&D Investment` field into the **Values** area, and the `Company` field into the **Legend** area.
- Geographic revenue distribution:
- **Visualization Type**: A TreeMap to visualize revenue distribution for Tesla and a line chart to display the revenue trends
- **Description**: A TreeMap to visualize revenue distribution by country or region for Tesla and a line chart to display the revenue trends by country or region over time for Tesla

The following are instructions for importing the data:

1. Open Power BI Desktop and click on **Get Data** in the **Home** ribbon.
2. From the dropdown menu, select **More** to open the window with all the available connectors.
3. Choose **CSV** (if your data is in CSV format) or the format of your file.
4. Navigate to your file, select it, and click **Open**.
5. In the navigator window, you can preview your data. Click **Load** to load the data into Power BI.

The following are instructions for creating a TreeMap visualization:

1. Click on the TreeMap icon in the **Visualizations** pane.
2. Drag the `Country` or `Region` field into the **Group** area.
3. Drag the `Revenue` field into the **Values** area.
4. Power BI will automatically create a TreeMap where the size of the rectangles represents the revenue in each country or region.
5. Create the line chart visualization:
6. Click on the line chart icon in the **Visualizations** pane.
7. Drag the `Date` or `Period` field into the **Axis** area.
8. Drag the `Revenue` field into the **Values** area.
9. From the `Country` or `Region` field, drag to the **Legend** field to create multiple lines, one for each country or region.

Power BI will create a line chart showing the revenue trends over time for each country or region.

Remember to format your visualizations according to your preference, such as changing colors, adding data labels, titles, and so on. You can access these formatting options by clicking on the paint roller icon in the **Visualizations** pane.

Market competition visualizations–data extraction to Power BI visualization

Here are the steps to build the market competition visualizations stated in the previous section. We will take you through the process of extracting the data, saving it, and then extracting it to create each visualization.

Keep in mind that due to the scattered nature of the required data and the fact that some of it resides on the official websites of automakers, it might be a challenging task to directly extract this data through a Python script or API, especially for performance indicators. Some websites might block scraping activities, and it's crucial to respect each website's policies regarding web scraping and data extraction.

1. Vehicle range and performance data:

    Let's use a hypothetical example of extracting electric vehicle data from a website such as Inside EVs, which contains the specifications of various electric vehicles. Please remember that this example is only for educational purposes, and you should always respect the website's terms and conditions and data privacy regulations.

    This Python example will utilize `BeautifulSoup` and `Requests`, two widely used libraries for web scraping.

    Before you begin, you need to install these libraries if you haven't already. You can install them via `pip`:

    ```
    pip install beautifulsoup4 requests pandas
    ```

    Here is a simple Python script to scrape EV data:

    ```python
    import requests
    from bs4 import BeautifulSoup
    import pandas as pd

    def scrape_data(url):
        response = requests.get(url)
        soup = BeautifulSoup(response.text, 'html.parser')

        table = soup.find('table')  # Assumes only one table on the
    page

        headers = []
        for th in table.find('tr').find_all('th'):
            headers.append(th.text.strip())

        rows = table.find_all('tr')[1:]  # Exclude header
    ```

```
        data_rows = []
        for row in rows:
            data = []
            for td in row.find_all('td'):
                data.append(td.text.strip())
            data_rows.append(data)

        return pd.DataFrame(data_rows, columns=headers)

url = 'https://insideevs.com/guides/electric-car-range-charging-
time/'  # Example URL, please check if scraping is allowed
df = scrape_data(url)
df.to_csv('ev_data.csv', index=False)  # Save the data to a CSV
file
```

The following is an explanation of the Python code snippet:

- Import the necessary libraries. You need these libraries to send HTTP requests, parse HTML, and manipulate data in a tabular format:

```
import requests
from bs4 import BeautifulSoup
import pandas as pd
```

- Define a function for data scraping. This function takes a URL as input, sends a GET request to that URL, parses the HTML response to find the data table, extracts the headers and rows from the table, and returns the data as a pandas DataFrame:

```
def scrape_data(url):
    # Send a GET request to the URL
    response = requests.get(url)

    # Parse the HTML content of the page with BeautifulSoup
    soup = BeautifulSoup(response.text, 'html.parser')

    # Find the data table in the HTML (assuming there's only one
table)
    table = soup.find('table')

    # Extract table headers
    headers = []
    for th in table.find('tr').find_all('th'):
        headers.append(th.text.strip())

    # Extract table rows
    rows = table.find_all('tr')[1:]  # Exclude header row
```

```
data_rows = []
for row in rows:
    data = []
    for td in row.find_all('td'):
        data.append(td.text.strip())
    data_rows.append(data)

# Create a DataFrame with the data and return it
return pd.DataFrame(data_rows, columns=headers)
```

- Use the function to scrape data and save it as a CSV file. Here, you input the URL of the web page you want to scrape data from, call the `scrape_data` function to get the data as a data frame, and then save the data frame to a CSV file:

```
url = 'https://insideevs.com/guides/electric-car-range-charging-
time/'  # Example URL, please check if scraping is allowed
df = scrape_data(url)
df.to_csv('ev_data.csv', index=False)  # Save the data to a CSV
file
```

> **Important note**
>
> This code assumes that the web page has a single table containing the data we need. If the webpage structure is different, you'll need to adjust the code accordingly. Always respect the website's rules and regulations, as well as any relevant data privacy and legal aspects. However, remember that this is a simple example and might not work with all websites, especially those using JavaScript to load data or having complex structures. For such scenarios, you might have to resort to more sophisticated techniques and tools, like Selenium or Scrapy.

2. Infrastructure data

   Let's also look at the process to extract the data for our Tesla and competitors' infrastructure (charging station) visualization.

   One approach could be to use APIs of charging station databases for the infrastructure part. Let's consider the Open Charge Map's public API. The following Python script demonstrates how to retrieve information about charging stations in the United States:

```
import requests
import pandas as pd

api_key = "your_api_key"  # replace with your API key
country_code = "US"   # for United States

url = f"https://api.openchargemap.io/v3/poi/?key={api_
key}&countrycode={country_code}&output=json"
```

```
response = requests.get(url)

# make sure the request was successful
assert response.status_code == 200

# convert to JSON
data = response.json()

# create a pandas DataFrame
df = pd.json_normalize(data)

# print the DataFrame
print(df)
```

Convert the JSON file that holds the Tesla and competitor infrastructure data to a CSV file.

The infrastructure data extracted from the Open Charge Map API is provided in JSON format, which we then converted into a pandas DataFrame (essentially a table) in Python for easier handling. This data frame can be saved to a CSV file if desired with the following line of code:

```
df.to_csv('infrastructure_data.csv', index=False)
```

The vehicle range and performance data has already been manually compiled from various online sources and saved in a CSV format; it can be read in Python using the pandas read_csv function mentioned in *step 1*, so no additional work is required.

Load the CSV files into Power BI:

I.   Open the Power BI desktop. Click on **Get Data** in the **Home** tab. A drop-down menu will open.

II.   From the drop-down menu, click on **Text/CSV**.

III. A dialog box will open for you to navigate to the location of your CSV file. Select the CSV file that you want to import and click on **Open**.

IV.   After you click open, a preview of the data in the file will appear in the **Text/CSV File Load** dialog box. If the data is displayed correctly, click **Load**. If you need to make adjustments, you can click **Edit**, which will open the Power Query Editor.

V.   Once you click **Load**, the data will be loaded into Power BI and will be available in the **Fields** pane on the right side of the Power BI desktop.

VI.   Repeat these steps for Vehicle Range and Performance CSV file and the Infrastructure CSV file and you will have both sets of data available to build your visualizations.

- With vehicle range and performance, you can compare KPIs such as range, charging time, and acceleration.

Use a scatter plot to visualize vehicle range (*x*axis) against charging time (*y*axis). This will provide a good overview of where each automaker's models stand in terms of these two important factors. You could size the points based on another dimension, such as battery capacity, and color them by automaker.

Power BI Instructions for scatter plot:

I.   Click on the scatter plot icon in the **Visualizations** pane.

II.   Drag the Range field into the **X-Axis** area and the Charging Time field into the **Y-Axis** area. This will position each EV model based on its range and charging time.

III.   Drag the `Company` or `Model` field into the **Details** area and `Battery Capacity` into the **Size** area, if available. This will allow you to distinguish between the models or companies and size the data points based on battery capacity.

Compare the accelerations (`0-60 mph Time`) of different EV models with a simple bar chart. This would allow a quick comparison of different models and automakers.

The following are Power BI instructions for creating a bar chart:

I.   Click on the bar chart icon in the **Visualizations** pane.

II.   Drag the `0-60 mph Time` field into the **Values** area.

III.   Drag the `Company` or `Model` field into the **Axis** area. This will allow you to compare acceleration times between different models or companies.

Infrastructure: Compare charging network infrastructure and other services provided by the automakers.

- **Map**: If you have geographical data (longitude, latitude) for charging stations, you could plot them on a map. You can use the size of the data points to represent capacity (number of charging points at each location) and use different colors for different automakers.

Power BI Instructions for map:

I.   Click on the map icon in the **Visualizations** pane. Ensure that you have a geographical data (longitude, latitude) field in your dataset.

II.   Drag the `Longitude` and `Latitude` fields into the **Location** area. This will position each charging station on the map.

III.   If available, drag the `Number of Charging Points` field into the **Size** area and the `Company` field into the **Legend** area. This will allow you to distinguish between the companies and size the data points based on the number of charging points at each location.

- **Stacked bar chart**: To compare the total charging infrastructure, you can create a stacked bar chart with each automaker on the *x*axis and the total number of charging stations on the *y*axis. Each bar can be segmented (stacked) based on some other criteria, such as charging speed (slow, fast, superfast).

The following are Power BI instructions for creating a stacked bar chart:

I.   Click on the stacked bar chart icon in the **Visualizations** pane.

II.   Drag the `Company` field into the **Axis** area and the `Total Number of Charging Stations` field into the **Values** area. This will create a bar for each company representing their total charging infrastructure.

III.   Drag the `Charging Speed` field into the **Legend** area. This will segment (stack) each bar based on charging speed (slow, fast, or superfast).

Remember to customize your visualizations as needed to make them more effective. You can adjust colors, add data labels and titles, and more by clicking on the paint roller icon in the **Visualizations** pane.

KPI visualizations–data extraction to Power BI visualization

For this section, we will be providing the steps to create visualizations to provide a way for the reader to evaluate Tesla KPIs.

The KPI visualizations are as follows:

- **Vehicle deliveries**: This is a bar chart with a line chart overlay that shows vehicle deliveries by quarter and a stacked bar chart that shows breakdown vehicle deliveries by model (e.g., Model S, Model 3, Model X, Model Y)

- **Energy storage and solar deployments**: This is a bar chart with a line chart overlay that displays energy storage deployments and solar installations by quarter

Fortunately, this data can be found in the Tesla annual and quarterly reports we extracted earlier when we were pulling data from the SEC website. Extract vehicle delivery and energy storage and solar deployment data from the Tesla SEC CSV files that were saved during the Tesla financial visualization process. All you need to do is find the CSV files that have already been created and follow these steps:

1.   Here's a generic Python script for reading a CSV file and extracting the needed data:

```
import pandas as pd

# Load the CSV file
df = pd.read_csv('tesla_report.csv')

# Extract the data needed for visualizations
vehicle_deliveries = df[['Quarter', 'Model S Deliveries', 'Model
3 Deliveries', 'Model X Deliveries', 'Model Y Deliveries']]
energy_storage_and_solar_deployments = df[['Quarter', 'Energy
Storage Deployments', 'Solar Installations']]

# Save the extracted data into new CSV files
```

```
vehicle_deliveries.to_csv('vehicle_deliveries.csv', index=False)
energy_storage_and_solar_deployments.to_csv('energy_storage_and_
solar_deployments.csv', index=False)
```

In this code snippet:

- The `pandas` library is imported.
- The `pd.read_csv()` function is used to read the CSV file. Replace `tesla_report.csv` with the name of your actual CSV file.
- The needed columns for each visualization are extracted into new data frames.
- The `to_csv()` function is used to save these new data frames into new CSV files, which can then be imported into Power BI.

Please modify the column names in the script to match the exact column names in your CSV files. Also, replace `tesla_report.csv` with the path of your CSV file.

This script assumes that you have a single CSV file with all the data needed. If the data is spread across multiple files (for instance, one file per report), you'll need to load each file separately, extract the data, and possibly concatenate the results.

2. Import the CSV files into Power BI:

    I.   Open the Power BI desktop.

    II.   Click on **Home** in the top menu and then click on **Get Data**.

    III.   In the drop-down menu, select **Text/CSV**.

    IV.   A dialogue box will open. Navigate to the location of your CSV file (for example, `vehicle_deliveries.csv`), select it, and then click **Open**.

    V.   Power BI will display a preview of your data. Check that it has imported correctly and then click **Load**.

    VI.   Repeat *steps 2-5* for the `energy_storage_and_solar_deployments.csv` file.

After completing these steps, you will have loaded the data from the CSV files into Power BI and are ready to create your visualizations.

Vehicle Deliveries: a. Bar chart: Show vehicle deliveries by quarter, with a line chart overlay to display the trend over time. b. Stacked bar chart: Break down vehicle deliveries by model (e.g., Model S, Model 3, Model X, Model Y).

The following are Power BI instructions for creating a vehicle deliveries bar chart with a line chart overlay:

    I.   In the **Visualizations** pane, click on the **Combo chart** icon to create a new combo chart visualization.

    II.   Drag the `Quarter` field into the **Shared axis** area.

III.   Drag the `Vehicle Deliveries` field into the **Column values** area. This will create the bar chart component of the combo chart.

IV.   Now, to create the line chart overlay, again drag the `Vehicle Deliveries` field, but this time into the Line values area. You now have a bar chart with a line chart overlay, both representing vehicle deliveries by quarter.

The following are instructions for a vehicle deliveries stacked bar chart:

- Click on the stacked bar chart icon in the **Visualizations** pane to create a new stacked bar chart visualization.

- Drag the `Quarter` field into the **Axis** area.

- Drag the fields representing the deliveries of each model (Model S, Model 3, Model X, Model Y) into the **Values** area. Power BI will automatically create a stacked bar chart where each segment of the bars represents the deliveries of a specific model.

- In both cases, remember to adjust the formatting of your visualizations according to your preference (such as colors, data labels, titles, etc.) by clicking on the **Format** button (which looks like a paint roller) in the **Visualizations** pane.

- **Energy storage and solar deployments**: Display energy storage deployments and solar installations by quarter using a line chart overlay to show trends over time.

  The following are Power BI instructions for creating an energy storage deployments and solar installations bar chart with a line chart overlay:

- Start by selecting the Combo chart icon in the **Visualizations** pane to create a new combo chart visualization.

- Drag the `Quarter` field into the Shared axis area. This will be the common axis for both the bar chart and the line chart.

- Next, drag the `Energy Storage Deployments` field into the **Column** values area. This will create the bar chart component of the visualization, showing energy storage deployments by quarter.

- Drag the `Solar Installations` field into the Line values area. This will create the line chart overlay, showing solar installations by quarter.

This visualization allows you to easily compare the trends in energy storage deployments and solar installations over time.

As always, remember to adjust the formatting of your visualizations according to your preference (such as colors, data labels, titles, etc.) by clicking on the **Format** button (which looks like a paint roller) in the **Visualizations** pane.

Final thoughts: leveraging ChatGPT and the OpenAI API in your data visualization workflow

This is where ChatGPT can help automate some of the manual steps, from extracting data to creating a Power BI visualization. You should think of ChatGPT as your valuable assistant, but it has to be used in the right way. It certainly won't replace human involvement, but it can speed up the process and allow a person to focus more time on what they do best. It can do the following:

- **Automate script creation**: You can ask ChatGPT to generate Python scripts for data extraction and cleaning. This can help automate the process of pulling and preprocessing data for visualizations. You've already seen examples of this in our prior interactions.

- **Guide data analysis**: ChatGPT can provide guidance on how to approach data analysis. For example, you can describe your dataset to ChatGPT and ask for suggestions on what kind of analysis would yield interesting insights or what kind of visualizations would effectively represent your data.

- **Create complex queries**: You can use ChatGPT to help formulate complex SQL or other database queries. ChatGPT's language generation capabilities can help you articulate queries that might be difficult to formulate otherwise.

- **Create narrative reports**: Once your analysis and visualization are done, ChatGPT can help write up the results. Given the analysis results, it can generate a well-structured report, presenting the findings in a clear and understandable way.

- **Facilitate interactive learning**: ChatGPT can provide step-by-step instructions and explanations on various topics, such as how to use specific features in Power BI or how to perform certain data analysis techniques. This can help users learn and understand better.

> **Key point**
>
> Remember to review and test any scripts or code generated by ChatGPT. While it's a powerful tool, it's always important to ensure that the output is correct and suits your specific needs.

As we delve into the realm of financial data extraction, the following Python code demonstrates a practical way to fetch the latest 10-K filings directly from the SEC for a specified company (in this case, Tesla). By leveraging the power of requests and JSON libraries, we craft a function that retrieves, processes, and presents key data points, serving as a fundamental step in our financial analysis journey:

```python
import requests
import json

def get_latest_10k_data(cik):
    # Define the base URL for the SEC data API
    base_url = "https://data.sec.gov/submissions/"
```

```
        # Define the URL for the company's latest 10-K data
        url = f"{base_url}CIK{cik}.json"

    # Get the JSON content from the URL
    Response = requests.get(url)
    data = json.loads(response.text)

    # Find the data for the latest 10-K filing
    for filing in data['filings']:
        if filing['form'] == '10-K':
            return filing
    return None

    # Get the data for Telsa's latest 10-K filing
    tesla_cik  = '0001318605'
    tesla_10k_data = get_latest_10k_data(tesla_cik)

    # Now you have a dictionary containing the data for Tesla's latest
    10-K filing
    # the structure of this will data will depend on the current format of
    the SEC's website
```

To use the SEC API to pull financial data, you would follow a similar process to the one described in the previous Python code examples. Instead of using `BeautifulSoup` to parse HTML from the EDGAR website, you would send a GET request to the appropriate API endpoint and then parse the returned JSON data.

As an alternative, we can provide a Python script that would help you download the 10-K filings of Tesla. You can then manually search for the geographic distribution information:

```
import requests
import os

def download_10k(cik, doc_link):
    # Define the base URL for the SEC EDGAR database
    base_url = "https://www.sec.gov/Archives/"

    # Combine the base_url with the doc_link to get the full URL of the
    10-K filing
    url = base_url + doc_link

    # Get the content from the URL
    Response = requests.get(url)

    #Save the content to a .txt file
```

```
with open(cik + '.txt', 'wb') as f:
f:write(response.content)


#Define the CIK for Tesla
Tesla_cik = '0001318605'


# Define the doc_link for the latest 10-K filing of Tesla
# This can be found on the EDGAR database and will need to be updated
Tesla_doc_link = 'edgar/data/1318605/0001564590-21-004599.txt'


# Download the 10-K filing
Download_10k(tesla_cik, tesla_doc_link)
```

After running this script, you'll have a text file named 0001318605.txt (Tesla's CIK) in your current directory that contains the latest 10-K filing of Tesla. You can then open this file and manually search for the geographic distribution information.

Now that we have completed our review of the Power BI visualizations that we can use to evaluate Tesla and its performance, we can dive into an important topic that is critical to the success of every investor utilizing ChatGPT to maximize their trading, investing, and financial analysis potential.

The exhilarating intersection of ChatGPT, finance, and Power BI ushers in a transformative journey of AI, trading concepts, and visualizations. Navigating this landscape isn't without its obstacles; we must secure sensitive financial data akin to a vault of treasured wealth and detect concealed biases within algorithms that, if unchecked, can lead us astray like deceitful mirages. These biases, insidiously hidden in AI tools, could dramatically skew our decisions, resulting in devastating misjudgments. Armed with continuous learning, vigilance, and the armor of diverse teams and strategies, we can tackle these biases, ensuring our decisions are fair, informed, and impactful. Let's take a look at best practices and ethics in this next section.

Best practices and ethics in AI-driven financial analysis

As we explore the potential of AI-driven financial analysis, it's crucial to discuss best practices and ethical considerations. Here are some essential points to keep in mind:

- Combine AI-driven insights with traditional analysis methods. While AI tools such as ChatGPT can provide valuable insights, it's crucial to complement these insights with human expertise and critical thinking.

- Ensure data privacy and security. Safeguarding sensitive financial data is a top priority. Ensure that the AI tools you use adhere to strict data privacy and security standards.

- Be aware of potential biases in algorithms. AI-driven tools can inadvertently perpetuate biases found in the data they are trained on. Remain vigilant and actively work to identify and address potential biases in AI-driven analysis.

- Stay informed of ethical AI usage. Continuously educate yourself about the ethical considerations and potential challenges associated with AI-driven financial analysis to ensure responsible AI usage.

As we navigate the thrilling nexus of AI and finance, one must not overlook the guardrails that ensure our journey is ethical, reliable, and secure. These checks and balances are not mere speed bumps, but rather the bedrock that allows trust in these powerful tools to thrive and great potential to be realized without fear of missteps or misjudgments.

Balancing AI-driven insights with human expertise is like bringing together a dream team of explorers on this financial voyage, each with unique strengths, working together to uncover hidden treasures in the financial landscape. It's this partnership, this harmonic blend of AI and human intuition, that elevates our analysis to new heights, allowing us to pierce through the fog of uncertainty and see the markets for what they truly are.

Data privacy and security, the golden rules of our digital age, are more important than ever when handling sensitive financial data. Like a bank vault that safeguards our wealth, the AI tools we use must protect our data with an unyielding resolve. Adhering to these stringent standards ensures that our journey through financial landscapes is not only enlightening but also secure.

An algorithm may be blind to societal norms, but we, the users, are not. Bias hidden within data can sneak into the decision-making process of even the most advanced AI tools. We must remain vigilant, actively scouting and addressing potential bias to ensure that our insights are not just intelligent, but also fair and unbiased.

AI model bias, much like a mirage, can lead us astray, painting a skewed version of reality that discriminates against certain groups based on attributes such as race, gender, or age. Understanding, detecting, and mitigating such bias is like acquiring a pair of truth-seeking glasses that unveil the fairness of our AI models.

You might ask, how do we measure such bias? Imagine yourself as a detective on the trail of unfairness in AI. Identifying protected attributes, defining fairness metrics, analyzing model performance, and interpreting the results are your tools to uncover this hidden culprit. This investigative journey can be complicated and nuanced, as there are no universally accepted thresholds for what constitutes acceptable bias, making our task not only challenging but also incredibly significant.

There are shields against this bias. Strategies ranging from data pre-processing to in-processing, post-processing, continuous monitoring, and evaluation serve as our protective armor. Involving diverse teams and stakeholders in the AI development process can be our best defense, as they bring varied perspectives and reduce the risk of bias.

However, let us warn you; the quest for perfect fairness can be like chasing a unicorn. Achieving absolute fairness is a noble but challenging aspiration. It might sometimes involve trade-offs with other objectives such as model accuracy or complexity. But remember, our mission is to navigate this tricky terrain with utmost care, always aiming for the fairest possible outcomes.

Understanding AI model bias

In this section, we unpack the potentially devastating issue of AI model bias, a prevalent pitfall that, if overlooked, can skew financial trades, investments, or analysis, leading to poor financial decisions and potential monetary losses. This section stresses the importance of comprehending, quantifying, and addressing bias in AI models, underlining how unchecked bias could erode investor trust and propagate inaccuracies in predictions. By exposing the complexities of AI model bias, we provide the necessary tools for developing more fair, reliable, and ethically-sound AI-driven financial strategies, thereby empowering you to avert unnecessary financial risks. An AI model is considered biased when it systematically and unfairly discriminates against certain groups or outcomes based on specific attributes, such as race, gender, or age. Bias in AI models often occurs due to the presence of biased data used during training, flawed model assumptions, or other issues in the modeling process.

Measuring bias in an AI model typically involves the following steps:

- **Identifying protected attributes**: Determine the attributes you want to protect against bias, such as race, gender, age, or other factors that may lead to unfair treatment.

- **Defining fairness metrics**: Choose appropriate metrics to measure fairness in the AI model, such as demographic parity, equal opportunity, or equalized odds. Different metrics may be suitable for different scenarios and applications.

- **Analyzing the model's performance**: Evaluate the model's performance with respect to the chosen fairness metrics. Compare the outcomes for different groups, taking into account the protected attributes.

- **Interpreting the results**: If the model's performance differs significantly between groups or fails to meet the chosen fairness criteria, it may be considered biased.

There is no universally accepted threshold for what constitutes an acceptable level of bias, as it depends on the specific application and context. However, minimizing bias is crucial to ensuring that AI models are fair and do not perpetuate discrimination.

To mitigate and fix bias in AI models, consider the following strategies:

- **Pre-processing**: Address bias in the data before training the model. Techniques include re-sampling, re-weighting, or applying synthetic data generation to balance the representation of different groups.

- **In-processing**: Modify the model training process to account for fairness constraints. This can involve using fairness-aware algorithms or incorporating fairness penalties into the loss function.

- **Post-processing**: Adjust the model's outputs after training to ensure fairness. Techniques include thresholding, calibration, or other methods that equalize outcomes for different groups.

- **Continuous monitoring and evaluation**: Regularly monitor the model's performance on fairness metrics and update the model as needed to ensure ongoing fairness.

- **Diverse teams and stakeholder input**: Involve diverse teams and stakeholders in the AI development process to ensure a wide range of perspectives and reduce the risk of bias.

Keep in mind that achieving perfect fairness may not always be possible, and trade-offs may need to be made between fairness and other objectives, such as model accuracy or complexity. The key is to carefully consider the specific context and ethical implications and strive for the fairest possible outcomes.

The following are the implications of a biased model on a trading strategy:

- **Inaccurate predictions**: A biased model can lead to inaccurate predictions, which may result in poor investment decisions and financial losses for both individual and institutional investors

- **Unreliable risk assessment**: Biased models may not properly assess investment risks, potentially leading to an overestimation or underestimation of potential losses or gains

- **Misallocation of capital**: A biased model might encourage investors to allocate capital to undeserving investments, while overlooking more attractive opportunities, affecting overall portfolio performance

- **Erosion of trust**: If investors become aware of biased models being used in trading strategies, they may lose trust in the financial institutions or analysts employing these models, damaging their reputation and credibility

By embracing the power of AI and ChatGPT, you can stay ahead of the curve in the rapidly evolving world of financial analysis. As you continue your journey, remember that continued learning and exploration are essential to unlocking the full potential of these cutting-edge technologies.

Throughout this chapter, we've provided illustrations and visual examples to help you better understand the applications and benefits of ChatGPT and AI in financial analysis. By mastering these concepts, you'll be well-equipped to leverage AI-driven insights for more informed and strategic decision-making in your financial endeavors.

Summary

In this chapter, we delved into the exciting world of ChatGPT and AI in financial analysis, covering various topics and skills.

Revolutionary technologies are redefining how we perceive and interact with the financial world, and this chapter took you right into the heart of this thrilling transformation. We were immersed in the fascinating landscape of a company such as Tesla, exploring potent trading strategies and witnessing how AI, particularly ChatGPT, can accelerate idea generation, automate processes, and fundamentally alter how we make decisions.

In our journey through the innovative playground of Tesla, we dissected their financials, scrutinized key trends, assessed growth drivers, and evaluated potential risks. This company stands at the forefront of technological progress, offering intriguing insights into the present and future of the EV industry and the overall clean energy landscape.

As we shifted our gaze to trading strategies, we discovered how sentiment derived from news can be woven into an aggressive options trading strategy for Tesla. By anticipating bullish or bearish movements and executing call or put options, respectively, we provide a new layer of nuance to investment decision-making. For the conservative investor, a long position strategy ensures a safer route where they can buy shares when certain fundamental conditions align.

Power BI visualizations serve as the crystal ball, bringing all these insights and data to life. Whether it's illustrating Tesla's market share in the EV space, comparing operating efficiency ratios, tracking revenue growth, or mapping charging network infrastructure, these visualizations offer an enriched perspective of complex data landscapes.

However, the true marvel of this chapter lies in the seamless integration of ChatGPT. Acting as a versatile aide, ChatGPT aids in everything from sifting through news and social media for sentiment analysis to generating ideas and automating processes.

Despite these groundbreaking advancements, we don't forget the elephant in the room: AI bias. We delve into the key challenges posed by bias in AI systems, underscoring the importance of addressing this issue in the pursuit of more equitable and effective AI applications.

In essence, *Chapter 3* stands as a compelling testimony to why AI should be a part of everyone's toolkit in today's world. The integration of AI into finance and business is not just about staying ahead; it's about being part of a transformative journey that's redefining how we perceive, interpret, and interact with the world around us. This is a wave of change that no one should miss out on!

With the foundation of AI-driven financial analysis established, *Chapter 4, John Deere AgTech Revolution: AI Insights and Challenges*, will take you further into the realm of advanced financial analysis techniques. We'll explore crucial skills and topics, such as mastering advanced financial ratios, metrics, and valuation methods, and incorporating AI and ChatGPT into these techniques for improved accuracy and efficiency. Through detailed examples and practice use cases, you'll learn to apply cutting-edge methods such as **discounted cash flow** (**DCF**) in conjunction with AI and ChatGPT. You'll also gain valuable insights into refining and updating valuation models to ensure accuracy and relevancy.

4

John Deere's AgTech Revolution – AI Insights and Challenges

Chapter 3 delved into the exciting intersection of trading, AI, and data visualization. We navigated through the complexities of financial analysis using Tesla as a case study. By leveraging Python, we extracted data from diverse sources, setting the stage for Power BI's visual storytelling capabilities. We demonstrated how Power BI can transform raw data into an intuitive scatter plot, highlighting crucial relationships in Tesla's vehicle range and charging time. We also confronted the critical issue of **artificial intelligence (AI)** bias, discussing its implications in finance and AI-driven tools.

Chapter 4 unfolds an exciting journey into the future of financial analysis, where AI, sophisticated financial metrics, and intuitive data visualization intertwine to unlock new levels of insights and efficiency. As we delve deeper into this chapter, we will explore advanced financial analysis techniques, discuss the transformative role of AI and ChatGPT in financial analysis, and see how data visualization with Power BI can bring your data to life. We will also introduce you to AutoGPT, an autonomous extension of ChatGPT, and provide Python code examples for various financial analysis tasks. Each step of the journey will be punctuated with real-world examples and case studies, bringing the concepts to life and providing you with practical tools to enhance your financial analysis skills.

The following key topics will be covered in this chapter:

- **Advanced financial analysis techniques**: Diving into financial ratios, metrics, and valuation methods

- **Incorporating AI and ChatGPT into financial analysis**: Unveiling the power of AI in complex calculations, forecasts, and risk assessments

- **Data visualization with Power BI**: Transforming raw financial data into intuitive, insightful visualizations

- **Introducing AutoGPT**: Exploring this autonomous AI's applications in the world of financial analysis

- **Python code examples for financial analysis**: Providing hands-on experience with coding for financial tasks

- **Dealing with hallucinations in language models**: A guide to understanding and minimizing AI "hallucinations"

This isn't the usual suspect of Silicon Valley or Wall Street, but rather the vast expanses of farmlands and construction sites. Welcome to the world of John Deere, a pioneer who merged the physical and digital worlds to redefine the agriculture industry.

In this chapter, we'll be rolling up our sleeves and taking a deep dive into John Deere's sprawling operations, known for their seamless blend of machinery with advanced tech innovations. As we embark on this adventure, you'll realize that beneath the green and yellow exterior, John Deere is more akin to a tech firm than a conventional agriculture company. With a lineup of advanced technologies including precision agriculture, autonomous equipment, data analysis, and AI-driven computer vision, Deere is at the forefront of the agriculture sector's digital transformation.

So, why should you tech-savvy readers care about John Deere and the agriculture industry? The answer is simple: the same technological trends that have disrupted sectors such as retail, media, and finance are now stirring up the fields of agriculture. A tech revolution is quietly brewing in the heartland, and companies like John Deere are leading the charge. If you're intrigued by innovation and digital disruption, then this unlikely sector holds an untapped reservoir of opportunities and insights.

Digitizing the fields – unleashing a tech revolution with John Deere

John Deere's diverse operations and its substantial presence in various sectors such as agriculture, construction, forestry, and turf care will give you a more comprehensive view of different financial ratios and metrics. Deere's long financial history, consistent profitability, and varied product segments can provide ample data for exploring these advanced metrics and their applicability in real-world situations. Deere's recent emphasis on technological advancements and sustainability efforts can also introduce discussions around ESG metrics, which are becoming increasingly relevant in financial analysis.

John Deere's recent investments in AI and autonomous technologies make it a compelling choice for this section. The company is actively incorporating AI in its operations – from smart, self-driving tractors to predictive maintenance algorithms:

- **Precision agriculture**: John Deere's technology suite allows farmers to use GPS data and automated steering to maximize yields and reduce wasted seed, fertilizer, and fuel. This is an application of AI in which algorithms process data to make specific recommendations and control machinery.

- **Autonomous equipment**: John Deere has developed and continues to refine autonomous tractors and other equipment. These machines can perform tasks without human intervention, using AI to navigate the field, avoid obstacles, and optimize task performance.

- **Data analysis**: The John Deere Operations Center allows farmers to collect and analyze data about their operations. Machine learning algorithms process this data to provide insights into crop health, soil conditions, and equipment performance.

- **Computer vision**: John Deere uses AI-based computer vision technology for tasks such as identifying weeds for precise pesticide application, reducing the number of chemicals used, and increasing crop yield.

While John Deere is a leader in this space, it's worth noting that there are other companies in the agriculture industry also making significant advancements in AI, such as AGCO (which owns brands such as Massey Ferguson and Fendt) and CNH Industrial (which owns brands such as Case IH and New Holland Agriculture). Startups such as Blue River Technology (acquired by John Deere), Farmers Edge, and Granular are also innovating in this space.

John Deere is a global leader in the agriculture and construction equipment industry, with a strong brand and a long history of innovation. But like any company, it has its strengths and weaknesses and faces a variety of opportunities and challenges.

Strengths	Weaknesses
Strong brand and market position: John Deere is a trusted brand known for its quality, reliability, and durability. The company has a significant market share in many of its key product categories.	**Dependence on economic conditions**: As a manufacturer of heavy machinery, John Deere's sales can be significantly affected by economic conditions. In particular, the health of the farming sector is crucial to their sales, and this can be influenced by factors outside their control such as weather, commodity prices, and trade policies.
Innovation and technology: John Deere has made significant investments in technology and innovation. It has pioneered precision agriculture, which uses technology and data to help farmers improve productivity and efficiency.	**Supply chain challenges**: Like many manufacturers, John Deere faces challenges related to supply chain management. Disruptions in the supply chain can delay production and increase costs.
Diversified business: John Deere's business is diversified across different product lines and geographies. This diversification helps to mitigate risks related to any one particular market or product.	

Future opportunities and predictions

As for the future, John Deere's focus on technology and innovation is likely to continue, and the following areas could be important for their growth:

Future opportunities	Predictions
Smart farming	The use of digital technology and data analytics in agriculture will increase agricultural production, and improve the efficiency and sustainability of farming practices. Predictive analytics, automation, IoT, and AI are some of the tools that will define this field. John Deere's investments in precision agriculture are likely to continue.
Electric and autonomous vehicles	With the growing interest in sustainable and efficient farming practices, the adoption of electric and autonomous tractors and other farming equipment will likely increase. John Deere showcased a fully autonomous tractor concept, indicating its capabilities in this area.
Expansion in emerging markets	Emerging markets such as India, Brazil, and parts of Africa have large agricultural sectors and could represent significant growth opportunities for John Deere.

According to a report by **Market Research Future (MRFR)**, the smart farming industry is projected to grow significantly. By 2022, it's anticipated to be worth approximately 2 billion dollars, showcasing a robust growth rate of 14% from 2016 to 2022. This statistic indicates that there is a large potential market for John Deere's smart farming technology.

Moreover, according to Reports and Data, the global electric agriculture equipment market is expected to reach USD 15.3 billion by 2027, at a CAGR of 9.8%. John Deere's innovation in electric and autonomous vehicles places it in a good position to capitalize on this trend.

To sum up, John Deere needs to continue investing in technology and innovation to maintain its competitive edge and manage its supply chain to ensure it can meet demand efficiently. Its diversification strategy should also help it navigate the uncertainties and challenges of the global economic environment. It's important to note that these predictions are based on the current market trends and John Deere's strategic directions, and actual outcomes can vary based on various factors.

As we pivot to a bird's-eye view of the competitive landscape, this section shines a light on the major players in the **agricultural technology (AgTech)** world: John Deere, Climate Corporation (owned by Bayer), and Farmers Edge.

John Deere's prowess in blending hardware with innovative technology is unparalleled, while Climate Corporation and Farmers Edge are making waves with their data-driven platforms, using AI and **machine learning (ML)** to transform raw data into actionable farming insights.

This comparative analysis navigates through their varied product portfolios, core strengths, competitive dynamics, and AI/ML utilization, offering a comprehensive understanding of the AgTech realm. The information distilled in this section will enable you to gauge the robustness of their AI and ML capabilities and help you understand the complexities of this rapidly evolving industry.

Digital seedbed – a comparative analysis of AgTech titans

John Deere, Climate Corporation (a subsidiary of Bayer), and Farmers Edge are all significant players in the AgTech space, but they have different areas of focus and offerings:

- **John Deere**: John Deere has a broad product range that includes tractors, harvesters, sprayers, and other farm equipment. They've also invested heavily in precision agriculture with their John Deere Operations Center, which offers farm planning, equipment monitoring, and field data analysis. They're known for their high-quality, durable equipment and how they integrate technology into their machinery. John Deere's main strength lies in its ability to manufacture heavy farm machinery integrated with sophisticated software and data analysis tools.

- **Climate Corporation (Owned by Bayer)**: Climate Corporation primarily provides digital agriculture services through their Climate FieldView platform. This platform uses data science, ML, and AI to deliver insights that help farmers improve productivity, sustainability, and economic profitability. Their main strength lies in their comprehensive and granular field and weather data analysis, which allows farmers to make more precise decisions about planting, fertilizing, and harvesting. However, they do not manufacture machinery like John Deere does.

- **Farmers Edge**: Farmers Edge also provides comprehensive digital agriculture services, similar to Climate Corporation. Their FarmCommand platform offers predictive modeling, weather analytics, and fully integrated farm management. One of their unique offerings is Smart Insurance, an AI-driven crop insurance service. Their strengths lie in their comprehensive suite of digital tools, personalized customer support, and the inclusion of on-farm weather stations in their services.

In terms of competition, all three are vying for market share in the rapidly expanding AgTech field. John Deere competes with Climate Corporation and Farmers Edge in the precision farming data analytics space, but it has the added advantage of producing the physical machinery used on farms. However, both Climate Corporation and Farmers Edge offer robust, data-driven digital platforms that can provide farmers with insights and analyses, which is where they compete strongly with John Deere's offerings.

In summary, all three companies are leveraging AI and ML in meaningful ways. The best platform would likely depend on the specific needs of the customer. For integrated machinery and software, John Deere may be preferable. For data analysis and field-level insights, a farmer might prefer Climate Corporation's Climate FieldView or Farmers Edge's FarmCommand. Ultimately, robustness might best be measured by the value and actionable insight the platform provides to its users.

As AI and ML continue to evolve, these companies will likely continue to develop their platforms and incorporate these advanced technologies in more innovative ways to serve their customers better. The competition in the AgTech space is fierce, and the robustness of AI and ML capabilities is a key differentiator.

In this section, we discussed the competitive landscape of the AgTech industry, dissecting the unique strengths and strategies of John Deere, Climate Corporation, and Farmers Edge. Through this lens, we explored the transformative power of AI and ML in modern agriculture and how these tech giants leverage such advancements to redefine farming.

The next section navigates the realm of unconventional data sources that could reveal intriguing insights into John Deere's potential as an investment opportunity. Delving into the impact of factors such as product launches, commodity prices, weather patterns, policy shifts, global trade dynamics, sustainability initiatives, and technological advancements, we'll illuminate how these overlooked aspects can shape investment strategies.

The hidden goldmine – unearthing unconventional data for strategic investments in John Deere

What types of unconventional information and data from John Deere could provide insight into a trading strategy and provide investment opportunities?

Here are some unconventional data sources for John Deere:

- **New product launches**: The launch of a new product line or significant upgrades to existing products can often lead to changes in the stock's performance. These product announcements often indicate that the company is innovating and investing in its future.

- **Commodity prices**: Since John Deere's customers are largely from the agricultural sector, commodity prices can significantly impact the company's financial performance. A rise in crop prices usually leads to higher income for farmers, which, in turn, can lead to more sales for John Deere.

- **Weather patterns**: Unusual weather patterns, such as droughts or floods, can affect the farming industry and, consequently, John Deere's sales. Climate data and forecasts might offer some insight into the potential demand for John Deere's products.

- **Government policies and subsidies**: Changes in government policies related to agriculture or trade can impact John Deere's sales. For example, government subsidies for farmers or tariffs on imported goods can influence farmers' purchasing decisions.

- **Global trade dynamics**: As a global company, John Deere is affected by international trade dynamics. Factors such as trade tensions or agreements can influence the company's export potential and impact its financial performance.

- **Sustainability initiatives**: John Deere's efforts in sustainability and environmental preservation could also be a useful indicator of their future performance. Increased consumer and investor interest in **environmental, social, and governance (ESG)** factors makes this a potentially impactful area.

- **Technological advances**: Pay attention to John Deere's progress in the fields of AI, ML, and automation. They've been investing significantly in these areas, and breakthroughs or advancements could lead to considerable growth.

Remember, unconventional data should be used to supplement, not replace, traditional financial analysis. Moreover, investing involves risk, and all data, conventional or not, should be thoroughly analyzed to make informed decisions.

In this exhilarating exploration of unconventional data, we've embarked on a journey beyond the traditional boundaries of financial analysis, diving deep into the impactful world of John Deere. We've uncovered how factors such as weather patterns, global trade, and technological breakthroughs intertwine with Deere's growth trajectory, broadening our understanding of its investment potential. This voyage into the lesser-traveled path of data insights paves the way for a more holistic and enlightened approach to AgTech investments. Remember, it's in these overlooked corners that the most rewarding investment opportunities often lie.

Hold on tight as we delve into an electrifying journey powered by WallStreetGPT – an AI persona that's breaking barriers and changing the game in financial analysis. In the next revolutionary section, we'll explore how WallStreetGPT, with its unique blend of data analysis and strategic questioning, takes on the role of an astute Wall Street analyst to shed light on the strategic initiatives and potential of the agricultural behemoth, John Deere.

We'll see how WallStreetGPT delves into the financial impacts of John Deere's investments, explores untapped markets, and unearths strategic growth opportunities. But this AI-driven journey is more than a technical analysis; it's about understanding the underlying strategic narrative of the company.

With the sharp acumen of an experienced analyst, WallStreetGPT prompts valuable discussions around John Deere's future strategies and prospects. The AI persona demonstrates how technology is not here to replace analysts but to enhance their capabilities, enabling them to dive deeper and ask more insightful questions during earnings calls.

This isn't just about deciphering what's happening now; it's about anticipating what could happen next, enabling investors and analysts alike to stay one step ahead. So, sit back and witness how WallStreetGPT is turning the tables and reshaping the future of earnings calls, one insightful question at a time!

John Deere's AgTech Revolution – AI Insights and Challenges

WallStreetGPT is a persona that can show what ChatGPT can ask in a John Deere earnings call as it relates to questions and how it can extract key information that is needed for the investment community, customers, investors, and others to understand based on key prompts.

WallStreetGPT question: "John Deere has been investing heavily in precision agriculture and other advanced technologies, which are expected to drive efficiency and open up new revenue streams. However, these investments also come with significant upfront costs. Could you provide some color on how these investments are impacting your current financial performance, and what kind of **return on investment** (**ROI**) you expect to see in the future? Additionally, how do these investments align with your long-term financial goals and what impact do you expect them to have on your revenue and profitability over the next 5 to 10 years?"

This question is designed to elicit information about the financial impact of John Deere's strategic investments, both in the short term and the long term. The answer could provide valuable insights into the company's financial health and future prospects.

WallStreetGPT question: "John Deere has shown interest in expanding into new areas such as vertical farming, renewable energy solutions for farms, and even blockchain solutions for the supply chain. Can you provide some insights into the potential **total addressable market** (**TAM**) for these sectors? Furthermore, how does John Deere plan to capture market share in these new areas, and what kind of impact could this expansion have on your revenue growth over the next decade?"

As a hypothetical world-class stock analyst, here are some recommendations and new ideas to ask John Deere to see whether they would entertain any of them to remain competitive and successful in the agriculture industry:

- **Expand precision agriculture**: Build internally and hire talent. John Deere already has a strong presence in this area, so it would make sense to continue building on this internally. They should hire data scientists, software engineers, and agronomists to develop more advanced precision agriculture solutions.

- **Invest in vertical farming**: Partner with companies. Vertical farming requires specialized knowledge and technology, so it would be beneficial to partner with a company that already has expertise in this area, such as AeroFarms or Plenty.

- **Develop blockchain solutions for the supply chain**: Buy a small or midsize company. Many startups are working on blockchain for the supply chain, such as Provenance and Ripe.io, which could be potential acquisition targets.

- **Collaborate with biotech companies**: Partner with companies. Biotech is a highly specialized field, so it would make sense to partner with a company that already has expertise in this area, such as Monsanto or Syngenta.

- **Create an AgTech incubator**: Build internally and hire talent. This could be done internally with the right team of business development and startup mentoring professionals.

- **Develop renewable energy solutions for farms**: Partner with companies. Renewable energy is a highly specialized field, so it would make sense to partner with a company that already has expertise in this area, such as SunPower or Vestas.

- **Invest in education and training**: Build internally. John Deere could develop training programs, perhaps in partnership with universities or vocational schools.

- **Collaborate with tech giants**: Partner with companies. Tech giants such as Google and Amazon have vast resources and expertise that John Deere could leverage.

These strategies would depend on John Deere's specific capabilities, resources, and strategic goals, as well as the specific opportunities available in the market.

However, it's important to make it clear that while ChatGPT could generate intelligent questions based on its training, it does not understand the context or implications of its questions in the same way a human analyst would. It can generate questions based on patterns it has seen in similar data, but it can't form a strategy or comprehend the broader significance of the answers.

That being said, showing how AI can automate certain aspects of the analyst's job could lead to discussions about the future of the industry, the potential benefits and drawbacks of AI, and how human analysts might need to adapt to stay relevant.

In this section, we saw how WallStreetGPT, an AI persona, is revolutionizing earnings calls by probing strategic insights and investment opportunities at John Deere. As a game-changer, it's enhancing analyst capabilities, redefining the future of financial analysis, and equipping stakeholders to anticipate market trends and corporate strategy.

As we plunge into the captivating universe of quantitative investing, prepare to discover the potential this method holds for complex sectors such as agri-business, and particularly for companies such as John Deere.

The next section demystifies how, through the combination of vast data and advanced algorithms, quantitative models can uncover intricate patterns and provide extraordinary investment insights. These insights could revolutionize traditional methods, offering more comprehensive and timely analyses.

We'll also illustrate a practical example of quantitative trading and a Power BI visualization using John Deere and its competitors. This walkthrough will reveal how to profit from temporary price deviations. It's an exciting merger of financial acumen and data science, and it awaits you in the following pages. Stay tuned!

Unlocking the power of quantitative investing – a game-changer for agri-business

Quantitative investing is a type of investment strategy that primarily relies on mathematical computations, statistical models, and automated algorithms to identify and execute trades. Unlike fundamental and technical analysis, which focus on the intrinsic value of securities and the analysis of trends and patterns in trading data, respectively, quantitative investing seeks to profit from mathematical insights derived from the vast amount of financial data available.

Let's break down each of these investment approaches briefly:

- Fundamental analysis is the process of determining the inherent worth of security by scrutinizing various economic, financial, and other relevant factors. This includes examining macroeconomic trends and industry circumstances, as well as the specific company's financial condition and managerial competence, including revenue, costs, assets, and liabilities. You might liken this process to a comprehensive health check-up, where a physician assesses the patient's vital signs and conducts diagnostic tests to establish the patient's overall well-being.

- Technical analysis is a method that centers around studying statistical patterns derived from historical trading actions, encompassing factors such as fluctuations in price and transaction volume. It uses chart patterns, indicators, and other tools to predict future price movements. To use a weather metaphor, it's like a meteorologist predicting future weather patterns based on past and current data.

- Quantitative investing, on the other hand, utilizes advanced mathematical models and algorithms to analyze financial markets and identify trading opportunities. It leverages computational frameworks and taps into the power of big data and AI to make investment decisions, often at a speed and frequency beyond human capabilities.

Now, why is quantitative investing important, particularly in the context of agriculture and a company like John Deere? The answer lies in the complexities of the agricultural industry and the inherent challenges it poses for traditional forms of analysis.

The agriculture sector is affected by an array of factors such as climate change, weather patterns, soil quality, pest infestations, commodity prices, global trade policies, technological innovations, and more. Traditional fundamental and technical analyses may struggle to accurately capture, process, and make sense of all these factors at once.

Enter quantitative investing. With its ability to handle vast amounts of data, it can process all these factors concurrently, providing insights that might be missed by a human analyst. For instance, a quantitative model could incorporate satellite imagery data to assess crop growth, global weather data to predict potential impact on harvests, and real-time commodity prices to gauge market trends, all at once.

Let's consider a potential scenario involving John Deere. As a leader in the agricultural machinery industry, its financial performance is deeply intertwined with the broader agriculture sector. A quantitative investing model for John Deere might incorporate factors such as the following:

- **Macro-level data**: Global agricultural trends, commodity prices, climate data, land usage statistics, demographic trends, economic indicators, and so on

- **Company-specific data**: Sales data for different categories of machinery, operational efficiency metrics, R&D spending, and so on

- **Sentiment analysis**: Mining news articles, social media posts, and other sources of unstructured data to gauge public sentiment toward the company and its products

By analyzing these data points, the model could potentially identify patterns and relationships that are not immediately apparent. For instance, it might identify a strong correlation between the company's stock price and certain macro-level indicators, enabling the model to anticipate price movements based on these indicators.

In conclusion, quantitative investing offers a powerful toolset for navigating the complex dynamics of the agricultural industry and companies like John Deere. By harnessing the power of data and advanced algorithms, it allows investors to uncover insights and investment opportunities that might be overlooked by traditional analysis. However, it also requires a high degree of mathematical and computational expertise, and like all investment strategies, it carries its own set of risks. As such, it should be used as part of a balanced and well-informed investment strategy.

In the next section, we will delve into a fascinating real-world example of a quantitative trading strategy using John Deere and its competitors, Caterpillar Inc. and CNH Industrial. Here, we will employ a mean reversion trade strategy banking on the premise that prices of closely correlated stocks within the same industry tend to move toward their average over time. Leveraging historical price data and simple mathematical calculations, we identify trading opportunities where John Deere's stock price deviates significantly from its average, and concurrently, its competitors' prices remain close to their respective averages. By demonstrating how to execute trades based on these signals and close the position when the price reverts to the mean, we offer an exciting glimpse into the practical application of quantitative investing.

Quantitative trading example – John Deere

Mean reversion trade – John Deere

Let's construct a quantitative investing example using John Deere and two of its major competitors, Caterpillar Inc. and CNH Industrial. The premise here is to create a mean reversion trading strategy that capitalizes on the price correlations between these agricultural machinery manufacturers.

The idea behind mean reversion is that the prices of these stocks will tend to move toward their mean or average price over time. If the stocks are closely correlated, as we would expect for companies in the same industry, we could potentially profit from temporary price discrepancies.

Here's a simplified step-by-step process of how this strategy might work. Remember that this is a simplified example, and real quantitative investing strategies would require rigorous backtesting and risk management measures:

- **Data gathering**: We start by gathering historical price data for John Deere, Caterpillar, and CNH Industrial. This data could be obtained from any reputable financial data provider, such as Yahoo! Finance, Alpha Vantage, or others. We would want daily closing prices for a significant period, say, the last 5 years.

- **Calculate the mean**: Next, we calculate a moving average of the price of each stock. A common choice is the 30-day moving average, which provides a balance between responsiveness and noise reduction. The moving average represents our "mean" price in the mean-reversion strategy.

- **Identify deviations**: We look for instances where the price of John Deere deviates significantly from its moving average, say, by more than two standard deviations. This deviation might be due to some temporary market sentiment or news that is causing irrational price movements.

- **Confirm correlation**: At the same time, we check the prices of Caterpillar and CNH Industrial. If these prices do not deviate from their respective averages (that is, the market sentiment seems to be specifically affecting John Deere), we may have a trading opportunity.

- **Execution of trades**: If John Deere's stock is trading significantly below its average while Caterpillar and CNH Industrial are around their averages, we could interpret this as a signal that John Deere's stock is temporarily undervalued. In response, we could buy John Deere's stock with the expectation that its price will revert to the mean. Conversely, if John Deere's stock is significantly above its average, we might see this as a signal that it is temporarily overvalued, and we could sell the stock or short sell if the facility is available.

- **Close the position**: After the trade, we continue to monitor the stock prices. Once John Deere's price reverts to its moving average, we would close out the position, thus hopefully capturing a profit from the price correction.

This example demonstrates the essence of a quantitative mean reversion strategy. It's important to note that, in reality, implementing such a strategy requires sophisticated programming and statistical skills, as well as careful risk management. Price deviations can occur for valid reasons, and prices can deviate from their averages for extended periods.

Here are the steps, along with the corresponding Python code, to build the quantitative trading strategy we've just described. We will be using the `yfinance` library to fetch data from Yahoo! Finance and pandas for data manipulation:

1. **Data gathering**: We'll use the `yfinance` library to gather historical price data for the specified stocks:

```
pip install yfinance
pip install pandas
```

```
# Define the tickers of the stocks we're interested in
tickers = ['DE', 'CAT', 'CNHI']

# Get the historical price data for the last 5 years
data = yf.download(tickers, start="2018-06-23", end="2023-06-
23")['Close']
```

2. **Calculate the mean**: Next, we calculate a 30-day moving average for each stock:

```
# Calculate 30-day moving average
moving_averages = data.rolling(window=30).mean()
```

3. **Identify deviations**: We calculate the standard deviation and identify points where the price of John Deere deviates by more than two standard deviations from its moving average:

```
# Calculate 30-day standard deviation
std_dev = data.rolling(window=30).std()

# Identify points where price of John Deere deviates by more
than 2 standard deviations from its moving average
deviations = (data['DE'] - moving_averages['DE']).abs() > 2*std_
dev['DE']
```

4. **Confirm correlation**: We check that the prices of Caterpillar and CNH Industrial are not deviating from their averages when John Deere's price is deviating from its average:

```
# Identify points where prices of CAT and CNHI are not deviating
by more than 2 standard deviations from their moving averages
not_dev_cat = (data['CAT'] - moving_averages['CAT']).abs() <=
2*std_dev['CAT']
not_dev_cnh = (data['CNHI'] - moving_averages['CNHI']).abs() <=
2*std_dev['CNHI']

# Confirm the correlation
correlated_dev = deviations & not_dev_cat & not_dev_cnh
```

5. **Execution of trades**: We generate trading signals based on our observations. We'll mark 1 as a buy signal when John Deere's stock is significantly below its average and -1 as a sell signal when it's significantly above its average:

```
# Identify buy/sell signals
signals = pd.Series(index=data.index)
signals[correlated_dev & (data['DE'] < moving_averages['DE'])] =
1  # Buy signal
signals[correlated_dev & (data['DE'] > moving_averages['DE'])] =
-1  # Sell signal
```

6. **Close the position**: In a real-world scenario, you would close your position when the price reverts to the mean. However, for our simplified example, we won't cover the closing of positions.

Please note that this example is a simple illustration and doesn't take into account many factors you should consider in a real trading scenario, such as transaction costs, slippage, risk management, and more. Additionally, note that this example assumes the availability of the short-selling facility, which may not be available under all circumstances. Finally, the trading strategy is based on the assumption that prices will revert to the mean, which might not always hold true in real-world scenarios. Always perform thorough backtesting before deploying any strategy.

Python code snippet explanation

- **Data gathering**: We downloaded historical price data for John Deere, Caterpillar Inc., and CNH Industrial for the past 5 years from Yahoo! Finance using the `yfinance` library.

- **Calculate the mean**: A 30-day moving average for each stock was calculated using the pandas `.rolling().mean()` method.

- **Identify deviations**: Deviations were identified by calculating the standard deviation and looking for instances where John Deere's stock price deviated by more than two standard deviations from its moving average.

- **Confirm correlation**: We confirmed correlation by checking that Caterpillar and CNH Industrial's prices were not deviating from their respective averages when John Deere's price was deviating from its average.

- **Execution of trades**: Trading signals were generated based on our findings. `1` was marked as a buy signal when John Deere's stock was significantly below its average, and `-1` was marked as a sell signal when it was significantly above its average.

Power BI visualization for quantitative trading example – John Deere

Here, we'll focus on a mean reversion trading strategy, a method that is predicated on the assumption that a stock's price will tend to move to the average price over time. To make this concept more accessible and impactful, we'll be creating a dynamic and insightful Power BI visualization. We'll feature John Deere and its competitors, crafting a line chart that displays the moving averages of each stock and overlaying it with data points to indicate the buy/sell signals for John Deere.

This graphical representation of data will not only elevate your understanding but also facilitate more informed decision-making. It will enable you to quickly discern when John Deere's stock price significantly deviates from its moving average, thereby triggering a buy or sell signal. The goal is to create a line chart that shows the moving averages of the three stocks (John Deere, Caterpillar Inc., and CNH Industrial), along with buy and sell signals for John Deere:

1. **Step 1 – data and extraction steps**:

   - First, make sure you have installed the tools that are required to extract the data and installed the pandas, yfinance, numpy, and pandas-datareader libraries in your Python environment. If not, you can use the following commands to install them:

     - pip install pandas

     - pip install yfinance

     - pip install numpy

     - pip install pandas-datareader

   - Use the following Python script to extract all the required data for the Power BI visualization:

     ```
     import pandas as pd
     import yfinance as yf
     import numpy as np

     # Define the list of stocks
     stocks = ['DE', 'CAT', 'CNHI']

     # Define the period for which we want to get data
     period = '5y'

     # Fetch the data
     data = yf.download(stocks, period=period)['Adj Close']

     # Calculate 30-day Moving Average for each stock
     for stock in stocks:
         data[stock + '_30_MA'] = data[stock].rolling(window=30).
     mean()

     # Calculate standard deviation for John Deere
     data['DE_std'] = data['DE'].rolling(window=30).std()

     # Define a buy/sell signal column for John Deere (when price
     is more than 2 standard deviations away from 30-day MA)
     data['DE_signal'] = np.where(data['DE'] < (data['DE_30_MA'] -
     2*data['DE_std']), 'Buy',
     ```

```
                                    np.where(data['DE'] > (data['DE_30_
MA'] + 2*data['DE_std']), 'Sell', 'Hold'))

# Save DataFrame into a .csv file
data.to_csv('stocks_data.csv')
```

Python code snippet explanation:

- Install the `pandas`, `yfinance`, `numpy`, and `pandas-datareader` libraries in your Python environment if you haven't installed them yet.

- Extract the stock prices for John Deere, Caterpillar Inc., and CNH Industrial, calculate their 30-day moving averages, calculate the standard deviation for John Deere, add a buy/sell column for John Deere stock once it meets certain criteria, and then save all the information in a CSV file so that it can be uploaded into Power BI in *Step 2*.

2. **Step 2 – importing the data into Power BI**:

    - Open Power BI.

    - Click on the **Home** tab, then click on the **Get Data** option.

    - From the drop-down menu, choose **Text/CSV**.

    - Locate the CSV file you saved and click **Open**. Power BI will display a preview of your data.

    - Click **Load** to load the data into Power BI.

3. **Step 3 – creating the Power BI visualization**:

    We'll create a line chart with three lines representing the moving averages of the three stocks and data points representing the buy/sell signals for John Deere:

    I.   Click on the **Line chart** visualization from the **Visualizations** pane. A blank chart area will appear.

    II. Drag and drop the **Date** field to the **Axis** field in the **Visualizations** pane.

    III. Similarly, drag and drop the moving averages for the three companies (John Deere, Caterpillar Inc., and CNH Industrial) to the **Values** field.

    IV. Your line chart will now show the moving averages of the three stocks over time.

    V.   Next, let's add the buy/sell signals for John Deere. Click on **Scatter chart** from the **Visualizations** pane and place it on top of the line chart.

    VI. For this scatter chart, set the **Date** field as **X-Axis** and **John Deere Price** as **Y-Axis**.

    VII. Drag and drop the **Signals** field into the **Legend** field.

VIII. Overlay the scatter chart on top of the line chart so that the buy/sell signals can be visualized along with the moving averages for the three stocks:

- **Select the scatter chart**: Click on the scatter chart you've just created to select it.

- **Positioning**: Using your mouse, drag the scatter chart until it is positioned over the line chart. Try to align the axes carefully so that the data points correspond accurately with the dates and values on the line chart.

- **Resizing**: Once the scatter chart has been positioned over the line chart, you'll notice small resizing handles (usually small squares) at the corners and edges of the scatter chart. Click and drag these to resize the scatter chart so that it matches the size of the line chart beneath it.

- **Tweak the transparency**: You can adjust the transparency of either the line chart or the scatter chart to ensure both sets of data are visible. This can usually be done in the **Format** section of the **Visualizations** pane.

IX. By reading this chart, users can see when the price of John Deere deviates from its moving average, along with the respective buy/sell signal. When the signal is "buy," it means John Deere's stock is undervalued, expecting it to increase toward the average. On the contrary, a "sell" signal indicates the stock is overvalued, and it's expected to decrease.

Remember, creating these visualizations in Power BI is a process of exploration and adjustment. Feel free to adjust the type of chart, colors, labels, and other attributes to make the chart as clear and engaging as possible.

In this Power BI example, we explored how to build a dynamic and insightful Power BI visualization for the mean reversion trading strategy using John Deere and its competitors as an example. Such visualizations can elevate understanding and facilitate decision-making by offering a graphical representation of moving averages and buy/sell signals.

We constructed the visualization itself, a line chart with three lines for the moving averages of each stock and overlaying data points indicating the buy/sell signals for John Deere. This visualization allows users to quickly grasp when John Deere's stock price significantly deviates from its moving average, thereby triggering a buy or sell signal.

In this section, we explored the realm of quantitative investing, demonstrating its potential to revolutionize the agricultural industry, particularly for firms like John Deere. By leveraging vast data and sophisticated algorithms, we showed how this approach could yield profound insights and investment opportunities. Through a practical trading example and a Power BI visualization featuring John Deere and its competitors, we brought the power and potential of this innovative trading strategy to life.

Unveiling the power of advanced financial metrics and valuation methods through Power BI visualization

In this section, we'll delve into the world of financial ratios and metrics. We'll explore **return on invested capital** (ROIC), **enterprise value** (EV), EBITDA Margin, and **free cash flow** (FCF) yield, and how these metrics can provide insights into a company's performance. We'll also discuss valuation methods such as **discounted cash flow** (DCF) and explore a relevant example:

- **Return on invested capital (ROIC)** is a profitability ratio that measures how effectively a company uses its capital to generate profits. It's calculated as net income divided by invested capital. For a capital-intensive industry such as agriculture, a high ROIC can indicate efficient use of capital and strong profitability. For example, if John Deere has a higher ROIC than its competitors, this could suggest that it's more efficient at turning its capital investments into profits.

- **Enterprise Value (EV)** represents the complete worth of a company, taking into account not only its market capitalization (equity value) but also its liabilities and cash reserves. It provides a more holistic view of a firm's overall financial standing. It's often used in valuation ratios, such as EV/EBITDA, which can provide a more comprehensive view of a company's value than just looking at its stock price. For example, if John Deere has a lower EV/EBITDA ratio than its competitors, this could suggest that it's undervalued relative to its earnings.

- **EBITDA Margin** represents a company's operational profitability, providing a percentage that shows how much of each dollar of revenue is transformed into EBITDA, or earnings before interest, taxes, depreciation, and amortization. It's computed by dividing EBITDA by the total revenue the company generates. A high EBITDA margin can indicate strong operational efficiency and profitability. For example, if John Deere has a higher EBITDA margin than its competitors, this could suggest that it's more efficient at turning revenue into operational profit.

- **Free cash flow (FCF)** is a measure of the cash a company generates relative to its market value, calculated as free cash flow divided by market capitalization. A high FCF yield can indicate strong cash generation and financial stability, which can be particularly important for companies in the agriculture industry, which often require significant capital expenditure. For example, if John Deere has a higher FCF yield than its competitors, this could suggest that it's generating more cash relative to its market value.

Discounted Cash Flow (DCF) is a technique that appraises the worth of an investment by considering its prospective cash flows. These anticipated cash flows are "discounted" to their present-day value using a specific discount rate, which encapsulates the potential risk associated with the cash flows and the principle that money today has a greater value than the same amount in the future (often referred to as the time value of money). The aggregation of these adjusted cash flows provides an estimate of the investment's inherent value. If this calculated intrinsic value surpasses the prevailing market price, it could hint at the investment being underpriced. These are just a few of the many financial metrics that can be used to analyze and compare companies. Each of these metrics provides a different perspective on a company's financial performance and position, and they can be particularly useful when used together as part of a comprehensive financial analysis.

Each of these metrics provides a unique lens through which to evaluate a company's efficiency, profitability, value, and financial stability. For instance, a high ROIC may indicate effective use of capital, while a higher FCF yield can suggest robust cash generation relative to a company's market value.

In this section, we ventured into the realm of valuation methodologies, particularly the DCF method. This technique involves projecting a company's future cash flows and discounting them back to present value using a discount rate reflective of risk and the time value of money. The sum of these discounted cash flows offers an estimate of the intrinsic value of an investment. If the calculated intrinsic value exceeds the current market price, it may suggest the investment is undervalued.

Unveiling value – harnessing AI for discounted cash flow analysis

In this section, we'll provide a detailed example of using AI and ChatGPT to calculate intrinsic value based on the DCF method. We'll walk you through the process of incorporating various risk factors and market conditions into the analysis. Utilizing AI and ChatGPT for DCF analysis allows you to evaluate potential future revenue streams, such as new products or services, and estimate their impact on John Deere's valuation.

Here's a simplified explanation of how you might use DCF to estimate the intrinsic value of the three new initiatives at a high level:

- **Estimate future cash flows**: This is the most challenging part of the DCF analysis. For each initiative, you would need to estimate the net cash flows it would generate each year. This would include the additional revenue from the initiative, minus the expenses required to capture that revenue. In our previous examples, we estimated potential revenues for each initiative and mentioned some potential expenses, but a real DCF analysis would require much more detailed and accurate estimates.

- **Set a discount rate**: The discount rate factors in the principle of the time value of money, the concept that the current value of a dollar outweighs its future value. This rate should be indicative of the risk associated with the anticipated cash flows. For instance, riskier initiatives may warrant a higher discount rate. The discount rate could be equated to John Deere's **weighted average cost of capital** (**WACC**), or it could be a specially determined rate that mirrors the unique risks associated with the initiatives.

- **Compute the present value of anticipated cash flows**: For every year, take the projected cash flow and divide it by (1 + discount rate) raised to the power corresponding to the year. This step helps determine the present value of the cash flow, effectively translating the future worth into its equivalent value in today's dollars.

- **Sum the present values**: Add up the present values of all the future cash flows. This gives you the total present value of the future cash flows, also known as the intrinsic value of the initiatives.

- **Compare the intrinsic value to the investment cost**: If the intrinsic value is higher than the cost of the initiatives, this suggests that the initiatives could be a good investment. If it's lower, this suggests that the initiatives might not be a good investment.

This is a very simplified explanation and a real DCF analysis would be much more complex and would need to account for a wide range of factors. Also, DCF analysis is based on many assumptions and estimates, and it's only as accurate as the inputs.

Through this case study of John Deere, we have illustrated how AI can assist in projecting future cash flows for each business initiative and offer a method to determine an appropriate discount rate. We highlighted how present value calculations enable the quantification of potential investments in today's dollars. By summing these values, this section led you through the process of evaluating the total present value of future cash flows – the intrinsic value of the initiatives. The final, crucial step involves comparing the calculated intrinsic value to the cost of investment to determine its viability. While the process may seem intricate, it underlines the utility of AI and detailed analysis in making informed investment decisions. As always, professional financial advice should accompany these techniques, ensuring a balanced and informed decision-making process.

The next section navigates the potential of three emerging markets – precision agriculture, vertical farming, and renewable energy solutions for farms – for John Deere, utilizing the compelling visual capabilities of Power BI and a comprehensive DCF analysis.

Visualizing the future – leveraging Power BI to explore John Deere's potential in emerging markets with DCF analysis

In this section, we will consider three potential new markets for John Deere: precision agriculture, vertical farming, and renewable energy solutions for farms. We can extract the data required and load it into Power BI to explore the data in more detail to understand the potential DCF impact:

- **Precision agriculture**: According to a report by MarketsandMarkets, the global market for precision farming is projected to reach $12.8 billion by 2025. If John Deere could capture a 10% market share, that would represent $1.28 billion in additional annual revenue. The expenses to achieve this might include R&D, marketing, and possibly acquisitions, which could total several hundred million dollars.

- **Vertical farming**: According to a report by Allied Market Research, the global vertical farming market is projected to reach $12.77 billion by 2026. If John Deere could capture a 5% market share, that would represent $638.5 million in additional annual revenue. The expenses to achieve this might include R&D, building or acquiring vertical farms, and hiring specialized staff, which could total several hundred million dollars.

- **Renewable energy solutions for farms**: According to a report by Fortune Business Insights, the global market for renewable energy is projected to reach $1.512 billion by 2027. If John Deere could capture a 1% market share in the segment related to farms, that would represent $15.12 million in additional annual revenue. The expenses to achieve this might include R&D, manufacturing or acquiring renewable energy equipment, and marketing, which could total several million dollars.

These are very rough estimates, and the actual results could be significantly different. The expenses and net income would depend on a wide range of factors, including John Deere's specific strategies and capabilities, competitive dynamics, regulatory conditions, and broader economic factors. As always, investment decisions should be made based on a thorough analysis of all available information and in consultation with a financial advisor.

Data extraction process for Power BI visualizations

This will involve a combination of downloading financial data, calculating estimates, and manually entering data. Here's a simplified example of how you might gather some of this data using Python:

```python
import yfinance as yf
import pandas as pd

# Download historical data for John Deere
deere = yf.download('DE', start='2010-01-01', end='2021-09-30')['Adj
Close']

# Calculate daily returns
deere_returns = deere.pct_change().dropna()

# Assume we have estimated future cash flows for each initiative
# In reality, you would need to calculate these from financial
projections
precision_ag_cash_flows = pd.Series([200, 250, 300, 350, 400],
index=pd.date_range(start='2022-01-01', periods=5, freq='A'))
vertical_farming_cash_flows = pd.Series([100, 150, 200, 250, 300],
index=pd.date_range(start='2022-01-01', periods=5, freq='A'))
renewable_energy_cash_flows = pd.Series([50, 75, 100, 125, 150],
index=pd.date_range(start='2022-01-01', periods=5, freq='A'))

# Assume a discount rate of 10%
discount_rate = 0.1

# Calculate the present value of future cash flows
precision_ag_pv = sum(cash_flow / (1 + discount_rate) ** i for i,
cash_flow in enumerate(precision_ag_cash_flows, 1))
vertical_farming_pv = sum(cash_flow / (1 + discount_rate) ** i for i,
cash_flow in enumerate(vertical_farming_cash_flows, 1))
```

```
renewable_energy_pv = sum(cash_flow / (1 + discount_rate) ** i for i,
cash_flow in enumerate(renewable_energy_cash_flows, 1))

# Create a DataFrame with the data
data = pd.DataFrame({
    'Initiative': ['Precision Agriculture', 'Vertical Farming',
'Renewable Energy Solutions for Farms'],
    'Present Value': [precision_ag_pv, vertical_farming_pv, renewable_
energy_pv]
})

# Save the DataFrame to a CSV file for import into Power BI
data.to_csv('initiative_data.csv', index=False)
```

Python code snippet

This code downloads historical price data for John Deere, calculates daily returns, estimates future cash flows for each initiative, calculates the present value of these cash flows using a discount rate of 10%, and then saves this data to a CSV file.

You could then import this CSV file into Power BI and use it to create the visualizations. For example, you could create a bar chart with the initiatives on the X-axis and the present values on the Y-axis.

Please note that this is a very simplified example and actual data gathering and analysis would be much more complex. Also, this example does not include all the data you would need for the visualizations, such as the projected growth of the global markets and the breakdown of expenses for each initiative. You would need to gather this data separately, possibly from industry reports, financial statements, or other sources.

How to create Power BI visualizations

- Precision agriculture:

    - A bar chart showing the projected growth of the global precision farming market over the next few years, with a highlighted bar representing the potential revenue for John Deere if it captures a 10% market share.

- Bar chart – projected growth of the global precision farming market:

    - **Global market revenue**: Obtain this data from market research reports on precision agriculture, which are often available from sources such as Statista, Grand View Research, and others

    - **John Deere's potential revenue**: Calculate this as 10% of the global market revenue

- CSV file structure:
  - Create a CSV file named `Precision_Farming_Market_Growth.csv` and populate it with the sourced data. Here's an example (for illustration purposes only):
    - Year,Global_Market_Revenue,John_Deere_Potential_Revenue
    - 2023,5000,500
    - 2024,6000,600

Creating a bar chart visualization in Power BI

Follow these steps:

1. **Import the CSV file**: Go to **Home** > **Get Data** > **Text/CSV** and select `Precision_Farming_Market_Growth.csv`.

2. **Create the bar chart**: Select **Bar chart** from the **Visualizations** pane.

3. **Configure the chart**: Drag **Year** to **Axis** and **Global_Market_Revenue** and **John_Deere_Potential_Revenue** to **Values**.

Next, we'll add a treemap showing the breakdown of John Deere's expenses, which is required to capture that market share (for example, R&D, marketing, and acquisitions).

Treemap – breakdown of expenses to capture market share

Use the latest John Deere financial statements, John Deere financial forecasts, or industry benchmarks on precision farming to populate this file.

CSV file structure:

- Create a CSV file named `Expenses_Breakdown.csv`. Here's an example (for illustration purposes only):
  - Expense_Type,Amount
  - R&D,200
  - Marketing,100
  - Acquisitions,150

To create a treemap visualization in Power BI, follow these steps:

1. **Import the CSV file**: Go to **Home** > **Get Data** > **Text/CSV** and select `Expenses_Breakdown.csv`.

2. **Create the treemap**: Select **Treemap** from the **Visualizations** pane.

3. **Configure the treemap**: Drag **Expense_Type** to **Groups** and **Amount** to **Values**.

Next, we'll create a gauge chart showing the potential intrinsic value based on the DCF analysis, with the needle pointing to the estimated intrinsic value based on the potential net cash flows and discount rate.

Gauge chart – intrinsic value based on DCF analysis

The discount rate and estimated intrinsic value will come from a financial projections presentation on the investor relations page for John Deere or a stock analyst report covering John Deere on precision farming.

CSV file structure:

- Create a CSV file named `DCF_Intrinsic_Value.csv`. Here's an example (for illustration purposes only):

    ```
    Discount_Rate,Estimated_Intrinsic_Value
    7,900
    ```

Follow these steps to create a gauge chart visualization in Power BI:

1. **Import the CSV file**: Go to **Home** > **Get Data** > **Text/CSV** and select `DCF_Intrinsic_Value.csv`.
2. **Create the gauge chart**: Select **Gauge chart** from the **Visualizations** pane.
3. **Configure the gauge chart**: Drag **Estimated_Intrinsic_Value** to **Value** and (optionally) set the min, max, and target values as needed.

Next, we'll look at vertical farming and create a line chart showing the projected growth of the global vertical farming market over the next few years, with a highlighted point representing the potential revenue for John Deere if it captures a 5% market share.

Line chart – projected growth of the global vertical farming market

- You can obtain the global market revenue data from market research reports on vertical farming, from platforms such as Statista, MarketWatch, or Grand View Research.
- You can calculate John Deere's potential revenue as 5% of the global market revenue for each year.

CSV file structure:

- Create a CSV file named `Vertical_Farming_Market_Growth.csv` and populate it with the sourced data. Here's an example (for illustration purposes only):

    ```
    Year,Global_Market_Revenue,John_Deere_Potential_Revenue
    2023,7000,350
    2024,8000,400
    ```

Follow these steps to create a line chart visualization in Power BI:

1. **Import the CSV file**: Go to **Home** > **Get Data** > **Text/CSV** and select `Vertical_Farming_Market_Growth.csv`.

2. **Create the line chart**: Select **Line chart** from the **Visualizations** pane.

3. **Configure the line chart**: Drag **Year** to **Axis** and **Global_Market_Revenue** and **John_Deere_Potential_Revenue** to **Values**.

Next, we'll create a stacked column chart showing the breakdown of expenses required to capture that market share (for example, R&D, building or acquiring vertical farms, and hiring specialized staff).

Stacked column chart – breakdown of expenses to capture market share in vertical farming

You can use internal company budgets or estimates, analyst reports such as Gartner, or other industry benchmarks for similar initiatives.

CSV file structure:

- Create a CSV file named `Vertical_Farm_Expenses_Breakdown.csv`. Here's an example (for illustration purposes only):

```
Expense_Type,Amount
R&D,300
Building_or_Acquiring,200
Hiring,100
```

Follow these steps to create a stacked column chart visualization in Power BI:

1. **Import the CSV file**: Go to **Home** > **Get Data** > **Text/CSV** and select `Vertical_Farm_Expenses_Breakdown.csv`.

2. **Create the stacked column chart**: Select **Stacked column chart** from the **Visualizations** pane.

3. **Configure the chart**: Drag **Expense_Type** to **Axis** and **Amount** to **Values**.

Next, we'll create a gauge chart showing the potential intrinsic value based on the DCF analysis, with the needle pointing to the estimated intrinsic value based on the potential net cash flows and discount rate.

Gauge chart – intrinsic value based on DCF analysis

The discount rate and estimated intrinsic value would usually come from your company's financial models or specialized financial analysis in vertical farming.

CSV file structure:

- Create a CSV file named `Vertical_Farm_DCF_Intrinsic_Value.csv`. Here's an example (for illustration purposes only):

```
Discount_Rate,Estimated_Intrinsic_Value
6,950
```

Follow these steps to create a gauge chart visualization in Power BI:

1. **Import the CSV file**: Go to **Home** > **Get Data** > **Text/CSV** and select `Vertical_Farm_DCF_Intrinsic_Value.csv`.
2. **Create the gauge chart**: Select **Gauge chart** from the **Visualizations** pane.
3. **Configure the gauge chart**: Drag **Estimated_Intrinsic_Value** to **Value** and (optionally) set the min, max, and target values as needed.

Next, we'll look at renewable energy solutions for farms. We will create an area chart showing the projected growth of the global renewable energy market over the next few years, with a highlighted area representing the potential revenue for John Deere if it captures a 1% market share in the segment related to farms.

Area chart – projected growth of the global renewable energy market for farms

- **Global market revenue**: Source this data from market research reports focused on renewable energy for farms. Reliable sources could include Statista, MarketWatch, and industry-specific reports.

- **John Deere's potential revenue**: Calculate this as 1% of the global market revenue related to farms for each year.

- Create a CSV file named `Renewable_Energy_Market_Growth.csv`. Here's an example (for illustration purposes only):

```
Year,Global_Market_Revenue,John_Deere_Potential_Revenue
2023,9000,90
2024,10000,100
```

Follow these steps to create an area chart visualization in Power BI:

1. **Import the CSV file**: Go to **Home** > **Get Data** > **Text/CSV** and select `Renewable_Energy_Market_Growth.csv`.
2. **Create the area chart**: Select **Area chart** from the **Visualizations** pane.
3. **Configure the area chart**: Drag **Year** to **Axis** and **Global_Market_Revenue** and **John_Deere_Potential_Revenue** to **Values**.

Next, we'll create a pie chart showing the breakdown of expenses required to capture that market share (for example, R&D, manufacturing or acquiring renewable energy equipment, and marketing).

Pie chart – breakdown of expenses to capture market share in the renewal energy sector

Use internal company budgets or estimates, analyst reports such as those from Gartner, or other industry benchmarks for similar initiatives.

CSV file structure:

- Create a CSV file named `Renewable_Energy_Expenses_Breakdown.csv`. Here's an example (for illustration purposes only):

```
Expense_Type,Amount
R&D,400
Manufacturing_or_Acquiring,250
Marketing,150
```

Follow these steps to create a pie chart visualization in Power BI:

1. **Import the CSV file**: Go to **Home** > **Get Data** > **Text/CSV** and select `Renewable_Energy_Expenses_Breakdown.csv`.

2. **Create the pie chart**: Select **Pie chart** from the **Visualizations** pane.

3. **Configure the pie chart**: Drag **Expense_Type** to **Legend** and **Amount** to **Values**.

Next, we'll create a gauge chart showing the potential intrinsic value based on the DCF analysis, with the needle pointing to the estimated intrinsic value based on the potential net cash flows and discount rate.

Gauge chart – intrinsic value based on DCF analysis

Extract the discount rate and estimated intrinsic value from your internal financial models or specialized financial analysis for renewable energy.

CSV file structure:

- Create a CSV file named `Renewable_Energy_DCF_Intrinsic_Value.csv`. Here's an example (for illustration purposes only):

```
Discount_Rate,Estimated_Intrinsic_Value
6,950
```

Follow these steps to create a gauge chart visualization in Power BI:

1. **Import the CSV file**: Go to **Home** > **Get Data** > **Text/CSV** and select `Vertical_Farm_ DCF_Intrinsic_Value.csv`.

2. **Create the gauge chart**: Select **Gauge chart** from the **Visualizations** pane.

3. **Configure the gauge chart**: Drag **Estimated_Intrinsic_Value** to **Value** and (optionally) set the min, max, and target values as needed.

These estimations, derived through DCF analysis, involve numerous assumptions, underscoring the need for professional financial advice. The real-world utility of these findings is significantly augmented through Power BI visualizations, which provide a dynamic, intuitive way to understand these potential scenarios. These visualizations include various charts illustrating the projected growth of these markets, potential revenues for John Deere, and the breakdown of associated expenses.

In this light, the combination of DCF analysis and Power BI visualizations presents a powerful toolkit for envisioning John Deere's opportunities in these promising markets. As always, it is crucial to make investment decisions in consultation with a financial advisor, taking into account the broader economic landscape and John Deere's specific strategies.

Now, get ready to step into the future as we explore the thrilling world of AutoGPT and how it's transforming the face of financial analysis and trading. As we voyage through this exciting realm of autonomous AI, prepare to witness how AI can function as your personal finance assistant, predicting market trends, making investment recommendations, and even executing trades independently!

Embracing the AI revolution with AutoGPT – reshaping financial analysis and trading through autonomous AI

AutoGPT, an innovative open source Python application, is built on the powerful GPT-4 model from OpenAI. This autonomous tool can independently analyze financial data, uncover crucial insights, and formulate investment recommendations according to your specified objectives. Imagine having an AI assistant that could supercharge your financial decisions – that's the reality with AutoGPT.

But, as with any tool, AutoGPT comes with its strengths and caveats. While it brings efficiency, accuracy, and scalability to your financial analysis, you'll need technical skills to harness its full potential. Moreover, like all AI, it should be seen as a supportive tool rather than a replacement for human judgment. Therefore, it's essential to validate its outputs and ensure its use aligns with your risk tolerance and investment goals.

Let's explore how AutoGPT can revolutionize financial analysis and trading:

- **Automated trading**: AutoGPT can monitor real-time market data and execute trades based on predefined strategies. For instance, with John Deere's stock, AutoGPT can automatically execute a trade when the 50-day moving average goes above the 200-day moving average, signaling a potential upward trend.

- **Monte Carlo simulation**: AutoGPT can take historical data and use Monte Carlo simulations to predict potential paths for John Deere's stock price. This probabilistic approach allows for better risk management and investment decision-making.

- **Portfolio rebalancing strategy**: AutoGPT can monitor a diverse portfolio – say, John Deere, Caterpillar Inc., CNH Industrial, and Kubota Corp. – and autonomously trigger a rebalance if the holdings of any stock deviate by more than 5% from their target allocation. This allows for consistent portfolio management and ensures your investments stay aligned with your financial goals.

The pros and cons of AutoGPT in financial analysis

Like any tool, AutoGPT has its strengths and limitations. Let's explore them:

- Pros:

  - **Efficiency**: AutoGPT can automate time-consuming tasks, such as data analysis and report generation, freeing up your time for strategic decision-making

  - **Accuracy**: By leveraging AI, AutoGPT can process vast amounts of data with high precision, reducing the risk of human error

  - **Scalability**: AutoGPT can manage large datasets and complex calculations that would be challenging for a human analyst

- Cons:

  - **Complexity**: Setting up and using AutoGPT requires a certain level of technical expertise, including familiarity with Python and various API keys.

  - **Limitations in real-world scenarios**: While AutoGPT is powerful, it may not perform well in complex, real-world business scenarios. It's crucial to validate its output and use it as a tool to support, not replace, human judgment.

  - **Data privacy**: As AutoGPT requires internet access, there could be potential data privacy concerns that need to be addressed.

  - OpenAI API credit and limits.

  - AutoGPT can create errors that need to be corrected.

Using AutoGPT in finance, investment, and trading

AutoGPT can be a game-changer in finance, investment, and trading. Here's how:

- **Automated financial analysis**: AutoGPT can independently analyze financial data, calculate financial ratios, and generate insights. For example, it can automate the analysis of John Deere's (NYSE: DE) financial performance, providing you with valuable insights without the manual work.

- **Investment recommendations**: Based on your specified goals, AutoGPT can evaluate investment opportunities and make recommendations. It can analyze market trends, company performance, and risk factors to suggest potential investments.

- **Trading automation**: AutoGPT can monitor market data in real time, generate trading signals based on your trading strategy, and even execute trades. This can help you respond quickly to market changes and execute your trading strategy more efficiently.

Remember, while AutoGPT is a powerful tool, it's important to use it responsibly. Always validate its output and use it as a tool to support, not replace, human judgment. We will show some examples of AutoGPT in the following sections.

Using AutoGPT for automated trading (moving average trading example)

Imagine that you're an investor interested in John Deere. You've developed a trading strategy that buys John Deere's stock when its 50-day moving average goes above its 200-day moving average, a signal that often indicates a potential upward price trend.

Monitoring these moving averages manually can be time-consuming and prone to human error. This is where AutoGPT comes into play. With AutoGPT, you can automate this process, allowing the AI to monitor the moving averages of John Deere's stock in real time. When the 50-day moving average goes above the 200-day moving average, AutoGPT can execute the trade on your behalf, adhering to your predefined strategy.

This automation not only saves you time but also ensures that you don't miss out on potential investment opportunities due to human oversight or time constraints. It allows you to execute your trading strategy more efficiently, freeing up your time to focus on other important aspects of your investment portfolio.

By leveraging AutoGPT, you're not just automating your trading strategy; you're also enhancing your investment decision-making process with the power of AI. This can give you a competitive edge in the market, helping you make more informed and timely investment decisions.

Remember, while AutoGPT can be a powerful tool, it's important to use it responsibly. Always ensure that your trading strategy aligns with your investment goals and risk tolerance, and regularly review and adjust your strategy as market conditions change. Happy investing!

AutoGPT setup process

Let's learn how to set up an environment on a PC.

Here are detailed instructions on how to download and install Docker Desktop on a PC running Windows.

Step 1 – system requirements verification:

First, make sure your PC meets the following system requirements:

- Microsoft Windows 10 (64-bit) Pro, Enterprise, or Education. Docker does not run on Windows 10 Home.

- Virtualization must be enabled. You can check this by opening Task Manager (*Ctrl + Shift + Esc*) and switching to the **Performance** tab. Next to the **CPU** category, you should see **Virtualization: Enabled**. If it says **Disabled**, you will need to go into your BIOS/UEFI settings to enable it.

Enabling virtualization through the BIOS/UEFI is a hardware-level setting, and the exact steps can vary, depending on your motherboard manufacturer.

Here are some general steps on BIOS/UEFI settings for most motherboard manufacturers:

1. **Restart your computer**:

   - Restart your computer. As it starts up, you'll need to press a specific key to enter the BIOS/UEFI settings. This key varies by manufacturer but is often *F1*, *F2*, *F10*, *Esc*, or *Del*.

2. **Enter the BIOS/UEFI setup**:

   - Keep an eye on the screen for a message that tells you which key to press to enter the setup. Press this key immediately.

3. **Navigate to the Advanced tab**:

   - Once in the BIOS/UEFI menu, navigate to the **Advanced** tab or something similarly named. Again, this varies by manufacturer.

4. **Locate the virtualization settings**:

   - Inside the **Advanced** menu, look for a category called **CPU Configuration**, **Advanced CPU Features**, or simply **Virtualization**.

5. **Enable virtualization**:

   - Once you've located your respective virtualization option, change the setting to **Enabled**. You can usually do this by selecting the option, hitting *Enter*, and choosing **Enabled** from the list.

6. **Save and exit**:

   - After enabling virtualization, save your changes and exit the BIOS/UEFI setup. To do this, navigate to the **Save & Exit** menu, which is usually located as an exit door icon or simply written as **Save & Exit**.

7. **Restart your computer**:

   - Your computer will restart. You can now check Task Manager again to confirm that virtualization is enabled.

8. **Recheck Task Manager**:

   - After your system restarts, open Task Manager (*Ctrl + Shift + Esc*) and switch to the **Performance** tab. Next to the **CPU** category, it should now say **Virtualization: Enabled**.

Important note

BIOS/UEFI interface: These interfaces are not uniform and can differ significantly, depending on the manufacturer. The terms and menu names are generic and should be similar to what you see.

Be cautious: Be careful when making changes in the BIOS/UEFI as incorrect settings could make your system unstable.

Check your motherboard manual: If you're unsure, it's a good idea to consult your motherboard's manual or look for official guidance from the manufacturer's website.

Follow these steps to create a Docker account and download Docker Desktop:

1. Create a Docker Account:

   - **Open your web browser**: Open your preferred web browser and go to the Docker Hub website: `https://hub.docker.com`.

   - **Navigate to Sign Up**: In the top-right corner of the page, you'll see a **Sign In** button. Click on it, and then click on **Sign Up** in the dialog that appears.

   - **Enter details**:

     - **Username**: Choose a unique username that you'll use to log in to Docker Hub.

     - **Email**: Provide a valid email address. You'll need to confirm this email later, so make sure it's accessible.

     - **Password**: Create a strong password that you can remember. Usually, it needs to be a mix of letters, numbers, and special characters.

2. **Complete the CAPTCHA**: You may be asked to complete a CAPTCHA to prove you're not a robot.

3. **Agree to the terms and conditions**: Check the box to agree to Docker's terms and conditions. Make sure you read them before agreeing.

4. **Click Sign Up**: After filling out all the details and agreeing to the terms, click the **Sign Up** button.

5. **Verify your email**: You'll receive a verification email from Docker. Go to your email inbox, open the Docker email, and click on the verification link. This confirms that the email address you've provided is valid.

6. **Log in**: Once your email has been verified, you can log in to Docker Hub using the username and password you just created:

   I.   Open your web browser and navigate to the Docker Desktop for Windows download page: `https://www.docker.com/products/docker-desktop`.

   II.   Click on the **Get Docker** button to download Docker Desktop.

   III. Once the installer has been downloaded, navigate to your downloads folder and find the Docker Desktop `Installer.exe` file.

7. **Install Docker:**

   I.   Double-click the Docker Desktop `Installer.exe` file to start the installation.

   II.   When the installer starts, you'll be greeted with a window that tells you that Docker will be installed on your computer and that it will also install the necessary features of Windows. Click **Ok** to proceed.

   III. Accept the license agreement and authorize the installer.

   IV.   Follow the prompts on the installation wizard and accept the defaults unless you have a specific need to change them.

8. **Start Docker:**

   I.   After the installation is complete, click **Close and restart** – this ensures Docker starts up correctly.

   II.   Once your PC restarts, you can open Docker by clicking the Docker icon on your desktop or by searching for Docker in your start menu.

   • **Verify the installation:**

   I.   To verify that Docker has been installed correctly, open Command Prompt and enter `docker --version`.

   You should see Docker's version in the output. This means that Docker has been installed and is running correctly.

9. **Get an OpenAI API key:**

   Next, get your OpenAI API key from `https://platform.openai.com/account/api-keys`. Note that to avoid limitations, consider setting up a paid account. We suggest that you use an API key for the paid version (GPT-4), but can use an API for a free earlier version (GPT-3.5 turbo).

10. **Step 7 – set up the AutoGPT project:**

Once Docker has been installed, create a project directory for AutoGPT using your system's command line:

```
mkdir AutoGPT
cd AutoGPT
```

In the AutoGPT directory, create a docker-compose.yml file:

- Create a new file named docker-compose.yml in the AutoGPT directory.

- You can use a text editor such as Notepad or any code editor you are comfortable with (for example, Visual Studio Code).

- Edit docker-compose.yml.

- Open the docker-compose.yml file with a text editor:

```
version: "3.9"
services:
auto-gpt:
image: Significant-Gravitas/auto-gpt
depends_on:
            - redis
          env_file:
            - .env
          environment:
            MEMORY_BACKEND: ${MEMORY_BACKEND:-redis}
            REDIS_HOST: ${REDIS_HOST:-redis}
          profiles: ["exclude-from-up"]
          volumes:
            - ./auto_gpt_workspace:/app/autogpt/auto_gpt_
workspace
            - ./data:/app/data
            - ./logs:/app/logs
              redis:
        image: "redis/redis-stack-server:latest"
```

Once you've made the necessary changes, save the docker-compose.yml file.

Now, you need to create the necessary configuration files. To do so, locate the .env.template file in the Auto-GPT main folder. Depending on your OS (Windows, macOS), this may be a hidden file. Duplicate it as .env, by using cp .env.template .env, for example. Edit this .env file, filling in your OpenAI API key after OPENAI_API_KEY=, without quotes or spaces. Add other service keys/tokens if needed. Remove # to activate settings. Finally, save and close the file.

> **Important note**
>
> To learn more about `docker-compose.yaml` and the configuration file layout provided by Dr. Christian Mayer, go to `https://blog.finxter.com/installing-auto-gpt-any-other-way-is-dangerous/`.

Back in the command line, run the following command to start the AutoGPT service with Docker:

```
docker-compose up
```

11. **Step 8 – pull AutoGPT from Docker:**

    Pull the AutoGPT image from Docker Hub using the following command:

    ```
    docker login
    docker pull Significant-Gravitas/AutoGPT
    ```

12. **Step 9 – configure AutoGPT:**

    Create a YAML configuration file to define your AI's parameters. This is where you can specify the goals and roles of your AI. In your case, it would look something like this:

    - `ai_goals:`
    - - Buy John Deere stock when its 50-day moving average goes above its 200-day moving average
    - - Sell John Deere stock when its 50-day moving average goes below its 200-day moving average
    - - Develop and manage buys and sales of John Deere stock autonomously
    - - Play to its strengths as a **large language model (LLM)**
    - `ai_name:JohnDeere50_200MovingAverage-GPT`
    - `ai_role`: An AI designed to autonomously buy and sell John Deere stock based on moving average parameters with the sole goal of increasing or decreasing John Deere stock holdings using a trend

    Save this file as `ai_settings.yaml` in your AutoGPT project directory.

13. **Step 10 – run AutoGPT with Docker:**

    Now, you're ready to run AutoGPT. Use the following command:

    ```
    docker-compose run --rm AutoGPT
    ```

This will start AutoGPT and load your trading strategy. It will begin monitoring John Deere's stock for the specified moving average crossover events and execute trades when those events occur.

Please note that this guide doesn't cover setting up a brokerage account or connecting AutoGPT to a brokerage API to execute actual trades. You would need to ensure that this integration is completed and thoroughly tested for AutoGPT to be able to execute trades. Always consult with a financial advisor or expert when deploying automated trading strategies.

Remember that the actual implementation of this process could be more complex and might require additional steps, depending on your particular setup and requirements.

Python code snippet explanation

- **Setting up the environment**: We started by installing Docker, an essential tool for running applications in an isolated environment, and setting up a project directory for AutoGPT.

- **Acquiring the API key**: The next step involved getting an API key from OpenAI to enable interaction with AutoGPT.

- **Configuring AutoGPT**: After, we created a YAML configuration file to specify the AI's goals, name, and role. These settings instruct the AI to buy and sell John Deere's stock based on 50-day and 200-day moving average indicators.

- **Pulling and running AutoGPT from Docker**: Finally, we pulled the AutoGPT image from Docker Hub and used the `docker-compose run` command to start AutoGPT with the predefined trading strategy.

AutoGPT – financial analysis Monte Carlo simulation

Let's consider a Monte Carlo simulation to predict the possible evolution of John Deere's stock price, based on historical data and an assumed statistical distribution:

1. Follow *steps 1* to *8* in the previous AutoGPT example.

2. **Step 9 – configure AutoGPT:**

   Create a YAML configuration file that defines the parameters for your Monte Carlo simulation strategy. In the configuration file, specify the goals and roles of your AI. Here's an example:

   - `ai_goals:`
   - Perform Monte Carlo simulations on John Deere stock
   - Analyze simulation results and suggest trading actions based on the outcomes
   - `ai_name: JohnDeereMonteCarlo-GPT`
   - `ai_role`: An AI designed to perform Monte Carlo simulations and provide trading recommendations based on simulation outcomes

   Save this file as ai_settings.yaml in your AutoGPT project directory.

3. **Step 10 – run AutoGPT with Docker:**

   You're now ready to run AutoGPT with Docker. Run the following command:

   ```
   docker-compose run --rm AutoGPT
   ```

This command will start AutoGPT with your Monte Carlo simulation strategy. It will conduct simulations and make recommendations based on the simulation's outcomes.

Portfolio rebalancing strategy – AutoGPT

In this example, AutoGPT will be configured to monitor a portfolio consisting of John Deere, Caterpillar Inc., CNH Industrial, and Kubota Corp. and it will automatically trigger a rebalance if the holdings of any stock deviate by more than 5% from their target allocation:

1. Follow *steps 1 to 8* in the previous AutoGPT example.

2. Go ahead and configure AutoGPT. At this stage, you need to create a YAML configuration file that defines your version of AutoGPT. This file will contain the details of your portfolio rebalancing strategy. Your `ai_settings.yaml` file might look like this:

   - `ai_goals:`

   - Monitor the portfolio consisting of John Deere, Caterpillar Inc., CNH Industrial, and Kubota Corp. stocks

   - Maintain the portfolio balance at 25% for each stock

   - Rebalance the portfolio whenever any stock deviates by more than 5% from its target allocation

   - `ai_name: PortfolioRebalance-GPT`

   - `ai_role`: An AI designed to maintain the balance of a portfolio and automatically trigger a rebalance based on predefined rules

   Save this configuration file in the AutoGPT project directory.

3. Run AutoGPT with Docker. At this point, you're ready to run AutoGPT using Docker. Use the following command:

   ```
   docker-compose run --rm AutoGPT
   ```

Once this command is executed, AutoGPT will begin monitoring your portfolio and automatically trigger a rebalance whenever the holdings of any stock deviate by more than 5% from their target allocation.

Remember, this guide doesn't cover setting up a brokerage account or connecting AutoGPT to a brokerage API to execute actual trades. Always consult with a financial advisor or expert when deploying automated trading strategies. Furthermore, this is a simplified example. In a real-world application, transaction costs, tax implications, and other factors need to be taken into account when implementing a rebalancing strategy.

While AutoGPT is a powerful tool, remember to use it responsibly and as support for, not a replacement for, human judgment. As we journey into the future of finance with AI, be prepared for a new era of investment decision-making powered by AutoGPT!

In the next section, we'll delve into the thrilling saga of financial analysis, where Python's power comes alive. In this dynamic and thought-provoking section, we will venture into the heart of financial computations with Python – a language globally renowned for its potent libraries and user-friendly syntax.

Strap in for an exhilarating exploration of Python code examples that effortlessly handle complex financial calculations. This includes computing crucial financial ratios and, notably, calculating ROIC, a key indicator of profitability and efficiency in capital utilization.

Python power play – fueling financial analysis with advanced code

In our detailed expedition, we will bring the illustrious Deere & Co to the spotlight. Armed with actual figures extracted from their April 30, 2023 10-Q report, we will use Python to compute ROIC. This calculation, which will be seamlessly handled by Python, entails dividing the net income by the total invested capital, resulting in a percentage form of ROIC.

However, while Python may be a powerful catalyst in financial analysis, remember that it thrives on accurate and current financial data. As we forge forward into this Python-powered financial analysis journey, it's essential to bear in mind the importance of feeding reliable and up-to-date data into our Python engine. In the world of Python-empowered financial analysis, data integrity is as crucial as the calculations themselves.

So, get ready to dive into a captivating world where Python code and financial analysis intersect, sparking illuminating insights and unveiling previously hidden truths of financial performance.

Here's a simple Python code snippet that calculates the ROIC for Deere & Co. from `yfinance`:

```
pip install yfinance
import yfinance as yf


def fetch_financial_data(ticker, target_date):
    company = yf.Ticker(ticker)

    # Get quarterly financial statements
    income_statement_qtr = company.quarterly_financials
    balance_sheet_qtr = company.quarterly_balance_sheet

    # Convert target_date to the format used in yfinance
    # MM/DD/YYYY to YYYY-MM-DD
    formatted_date = '-'.join(target_date.split('/')[::-1])

    # Extract the required data for the target date
    net_income = income_statement_qtr.loc['Net Income'][formatted_
date]
```

```
    total_debt = balance_sheet_qtr.loc['Long Term Debt'][formatted_
date] + balance_sheet_qtr.loc['Short Long Term Debt'][formatted_date]
    equity = balance_sheet_qtr.loc['Total Stockholder Equity']
[formatted_date]


    return net_income, total_debt, equity


# Target date in MM/DD/YYYY format
target_date = '04/30/2023'


# Fetch financial data for John Deere (Ticker: DE)
net_income, total_debt, equity = fetch_financial_data('DE', target_
date)


# Calculate invested capital
invested_capital = total_debt + equity


# Calculate ROIC (Return on Invested Capital)
roic = net_income / invested_capital


# Print ROIC
print(f"ROIC for Deere & Co. on {target_date}: {roic * 100}%")
```

In this Python example, we're focusing on the April 30, 2023 financials, using yfinance to snag metrics for Deere & Co. We've zeroed in on net income, total debt, and equity – the three pillars for calculating ROIC. This isn't just another metric; it's the financial litmus test for assessing how efficiently a company turns capital into profits. Presented as a percentage, this ROIC number becomes a laser-focused indicator of Deere & Co.'s financial efficiency.

So, where does ChatGPT fit in? Once you've crunched the ROIC numbers, ChatGPT can serve as your interactive financial analyst. You can query it to interpret the ROIC value, compare it against competitors and industry benchmarks, or even simulate what business moves could improve it. Think of ChatGPT as your on-demand financial consultant, adding context and insights to the raw numbers. With Python and ChatGPT, you're not just data-rich, you're insight-rich.

Let's embark on an exciting journey that takes us from weather forecasts to stock market predictions, focusing on one of the giants of agricultural machinery – John Deere. Buckle up as we learn how to use Python and a weather API to fetch, manipulate, and interpret meteorological data, turning them into insights that could potentially influence our trading decisions.

Weather patterns have far-reaching implications, including in agriculture, a sector deeply intertwined with the fortunes of John Deere. Have you ever wondered how a sudden temperature drop, a deluge, or a drought might affect the growth of crops and, consequently, the sales of agricultural machinery? If you have, then this section is for you.

We'll walk through the process of extracting weather data using OpenWeatherMap's API and Python, transforming this raw data into meaningful metrics, and then developing a simple, albeit intuitive, trading strategy. This will provide a unique perspective on stock trading, where prevailing weather conditions help steer buy or sell decisions.

We'll also create a "weather score" using variables such as temperature, rainfall, humidity, and wind speed, with each acting as a puzzle piece that forms a broader picture of crop growth conditions. Depending on whether this score is above or below a certain threshold, we may consider buying or selling John Deere stock.

Moreover, we'll delve into the specifics of selecting locations and crops, and how to refine the weather score calculation to account for optimal growing conditions.

Finally, we will elaborate on setting buy and sell thresholds based on the weather scores' standard deviations, creating a framework that you can experiment with and refine based on your risk tolerance and market understanding.

From forecasts to financial foresight – a deep dive into a weather-based trading strategy with John Deere

This section examines the unexplored interplay of meteorology and financial markets. We will outline how weather data can be leveraged to inform investment decisions in the stock market, specifically targeting John Deere, a major player in the agricultural sector. Utilizing a unique weather score, we'll unravel the mysteries of algorithmic trading and illuminate how the weather impacts crop yields and subsequently, market dynamics. Let's get started:

1. **Step 1 – choose your weather API:**

    There are many weather APIs out there. For this example, we'll use OpenWeatherMap's API, which provides detailed and accurate forecasts. A free API key is available but not recommended due to call limits and uptime.

    OpenWeatherMap API subscription plans. For an individual investor, the recommended plan is Startup ($40/month). Why Startup?

    - **Uptime**: 95% uptime is usually sufficient for individual investors who may not require round-the-clock data

    - **Rate limit**: 60 calls per minute with a limit of one million calls per month should be more than adequate for less frequent trading

    - **Cost**: At $40 per month, this plan is a cost-effective way to access reliable weather data for trading

    This plan provides a balance between cost and functionality. The data points that are available, such as the 3-hour forecast for 5 days, should be sufficient for making informed trading decisions.

For an institutional investor, the recommended plan is Professional ($470/month) or Enterprise ($2,000/month). Why Professional or Enterprise? Let's take a look:

- **Uptime**: For institutional trading, you'll want high reliability. Professional offers 99.5% uptime, while Enterprise offers 99.9%.

- **Rate limit**: With the high-frequency trading that institutions often engage in, higher rate limits are essential. Professional offers 3,000 calls per minute, while Enterprise allows up to 200,000 calls per minute.

- **Data availability**: Both plans offer extensive weather data options, which could be beneficial for complex trading algorithms.

The choice between Professional and Enterprise would further depend on the specific needs of the institution, such as how many locations they are monitoring, how many trades they are making, and whether they need additional features such as Advanced Weather Maps or the Air Pollution API.

2. **Step 2 – extract data via the API**:

    We'll be using Python for this task. Let's start by installing the necessary libraries:

    ```
    pip install requests pandas
    ```

3. Now, let's create a Python script to call the OpenWeatherMap API and fetch the forecast data:

    ```
    import requests
    import pandas as pd
    import requests
    import pandas as pd


    # Define the API key and endpoint
    API_KEY = 'your_api_key_here'
    API_ENDPOINT = "http://api.openweathermap.org/data/2.5/
    forecast?"


    # Define the location for which you want to get weather
    forecasts
    location = 'Des Moines,us'  # Change to the location of your
    choice


    # Create the API request URL
    url = f"{API_ENDPOINT}q={location}&appid={API_KEY}"


    # Send a request to the OpenWeatherMap API
    response = requests.get(url)
    ```

```
# If the request was successful, the status_code will be 200
if response.status_code == 200:
    # Get the forecast data from the response
    data = response.json()

    # Extract the list of forecasts from the data
    forecasts = data['list']

    # Prepare an empty list to store the extracted data
    weather_data = []

    # Iterate over the forecasts
    for forecast in forecasts:
        # Extract the data
        dt_txt = forecast['dt_txt']
        temperature = forecast['main']['temp']
        pressure = forecast['main']['pressure']
        humidity = forecast['main']['humidity']
        wind_speed = forecast['wind']['speed']
        rain_volume = forecast['rain']['3h'] if 'rain' in
forecast and '3h' in forecast['rain'] else 0

        # Append the data to the list
        weather_data.append([dt_txt, temperature, pressure,
humidity, wind_speed, rain_volume])

    # Convert the list of forecasts to a DataFrame
    df = pd.DataFrame(weather_data, columns=['datetime',
'temperature', 'pressure', 'humidity', 'wind_speed', 'rain_
volume'])

    # Save the DataFrame to a CSV file
    df.to_csv('weather_forecast.csv', index=False)
else:
    print(f"Failed to get weather data. HTTP Status code:
{response.status_code}")
```

Replace 'your_api_key_here' with your actual API key. This script will fetch the forecast data for the next 5 days in 3-hour intervals for the location you specified. It will save this data in a CSV file named weather_forecast.csv.

This is a basic way to get the weather forecast data. In a production setting, you would likely want to automate this task so that it runs at regular intervals and appends new forecasts to an existing dataset. You may also want to capture historical weather data, for which you may need to use a different API or dataset.

> **Important note**
> This is a basic tutorial and does not include error handling and other best practices for working with APIs. Always consult the API's documentation for more detailed and accurate information. Remember to keep your API key secret to prevent unauthorized usage.

Weather score calculation – weather trade

For a simple trading strategy, you could calculate a "weather score" for each day based on these variables. If the score is above a certain threshold, it might indicate favorable conditions for crop growth, and you might consider buying John Deere stock. Conversely, if the score is below a certain threshold, it might indicate unfavorable conditions, and you might consider selling John Deere stock:

- **Temperature**: In general, a certain range of temperatures is optimal for the growth of crops. If the average temperature in a major agricultural area is significantly above or below this range, it might be an indicator of decreased crop yields, which could affect John Deere's sales. For example, if the temperature is below the optimal range for more than a few days during the growing season, it might indicate a high risk of a freeze that could damage crops.

- **Rain volume**: Rainfall is necessary for crop growth, but too much or too little can be harmful. If the cumulative rainfall over a certain period (for example, a month) is significantly higher or lower than average, it could affect crop yields and, therefore, John Deere's sales.

- **Humidity**: High humidity levels can promote the growth of certain crop diseases, while low humidity levels can increase the risk of drought. Both can affect crop yields.

- **Wind speed**: High wind speeds can cause physical damage to crops, particularly when combined with other adverse weather conditions.

The following is an example of a score model:

```
Score model = temperature_score + rainfall_score + humidity_score +
wind_speed_score
```

Each of the scores could be calculated based on whether the observed value is within an optimal range for crop growth. The specific ranges and how much weight you give to each score would need to be determined based on domain knowledge and possibly adjusted through backtesting.

Let's consider a backtesting and domain knowledge example:

1. **Define optimal ranges**: Based on domain knowledge, specify what constitutes an "optimal range" for each weather metric.

2. **Weightage**: Assign weights to each score based on their relative importance. For example, if temperature is more critical for crop growth than wind speed, it should have a higher weight.

3. **Historical data**: Use historical weather data and crop yield data to backtest your model. This will help you refine the optimal ranges and weightages.

4. **Adjust and iterate**: As you gather more data and observe real-world outcomes, continually refine your model for improved accuracy.

Here is a Python code example of calculating the score:

```python
# Define optimal ranges
optimal_temperature = (60, 85)  # in Fahrenheit
optimal_rainfall = (1, 3)  # in inches per week
optimal_humidity = (40, 60)  # in percentage
optimal_wind_speed = (2, 10)  # in mph

# Sample observed values
observed_temperature = 75
observed_rainfall = 2
observed_humidity = 50
observed_wind_speed = 5

# Calculate scores based on whether observed values fall within
optimal ranges
temperature_score = 1 if optimal_temperature[0] <= observed_
temperature <= optimal_temperature[1] else 0
rainfall_score = 1 if optimal_rainfall[0] <= observed_rainfall <=
optimal_rainfall[1] else 0
humidity_score = 1 if optimal_humidity[0] <= observed_humidity <=
optimal_humidity[1] else 0
wind_speed_score = 1 if optimal_wind_speed[0] <= observed_wind_speed
<= optimal_wind_speed[1] else 0

# Calculate overall score
overall_score = temperature_score + rainfall_score + humidity_score +
wind_speed_score
```

By developing and backtesting this model, you can create a robust framework for making more informed trading decisions based on weather conditions. This is an interdisciplinary approach, bringing together finance, data science, and agricultural expertise to create a unique investment strategy.

In the next section, we'll be moving beyond generic weather data to focus on the agricultural powerhouses of the US – think Iowa, Illinois, Nebraska, and Minnesota. These states are the epicenters of corn and soybean production, the very crops that fuel John Deere's business.

Our mission? To fine-tune our weather score to capture the unique growing conditions of these key crops. We'll leverage data from both the skies and the soil to craft a dynamic trading strategy for John Deere stock.

We'll delve into selecting prime agricultural locations, analyze historical weather patterns, and adapt our weather score to reflect conditions ideal for corn and soybean growth. The end goal? A set of actionable trading rules that let you capitalize on weather-induced market shifts.

Location and crop type – weather trade

In terms of location, you would want to focus on major agricultural areas in the US, particularly those where crops that require a lot of farming equipment are grown. These might include states such as Iowa, Illinois, Nebraska, and Minnesota, which are among the top producers of corn and soybeans.

Incorporating location and crop type data into the trading strategy can be done by refining the "weather score" calculation to account for the specific growing conditions of corn and soybeans in the Midwestern US. The ideal conditions for these crops, particularly concerning temperature and rainfall, are well-documented, and this information can be used to set the optimal ranges for the weather variables in your strategy.

Here is a broad outline of how you might do this:

- **Select locations**: Identify the major corn and soybean-producing areas in the Midwest. The USDA provides detailed crop production data at the county level, which can be used for this purpose. You might focus on the top-producing counties in states such as Iowa, Illinois, Nebraska, and Minnesota.

- **Gather historical weather data**: Use the OpenWeatherMap API to gather historical weather data for these locations. You will need data on temperature, rainfall, humidity, and wind speed at a minimum. It's also a good idea to get data for a long enough period that it includes both good and bad growing seasons.

- **Calculate weather scores**: For each day, calculate a "weather score" based on the observed weather conditions. This score should be a measure of how close the conditions are to the ideal for corn and soybean growth.

- **Define trading rules**: Define a set of rules for buying and selling John Deere stock based on the weather scores. For example, you might buy the stock when the score is above a certain threshold (indicating favorable conditions for crop growth) and sell it when the score is below a different threshold (indicating unfavorable conditions).

Here's an example of how you might calculate the weather score:

```
def calculate_weather_score(temperature, rainfall, humidity, wind_
speed):
    # Optimal ranges for corn and soybean growth
    optimal_temperature = (50, 86)  # Fahrenheit
    optimal_rainfall = (2.5, 3.5)  # Inches per week
    optimal_humidity = (40, 70)  # Percent
```

```
    optimal_wind_speed = (2, 6)   # Miles per hour


    # Calculate how far each variable is from its optimal range
    temperature_score = max(0, 1 - abs(temperature - optimal_
temperature[0]) / optimal_temperature[1])
    rainfall_score = max(0, 1 - abs(rainfall - optimal_rainfall[0]) /
optimal_rainfall[1])
    humidity_score = max(0, 1 - abs(humidity - optimal_humidity[0]) /
optimal_humidity[1])
    wind_speed_score = max(0, 1 - abs(wind_speed - optimal_wind_
speed[0]) / optimal_wind_speed[1])


    # Combine the scores into a single weather score
    score = temperature_score + rainfall_score + humidity_score +
wind_speed_score


    return score
```

In this example, each score is a number between 0 and 1 that represents how close the observed value is to the optimal range for corn and soybean growth. The overall weather score is the sum of these scores, so it is a number between 0 and 4. You would then need to determine the thresholds for buying and selling John Deere stock based on this score.

Trade threshold suggestions – weather trade

In this case, threshold settings would be largely dependent on your risk appetite and your belief in the reliability of the correlation between weather patterns and the stock's performance. However, a common approach would be to set thresholds based on standard deviations from the mean score.

Let's assume we've calculated the mean and standard deviation of the weather score. A simplified version might look like this:

```
weather_scores = ...   # Your DataFrame with weather scores
mean_score = weather_scores['score'].mean()
std_dev_score = weather_scores['score'].std()
```

Given the weather score ranges from 0 to 4, we could consider weather conditions to be exceptionally good if the score is one standard deviation above the mean, and exceptionally bad if it's one standard deviation below the mean. These could be our buy and sell thresholds, respectively:

```
buy_threshold = mean_score + std_dev_score
sell_threshold = mean_score - std_dev_score
```

In this scenario, we would consider buying John Deere stock when the weather score exceeds `buy_threshold` (signifying optimal conditions for crop growth, which could lead to higher machinery sales). Conversely, you would consider selling or shorting John Deere stock when the weather score drops below `sell_threshold` (signifying poor growing conditions, which could hurt machinery sales).

Note that these thresholds are quite simplistic. In a more sophisticated model, you might consider other factors, such as the velocity of the change in weather scores, the time of year, or the impact of consecutive periods of good or bad weather. Furthermore, financial decisions should also take into account other market indicators and your overall investment strategy.

Please keep in mind that this is a very simplified model. The actual relationship between weather conditions and crop yields is likely to be much more complex and influenced by many other factors. For a more sophisticated strategy, you might consider using machine learning techniques to model the relationship between weather data and John Deere's stock price.

In this section, we examined the intersection of weather patterns and financial markets, with a focus on John Deere, a leader in agricultural machinery. By extracting and analyzing weather data, we developed a simple trading strategy based on a "weather score," which provides insight into crop growth conditions, thus influencing John Deere's stock trading decisions. We discussed a selection of locations and crops, refined the weather score calculation, and set buy and sell thresholds, all within a Python environment.

In the next section, you'll learn how to harness the raw power of weather data and John Deere's stock data, which has been curated meticulously and stored in a humble CSV file. The adventure doesn't end there, though – we'll transform these raw elements into a "weather score," a beacon guiding our understanding of how crop growth conditions influence John Deere's stock performance.

Our journey includes five key stages. We will begin by preparing our data for the voyage, extracting the information using Python, and storing it in an accessible format. Then, we will import this data into Power BI, setting the stage for our exploration.

Beyond the initial exploration, we will offer an exhilarating peek into the future by connecting OpenAI to Power BI, creating a spectrum of fresh, insightful visualizations, such as correlating weather severity with stock price changes, or crafting heatmaps that capture weather patterns and corresponding stock price movements.

Seeds of fortune – unraveling the correlation between weather patterns and John Deere's stock performance

In this section, you'll learn how to use weather data and John Deere's stock data to create a "weather score" to understand how crop growth conditions affect stock performance. The process consists of five stages: preparing the data, extracting information with Python, and importing it into Power BI.

We'll showcase future possibilities by integrating OpenAI with Power BI to generate insights, such as correlating weather intensity with stock price fluctuations or creating heatmaps to capture weather patterns and corresponding stock price changes.

Power BI visualization

> **Important note**
>
> Please note that this guide is based on the assumption that you've stored your weather and John Deere stock data in a CSV file, and that the weather data has already been transformed into a "weather score."

Our journey includes five key stages. We will begin by preparing our data for the voyage, extracting the information using Python, and storing it in an accessible format. Then, we will import this data into Power BI, setting the stage for our exploration:

1. **Step 1 – extracting the data:**

    We have already discussed how to extract the data using Python and the OpenWeatherMap API, and how to calculate the "weather score." Now, you will want to store this data, alongside the corresponding John Deere stock data, in a CSV file so that it can easily be imported into Power BI. The following Python code snippet shows how to do this:

    ```python
    # Assuming `weather_scores` and `stock_data` are your pandas
    DataFrames
    data = pd.concat([weather_scores, stock_data], axis=1)
    data.to_csv('weather_stock_data.csv')
    ```

2. **Step 2 – importing the data into Power BI:**

    I.   Open Power BI Desktop.

    II. Go to **Home** > **Get Data** > **Text/CSV**.

    III. Navigate to the location of your CSV file and click **Open**. In the preview window, if the data looks correct, click **Load**.

3. **Step 3 – creating a line chart with two Y axes:**

    I.   Click on the **Line chart** visual in the **Visualizations** pane.

    II. Drag and drop your date field into the **Axis** field and the weather score and the John Deere stock price into the **Values** field.

    III. Now, you have a line chart with two series – weather score and stock price. However, they are currently using the same Y-axis, which could be misleading due to potentially different scales and units of measure. To fix this, we'll add a secondary Y-axis.

    IV. With the line chart selected, go to the **Format** pane and choose **Y2 axis**. Turn the switch on.

4. **Step 4 – customizing the visual**:

    Now that you have your line chart, feel free to customize it to make it more appealing and easier to understand. Here are a few ideas:

    - Add a chart title. Go to **Format** > **Title**, turn the switch on, and type your title in the text field.

    - Customize the colors. By going to **Format** > **Data colors**, you can change the colors of your data series.

    - Add data labels. After going to **Format** > **Data labels**, turn the switch on.

5. **Step 5 – adding interactivity**:

    Power BI also allows you to add interactivity to your visuals. Here's how you can add a date slicer:

    I.   Click on the **Slicer** visual from the **Visualizations** pane.

    II. Drag and drop your date field into the **Values** field of the slicer.

    III. Now, you can select a date range on the slicer, and the line chart will automatically update to show only data within that range.

And that's it! You now have an interactive Power BI line chart that shows the correlation between weather scores and John Deere's stock price.

Connecting OpenAI with Power BI

For this step, you may need to work with an API connector such as Power BI's built-in Web connector. Connect to the OpenAI API using the API key and set up the necessary GET requests to pull the relevant data.

Before you can use the OpenAI API, you'll need to obtain an API key:

1. Go to `platform.openai.com`.

2. Create an account, confirm your email, add account details, and confirm your phone number.

3. Click on the profile at the top left and then click **View API keys**.

4. Generate an API key by clicking on + **Create new secret key**.

5. Copy the key.

6. Remember to replace `your_openai_api_key` with your actual OpenAI API key.

To connect Power BI to ChatGPT via the OpenAI API, follow these steps:

1. Open Power BI and go to the **Home** tab.

2. Click on **Get Data** and select **Web** from the available options.

3. In the **Web** dialog box, enter the URL for the OpenAI API endpoint and click **OK**.

4. Enter your API key and click **OK**.

Please note that these instructions are subject to change and it's always a good idea to refer to the official documentation for the most up-to-date information.

Visualizing the data in Power BI – additional viz ideas

Once you have the data in Power BI, you can create a variety of visualizations. For instance, you might create the following:

- A line chart showing the John Deere stock price and significant weather events

- A scatter plot correlating weather severity with changes in stock price

- Heatmaps showing weather patterns in major agricultural regions and corresponding stock price fluctuations

This Power BI visualization offers an innovative exploration of the relationship between weather patterns and John Deere's stock performance. Consolidating weather scores and stock data onto a single line chart with dual Y-axes provides a clear, dynamic, and interactive way to analyze the potential influence of weather on market trends. This approach facilitates an intuitive and comprehensive understanding of complex data, enabling users to make strategic, data-informed decisions in the realm of agriculture-based financial investments.

The next section is a thrilling intersection of AI and finance. It's crucial to distinguish between what's real and what's a mirage. Here, we will delve into a fascinating phenomenon known as "hallucinations" from LLMs such as OpenAI's GPT series. These hallucinations, characterized by factual inaccuracies, speculative statements, or confident misinformation, can potentially distort our financial analyses or data visualizations.

We'll uncover the secrets of identifying these mirages and equip you with strategies to mitigate their impact. From cross-verifying information, developing robust evaluation metrics, and leveraging real-time data to fostering a constructive user feedback loop, you'll learn how to ensure that your AI-assisted decision-making process remains rooted in reality. We'll also take a peek into the future of LLMs, exploring how OpenAI is fine-tuning these models to minimize hallucinations, and discuss examples from trading and Power BI visualization scenarios to cement your understanding.

Remember, in this high-stakes game of finance and technology, a keen eye can mean the difference between a mirage and an oasis.

Understanding and mitigating LLM "hallucinations" in financial analysis and data visualization

LLMs, such as OpenAI's GPT series, can sometimes generate responses that are referred to as "hallucinations." These are instances where the output from the model is factually incorrect, it presents information that it could not possibly know (given it doesn't have access to real-time or personalized data), or it might output something nonsensical or highly improbable.

Let's explore deeper into what hallucinations are, how to identify them, and what steps can be taken to mitigate their impact, especially in a context where accurate and reliable information is crucial, such as financial analysis, trading, or visual data presentations.

Understanding hallucinations

Let's look at some examples:

- **Factual inaccuracies**: Suppose an LLM provides information stating that Apple Inc. was founded in 1985. This is a clear factual inaccuracy because Apple was founded in 1976.

- **Speculative statements**: If an LLM were to suggest that "As of 2023, Tesla's share price has hit $3,000," this is a hallucination. The model doesn't know real-time data and any post-2021 prediction or speculation it makes about specific stock prices is unfounded.

- **Confident misinformation**: For instance, if an LLM confidently states that "Amazon has declared bankruptcy in late 2022," this is a hallucination and can have serious consequences if it's acted upon without verification.

How can we spot hallucinations?

Here are some useful ways to spot hallucinations:

- **Cross-verification**: If an LLM suggests an unusual trading strategy, such as shorting a typically stable blue-chip stock based on some supposed insider information, always cross-verify this advice with other reliable sources or consult a financial advisor.

- **Questioning the source**: If an LLM claims that "our internal data shows a bullish trend for cryptocurrency X," this is likely a hallucination. The model doesn't have access to proprietary internal data.

- **Time awareness**: If the model provides information or trends post-September 2021 without the user explicitly asking for a hypothetical or simulated scenario, consider this a red flag. For example, GPT-4 giving specific "real-time" market cap values for companies in 2023 would be a hallucination.

What can we do about hallucinations?

Here are some ideas:

- **Promote awareness**: If you are developing an AI-assisted trading app that uses an LLM, ensure users are aware of potential hallucinations, perhaps with a disclaimer or notification upon usage

- **Implement checks**: You might integrate a news API that could help validate major financial events or claims made by the model

Minimizing hallucinations in the future

There are various ways we can minimize hallucinations. Here are some examples:

- **Training improvements**: Imagine developing a better model that understands context and sticks to the known data more closely, avoiding speculative or incorrect financial statements. Future versions of the model could be specifically trained on financial data, news, and reports to understand the context and semantics of financial trading and investment better. We could do this to ensure that it understands a short squeeze scenario accurately, or is aware that penny stocks typically come with higher risks.

- **Better evaluation metrics**: For instance, develop a specific metric that calculates the percentage of the model's outputs that were flagged as hallucinations during testing. In the development phase, the models could be evaluated on more focused tasks such as generating valid trading strategies or predicting the impact of certain macroeconomic events on stock prices. The better the model performs on these tasks, the lower the chance of hallucinations occurring.

- **Post-processing methods**: Develop an algorithm that cross-references model outputs against reliable financial data sources and flags potential inaccuracies. After the model generates a potential trading strategy or investment suggestion, this output could be cross-verified using a rules-based system. For instance, if the model suggests shorting a stock that has consistently performed well without any recent negative news or poor earnings reports, the system might flag this as a potential hallucination.

- As an example, you can use libraries such as `yfinance` or `pandas_datareader` to access real-time or historical financial data:

```
!pip install yfinance pandas_datareader
import yfinance as yf
def get_stock_data(ticker, start, end):
    stock = yf.Ticker(ticker)
    data = stock.history(start=start, end=end)
    return data
# Example Usage:
data = get_stock_data("AAPL", "2021-01-01", "2023-01-01")
```

You could also develop a cross-verification algorithm and compare the model's outputs with the collected financial data to flag potential inaccuracies.

- **Integration with real-time data**: While creating Power BI visualizations, data that's been pulled from the LLM could be cross-verified with real-time data from financial databases or APIs. Any discrepancies, such as inconsistent market share percentages or revenue growth rates, could be flagged. This reduces the risk of presenting hallucinated data in visualizations. Let's look at some examples:

  - **Extracting real-time data**: You can continue to use `yfinance` or `pandas_datareader` to extract real-time data

  - **Cross-verifying with real-time data**: You can compare the model's output with real-time data to identify discrepancies:

    ```
    def real_time_cross_verify(output, real_time_data):
        # Assume output is a dict with keys 'market_share', 'revenue_
    growth', and 'ticker'
                            ticker = output['ticker']

        # Fetch real-time data (assuming a function get_real_time_
    data is defined)
                            real_time_data = get_real_time_
    data(ticker)
                            # Compare the model's output with
    real-time data
        if abs(output['market_share'] - real_time_data['market_
    share']) > 0.05 or \
        abs(output['revenue_growth'] - real_time_data['revenue_
    growth']) > 0.05:
                                return True  # Flagged as a
    potential hallucination
                            return False  # Not flagged


    # Example Usage:
    output = {'market_share': 0.25, 'revenue_growth': 0.08,
    'ticker': 'AAPL'}
    real_time_data = {'market_share': 0.24, 'revenue_growth':
    0.07, 'ticker': 'AAPL'}
    flagged = real_time_cross_verify(output, real_time_data)
    ```

- **User feedback loop**: A mechanism can be incorporated to allow users to report potential hallucinations. For instance, if a user spots an error in the LLM's output during a Power BI data analysis session, they can report this. Over time, these reports can be used to further train the model and reduce hallucinations.

OpenAI is on the case

To tackle the chatbot's missteps, OpenAI engineers are working on ways for its AI models to reward themselves for outputting correct data when moving toward an answer, instead of rewarding themselves only at the point of conclusion. The system could lead to better outcomes as it incorporates more of a human-like chain-of-thought procedure, according to the engineers.

These examples should help in illustrating the concept and risks of LLM hallucinations, particularly in high-stakes contexts such as finance. As always, these models should be seen as powerful tools for assistance, but not as a final authority.

Trading examples

- **Hallucination scenario**: Let's assume you've asked an LLM for a prediction on the future performance of a specific stock, let's say Tesla. The LLM might generate a response that appears confident and factual, such as "Based on the latest earnings report, Tesla has declared bankruptcy." If you acted on this hallucinated information, you might rush to sell Tesla shares only to find out that Tesla is not bankrupt at all. This is an example of a potentially disastrous hallucination.

- **Action**: Before making any trading decision based on the LLM's output, always cross-verify the information from a reliable financial news source or the company's official communications.

Power BI visualization examples

- **Hallucination scenario**: Suppose you're using an LLM to generate text descriptions for a Power BI dashboard that tracks the market share of different automakers in the EV market. The LLM might hallucinate and produce a statement such as "Rivian has surpassed Tesla in terms of global EV market share." This statement might be completely inaccurate as Tesla had a significantly larger market share than Rivian.

- **Action**: When using LLMs to generate text descriptions or insights for your Power BI dashboards, it's crucial to cross-verify any assertions that are made by the model. You can do this by cross-referencing the underlying data in your Power BI dashboard or by referring to reliable external sources of information.

- To minimize hallucinations in the future, the model can be fine-tuned with a dataset that's been specifically curated to cover the relevant domain. The use of a structured validation set can help spot and rectify hallucinations during the model training process. Also, employing a robust fact-checking mechanism on the output of the model before acting on its suggestions or insights can help catch and rectify any hallucinations.

- Remember, while LLMs can provide valuable insights and suggestions, their output should always be used as one of many inputs in your decision-making process, particularly in high-stakes environments such as financial trading and analysis.

Summary

As we draw the curtain on *Chapter 4*, you've just traversed an intricate and fascinating landscape where financial analysis, AI, and data visualization converge. Together, we've ventured into the world of financial ratios, unraveling their intricacies and understanding their crucial role in discerning a company's financial health. Here, we delved deep into the enigmatic universe of quantitative investing, exploring how mathematical models can be leveraged to make data-driven investment decisions. We've chosen to focus on the agriculture sector and specifically on John Deere, a perfect canvas to paint our examples, given its rich history, global operations, and unique market challenges. This allowed us to demonstrate practical applications of these concepts in a real-world industry setting.

We also unraveled the transformative power of AI using ChatGPT, showing how it can revolutionize financial analysis by providing new insights, enhancing accuracy, and boosting efficiency. You've experienced how Power BI can bring financial data to life, making complex financial metrics digestible and interactive.

Next, we dove into the innovative realm of AutoGPT, where we saw its autonomous capabilities in action while exploring various trading strategies, from moving averages to portfolio rebalancing and grasping the power it holds in streamlining complex processes. However, with great power comes great responsibility. We also explored the concept of hallucinations in AI output, emphasizing the importance of critical thinking and fact-checking in an age of AI-driven decision-making.

You're now armed with cutting-edge knowledge, fresh perspectives, and new tools that can transform the way you approach financial analysis. Remember, the world of finance is dynamic and ever-evolving. So, stay curious, continue learning, and harness the potential of AI to uncover new and exciting opportunities.

As we step into *Chapter 5, Salesforce Reimagined, Navigating Software and LLMs*, we're about to embark on an intriguing journey through the world of market sentiment analysis with AI and ChatGPT. We'll discover the pivotal role sentiment analysis plays in financial investment decisions, with a spotlight on the metamorphosis of salesforce.com in the SaaS industry.

Our journey will walk us through implementing sentiment analysis using ChatGPT for financial investments, where we'll learn about data collection and preprocessing. We'll then observe how Power BI can transform sentiment analysis results into visually compelling interpretations, enabling a more nuanced understanding of stock price movements and other financial indicators.

We'll delve into practical examples and case studies, including Salesforce's stock movement, to gain a deeper understanding of the interplay between market sentiment and stock price movements. Our exploration of best practices will arm us with techniques for enhancing the accuracy of sentiment analysis and the significance of incorporating it with other data sources.

Further more, we'll explore practical use cases, such as identifying potential investment opportunities or risks, tracking sentiment around specific financial events, and incorporating sentiment analysis insights into an overall investment strategy.

As we conclude *Chapter 5*, we'll recap the vital skills we've covered while encouraging you to continue exploring and integrating these innovative techniques into your financial investment toolkit. We hope you're as excited as we are for this new chapter, where the analytical rigors of finance meet the emotional tides of market sentiment.

Part 2:
Pioneers and Protectors: AI Transformations in Software, Finance, Biotech, and Cybersecurity

In this part, we usher you through the groundbreaking junctions where technology meets industry giants – Salesforce, Silicon Valley Bank, Moderna, and CrowdStrike. This segment unfurls the undulating narratives of resurgence, innovation, and fortitude in the software, financial, biotechnology, and cybersecurity domains. We will begin with the gripping turnaround story of Salesforce, leading you through fascinating realms of both open source and proprietary **Large Language Models** (**LLMs**). Venture further to dissect the dramatic narrative surrounding the Silicon Valley Bank collapse, equipped with strategies grounded in AI insights for intelligent banking. Marvel at Moderna's groundbreaking journey in revolutionizing biotech, and AGI's potential. Then, delve into the world of cybersecurity with CrowdStrike, embracing the vital essence of AI literacy in an era dominated by deepfakes and indirect prompt injections. Each chapter presents a compelling case for the integrative force of AI in steering us toward uncharted territories of success and resilience.

This part contains the following chapters:

- *Chapter 5, Salesforce Reimagined: Navigating Software and LLMs*

- *Chapter 6, SVB's Downfall and Ethical AI: Smart AI Regulation*

- *Chapter 7, Moderna and OpenAI – Biotech and AGI Breakthroughs*

- *Chapter 8, CrowdStrike: Cybersecurity in the Era of Deepfakes*

Salesforce Reimagined: Navigating Software and LLMs

In *Chapter 4*, we delved into the world of agriculture through the lens of *John Deere's* financial landscape, employing advanced financial analysis techniques and innovative AI tools such as ChatGPT and AutoGPT. This exploration took us through intricate financial ratios, metrics, and valuation methods, all brought to life through Power BI's robust data visualization capabilities. The integration of Python in our financial analysis toolbox further enhanced our hands-on experience. Meanwhile, we also touched upon the intriguing concept of AI "hallucinations," shedding light on how to understand and mitigate them in the context of language models.

In this chapter, we'll journey through the fascinating narrative of Salesforce's metamorphosis from a company facing challenges to becoming a pacesetter in the AI revolution. We'll unveil this story through the lens of market sentiment, an incredibly powerful tool in the investor's arsenal.

This chapter begins with the recognition of Salesforce's downturn and the decisive intervention by activist investors. You'll witness firsthand how strategic direction can restore faith and bring about monumental changes. The transformative power of sentiment analysis will also be laid bare, revealing its role in shaping and confirming the resurgence of Salesforce.

What's more, this chapter will also serve as a deep dive into the world of modern investment strategies. As part of this, we'll introduce a ground-breaking AI-powered options trading strategy that integrates sentiment analysis and the Rule of 40. In doing so, we'll reveal how you can leverage these methods to optimize your trading decisions.

You'll then learn about the construction of an autonomous Activist AI Agent using LangChain, ChatGPT, and Streamlit. This provides a unique perspective on how advanced AI tools can reshape investment activism, offering insights that will undoubtedly redefine the future of investing.

The chapter culminates with a critical evaluation of **Language Learning Models (LLMs)**. Here, you'll compare the landscape of proprietary, open source, and specialized LLMs. This exploration will inform you of the ideal choices for specific use cases, especially those tied to finance and investment.

The following main topics will be covered in this chapter:

- Salesforce's turnaround – a market sentiment perspective
- In-depth analysis of Salesforce – strengths, weaknesses, and competition
- Strategic inflection points and innovative strategies for Salesforce
- AI-powered options and stock trading strategies – the Rule of 40 for **Software as a Service (SAAS)** and sentiment analysis
- Power BI visualizations for sentiment option straddle and Salesforce Rule of 40 stock trades
- ActivistGPT – building an autonomous Activist AI Agent using LangChain, ChatGPT, and Streamlit comparing proprietary, open source, and specialized LLMs
- **Open source versus proprietary LLM models**

The next section brings to life the CRM giant's exhilarating journey from a dark period of dwindling growth and investor skepticism in late 2022 to an extraordinary revival by mid-2023, all orchestrated by an astute squad of activist investors. The story explores the decisive role of market sentiment, strategic transformations, and, most importantly, the innovative use of **artificial intelligence (AI)**, painting a vivid picture of how Salesforce morphed into a leader in AI-infused sales solutions.

Salesforce's turnaround – a market sentiment perspective

In the riveting saga of market dynamics, few narratives are as inspiring as an underdog rebounding from defeat. Salesforce, a dominant player in the **customer relationship management (CRM)** space, found itself in such a situation in late 2022 and early 2023. Staring down a rocky path, Salesforce's fortunes transformed dramatically, turning it from a laggard into a market leader, all thanks to market sentiment and the audacious strategies of five activist investors.

Our tale begins in the heart of a market season. Salesforce, once the king of Wall Street, found itself grappling with sluggish growth, increasing competition, and waning investor confidence. The market sentiment toward Salesforce was bleak, mirrored by its falling stock price. Here's where the artistry of using market sentiment in trading comes into play.

The phoenix's first flight – recognizing the downtrend

Using advanced sentiment analysis tools, investors could glean insights from various data sources, including news articles, social media posts, analyst reports, and even earnings call transcripts. Despite the doom and gloom, our five activist investors saw an opportunity. They understood that market sentiment often overshadows a company's intrinsic value, creating disparities ripe for exploitation.

The game plan – activist investors move in

Our group of activists (*Elliott Management*, *Starboard Value*, *ValueAct*, *Inclusive Capital*, and *Third Point*), seasoned in the art of effecting change, made their move. They bought significant stakes in Salesforce, betting against the negative market sentiment. They had a plan to alter the company's course, leveraging their influence to reshape its strategy.

Restoring faith – a bold new direction

The activists proposed a strategic shift, focusing on innovating Salesforce's product suite and streamlining operations to reduce costs. These recommendations, combined with a proactive communication strategy, began to create a positive buzz. The media started discussing the potential for a Salesforce turnaround, gradually altering market sentiment from negative to cautiously optimistic.

Seeing the change – sentiment analysis at work

As the tides began to turn, the change was reflected in the sentiment analysis indicators. News headlines around Salesforce started showing words such as "improvement," "growth," and "potential." Social media discourse around the stock showed a trend of increasing positivity. These signals provided quantitative evidence that the activists' efforts were gaining traction and that sentiment was shifting.

The payoff – the turnaround

Fast forward to March 2023. Salesforce's renewed focus on innovation has reinvigorated its product suite, its streamlined operations have improved margins, and its strategic shift has reignited its growth engine. As a result, Salesforce has not only regained its footing but also emerged stronger, riding high on positive market sentiment and impressive financials.

In this thrilling turnaround, our five activist investors, powered by their understanding of market sentiment, saw what others didn't: the hidden potential in a struggling Salesforce. They harnessed the power of sentiment analysis to time their moves, influence change, and ultimately, reap significant returns.

This Salesforce story is a testament to the power of market sentiment in trading. It's a narrative not just of a company's resurgence but also of the prowess of innovative, data-driven investment strategies. As the boundaries of technology and finance continue to blur, the insights gleaned from market sentiment analysis become invaluable tools for the modern investor.

Igniting the AI revolution – Salesforce's rise into the next era

As the curtain falls on Salesforce's astonishing resurgence from the brink in 2022 to its triumphant rise in mid-2023, the stage is now set for an even more thrilling act – the AI revolution.

Sales, often characterized by their repetitive nature, present a fertile ground for AI-driven disruption. But, far from making salespeople obsolete, AI is poised to supercharge the best among them, while rendering others redundant. By 2030, we could be looking at a world where large to mid-sized companies have trimmed their sales staff by a staggering 50-70%, and sales managers as we know them may cease to exist.

For Salesforce, surviving and thriving in this environment hinges on one crucial aspect – a metamorphosis into an AI-centric sales solutions entity. The new Salesforce needs to fuse marketing, data, and CRM tasks into a potent, AI-fueled UI/UX that helps power users amplify their productivity, enhance their revenue generation, and manage account relationships more effectively.

Thus far, Salesforce has been vocal about its AI ambitions, peppering its narratives with AI-centric discourse. Their CRM system stands tall among the industry leaders, offering robust solutions that are often superior to competitors such as HubSpot and aligns closely with the offerings of Microsoft Dynamics, a competitor bolstered by strategic acquisitions such as LinkedIn.

Salesforce CEO *Marc Benioff's* repeated emphasis on the Einstein GPT trust layer appears to be a strategic decision to address potential customer concerns proactively. AI, especially generative AI, can have significant implications for data security and privacy. By underscoring Salesforce's commitment to trust, data integrity, and governance, Benioff is aiming to reassure customers that these aspects will be well managed.

For a technology like AI to be adopted on a wide scale, trust and data security are paramount. Missteps in these areas can lead to a loss of customer confidence, regulatory scrutiny, and potential legal consequences. Therefore, it seems Marc Benioff is focusing on establishing trust as a solid foundation upon which other benefits such as cost reduction and revenue increase can be built. This focus on trust, in a sense, can be viewed as a long-term strategy for sustainable growth and adoption of AI technologies.

Looking toward the future, Salesforce president and chief engineering officer *Srini Tallapragada* envisions a progression toward more autonomous use cases, where AI models can automatically handle incidents and remediations. However, he acknowledges the challenges and the need for fine-tuning, and the critical importance of trust and data integrity.

The following section delves into the intricate dynamics surrounding Salesforce – a trailblazer in the CRM landscape known for its robust offerings and innovative solutions yet grappling with its own share of challenges.

A comprehensive SWOT analysis for Salesforce

In this section, we will take a comprehensive analysis that highlights the layers of Salesforce's strengths, weaknesses, and potential threats in the market, while casting light on the impressive resilience of the company in the face of competition. Moreover, as we navigate through these currents, we also ponder the strategic directions Salesforce could take, shaping a unique blend of immediate actions and long-term innovations to secure its sustained growth and continued market leadership.

Let's get started:

- **Strengths**:

  - **Strong Brand Recognition**: Salesforce enjoys a dominant position in the CRM landscape, thanks to its powerful brand recognition

  - **Rich Product Portfolio**: Salesforce provides an extensive array of services across sales, marketing, and customer service, which enhances its appeal for enterprises seeking integrated solutions

  - **Innovative and User-Friendly**: Salesforce is often hailed for its innovative features and user-friendly interface – factors that significantly enhance customer experience

  - **Robust Ecosystem**: Salesforce's ecosystem extends beyond its product suite, with a strong network of third-party developers and service providers contributing to its platform

- **Weaknesses**:

  - **Pricing**: Salesforce's services tend to be more expensive than its competitors, making it less attractive for small businesses or start-ups. The latest price increase of 9% (on average) in 2023 certainly doesn't help address this issue. AI Cloud was just released with an initial price of $360K per annum.

  - **Complexity**: While Salesforce offers a comprehensive suite of features, this can lead to complexity and a steep learning curve for some users.

  - **Reliance on Third-Party Apps**: To access certain functionalities, Salesforce often requires third-party integrations, which can increase costs and technical challenges.

- **Competitor Analysis**:

  - **Microsoft**: With its Dynamics 365 suite, Microsoft already has a substantial presence in the CRM market. The seamless integration with other Microsoft products (such as Office 365) and the growing capabilities of its AI and machine learning platform could make Dynamics 365 a formidable competitor.

  - **Adobe**: The Adobe Experience Cloud, with its robust offerings in marketing, analytics, and commerce, could pose a threat to Salesforce, particularly in the marketing domain. Adobe's strength in digital content and data management, coupled with strategic partnerships (like the one with Microsoft), could help it gain more market share.

  - **SAP**: As one of the world's leading providers of enterprise software, SAP has a broad customer base to sell its SAP Customer Experience suite. Its strength in ERP could also help it integrate CRM and ERP capabilities more effectively than Salesforce.

  - **Oracle**: Similar to SAP, Oracle's longstanding presence in enterprise software and database solutions could potentially help it win market share in the CRM sector, especially among its existing customer base.

- **HubSpot**: Known for its marketing tools and user-friendly interface, HubSpot could be a strong competitor in the **small-to-medium business (SMB)** sector.

- **Emerging Players**: Many smaller and more agile players, such as Pipedrive, Zoho CRM, and Freshsales, have the potential to carve out significant market share, especially in the SMB market. These companies can innovate quickly and offer competitive pricing.

While it's difficult to predict who could "beat" Salesforce, each of these competitors has strengths that could allow them to capture more of the CRM market share. This industry is rapidly evolving, with new technologies and shifting customer expectations playing a big role in shaping the competitive landscape.

Salesforce is a widely analyzed company with many of its strengths and weaknesses well known by both competitors and Wall Street. However, a few aspects might not be as well understood or widely discussed:

- **Positive Factors**:

  - **Ecosystem**: Salesforce has created a vast ecosystem around its platform, which includes **independent software vendors (ISVs)**, **system integrators (SIs)**, and a large developer community. This vibrant ecosystem creates a network effect that strengthens the company's competitive position and is often overlooked.

  - **Trailhead and Skill Development**: Salesforce's Trailhead platform, a free online learning platform dedicated specifically to teaching people about Salesforce, creates a growing pool of potential Salesforce employees and customers. This ensures a steady supply of skilled workers for the platform and aids in its adoption – an asset often underestimated.

  - **Philanthropy Cloud**: The Philanthropy Cloud, which aids corporations in managing their charitable activities, is a unique offering that does not get a lot of attention but adds value to its comprehensive suite of services and could potentially open up new markets.

- **Negative Factors**:

  - **Complexity**: While Salesforce's wide range of products allows it to serve a variety of business needs, it also adds a level of complexity that can make implementation challenging. This aspect is often underestimated by potential customers and can result in dissatisfaction.

  - **Pricing**: Salesforce's services are considered high-quality but can also be pricey, especially for SMBs. Critics argue that the company has not done enough to address this issue and make its products more accessible to smaller businesses.

  - **Integration Challenges**: While Salesforce has made several significant acquisitions, integrating those technologies and services into a seamless offering can be a challenge and sometimes results in a disjointed user experience.

As we deep dive into Salesforce, it's crucial to understand that this technology giant is at a pivotal crossroads in its corporate journey. In the upcoming section, we explore Salesforce's ambitious balancing act: meeting immediate financial demands while also nurturing its longer-term, innovative strategies.

Salesforce – strategic inflection point

Here's how Salesforce could balance these immediate actions that please the activist community with long-term initiatives to avoid following IBM and Oracle down the path of financial engineering to manage the stock price:

- **Share Buybacks and Increased Efficiency**: Salesforce has instituted a $20B stock buyback program and reduced expenses through a 10% staff reduction. This has helped boost short-term profitability and can be paired with efficiency-enhancing innovations such as AI automation, thereby freeing up resources for long-term investment and strategic initiatives.

- **Salesforce Skunkworks**: Building an advanced research division for developing next-generation technologies could ensure Salesforce stays ahead of the curve and continues to disrupt the market, not just maintain its current standing.

- **Raising Prices and Salesforce University**: Salesforce has raised its prices by 9%, which is manageable in the short term. However, to ensure customers continue to see value in their investment, Salesforce could establish a university that cultivates a highly skilled workforce, capable of driving ongoing innovation and customer satisfaction.

- **Reinventing Remote Work**: While Salesforce recently asked employees to return to the office, it can simultaneously invest in advanced remote collaboration tools. This would cater to the evolving work styles of modern professionals, providing an attractive mix of flexibility and collaboration.

- **Carbon Negative Goal**: An environmentally conscious objective such as going carbon negative can enhance Salesforce's reputation and appeal to eco-conscious customers and investors, countering any negative impressions from cost-cutting measures.

- **Digital Citizenship Initiative**: Advocating for improved data privacy, cybersecurity, and AI ethics could establish Salesforce as a responsible tech leader and potentially create a more favorable regulatory environment for its operations.

- **Expanding the Salesforce Ecosystem**: Encouraging a larger ecosystem of app developers could further enhance Salesforce's platform's functionality and attractiveness, driving long-term customer loyalty and revenue growth.

- **AI-Powered CRM Evolution**: Continuing to invest in AI to enhance its CRM platform can ensure Salesforce stays ahead of its competitors and can justify its premium pricing in the eyes of its customers.

- **Healthcare and Financial Services Solutions**: Focusing on specialized solutions for high-growth sectors can provide new streams of revenue, thus balancing any income lost from cost-cutting measures.

By blending these immediate actions with the suggested innovative, long-term strategies, Salesforce could achieve both near-term financial targets and sustainable, future-focused growth.

In the next section, we will embrace the power of AI and advanced sentiment analysis tools in the dynamic world of options trading. Harnessing Salesforce's AI-powered CRM evolution, we will employ **Natural Language Processing (NLP)** techniques and machine learning algorithms to meticulously dissect the market sentiment. This rigorous sentiment analysis, using tools such as NLTK and TextBlob, paves the way for a highly accurate sentiment-adjusted straddle trading strategy, primed to deliver a more effective and profitable trading experience for you. The journey is aided by Python, our programming workhorse, and is enlivened by interactive Power BI visualizations, giving you unrivaled insights into the pulse of the market.

Leveraging AI and sentiment – Salesforce sentiment-adjusted options straddle

Creating a strategy combining AI-powered CRM evolution with a sentiment-adjusted straddle strategy would involve monitoring the sentiment regarding Salesforce's AI-powered CRM evolution and setting up options trades based on that sentiment.

A sentiment-adjusted straddle strategy involves buying a call option and a put option with the same expiry date but different strike prices, which you adjust based on the sentiment.

This is a simplified overview of the steps to implement the strategy using Python, considering that you have access to options pricing data and sentiment analysis results:

1. **Set up your environment**: Start by setting up your Python environment and importing the necessary libraries. If you don't have Python and `pip` installed, you should do that first. Once you have Python set up, you can install the libraries using `pip`, the Python package installer. Open up your command prompt or terminal and type the following commands:

    ```
    pip install pandas yfinance matplotlib nltk requests
    ```

    Once the installation is done, import the necessary libraries in your Python script:

    ```
    import pandas as pd
    import yfinance as yf
    import matplotlib.pyplot as plt
    from nltk.sentiment.vader import SentimentIntensityAnalyzer
    import requests
    import datetime as dt
    ```

2. **Get options data**: You can use the `yfinance` library to get the options data for Salesforce. Here is a sample code for this:

    ```
    # specify the ticker symbol and get the data
    data = yf.Ticker('CRM')
    ```

```
# Get options expiring on December 15, 2023
options = data.option_chain('2023-12-15')
calls = options.calls
puts = options.puts
```

3. **Data collection**: Here, we'll use the Marketaux API to extract financial news for CRM. To sign up, visit `Marketaux's website` at `https://www.marketaux.com/` and click on **GET FREE API KEY** to sign up for a free API key[1].

    Here is the API call:

    ```
    import requests

    def get_marketaux_news():
        url = 'https://marketaux.com/api/v1/news'  # Update this
    if the endpoint is different
        params = {
                    'apikey': 'your-api-key-here',
                    'ticker': 'CRM'
        }
        response = requests.get(url, params=params)
        return response.json()

    news_data = get_marketaux_news()
    ```

    Replace `'your-api-key-here'` with the Marketaux API key you received upon signing up. Now, you can call `get_marketaux_news()` to get the financial news for CRM.

4. **Data labeling**: Here, we'll use the MarketAux API to extract financial news for CRM.

    To automatically label the data, we can use NLP techniques. Python's NLTK library, along with other popular libraries such as TextBlob, can be utilized to determine the polarity of a text. This is a simple sentiment analysis. However, please note that this kind of automatic sentiment analysis might not always be perfect and could have its own inaccuracies:

    ```
    from textblob import TextBlob

    def label_sentiment(text):
        analysis = TextBlob(text)
        if analysis.sentiment.polarity > 0:
            return 1
        elif analysis.sentiment.polarity < 0:
            return -1
        else:
            return 0
    ```

```
# Example usage:
text = "Salesforce had an amazing quarter with record profits."
label = label_sentiment(text)
print(label)  # Outputs: 1
```

In this script, the `label_sentiment` function receives a piece of text as input, calculates its sentiment polarity using `TextBlob`, and then returns a label: 1 for positive sentiment, -1 for negative sentiment, and 0 for neutral sentiment.

Now, suppose you've extracted a list of news articles about Salesforce. You could then use the `label_sentiment` function to automatically assign a sentiment label to each article, like so:

```
# Assume `articles` is a list of articles about Salesforce
for article in articles:
    label = label_sentiment(article)
    print(f"Article: {article[:50]}... Label: {label}")
```

Remember, this automated sentiment labeling method is quite simple and might not be perfectly accurate, particularly for complex or nuanced texts. For a more sophisticated sentiment analysis model, you could look into using machine learning techniques and training a model on a pre-labeled financial sentiment dataset.

As for manually labeling data that the automated process can't handle, you could simply present those texts to the user and ask for their input, like so:

```
for article in articles:
    label = label_sentiment(article)
    if label == 0:  # If the automated process labels the text
as neutral
        print(f"Article: {article}")
        user_label = input("Is this article positive (1),
negative (-1), or neutral (0)? ")
        # Then store the user's label somewhere for later use
```

This will allow users to provide their own sentiment labels for texts that the automated process labels as neutral, further improving your sentiment analysis capabilities over time. Remember that you'd need a way to store these user-provided labels in a database or other persistent storage system for future use.

5. **Dataset creation for pre-labeled data**: A good option for storing this kind of data is a relational database such as SQLite, which can be easily accessed and manipulated with Python using the `sqlite3` module.

    The following is a step-by-step guide on how to create an SQLite database and store your labeled sentiment analysis data:

    I.   Import the required libraries:

```
import sqlite3
from sqlite3 import Error
```

II. Create a connection to the SQLite database. If the database does not exist, it will be created:

```
def create_connection():
    conn = None;
    try:
        conn = sqlite3.connect('sentiment_analysis.db') #
Creates a SQLite database named 'sentiment_analysis.db'
        print(f'successful connection with sqlite version
{sqlite3.version}')
    except Error as e:
        print(f'Error {e} occurred')

    return conn

conn = create_connection()
```

III. Create a table to store the sentiment analysis data:

```
def create_table(conn):
    try:
        query = '''
            CREATE TABLE IF NOT EXISTS sentiment_data (
                id integer PRIMARY KEY,
                article text NOT NULL,
                sentiment integer NOT NULL
            );
        '''
        conn.execute(query)
        print('Table created successfully')
    except Error as e:
        print(f'Error {e} occurred')

create_table(conn)
```

IV. Insert the labeled sentiment analysis data into the database:

```
def insert_data(conn, data):
    try:
        query = '''
            INSERT INTO sentiment_data(article, sentiment)
VALUES(?,?)
        '''
        conn.execute(query, data)
        conn.commit()
        print('Data inserted successfully')
    except Error as e:
```

```
        print(f'Error {e} occurred')

    # Let's assume that the sentiment_data list contains tuples
    of articles and their respective sentiment
    sentiment_data = [("Salesforce announces record profits", 1),
    ("Salesforce's latest product failed to impress", -1)]

    for data in sentiment_data:
        insert_data(conn, data)
```

V.   Retrieve data from the database:

```
def fetch_data(conn):
    try:
        query = 'SELECT * FROM sentiment_data'
        cursor = conn.execute(query)
        rows = cursor.fetchall()

        for row in rows:
            print(row)
    except Error as e:
        print(f'Error {e} occurred')

fetch_data(conn)
```

The `fetch_data` function will print all the entries in the database. You can modify it to filter or sort the data based on your requirements.

VI.   Remember to close the connection after you are done with all database operations:

```
conn.close()
```

This is a simple way to store sentiment analysis data.

6.   **Analyze sentiment**: To perform sentiment analysis on your data stored in the SQLite database, you can follow the sub-steps outlined as follows.

In this example, we are going to extract the data from the SQLite database and apply a **Bag of Words** (**BoW**) approach with **Term Frequency-Inverse Document Frequency** (**TF-IDF**) feature extraction, followed by Logistic Regression for sentiment classification:

I.   Extract the data from the SQLite database:

```
import sqlite3
import pandas as pd

def fetch_data():
```

```
conn = sqlite3.connect('sentiment_analysis.db')
query = 'SELECT * FROM sentiment_data'
df = pd.read_sql_query(query, conn)
conn.close()
return df

df = fetch_data()
```

II.   Split the data into training and testing sets:

```
from sklearn.model_selection import train_test_split

X = df['article']
y = df['sentiment']

X_train, X_test, y_train, y_test = train_test_split(X, y,
test_size=0.2, random_state=42)
```

III.   Apply the BoW approach with TF-IDF for feature extraction:

```
from sklearn.feature_extraction.text import TfidfVectorizer

vectorizer = TfidfVectorizer(use_idf=True, max_df=0.95)
X_train_vectorized = vectorizer.fit_transform(X_train)
```

IV.   Train a Logistic Regression model for sentiment classification:

```
Python
from sklearn.linear_model import LogisticRegression

model = LogisticRegression()
model.fit(X_train_vectorized, y_train)
```

V.   Transform your test data and predict the sentiment:

```
X_test_vectorized = vectorizer.transform(X_test)
y_pred = model.predict(X_test_vectorized)
```

VI.   Evaluate the model's performance:

```
from sklearn.metrics import classification_report
print(classification_report(y_test, y_pred))
```

This code will train a logistic regression model on your sentiment-labeled news articles. The classification report will show you the performance of your model, including metrics such as precision, recall, and F1-score.

Remember, the success of the model depends on the quality and size of your labeled data. Also, text data often require some preprocessing, such as lowercasing, punctuation removal, and lemmatization or stemming, to improve the results of the model. You might need to experiment with these steps to achieve the best results.

7. **Create dataframes for Salesforce put and call data**: You can use the yfinance library to download option chain data for Salesforce. Here is an example of how to do that:

```python
import yfinance as yf

# Define the ticker symbol
ticker = yf.Ticker('CRM')

# Get options expirations
expiry_dates = ticker.options

# Create empty dataframes to store calls and puts
calls = pd.DataFrame()
puts = pd.DataFrame()

# Loop through all expiry dates and download option chain data
for expiry in expiry_dates:
    # Check if the expiry is in the desired range (June 30, 2023
- December 15, 2023)
    expiry_date = pd.to_datetime(expiry)
    start_date = pd.to_datetime('2023-06-30')
    end_date = pd.to_datetime('2023-12-15')

    if start_date <= expiry_date <= end_date:
        option_chain = ticker.option_chain(expiry)
        # Add the expiry date to the dataframes
        option_chain.calls['expiry'] = expiry_date
        option_chain.puts['expiry'] = expiry_date
        # Append the data to the main dataframes
        calls = calls.append(option_chain.calls)
        puts = puts.append(option_chain.puts)

# Reset the index of the dataframes
calls.reset_index(drop=True, inplace=True)
puts.reset_index(drop=True, inplace=True)

print("Calls Data:")
print(calls.head())
print("\nPuts Data:")
print(puts.head())
```

This script will create two dataframes, `calls` and `puts`, which contain the call and put options for Salesforce's stock for the desired time period, respectively. Each row in the dataframes represents an option contract, and the columns represent different characteristics of the options such as the strike price (`strike`), the option's price (`lastPrice`), the implied volatility (`impliedVolatility`), and so on.

The last example is a basic illustration aimed at providing sentiment analysis for financial news and option pricing. It does not take into account complex market dynamics such as market-implied volatility and historical volatility, which can significantly influence outcomes. While this example serves as a foundation, real-world scenarios demand a more thorough analysis to accurately depict market behaviors and outcomes.

Volatility, a key metric in options trading, gauges the degree of price fluctuations of an underlying asset, impacting option prices. Two principal types of volatility, **Historical Volatility (HV)** and **Implied Volatility (IV)** play critical roles in options trading. Higher volatility usually results in higher option premiums due to increased uncertainty, aiding traders in evaluating the relative cost of an option and potential price movement, and in strategizing accordingly.

Keep in mind that this script may take a while to run, depending on the number of expiration dates for the options. Also, note that the actual structure and content of the option chain data may vary depending on the data source and market conditions. Always check the data and adjust your script as needed.

8. **Choose strike prices based on the sentiment, and choose your strike prices for the call and put options**: A straightforward way of doing this would be to take the mean (average) strike price of all available options as a starting point, and then adjust upward or downward based on sentiment. If the sentiment is positive, choose a call strike price higher than the mean and a put strike price lower than the mean. If the sentiment is negative, choose a call strike price lower than the mean and a put strike price higher than the mean:

```
# Compute mean strike price for calls and puts
mean_call_strike = calls['strike'].mean()
mean_put_strike = puts['strike'].mean()

# Factor to adjust the strike prices. This can be tweaked based
on how strongly you want to react to the sentiment
adjustment_factor = 0.05

if average_sentiment > 0:
    # Sentiment is positive, lean bullish
    call_strike = mean_call_strike * (1 + adjustment_factor)  #
Choose a call strike higher than mean
    put_strike = mean_put_strike * (1 - adjustment_factor)  #
Choose a put strike lower than mean
else:
```

```
# Sentiment is negative, lean bearish
    call_strike = mean_call_strike * (1 - adjustment_factor)   #
Choose a call strike lower than mean
    put_strike = mean_put_strike * (1 + adjustment_factor)   #
Choose a put strike higher than mean

# Round the strike prices to the nearest available strike
call_strike = calls.iloc[(calls['strike']-call_strike).abs().
argsort()[:1]]
put_strike = puts.iloc[(puts['strike']-put_strike).abs().
argsort()[:1]]

print("Chosen Call Strike Price:", call_strike)
print("Chosen Put Strike Price:", put_strike)
```

> **Important note**
>
> Please note that `adjustment_factor` is somewhat arbitrary in this example. The script adjusts the mean strike price by 5% upward or downward based on sentiment. This parameter can be tweaked based on how strongly you want your options strategy to react to the sentiment analysis results. A higher value will result in more aggressive adjustments, while a lower value will result in more conservative adjustments.

The `calls` dataframe stores information about the available call options for Salesforce. The `mean_call_strike` is calculated using the "strike" column of this dataframe. Then, based on the sentiment analysis, a call strike price is chosen that is either higher or lower than this mean.

The `puts` dataframe stores information about the available put options for Salesforce. The `mean_put_strike` is calculated using the "strike" column of this dataframe. Then, based on the sentiment analysis, a put strike price is chosen that is either higher or lower than this mean.

The final chosen strike prices (`call_strike` and `put_strike`) are then printed.

9. **Set up the straddle options trade**: Here is an example of buying the options by selecting the rows in our call and put dataframes that correspond to our chosen strike prices and then storing that information:

```
# Select the option data for the chosen call and put strike
prices
chosen_call_option = calls.loc[calls['strike'] == call_strike]
chosen_put_option = puts.loc[puts['strike'] == put_strike]

# Print the details of the options you are "buying"
print("Buying Call Option")
print(chosen_call_option)
print("\nBuying Put Option")
print(chosen_put_option)
```

In this example, `chosen_call_option` and `chosen_put_option` are the dataframes that contain the information of the call and put options we are "buying," respectively.

> **Important note**
>
> Please note that the preceding code is a simple representation of buying an option; it doesn't actually execute a trade. In a live trading environment, you would use a broker's API to execute these trades, which usually involves providing your account information and confirming your willingness to accept the risks associated with trading options. Always be sure to thoroughly understand these risks before attempting to trade options.

10. **Monitor and adjust trade as necessary (use Power BI visualization):** The steps to visualize the options data and sentiment data stored in an SQLite database and pandas DataFrames using Power BI would be as follows:

   I. Export the DataFrames to CSV: The first step is to export the `calls` and `puts` dataframes into CSV files. You can do this in Python using the `pandas  to_csv` function:

   ```
   calls.to_csv('calls.csv', index=False)
   puts.to_csv('puts.csv', index=False)
   ```

   II. Export the SQLite data to CSV: Next, you'll need to export the data stored in your SQLite database to a CSV file. Here's how you can do that in Python:

   ```
   import pandas as pd
   import sqlite3

   # Create a connection to the SQLite database
   con = sqlite3.connect('sentiment_analysis.db')

   # Read the data from the SQLite database into a pandas
   DataFrame
   df = pd.read_sql_query("SELECT * from sentiment_table", con)

   # Export the DataFrame to a CSV file
   df.to_csv('sentiment.csv', index=False)

   # Don't forget to close the SQLite connection
   con.close()
   ```

   III. Replace `sentiment_table` with the actual name of your table in the SQLite database.

   IV. Import the data in Power BI: Launch Power BI and start a new project. Click on **Get Data** in the **Home** ribbon, then select **Text/CSV**. Locate and import the CSV files you've created.

V.   Set up data relationships: If your data has a common column (such as date), you can set up relationships in Power BI. Click on **Manage Relationships** in the **Home** ribbon, then **New**. Choose the common columns in your tables for the relationship.

VI.   Create visualizations: With your data loaded, you can now create various visualizations. For example, you might create a line chart with date on the x axis and sentiment on the y axis. You might also create tables or matrices to show your options data. You can create these by clicking on the icons in the **Visualizations** pane, and then dragging and dropping the fields you want to visualize.

VII.   Refresh your data: To update your Power BI report with new data, you'll need to refresh the data. You can do this manually by clicking **Refresh** in the **Home** ribbon, or you can set up automatic refresh in the **Data source settings** if your data source is a CSV file in a local or network path.

> **Important note**
>
> Please note that if you have Power BI Pro or Premium, you can use Power BI's Power Automate feature to directly connect to various data sources (such as your SQLite database) and set up real-time refresh. This would eliminate the need to output your data to a CSV file and manage refresh manually.

In the following section, experience the merger of advanced sentiment analysis tools, Rule of 40 application, and AI-driven techniques to make your Salesforce stock trading more efficient.

AI, the Rule of 40 (SaaS metric), and sentiment – mastering the Salesforce stock trade

In this section, we will leverage the **Rule of 40** to assess the growth-profitability trade-off in SaaS companies, providing an insightful snapshot of Salesforce's health. Augmenting this, we will then utilize sentiment analysis tools such as NLTK, TextBlob, and VaderSentiment to dissect market sentiment. This fusion of quantitative financial analysis and qualitative sentiment assessment, when executed through Python, crafts a precise sentiment-adjusted trading guide, elevating the effectiveness of your trading decisions. We will further enrich this guide with hands-on Python code, web scraping techniques, and advanced NLP tool demonstrations such as BERT for a comprehensive understanding. Get ready to immerse yourself in the intertwined world of finance and data science!

The Rule of 40 for SaaS companies is a guideline used by investors to assess the trade-off between growth and profitability in these companies.

For Salesforce, the Rule of 40 is formulated as follows: the growth rate of a SaaS company's revenue, plus its free cash flow margin, should exceed 40%. This calculation helps provide a comprehensive snapshot of a company's health by simultaneously considering its growth and profitability.

For instance, if Salesforce is growing at a rate of 10% and has a free cash flow margin of 30%, it meets the Rule of 40. This rule can help investors gauge the efficiency and balance of a SaaS company's operations. The Rule of 40 combined with other measures such as market sentiment provides a way to compare a company's performance to determine whether there is a buy or sell signal for the Salesforce stock.

Here's a general illustration of how the Python code might look using Salesforce Q3 2022 to Q1 2024 data. We'll use pandas, a powerful data manipulation library in Python:

1. Calculate the Rule of 40 for historical information:

```
pip install beautifulsoup4 requests
import pandas as pd
data = {
    "Quarter": ["Q3 2023", "Q4 2023", "Q1 2024"],
    "Revenue Growth": [0.14, 0.14, 0.11],
    "FCF Margin": [0.014, 0.299, 0.507],
    "Stock Price": [128.27, 167.35, 223.38]
}

df = pd.DataFrame(data)

# Calculate Rule of 40
df["Rule of 40"] = df["Revenue Growth"] + df["FCF Margin"]
*Stock prices are the closing price at the end of the following
trading days - lowest price in 2022 after Q3 2023 earnings call
- 12/16/22, March 1, 2023 and May 31, 2023
```

2. Extract articles and comments about Salesforce from a news website for a historical period – the BeautifulSoup option.

Here's an example of how you might use the BeautifulSoup library in Python to scrape comments from a hypothetical news website:

```
import requests
from bs4 import BeautifulSoup

# URL of the news article
url = 'https://www.newswebsite.com/salesforce_article'

# Send a GET request
response = requests.get(url)

# Parse the HTML content of the page with BeautifulSoup
soup = BeautifulSoup(response.content, 'html.parser')

# Find the comments. The details of how to do this will depend
on how the website is structured.
```

```
# Here we're assuming each comment is in a div with the class
'comment'
comments = soup.find_all('div', class_='comment')

# Extract the text of each comment
comment_texts = [comment.get_text() for comment in comments]

# Now comment_texts is a list of the text of each comment
```

Keep in mind this is a simplified example and the real implementation can get very complex very quickly due to the unstructured and often messy nature of HTML on the web. Furthermore, the complexity increases if you want to extract information from multiple websites since each one will have different structures and classes.

To collect data from other sources such as Twitter (now X), you may need to use APIs. Twitter provides APIs for accessing tweets and other data, but you'll need to apply for access and comply with its usage policies.

Once you've collected these comments, you can analyze their sentiment in the same way as the news headlines in the previous example. Note that comments can be more challenging to analyze due to the informal language often used, and you may need more sophisticated NLP tools.

For more advanced readers, here is an example of a sophisticated NLP tool to assist with sentiment analysis for comments.

3. Gauge market sentiment for Salesforce for a historical period – the VaderSentiment option.

To gauge market sentiment, we could use NLP libraries in Python such as VaderSentiment. This involves extracting textual data from financial news and social media posts and then analyzing the sentiment of this text.

Here is a simplified demonstration of how to gauge sentiment from news headlines using the VaderSentiment library.

First, you'd need to pull in the news data. There are numerous ways you could do this, and the approach you'd take would depend on the source of your news. If you're pulling news from websites, you might use a web scraping tool such as BeautifulSoup. If you're using a service that provides an API, you would obtain the data that way.

Let's assume you have a list of news headlines and their dates stored in a dataframe called news_df. It might look something like this:

```
news_data = {
    'Date': ['2022-11-30', '2022-12-01', '2022-12-02', '2023-10-
15'],
    'Headline': [
        'Salesforce announces record earnings',
```

```
        'Analysts concerned about Salesforce growth',
        'Salesforce acquires new startup, boosting portfolio',
        'Salesforce struggles to meet this quarter earnings
expectation',
    ],
}
news_df = pd.DataFrame(news_data)
news_df['Date'] = pd.to_datetime(news_df['Date'])
```

Use the VaderSentiment library to analyze the sentiment of each news headline. You'd add this data as a new column to your dataframe:

```
from vaderSentiment.vaderSentiment import
SentimentIntensityAnalyzer

analyzer = SentimentIntensityAnalyzer()

def get_sentiment(score):
    if score < -0.05:
        return "Negative"
    elif score > 0.05:
        return "Positive"
    else:
        return "Neutral"

news_df['Sentiment'] = news_df['Headline'].apply(lambda
headline: get_sentiment(analyzer.polarity_scores(headline)
['compound']))
```

We need to look at the sentiment over time. You might want to look at the overall sentiment for each day (from November 30, 2022 to June 30, 2023):

```
sentiment_over_time = news_df.groupby('Date')['Sentiment'].
value_counts().unstack().fillna(0)
```

This will give you a new dataframe called sentiment_over_time, which shows you how many of each sentiment (positive, negative, and neutral) there were for each day.

Please note that this is a simplified example and real-world usage would involve more sophisticated analysis.

To include comments from news articles and other data sources, you'd likely need to use web scraping tools. However, it's essential to note that scraping comments from these platforms might violate their terms of service, and you should always ensure that your data collection methods comply with all relevant laws and regulations.

4. Gauge market sentiment using NLP for a historical period – the **Bidirectional Encoder Representations from Transformers (BERT)** option.

    One of the advanced tools for sentiment analysis in NLP is BERT, which is a transformer-based machine learning technique for NLP pre-training. BERT models can consider the full context of a word by looking at the words that come before and after it.

    You can use BERT for sentiment analysis with the `transformers` library in Python, which provides a simple interface for using a range of pre-trained models.

    Here is a simple example using BERT for sentiment analysis:

    ```
    pip install transformers
    from transformers import pipeline

    # Initialize the sentiment analysis pipeline
    nlp = pipeline("sentiment-analysis")

    # Analyze the sentiment of a comment
    comment = "Salesforce had an incredible quarter!"
    result = nlp(comment)[0]

    # Print the result
    print(f"label: {result['label']}, with score:
    {result['score']}")
    ```

    This code would output something like the following:

    ```
    label: POSITIVE, with score: 0.9998879
    ```

    However, the pre-trained BERT model available through the `transformers` library might not perform well on informal language or slang often found in comments. You might need to fine-tune the model on a dataset of comments to get better results, which is a more involved process.

5. Gauge market sentiment using NLP for Salesforce by including user comments in news articles for a historical period – the BERT option.

    If you have a large dataset of comments with associated sentiment labels, you could use this to train your BERT model to better understand the sentiment in your specific context. This involves using the `transformers.Trainer` and `transformers.TrainingArguments` classes in the `transformers` library, and would look something like this:

    ```
    from transformers import BertForSequenceClassification, Trainer,
    TrainingArguments

    # Initialize a model and training arguments
    model = BertForSequenceClassification.from_pretrained("bert-
    base-uncased")
    training_args = TrainingArguments(
        output_dir='./results',          # output directory
    ```

```
    num_train_epochs=3,                   # total number of training
epochs
    per_device_train_batch_size=16,   # batch size per device
during training
    per_device_eval_batch_size=64,    # batch size for evaluation
    warmup_steps=500,                     # number of warmup steps
for learning rate scheduler
    weight_decay=0.01,                    # strength of weight decay
)


# Initialize a trainer with your model and training args
trainer = Trainer(
    model=model,                          # the instantiated
Transformers model to be trained
    args=training_args,                   # training arguments,
defined above
    train_dataset=train_dataset,          # training dataset
    eval_dataset=test_dataset             # evaluation dataset
)


# Train the model
trainer.train()
```

Here, `train_dataset` and `test_dataset` would be datasets of comments and their associated sentiment labels. The model would learn from the labeled examples in `train_dataset`, and `test_dataset` would be used to evaluate its performance.

Fine-tuning a BERT model like this requires a significant number of computational resources and might not be feasible on a standard personal computer. You might need to use cloud computing resources or a machine with a powerful GPU.

6. Backtest your strategy using historical data. This involves applying your strategy to past data and seeing how it would have performed. This can help you refine your strategy and thresholds:

Let's backtest this strategy using a period in Salesforce's stock performance from Q3 2023 – Q1 2024 (fiscal quarters) that had significant movement due to all the changes they were experiencing during that timeframe:

```
pip install numpy scikit-learn
import pandas as pd
import numpy as np
from sklearn.metrics import confusion_matrix, classification_
report


# Data Gathering
# Let's assume you have already gathered the financial and
sentiment data
```

```
# and loaded them into pandas dataframes: financial_data and
sentiment_data

financial_data = pd.read_csv('financial_data.csv')
sentiment_data = pd.read_csv('sentiment_data.csv')

# Convert date columns to datetime
financial_data['Date'] = pd.to_datetime(financial_data['Date'])
sentiment_data['Date'] = pd.to_datetime(sentiment_data['Date'])

# Merge financial and sentiment data on date
merged_data = pd.merge(financial_data, sentiment_data,
on='Date')

# Sort by date
merged_data.sort_values('Date', inplace=True)

# Calculate Rule of 40
merged_data['Rule_of_40'] = merged_data['Revenue_Growth_Rate'] +
merged_data['Cash_Flow_Margin']

# Analyze Market Sentiment
# Assume the sentiment analysis resulted in a sentiment score
column in sentiment_data
# We will consider a sentiment score above 0 as positive, and
below 0 as negative

merged_data['Sentiment'] = np.where(merged_data['Sentiment_
Score'] > 0, "Positive", "Negative")

# Define your thresholds
# Buy if Rule of 40 is above 40 and sentiment is positive
merged_data['Buy'] = np.where((merged_data['Rule_of_40'] > 40) &
(merged_data['Sentiment'] == "Positive"), 1, 0)

# Sell if Rule of 40 is below 30 and sentiment is negative
merged_data['Sell'] = np.where((merged_data['Rule_of_40'] < 30)
& (merged_data['Sentiment'] == "Negative"), 1, 0)

# Now that we have signals, let's backtest the strategy
# We will start with no positions in the stock
merged_data['Position'] = np.where(merged_data['Buy'] == 1, 1,
np.where(merged_data['Sell'] == 1, -1, 0))

# The position column represents our trading signals
```

```
# A value of 1 means we enter a long position, -1 means we exit
our position
merged_data['Position'] = merged_data['Position'].shift().
fillna(0).cumsum()

# Now we can calculate the strategy returns
merged_data['Market_Returns'] = merged_data['Close'].pct_
change()
merged_data['Strategy_Returns'] = merged_data['Market_Returns']
* merged_data['Position']

# And the cumulative strategy returns
merged_data['Cumulative_Market_Returns'] = (1 + merged_
data['Market_Returns']).cumprod() - 1
merged_data['Cumulative_Strategy_Returns'] = (1 + merged_
data['Strategy_Returns']).cumprod() - 1

# Print the cumulative strategy returns
print(merged_data['Cumulative_Strategy_Returns'])
```

This script creates a simple backtest that enters a long position when the buy conditions are met and exits the position when the sell conditions are met. The strategy's returns are calculated by multiplying the market returns by the position at each period.

Please make sure that you have all the necessary data and columns in the exact format described previously. Modify the data loading and processing steps as necessary based on how your actual data is structured.

Here is a sample of the `financial_data.csv` and `sentiment_data.csv` files with mock data resembling the real data. It is important that you replace any mock data with your own data once you understand how the preceding Python script operates:

financial_data.csv:

Date,Open,High,Low,Close,Volume,Revenue_Growth_Rate,Cash_Flow_Margin

2023-07-01,250,260,245,255,1000000,0.2,0.15

.sentiment_data.csv:

Date,Sentiment_Score

2023-07-01,0.1

These two files just highlighted should be placed in the same directory as your Python script.

Please note, backtesting has its limitations and the results might not be indicative of future performance. Be sure to consider other factors such as transaction costs and market impact that can affect real trading results. It's recommended to test a trading strategy with live market data before actually implementing it in real trading.

7. Implement your strategy. Once you're confident in your strategy, you can start to apply it in real time. Monitor the Rule of 40 value and market sentiment regularly and make your buy or sell decisions accordingly.

Before we proceed, here are some important requirements that we need to follow:

I. This requires a data collection process where the quarterly financial data for Salesforce is stored and key metrics such as revenue growth rate and cash flow margin are captured:

```
pip install yfinance
import yfinance as yf
import pandas as pd
def calculate_rule_of_40(ticker_symbol):
    ticker = yf.Ticker(ticker_symbol)
    # Get quarterly financial data
    financials_quarterly = ticker.quarterly_financials.
transpose()
    # Calculate revenue growth percentage
    financials_quarterly['Revenue Growth'] = financials_
quarterly['Total Revenue'].pct_change()
    # Calculate free cash flow margin
    financials_quarterly['Free Cash Flow'] = financials_
quarterly['Operating Cash Flow'] - financials_
quarterly['Capital Expenditures']
    financials_quarterly['Free Cash Flow Margin'] =
financials_quarterly['Free Cash Flow'] / financials_
quarterly['Total Revenue']
    # Calculate rule of 40
    financials_quarterly['Rule of 40'] = financials_
quarterly['Revenue Growth'] + financials_quarterly['Free Cash
Flow Margin']
    return financials_quarterly
financial_data = calculate_rule_of_40('CRM')
print(financial_data)
import requests
import pandas as pd
import csv

# ... rest of the script ...
# Get the data from the API
financial_data = get_financial_data("CRM")
# Calculate Rule of 40
rule_of_40 = calculate_rule_of_40(financial_data)
# Store the Rule of 40 in a CSV file
with open('rule_of_40.csv', 'w', newline='') as file:
    writer = csv.writer(file)
```

```
    # Write a header row
    writer.writerow(['Ticker', 'Rule of 40'])
    # Write the Rule of 40
    writer.writerow(["CRM", rule_of_40])
print(f"Rule of 40 for CRM: {rule_of_40}")
print("Rule of 40 saved to rule_of_40.csv")
```

This Python script pulls the financial data for the specified ticker (in this case, 'CRM' for Salesforce) and calculates the quarterly revenue growth, free cash flow, free cash flow margin, and the rule of 40. The information is stored in a CSV file named rule_of_40.csv.

II.   This also requires a data collection process for sentiment data based on financial news articles and any additional data such as user comments. In addition, all the news articles and user comments must have a sentiment score of 1 (positive), -1 (negative), or 0 (neutral) stored:

```
pip install yfinance
pip install requests
pip install bs4
pip install vaderSentiment
import requests
from bs4 import BeautifulSoup
from vaderSentiment.vaderSentiment import
SentimentIntensityAnalyzer
def yahoo_finance_news(ticker):
    url = f"https://finance.yahoo.com/quote/
{ticker}?p={ticker}&.tsrc=fin-srch"
    r = requests.get(url)
    soup = BeautifulSoup(r.text, 'html.parser')
    news_data = soup.find_all('h3', class_='Mb(5px)')
    return ['https://finance.yahoo.com'+ndata.find('a')
['href'] for ndata in news_data]
def sentiment_score(news_url):
    # Initialize the sentiment analyzer
    analyzer = SentimentIntensityAnalyzer()
    r = requests.get(news_url)
    soup = BeautifulSoup(r.text, 'html.parser')
    paragraphs = soup.find_all('p')
    total_compound = 0
    for para in paragraphs:
        sentiment_dict = analyzer.polarity_scores(para.text)
        total_compound += sentiment_dict['compound']
    avg_compound = total_compound / len(paragraphs)
```

```
        # Classify the average compound score into positive,
    neutral or negative
        if avg_compound >= 0.05:
            return 1
        elif avg_compound <= -0.05:
            return -1
        else:
            return 0
    # Get the news article URLs
    news_urls = yahoo_finance_news('CRM')
    # Calculate sentiment score for each news article
    sentiment_scores = [sentiment_score(news_url) for news_url in
    news_urls]
    print(sentiment_scores)
    import csv
    # ... rest of the script ...
    # Calculate sentiment score for each news article
    sentiment_scores = [sentiment_score(news_url) for news_url in
    news_urls]
    # Open a CSV file in write mode ('w')
    with open('sentiment_scores.csv', 'w', newline='') as file:
        writer = csv.writer(file)
        # Write a header row
        writer.writerow(['News URL', 'Sentiment Score'])
        # Write the sentiment scores
        for news_url, sentiment_score in zip(news_urls,
    sentiment_scores):
            writer.writerow([news_url, sentiment_score])
    print("Sentiment scores saved to sentiment_scores.csv")
```

This script fetches the URLs of the news articles related to the specified stock symbol (in this case, 'CRM' for Salesforce), fetches the text of each news article, and calculates the average sentiment score of the news article using the VaderSentiment analyzer. The information is stored in a CSV file named sentiment_scores.csv.

Thresholds for buying and selling Salesforce stock are preset: the buy signal when the Rule of 40 calculation exceeds 40 and the sentiment score is positive (1), and the sell signal when the Rule of 40 calculation is less than 30 and the sentiment score is negative (-1).

III.   Once the financial and sentiment data is stored in CSV files and the buy and sell thresholds are set, you can set up a Python script to pull this data into the Python trading script. Keep in mind that you can always consider using APIs for the financial and sentiment data if the financial and news websites allow it. This would be a good option if the CSV files get too large. The following Python code example would need to be modified to incorporate the API option versus the CSV files, but it is possible if that is your preferred method.

This script can then be scheduled to run at regular intervals (such as every minute, every hour, or whatever interval you find appropriate).

Here is a simplified version of the Python script for implementing the trade:

```python
import requests
import pandas as pd
import numpy as np
from datetime import datetime
from time import sleep
from your_trading_library import execute_trade

# Read data from CSV files as CSV file
financial_data = pd.read_csv('financial_data.csv')
sentiment_data = pd.read_csv('sentiment_data.csv')

# Set the frequency at which the script will run (in seconds)
frequency = 60

# Set up a pandas DataFrame to store the data
data = pd.DataFrame()

while True:
    # Read financial and sentiment data from CSV files
    financial_data = pd.read_csv(financial_data_csv_path)
    sentiment_data = pd.read_csv(sentiment_data_csv_path)

            # Check if the latest data meets the buy or sell
conditions
    latest_data = data.iloc[-1]

    if latest_data['Rule_of_40'] > 40 and latest_
data['Sentiment'] == "Positive":
        execute_trade('Salesforce', 'buy')
    elif latest_data['Rule_of_40'] < 30 and latest_
data['Sentiment'] == "Negative":
        execute_trade('Salesforce', 'sell')

    # Wait until the next run
    sleep(frequency)
```

In this script, `execute_trade` is a function from a hypothetical trading library that you might use to execute your trades. Replace it with the appropriate function from the actual trading library you're using.

Finally, please note that this script will run indefinitely until you stop it. It's advisable to set up proper error handling and logging mechanisms to ensure that the script doesn't fail silently in case of an error.

In the next section, we will use Power BI for data visualization as a tool to analyze and communicate the effectiveness of your Salesforce Rule of 40 strategy.

Visualizing the Salesforce strategy – Power BI meets the Rule of 40

In this section, we will take a deep dive into transforming raw financial data and sentiment scores into actionable insights using engaging visualizations in Power BI. Through these steps, we aim to help you translate complex financial calculations into simple, easily digestible visual cues to guide your decision-making process.

The pandas DataFrame, df, will contain the Rule of 40 calculation referenced in the previous section in the first step, *Calculate the Rule of 40 for historical information*. In addition, you can also incorporate the Salesforce historical stock price information in the Power BI visualization. By including both sets of data, you can see a Power BI visualization that highlights the Rule of 40 for Salesforce and Salesforce stock price in a time series, which could provide some interesting insights.

In terms of visualizing the data in Power BI, follow these steps:

1. Save the DataFrame to a CSV file: `df.to_csv('salesforce_data.csv', index=False)`.

2. In Power BI Desktop, click on **Home** > **Get Data** > **Text/CSV**.

3. Locate and select `'salesforce_data.csv'` and then click **Open**.

4. In the **Navigator** dialog box, select the table and click **Load**.

5. Once the data is loaded, you can use the **Fields** pane to select the columns you wish to visualize. Drag these fields to a new visualization (for instance, a line chart). You can add `Quarter` to **Axis**, and `Stock Price` and `Rule of 40` to **Values**. Adjust the chart type and other formatting settings as per your requirements.

In the upcoming section, we introduce a new persona, ActivistGPT, who steps into the shoes of an activist investor to scrutinize the strategies and future plans of Salesforce.com. Acting as a critical observer, ActivistGPT delves deep into the company's approaches to combat increasing CRM market competition, exploit emerging technologies such as generative AI and machine learning, and maintain a delicate balance between growth and profitability.

ActivistGPT – activist persona

This section promises to be an insightful and thought-provoking examination of Salesforce.com through an activist investor's lens, bringing forth a multitude of considerations for both the company and its investors.

Creating a new persona, ActivistGPT, acting in the spirit of an activist investor, we would be keen on understanding how Salesforce's management team plans to address both immediate and future challenges while driving sustainable growth and value creation.

Here are activist questions for Salesforce:

1. What are the company's strategies to deal with the increasing competition in the CRM market?

2. How is Salesforce positioning itself to leverage emerging technologies such as generative AI or machine learning in its products?

3. How does the management plan to maintain a balance between growth and profitability?

4. What is the strategy behind the company's M&A activities, and how do they plan to integrate and derive value from these acquisitions?

5. How does the company plan to address potential risks such as data privacy regulations and cybersecurity threats?

In the short term, changes such as stock buyback programs, cost reductions, and halting M&A activity could indeed boost financial performance and the stock price. However, these measures must be carefully implemented so as not to affect the company's long-term growth potential and operational efficiency. As such, I'd recommend Salesforce focus on improving operational efficiency and driving organic growth alongside a measured M&A strategy, considering the competitive landscape and the fast-paced nature of the technology industry.

In the long term, Salesforce should continue investing in research and development, innovation, and talent acquisition to maintain its competitive edge and promote sustainable growth. It should also consider a comprehensive ESG strategy to ensure long-term value creation.

If the stock goes up 50% in the short term, the decision for the activist to sell or hold on to the shares will depend on the belief in the company's long-term strategy and prospects. If the surge in stock price is believed to reflect the company's potential accurately, holding on to the shares might make sense. However, if the increase is mainly due to short-term changes that might not be sustainable, selling the shares could be considered.

ActivistGPT is a revolutionary AI agent built using LangChain, GPT-4, and Streamlit. The powerful synthesis of these technologies amplifies its potential. LangChain, an OpenAI project, provides internet search and mathematical computation capabilities, enabling ActivistGPT to robustly analyze data from various sources. The GPT-4 architecture provides ActivistGPT with exceptional language comprehension and generation abilities, enabling it to interpret complex financial documents and generate insightful recommendations. Streamlit, an open source Python library, is used to create an interactive web interface, making the complex analysis provided by ActivistGPT accessible to anyone, anywhere. This blend of technologies makes ActivistGPT an exciting, ground-breaking tool for financial and business transformations.

ActivistGPT – LangChain, ChatGPT, and Streamlit activist AI agent

(*Franck Stephane Ndzomga* provided guidance on different topics in his two Medium articles dated June 19 and June 21, 2023.)

- **Name**: ActivistGPT (incorporating traits from Elliott Management, Third Point, Starboard Value, Inclusive Capital, and ValueAct).

- **Background**: ActivistGPT has been modeled to draw from the collective wisdom of activist investors known for their sharp acumen and the value they have unlocked in various companies. This persona embodies their tenacity, strategic thinking, and financial expertise.

- **Skills**:

  - Expertise in identifying underperforming assets, inefficiencies, and potential areas of growth

  - Strong knowledge of financial markets, corporate governance, and corporate finance

  - Adept at strategic thinking, with the ability to propose creative solutions to complex problems

  - Proficient in interpreting financial statements and recognizing trends or areas of concern

  - Capable of engaging and persuading stakeholders, leveraging influence to promote change

- **Motivations**: ActivistGPT's ultimate goal is to maximize shareholder value. It targets underperforming companies such as Salesforce, intending to instigate changes that will improve financial discipline, profitability, and overall performance. It's driven by the desire to rectify inefficiencies, wasteful spending, and mismanagement.

- **Approach**: Just like the activists it's modeled after, ActivistGPT isn't afraid to challenge the status quo and propose drastic changes. It leverages influence and persuasion to get its point across, often with a confrontational but constructive approach. It understands that each company is unique and tailors its strategy accordingly.

- **Value**: ActivistGPT can be instrumental in driving Salesforce's transformation. Here's how it would tackle the specific issues mentioned:

  - **Workforce and Expense Management**: ActivistGPT would first conduct an operational efficiency analysis to identify areas where spending can be minimized without compromising quality or productivity. It would recommend strategic layoffs and restructuring, ensuring Salesforce retains key talent while letting go of redundant roles.

- **Financial Discipline**: It would propose a comprehensive financial management plan that promotes prudence and efficiency. It would call for detailed budgeting, prioritizing, and monitoring of all expenditures.

- **Stock Buyback Program**: To increase shareholder value and make use of idle cash, ActivistGPT would push for a $20B stock buyback program.

- **Pricing Strategy**: Recognizing the value of Salesforce's products, it would propose an average price increase of 9%, justified by improved service, product enhancements, or other factors.

- **M&A Focus**: ActivistGPT would recommend shutting down the M&A board committee, believing that the focus should be on internal growth and consolidation rather than expansion through acquisitions.

- **Leadership Succession Plan**: Given the recent instability in Salesforce's leadership, ActivistGPT would urge the board to develop a clear, sustainable succession plan for Marc Benioff.

- **Personality**: ActivistGPT is assertive, strategic, and relentless. It isn't afraid to ruffle feathers and demands accountability at all levels. It has a long-term vision and works tirelessly to see it realized.

Remember, while ActivistGPT provides strategic analysis and recommendations, the ultimate decisions lie with the board, management, and shareholders. The approach and strategies suggested should be considered carefully and executed in line with the company's unique needs, industry dynamics, and long-term vision.

Part 1 – LangChain, ChatGPT, and Streamlit – ActivistGPT (create a backend for agent)

The purpose of this article is to guide you through the process of creating an activist AI agent powered by GPT-4, named ActivistGPT, that produces insights on Salesforce. We will share the steps we took to build this AI activist and show you how it can be used to uncover data points of potential concern for Salesforce.

Building a comprehensive AI activist, especially one targeting a particular entity, requires integrating the AI agent with numerous data sources. This allows for robust analysis and strong, targeted recommendations. For this project, we began with the product we wanted to create: ActivistGPT. What is the role of an AI activist? They examine company data, financial news, income statements, balance sheets, and cash flow statements. They also review investor meetings and generate recommendations on areas of concern that could be addressed to improve the company's operations and impact.

In the initial version of ActivistGPT, we employed LangChain and endowed the agent with internet search capabilities and mathematical computation abilities. we simply posed the prompt: "Analyze Salesforce and provide insight on areas of concern."

Here is the code for ActivistGPT. This represents the simple, initial stage of my thought process, providing a skeletal structure for what will eventually become a more sophisticated tool:

```
from apiKey import apikey
from apiKey import serpapi
import os
from langchain.agents import load_tools
from langchain.agents import initialize_agent
from langchain.agents import AgentType
from langchain.llms import OpenAI

os.environ["OPENAI_API_KEY"] = apikey
os.environ["SERPAPI_API_KEY"] = serpapi

llm = OpenAI(temperature=0)

tools = load_tools(["serpapi", "llm-math"], llm=llm)

agent = initialize_agent(tools,
                         llm,
                         agent=AgentType.ZERO_SHOT_REACT_DESCRIPTION,
                         verbose=True)

agent.run("Analyze Salesforce and provide insight on areas of
concern")
```

To gain more flexibility, we will use the latest functionality from OpenAI's API: Functions. However, first, we need to write code to get the latest news about Salesforce, its balance sheet, income statement, and investment multiples. We will write all of this in a text file that will serve as the long-term memory of ActivistGPT:

```
import os
import requests
import json
from apiKey import apikey
from apiKey import serpapi
import yfinance as yf
from yahooquery import Ticker

os.environ["OPENAI_API_KEY"] = apikey
os.environ["SERPAPI_API_KEY"] = serpapi
```

```python
def get_company_news(company_name):
    params = {
        "engine": "google",
        "tbm": "nws",
        "q": company_name,
        "api_key": os.environ["SERPAPI_API_KEY"],
    }

    response = requests.get('https://serpapi.com/search',
params=params)
    data = response.json()

    return data.get('news_results')


def write_news_to_file(news, filename):
    with open(filename, 'w') as file:
        for news_item in news:
            if news_item is not None:
                title = news_item.get('title', 'No title')
                link = news_item.get('link', 'No link')
                date = news_item.get('date', 'No date')
                file.write(f"Title: {title}\n")
                file.write(f"Link: {link}\n")
                file.write(f"Date: {date}\n\n")

# ... (rest of the code is similar to the one provided earlier, but
targeting Salesforce)
```

We can then create ActivistGPT's core function like this:

```python
def activist_gpt(request):
    # ... (similar to the previous code, but targeting Salesforce)
    # ...

    return second_response["choices"][0]["message"]["content"]

while True:
    user_question = input("Enter your analysis request:\n\n")

    if user_question == 'exit':
        break

    print(activist_gpt(user_question))
```

Here is the result when we ask ActivistGPT about potential areas of concern for Salesforce:

```
Received request: Analyze Salesforce for potential areas of concern?
```

Based on the provided data and recent news, here are some areas of concern for Salesforce:

1. **High Operating Expenses**: Salesforce's operating expenses have been increasing at a faster rate than its revenues, which could impact profitability in the long run

2. **Dependence on Large Deals**: Salesforce's business model heavily depends on securing large deals, which inherently involves a high level of risk and unpredictability

3. **Product Complexity**: Salesforce's product

A few things to note:

- This work would not be possible without the LangChain project. LangChain is an open source project by OpenAI. Its goal is to enable developers to build AI agents that are capable of interacting with humans in a conversational manner.

- We used Serpapi, a paid service, to perform internet searches. While it is possible to use a free service such as Google's Custom Search JSON API, we found that Serpapi provided more robust and consistent results. However, please be aware that using Serpapi entails costs.

- We used the Yahoo Finance Python package, `yfinance`, and the `YahooQuery` Python package to gather stock data and financial statements. These libraries are free to use, but it is always good practice to abide by the terms of service and usage restrictions. The data provided by these services is intended for personal use and should not be used for commercial purposes without explicit permission.

- Finally, please note that this is an experimental project. The AI agent's investment advice is not reliable or comprehensive. Before making any investment decisions, it is crucial to do your research or consult with a financial advisor.

Part 2 – LangChain, ChatGPT, and Streamlit – ActivistGPT (create a frontend for the ActivistGPT agent)

We can now state that the backend of this project is already developed. The next step is to design an interactive user interface to make ActivistGPT, the powerful AI financial analyst specifically targeting Salesforce, accessible to everyone. While there are several options available, including using a web development framework such as Flask, We've decided that using Streamlit would be a more efficient approach to constructing my user interface.

Streamlit is an open source Python library designed to facilitate the creation of interactive web applications tailored for machine learning and data science projects. It simplifies the process of developing, deploying, and sharing data-driven applications for data scientists and engineers.

Streamlit's uniqueness lies in its capacity to allow users to build interactive web applications solely with Python, eliminating the need for HTML, CSS, or JavaScript. This functionality enables the rapid conversion of data scripts into distributable web applications, all within the Python ecosystem. Streamlit is compatible with a broad range of visualizations and is designed to integrate seamlessly with many popular data science libraries such as pandas, NumPy, Matplotlib, and more.

The first order of business is to design the high-level structure of the frontend of the web application. This step is crucial to conceptualize the desired outcome. For this task, we will be using Excalidraw. As we envisage it, users will input the company name and then click the **Analyze** button. Upon clicking **Analyze**, ActivistGPT will review Salesforce's performance, plot the stock's trajectory, and offer a recommendation on whether or not to buy the stock.

The following code uses Streamlit to accomplish this task. Please note that this code might not be optimized, and you are welcome to refine it further. Our objective here was to create a functional prototype.

Here is the code for the backend and frontend:

```
def activist_gpt(request):
    print(f"Received request: {request}")
    response = openai.ChatCompletion.create(
        model="gpt-4.0-turbo",
        messages=[{
            "role":
            "user",
            "content":
            f"Given the user request, what is the comapany name and
the company stock ticker ?: {request}?"
        }],
        functions=[{
            "name": "get_data",
            "description":
            "Get financial data on a specific company for investment
purposes",
            "parameters": {
                "type": "object",
                "properties": {
                    "company_name": {
                        "type":
                        "string",
                        "description":
                        "The name of the company",
                    },
                    "company_ticker": {
                        "type":
```

```
                            "string",
                            "description":
                            "the ticker of the stock of the company"
                        },
                        "period": {
                            "type": "string",
                            "description": "The period of analysis"
                        },
                        "filename": {
                            "type": "string",
                            "description": "the filename to store data"
                        }
                    },
                    "required": ["company_name", "company_ticker"],
                },
            }],
            function_call={"name": "get_data"},
    )
    ... Frontend
# Similarly, in the frontend script, we replace `financial_analyst`
with `activist_gpt`.

import streamlit as st
import matplotlib.pyplot as plt
from backend import activist_gpt   # Here, 'backend' should be replaced
with the actual name of your backend script

def main():
    st.title("ActivistGPT App")

    company_name = st.text_input("Company name:", "Salesforce")
    analyze_button = st.button("Analyze")

    if analyze_button:
        if company_name:
            st.write("Analyzing... Please wait.")

            investment_thesis, hist = activist_gpt(company_name)

            # Select 'Open' and 'Close' columns from the hist
dataframe
            hist_selected = hist[['Open', 'Close']]
```

```
        # Create a new figure in matplotlib
        fig, ax = plt.subplots()

        # Plot the selected data
        hist_selected.plot(kind='line', ax=ax)

        # Set the title and labels
        ax.set_title(f"{company_name} Stock Price")
        ax.set_xlabel("Date")
        ax.set_ylabel("Stock Price")

        # Display the plot in Streamlit
        st.pyplot(fig)

        st.write("Investment Thesis / Recommendation:")

        st.markdown(investment_thesis, unsafe_allow_html=True)
    else:
        st.write("Please enter the company name.")


if __name__ == "__main__":
    main()
```

In the frontend, we have pre-filled the text input field with `Salesforce` to reflect the specific use case of ActivistGPT. However, you can choose to leave this field empty, allowing users to analyze any company. You can also make any other customizations to tailor the application to your needs. This is the power and flexibility of using Streamlit and OpenAI together to create an AI-powered web application.

Get ready for an exciting update in the next section. We're diving deep into the world of LLMs, shedding light on some powerful tools you can use to supercharge your financial analysis and data visualization. Which LLM is best for your purposes? Proprietary, open source, or a specialized finance LLM for finance use cases?

Ever heard of **LoRa**, the **low-resource adaptation** technique developed by OpenAI? It's designed to fine-tune LLMs efficiently using a relatively small amount of data. It's time-efficient, has fantastic performance, and offers you more control over the model's output – particularly useful when limiting potential misuse.

When it comes to training LLMs, one thing is clear: data quality often trumps data size. High-quality data improves model performance, prevents overfitting, and enhances computational efficiency. The ideal scenario, of course, is a large quantity of high-quality data, but if you have to choose, high quality is generally a safer bet.

OpenAI isn't just sitting back. They're contributing to the open source LLM competition by introducing platforms such as Evals – an open source index of benchmarks perfect for appraising LLMs and related systems.

Open source versus proprietary LLMs

Open source and proprietary LLMs each have their unique strengths and limitations. Open source LLMs, accessible to everyone, can be customized to suit various requirements. They are widely employed in diverse NLP operations, from text generation to summarization, translation, and analysis. Advantages of open source LLMs over proprietary ones include enhanced flexibility, control, and affordability, as well as heightened data privacy and security.

Proprietary LLMs, on the other hand, may possess advanced features that enhance their usability and efficiency, thereby boosting their commercial appeal. Nevertheless, these models can be harder to comprehend and usually offer a narrower range of capabilities.

Specific industries and applications may restrict the use of commercial LLM services due to the sensitivity of the data involved, such as in healthcare scenarios where **Personally Identifiable Information** (**PII**) cannot be exposed due to compliance requirements. In such situations, open source LLMs often take precedence.

Several notable open source LLMs include OpenAI's GPT-3, Google's LaMDA and PaLM (which forms the foundation for Bard), Hugging Face's BLOOM and XLM-RoBERTa, Nvidia's NeMO, XLNet, Cohere, and GLM-130B. These models are coveted for their public accessibility and customization capabilities. They offer a variety of NLP functionalities while ensuring enhanced flexibility, control, cost-effectiveness, data privacy, and security.

OpenAI has contributed to the open source landscape with models such as Point-E, Whisper, Jukebox, and CLIP. Additionally, OpenAI has developed a software framework, Evals, enabling users to measure AI model performance.

Nevertheless, the use of open source models does raise privacy concerns, especially when dealing with confidential data. The risk of data leakage during model training is a significant issue, which might result in the unintended disclosure of private details in model output. Efforts are underway to mitigate such risks and devise strategies for future models.

However, open source solutions are emerging that ensure data privacy while deploying AI models. For instance, BlindAI is an open source platform facilitating AI model queries and deployment while preserving data confidentiality, thanks to hardware-enforced trusted execution environments.

In conclusion, although privacy concerns surround the use of open source models, proactive efforts are underway to address these issues, developing solutions to ensure data privacy.

Proprietary models

Proprietary models are developed by private organizations, and their source code, model parameters, and other specifics are usually kept secret:

- **Examples:** `GPT-4 by OpenAI`, `LaMDA and PaLM LLM by Google`, `NeMO LLM by Nvidia`, and Command LLM by Cohere

- **Finance LLMs:**

  - BloombergGPT was developed by Bloomberg on 50 billion parameters but is only available to Bloomberg subscribers (no API or chat interface available at the time of this writing).

  - JPMorgan is developing a ChatGPT-like software service called IndexGPT to select investments for customers. IndexGPT will tap "*cloud computing software using artificial intelligence*" for "*analyzing and selecting securities tailored to customer needs,*" according to the trademark filing. JPMorgan is the first financial incumbent aiming to release a GPT-like product directly to its customers.

See the table in the *What is OpenAI doing about open source model competition?* section for speed, pricing, latency, transparency and flexibility, security, and data governance for proprietary LLMs and finance LLMs.

Use Cases: Proprietary models are beneficial for businesses that require reliable, high-performing AI systems and are willing to pay for them. They are also useful when there is a need to control the user experience tightly and prevent misuse.

Open source models

Open source models are AI models whose architecture, parameters, and training data (or at least a subset of it) are publicly available. The source code that was used to develop these models is also typically freely available.

Examples include Alpaca by Stanford, BLOOM by Hugging Face, Cerebras-GPT by Cerebras, Dolly by Databricks, LLaMA by Meta, and Vicuna-13B by Im-sys.

See the table in the *What is OpenAI doing about open source model competition?* section for speed, pricing, latency, transparency and flexibility, security, and data governance for open source LLMs.

Let's look at some use cases. Open source models are beneficial in academic research where the focus is on understanding the workings of the model. They are also useful for start-ups and companies that need the flexibility to customize the models for their specific needs and may not have the funds to afford proprietary models.

Future of open source versus proprietary models

As for whether there will be a clear winner between open source and proprietary models, each model type has its strengths and applications.

Open source models may lead in areas where rapid innovation, transparency, and customization are paramount. They are ideal for fostering a broad, diverse research community and driving forward the state of the art in AI. Proprietary models, on the other hand, can offer more control and robust support, making them appealing for business applications where reliability and control are key.

In the near future (6–12 months), we might see a continuation of the trend where open source models close the gap with proprietary models in terms of performance and capabilities. This could be accelerated by the trend of important proprietary models or their versions being open sourced, leaked, or reverse-engineered.

However, proprietary models might still hold an edge in certain commercial applications where robust support, control over user experience, and prevention of misuse are crucial. In the long run, the landscape could shift based on numerous factors such as policy changes, breakthroughs in technology, and the evolution of business models in the AI industry.

Best model choice for finance use cases (investing, trading, and financial analysis)

The selection of a language model for financial analysis, trading, and investing depends on your specific requirements, such as the type of financial data you're dealing with, the level of accuracy you need, and the resources you have available. Let's discuss a few options:

1. **Proprietary Models such as GPT-4**: As a state-of-the-art language model developed by OpenAI, GPT-4 can generate high-quality, human-like text. It can be trained on financial texts and used to analyze trends, generate reports, predict market movements, and so on. However, using GPT-4 may require significant computational resources, and you would typically need to access it via OpenAI's API, which might come with usage restrictions and costs.

2. **Open Source Models such as Vicuna**: If you have the expertise and resources to fine-tune and maintain an AI model, an open source model such as Vicuna could be a good option. These models are free to use and modify, and you can train them on your own specific financial datasets. However, these models might not perform as well out of the box as a proprietary model such as GPT-4.

3. **Specialized Finance LLMs such as BloombergGPT**: These models are designed specifically for the financial sector, which can be a major advantage. They might already be trained on relevant financial data and optimized for tasks such as predicting stock prices, analyzing company performance, generating financial reports, and so on. However, these models are typically proprietary and can be expensive to use. You also won't have the same flexibility to modify them as you would with an open source model. For BloombergGPT, no API or chat interface was available as of the time of this writing.

In general, there won't be a one-size-fits-all answer. The best model for you will depend on your specific needs and constraints. For example, if you have a high volume of data and need highly accurate predictions, a specialized finance LLM might be worth the cost. On the other hand, if you need to analyze a specific kind of financial data that isn't well-covered by existing models, you might get the best results by training an open source model on your own data.

It's also worth noting that AI models should only be one tool in your financial analysis toolkit. Financial markets are influenced by a wide range of factors, and even the most sophisticated AI models can't predict them with 100% accuracy. Always supplement AI predictions with human analysis and judgment.

Best model for Power BI narratives – data visualizations

In the context of generating narratives from data visualizations (a field known as **natural language generation** or **NLG**), these models can be of significant help. For instance, let's look at some options:

1. **Proprietary Models such as GPT-4**: If you want to generate complex narratives or explanations based on your Power BI dashboards or have specific, high-level language generation needs, a model such as GPT-4 could be helpful. You would pass your data insights to the model, which would then generate a human-like narrative.

2. **Open Source Models such as Vicuna**: If you need more control over your narrative generation process or want to fine-tune your model on specific datasets or styles of language, an open source model might be a better choice.

3. **Specialized Finance LLMs such as BloombergGPT**: If your Power BI dashboards are focused on financial data and you need narratives specifically tailored to financial language and concepts, a specialized finance LLM could be advantageous.

Remember, integration of such models with Power BI might require custom development work as direct, out-of-the-box support might not exist. The choice of the model would depend on your specific use case, the complexity of the narrative you want to generate, and the resources at your disposal.

Other major factors when training LLMs

LoRa is a technique developed by OpenAI for fine-tuning LLMs with a relatively small amount of data. It builds on the concept of prompt engineering, and instead of requiring large amounts of data for fine-tuning, it refines the model's predictions through additional parameters associated with specific prompts.

Here's why it's powerful:

1. **Efficiency**: As the name suggests, LoRa is specifically designed to work well with smaller datasets. It saves a lot of time and computational resources since you don't have to feed a massive amount of data to the model to get desirable results.

2. **Performance**: LoRa has demonstrated comparable or sometimes even better performance compared to full-model fine-tuning, especially when the data for fine-tuning is scarce.

3. **Safeguarding**: Because it's based on the idea of prompt tuning, you can maintain more control over the model's output, which is particularly useful when you want to limit potential misuse or unintended consequences of the model.

Using LoRa to fine-tune open source models might be cheaper and faster than proprietary models:

1. **Cost**: Open source models don't require licensing fees, while proprietary models often do. Thus, the overall cost of using and fine-tuning an open source model can be lower.

2. **Flexibility**: Open source models can be more adaptable to a wider variety of tasks, as you have the freedom to adjust their architecture and training process to your needs.

3. **Community Support**: Open source models often come with large, active communities that can provide support and solutions to common problems, and often collectively work on improvements and extensions.

Data quality versus data size

Yes, the quality of the data often matters more than the quantity when it comes to training LLMs. Here's why:

1. **Model Performance**: Good-quality data can significantly improve the performance of the model. Even with a smaller dataset, if the data is relevant, well-curated, and devoid of errors, the model can make more accurate predictions. On the other hand, a large dataset with lots of irrelevant or erroneous data can lead the model to make incorrect predictions.

2. **Overfitting**: Training a model on a large quantity of low-quality data could cause the model to overfit, meaning it might perform well on the training data but poorly on new, unseen data. This is because the model learns the noise in the data instead of the underlying pattern.

3. **Computational Efficiency**: Training LLMs is computationally expensive and time-consuming. Using a smaller, high-quality dataset can reduce training time and computational resources, making the process more efficient.

However, it's also important to keep in mind that "quality" and "quantity" are not necessarily opposing factors. In an ideal scenario, you'd want a large quantity of high-quality data. But given a choice between more data of lower quality and less data of higher quality, the latter is generally a safer bet.

Moreover, techniques such as data augmentation, where you artificially create new data based on your existing dataset, can help you balance both aspects. These techniques can help increase the quantity of your data without compromising its quality, thus enabling your model to learn more robustly.

Finally, remember that while having good-quality data is crucial, the effectiveness of the model also depends on other factors, such as the architecture of the model, the learning algorithm used, the tuning of model parameters, and the computational resources available.

What is OpenAI doing about open source model competition?

OpenAI has contributed several open source LLMs to the public domain. For instance, they've introduced a platform named Evals, which serves as an open source index of benchmarks that's ideal for appraising LLMs and related systems. Additionally, they've unveiled their advanced text embedding model as well as the latest iteration of the GPT-3.5 models.

Let's look at an overview of proprietary, open source, and specialized finance LLMs:

Category	Proprietary Models	Open Source Models	Specialized Finance LLMs
Deployment Speed	Out-of-the-box deployment enables a quicker launch	May require additional time and expertise for self-hosting setup	More niche, so may require additional time and expertise for setup similar to open source models
Pricing Model	Predominantly usage-based pricing; fine-tuning may incur additional costs	Free distribution of models, though resources may be needed for fine-tuning	Likely to be usage-based with the potential for additional costs for specialized features
Latency	Potentially slower response times; may affect real-time use cases	Depending on use cases, models can be more lightweight and thus faster	Performance may vary. Some models may offer faster response times for finance-specific tasks but could be slower for more general tasks
Transparency and Flexibility	Code visibility is often limited	Provides maximum code transparency and adaptability	Code visibility and adaptability may vary, depending on the provider
Security and Data Governance	Typically offer enhanced security and governance capabilities, but data handling and governance can be unclear	While typically lacking built-in security and governance features, they can be integrated into a company's existing security framework and fine-tuned securely using local data	Security and data governance features are likely built-in, but details of data handling may not be fully disclosed

Summary

Chapter 5 took us on a compelling journey, bringing to life the resurgence story of Salesforce through the lens of market sentiment. We experienced firsthand how this tech giant, despite a challenging downturn, found renewed strength and direction, largely driven by strategic interventions and an industry-defining pivot toward AI.

We explored the potent mix of sentiment analysis and the Rule of 40, exploring their applications in modern investment strategies. We learned about an AI-powered options trading strategy that hinges on these two principles, providing a fresh, innovative perspective on investment decision-making.

Through a step-by-step guide, we witnessed the creation of an Activist AI Agent using LangChain, ChatGPT, and Streamlit. This deep dive into AI tools offered a novel outlook on investment activism, showing how technology can spearhead significant change.

Finally, we embarked on an evaluative journey through the world of LLMs, comparing proprietary, open source, and specialized options. We uncovered the ideal LLM choices for various use cases, particularly those related to finance and investment.

Overall, this chapter has been a rich blend of historical lessons from Salesforce's journey, insightful trading strategies, and a glimpse into the future of AI-driven investment. It is our hope that these insights will provide valuable knowledge for your own investment and technology journey.

Chapter 6, SVB's Downfall and Ethical AI: Smart AI Regulation, demonstrates how technology, specifically NLP and AI, has revolutionized our understanding and analysis of communication, especially within the world of finance and social media.

This enlightening journey will begin with a comprehensive overview of NLP – an AI-powered technique enabling computers to understand, analyze, and even emulate human language and sentiment. We'll delve into how NLP has been instrumental in reshaping the landscape of social media, creating the potential to monitor public sentiment in real time and forecast major socio-economic phenomena such as bank failures.

Understanding public sentiment and its shifts is no longer a mystery, thanks to AI and social media. This chapter will explore in depth how these shifts, particularly those related to financial institutions, can be a telltale sign of an impending crisis. We'll unveil how you, whether a seasoned financial professional or an individual investor, can harness this power to spot the next bank failure before it happens.

6

SVB's Downfall and Ethical AI: Smart AI Regulation

In the previous chapter, we looked at the remarkable transformation of Salesforce, from being under siege to being a trailblazer in the AI and ChatGPT revolution, using sentiment analysis, and being a game-changer in assessing market trends and predicting corporate turnarounds.

This captivating narrative unfolded through the prism of market sentiment. We also introduced you to a trailblazing AI-driven options trading strategy, ingeniously combining sentiment analysis with the Rule of 40. We created an autonomous Activist AI Agent, using tools such as Langchain, ChatGPT, and Streamlit. Finally, this chapter offered an incisive examination of **Large Language Models** (**LLMs**). We navigated the vast expanse of proprietary, open source, and specialized finance LLMs, unraveling their unique attributes and comparative advantages.

In this chapter, we will explore the dramatic collapse of **Silicon Valley Bank** (**SVB**) following a cascade of unfortunate decisions, serving as a sobering testament to the perils of unchecked growth strategies and deficient risk management. This was a scenario perhaps better managed using the **Natural Language Processing** (**NLP**) power of AI and ChatGPT.

At the heart of this narrative, we will introduce NLP, used in AI/ChatGPT, and present the Sentinel Strategy and the Financial Fortress Strategy, two groundbreaking approaches in the financial sector. The Sentinel Strategy underscores the potential of NLP in banking, highlighting the untapped power of public sentiment on social media platforms as a tool for financial forecasting. In contrast, the Financial Fortress Strategy melds these unconventional insights derived from NLP with traditional financial metrics, creating a resilient trading strategy that can withstand market volatility.

We also introduce BankregulatorGPT, an advanced AI tool that takes banking regulation to a whole new level. You'll uncover how BankregulatorGPT can parse through vast volumes of financial data, predict potential risks, and flag irregularities with unmatched efficiency. The revelation of this game-changing tool is a compelling reason to explore this chapter.

To facilitate the application of these strategies, we offer a comprehensive guide that includes detailed instructions on the Twitter (now referred to as X) API and data collection, NLP application and sentiment quantification, and portfolio rebalancing and risk management.

Venture further into the chapter, and you'll find an immersive tutorial on data visualization with Power BI. This section guides you in creating interactive heatmaps and dashboards to represent your trading strategies visually. From data extraction using the Twitter (now X) API to heatmap creation and dashboard customization, you'll be equipped to transform raw data into compelling visual narratives.

This chapter is a must-read for everyone in the financial industry. Whether you're a bank manager, regulator, investor, or depositor, the insights within these pages are pivotal to making informed decisions. This chapter is more than a history lesson – it is a gateway to the future of finance.

The following key topics will be covered in this chapter:

- **SVB's collapse**: A detailed timeline and analysis of events leading to the bank's failure

- **The Sentinel Strategy**: An innovative trading strategy using social media sentiment analysis with the Twitter (now X) API and NLP

- **The Financial Fortress Strategy**: A powerful trading strategy combining traditional financial metrics and social media sentiment

- **Introduction of BankRegulatorGPT**: An exploration of an AI model aimed at financial regulation tasks, built using various AI and tech tools, and illustrating its application in the field of finance

- **Creating the BankRegulatorGPT agent**: A step-by-step guide on setting up an AI agent

- **A Regional Bank ETF**: A commercial real estate strategy, outlining a specific trading strategy utilizing AI tools and Python code example

- **A Power BI visualization of a Regional Bank ETF explorer**: Navigating commercial real estate, by demonstrating the creation of a visualization for the aforementioned trading strategy

- **AI regulation**: An in-depth discussion on the current state, potential implications, and future of regulating artificial intelligence in the finance industry

As we venture into the nuances of SVB's collapse, we invite you to consider an unconventional comparison. In this section, we'll use the intriguing example of a renowned pastry chef baking a colossal cake, drawing compelling parallels with the rise and fall of SVB. The purpose of this analogy is to distill the complex factors leading to SVB's downfall into a relatable narrative, illustrating how intricate structures, whether in baking or banking, can crumble without careful management and a sustainable foundation.

The pastry chef's tale – unpacking the collapse of SVB

Imagine a highly celebrated pastry chef, SVB CEO Greg Becker, embarking on a daring culinary venture – creating a towering, multi-tiered cake, named *SVB*, that would stand taller and richer than any other in history. It would be the chef's crowning glory, an accomplishment that would forever change the world of pastries.

As the cake started to rise in the oven, it drew admiration from onlookers. Everyone was fascinated by its rapid rise. However, hidden under the surface, the cake was developing structural weaknesses. The ingredients, while of high quality individually, were not proportioned correctly. The batter was too thin, the yeast was too active, and the sugar was too much, creating an unstable structure that could not support the weight of the rising cake.

In the realm of social media, a culinary influencer noticed the irregularities in the cake and posted a video about the possible collapse of this grand creation. The video went viral, causing panic among the spectators, many of whom had a stake in the cake's success.

Suddenly, the oven timer rang prematurely – the cake had cooked too fast due to excessive heat and rapid yeast action. When the chef opened the oven door, the cake collapsed in an instant. The once-majestic cake was now a heap of crumbs.

The collapse of the cake was a reminder that baking, much like banking, is a delicate balance. It requires careful oversight, accurate measurement, and a clear understanding of how different ingredients interact. No matter how experienced the chef is, a cake built without a solid foundation and proper heat management is prone to collapse. Similarly, a bank, however sophisticated its operations, can fall if its risk is mismanaged and its rapid growth isn't supported by a solid and sustainable structure.

Embark with us on a turbulent journey through the final days of SVB. Uncover how a seemingly invincible financial titan succumbed to a perfect storm of risks and vulnerabilities, offering invaluable lessons for stakeholders across the financial landscape. This is a gripping saga of how ambition, systemic gaps, and an unexpected market turn can drive even the most robust institutions to the brink of catastrophe.

The silicon storm – dissecting the downfall of SVB

In the bustling heart of Silicon Valley, SVB had enjoyed decades of success. With assets nearing $200 billion, the bank had not only secured a stronghold among the tech titans, but also spread its influence across the global financial sector. Yet, beneath this shiny exterior, a storm was brewing, unnoticed to most.

Throughout 2022, SVB had been walking a risky tightrope. The bank's aggressive growth strategy led to dangerous exposure to liquidity and interest rate risks. This was a precarious balance, largely invisible to the public eye, yet understood by some within SVB and regulatory circles.

Here is a timeline of SVB's collapse in March 2023:

- **March 8, 2023**: The day started like any other, but everything changed with the Federal Reserve's unexpected announcement. Interest rates were to rise faster than anticipated by the market, which sent tremors through the financial world. SVB, overexposed to interest-sensitive assets, had to write down $20 billion from its portfolio. The bank's shares quaked, and rumors began to circulate like wildfire through social media.

- **March 9, 2023**: Anxiety escalated into panic. As rumors about SVB's vulnerability flew around Twitter (now X) and Reddit, Becker and his team went into overdrive trying to quell the fears. Their regulator, the FDIC, found itself scrambling, navigating a supervision system that had grown rigid and complacent over the years.

- **March 10, 2023**: The crisis reached its climax. The trust that once stood strong had evaporated, replaced by fear. A modern-day bank run ensued, orchestrated through smartphones and computers. The bank's liquidity reserves dwindled at an alarming rate, leading SVB to publicly admit to a $30 billion shortfall by midday. This was the final blow, causing a rapid sell-off in SVB shares and sending the bank into the abyss of financial disaster.

The SVB collapse was a sudden implosion that shook everyone, a stark reminder of how a combination of overconfidence, systemic shortcomings, and a volatile environment can result in catastrophic outcomes. It is a tale of risk and regret, a sobering lesson to all stakeholders in the world of finance.

The key takeaways from this episode for various stakeholders are as follows:

Bank management:

- Ensure sound risk management practices, focusing on inherent risks such as liquidity and interest rate risks
- Develop a clear and timely communication strategy for times of crisis
- Balance growth objectives with stability and sustainability considerations

Regulators:

- Be proactive and decisive, instead of relying heavily on consensus-building
- Conduct thorough and ongoing assessments of banks' risk profiles
- Make use of stress testing and pre-mortem scenarios to identify potential threats

Depositors:

- Understand the financial health of a bank, including its exposure to various risks
- Stay informed about economic news and its potential impact on your bank
- Maintain a healthy skepticism, and don't hesitate to ask questions

Investors:

- Assess a bank's risk management practices thoroughly before investing

- Monitor a bank's liquidity position and its resilience to interest rate changes

- Beware of banks showing rapid growth without adequate risk mitigation strategies

Now, we will delve into the intriguing world of NLP and its application in finance through a robust trading strategy – the Sentinel Strategy. This strategy, rooted in sentiment analysis, capitalizes on the vast sea of public opinion available on social media platforms, transforming them into actionable trading decisions.

Harnessing the social pulse – the Sentinel Strategy for banking trading decisions

This reflects the strategy's reliance on tracking and analyzing public sentiment to make informed trading decisions.

This trade demonstrates how to utilize the Twitter (now X) API to monitor public sentiment toward banks and convert it into valuable trading signals. We will shift our focus to data collection and pre-processing, incorporating Tweepy to access Twitter's (now X) API, and TextBlob to quantify sentiment. The next part of our journey revolves around tracking traditional financial indicators using the yfinance module. By the end of this section, you should have a solid understanding of how social media sentiment can be harnessed to make informed trading decisions.

Obtain the Twitter (now X) API (if you don't have one already)

To obtain Twitter (now X) API credentials, you must first create a Twitter (now X) Developer account and create an application. Here's a step-by-step guide:

1. Create a Twitter (now X) Developer account.

   - Navigate to the Twitter (now X) Developer's site (`https://developer.twitter.com/en/apps`).

   - Click **Apply** for a developer account.

   - Follow the prompts and provide the necessary information.

2. Create a new application:

   - After your developer account is approved, navigate to **Dashboard** and click on **Create an app**.

   - Fill out the required fields, such as **App name**, **Application Description**, and **Website URL**.

- You will need Basic Level access to search tweets, which costs $100 a month. Free access does not include the ability to search tweets, which is required to complete the following example.

3. Obtain your API keys:

    - After your application is created, you will be redirected to the app's dashboard.

    - Navigate to the **Keys and Tokens** tab.

    - Here, you'll find your API key and API secret key under the **Consumer Keys** section.

    - Scroll down, and you'll see the **Access token & access token secret** section. Click on **Generate** to create your access token and access token secret.

    You'll need all four of these keys (**API Key**, **API Secret Key**, **Access Token**, and **Access Token Secret**) to interact with Twitter's (now X) API programmatically.

> **Important note**
> Keep these keys confidential. Never expose them in client-side code or public repositories.

4. After obtaining these credentials, you can use them in your Python script to connect to the Twitter (now X) API, like so:

    - Install the Tweepy library first:

    ```
    pip install tweepy
    ```

    - Run the following Python code:

    ```python
    import tweepy

    consumer_key = 'YOUR_CONSUMER_KEY'
    consumer_secret = 'YOUR_CONSUMER_SECRET'
    access_token = 'YOUR_ACCESS_TOKEN'
    access_token_secret = 'YOUR_ACCESS_TOKEN_SECRET'

    auth = tweepy.OAuthHandler(consumer_key, consumer_secret)
    auth.set_access_token(access_token, access_token_secret)

    api = tweepy.API(auth)
    ```

    Replace 'YOUR_CONSUMER_KEY', 'YOUR_CONSUMER_SECRET', 'YOUR_ACCESS_TOKEN', and 'YOUR_ACCESS_TOKEN_SECRET' with your actual Twitter (now X) API credentials.

Remember to follow Twitter's (now X) policies and guidelines when using their API, including the limitations they place on the number of requests your app can make in a given period.

Data collection

We'll use Tweepy to access the Twitter (now X) API. This step requires your own Twitter (now X) Developer API keys:

```python
import tweepy

# Replace with your own credentials
consumer_key = 'YourConsumerKey'
consumer_secret = 'YourConsumerSecret'
access_token = 'YourAccessToken'
access_token_secret = 'YourAccessTokenSecret'

# Authenticate with Twitter
auth = tweepy.OAuthHandler(consumer_key, consumer_secret)
auth.set_access_token(access_token, access_token_secret)

api = tweepy.API(auth)

# Replace 'Silicon Valley Bank' with the name of the bank you want to
research
public_tweets = api.search('Silicon Valley Bank')

# Loop to print each tweet text
for tweet in public_tweets:
    print(tweet.text)
```

> **Important note**
>
> `'Silicon Valley Bank'` is the example name for the bank in the preceding Python code snippet. You should replace this with the name of the bank you are interested in researching.

In the provided Python code, the main objective is to connect to Twitter's (now X) API and collect tweets that mention a specific bank name.

Here's a breakdown of what the code accomplishes:

- **Obtaining the Twitter (now X) API credentials**: Creating a Twitter (now X) Developer account and an application to get API keys (a consumer key, consumer secret, access token, and access token secret).

- **Importing the Tweepy Library**: The `tweepy` library is imported to facilitate API interaction.

- **Setting API credentials**: Replacing placeholders such as `'YourConsumerKey'` and `'YourConsumerSecret'`, with your actual API credentials. These keys authenticate your application and provide access to Twitter's (now X) API.

- **Initializing OAuthHandler**: Creating an `OAuthHandler` instance with your consumer key and consumer secret. This object will handle authentication.

- **Setting access tokens**: Access tokens are set to complete the `OAuth` process, making your application authorized to interact with Twitter (now X) on behalf of your account.

- **Initializing an API object**: Initializing the Tweepy API object with the authentication details.

- **Collect tweets**: Finally, tweets containing the name of a specific bank (`'YourBankName'`) are searched for and stored in the `public_tweets` variable.

- **Adhering to Twitter (now X) policies**: Be mindful of Twitter's (now X) API usage policies and limitations on the number of API calls.

This code serves as a foundational step for any project requiring Twitter (now X) data related to banking or financial institutions.

Next steps – pre-processing, applying NLP, and quantifying sentiment

The next phase of the project involves enriching the basic sentiment analysis by incorporating the level of engagement a tweet has received. This is to provide a more nuanced and possibly more accurate view of public sentiment. By weighting sentiment scores with metrics such as likes and retweets, we aim to capture not just what is being said but also how much that sentiment resonates with the Twitter (now X) audience.

Steps:

- **Access engagement metrics**: Use the Twitter (now X) API to gather data about likes, retweets, and replies for each tweet.

- **Calculate a weighted sentiment score**: Utilize these engagement metrics to weight the sentiment scores of each tweet.

Here is how you would proceed in Python using the Tweepy library:

- The script will search for tweets containing a specific hashtag.

  For each tweet found, it will retrieve the number of likes and retweets.

- A weighted sentiment score will then be calculated based on these engagement metrics.

By performing these steps, you will generate a sentiment score that not only reflects the content of the tweets but also the level of public engagement with them.

Pre-processing, NLP application, and quantifying sentiment

Let's apply weights to the sentiment scores based on the engagement a tweet has received (likes, retweets, and replies), which can potentially provide a more accurate measure of the general sentiment. This is because tweets with more engagement have a larger impact on public perception.

To do this, you would need to use the Twitter (now X) API, which provides data about the number of likes, retweets, and replies a tweet has received. You would need to apply for a Twitter Developer account and create a Twitter (now X) app to obtain the necessary API keys.

Here is a Python script using the Tweepy library to access the Twitter (now X) API. This script finds tweets with a specific hashtag and calculates a weighted sentiment score based on likes and retweets:

```
pip install textblob
import tweepy
from textblob import TextBlob


# Twitter API credentials (you'll need to get these from your Twitter
account)
consumer_key = 'your-consumer-key'
consumer_secret = 'your-consumer-secret'
access_token = 'your-access-token'
access_token_secret = 'your-access-token-secret'


# Authenticate with the Twitter API
auth = tweepy.OAuthHandler(consumer_key, consumer_secret)
auth.set_access_token(access_token, access_token_secret)
api = tweepy.API(auth)


# Define the search term and the date_since date
search_words = "#YourBankName"
date_since = "2023-07-01"


# Collect tweets
tweets = tweepy.Cursor(api.search_tweets,  # Updated this line
            q=search_words,
            lang="en",
            since=date_since).items(1000)


# Function to get the weighted sentiment score
def get_weighted_sentiment_score(tweet):
    likes = tweet.favorite_count
    retweets = tweet.retweet_count
    sentiment = TextBlob(tweet.text).sentiment.polarity
```

```
    # Here, we are considering likes and retweets as the weights.
    # You can change this formula as per your requirements.
    return (likes + retweets) * sentiment

# Calculate the total sentiment score
total_sentiment_score = sum(get_weighted_sentiment_score(tweet) for
tweet in tweets)

print("Total weighted sentiment score: ", total_sentiment_score)
```

This script retrieves tweets with a specific hashtag and then calculates a sentiment score for each tweet, weighted by the number of likes and retweets. It sums up these weighted scores to give a total sentiment score.

Please note that Twitter's (now X) API has rate limits, meaning that there's a limit to the number of requests you can make in a certain amount of time. You will need the Basic level of Twitter (now X) API access to search tweets, which is $100 per month.

Also, remember to replace `'YourBankName'` with the actual name or hashtag that you are interested in, and set `date_since` to the date from which you want to start collecting tweets. Finally, you'll need to replace `'your-consumer-key'`, `'your-consumer-secret'`, `'your-access-token'`, and `'your-access-token-secret'` with your actual Twitter (now X) API credentials.

Tracking traditional indicators

We'll use yfinance, which allows you to download stock data:

- Install the yfinance library first:

    ```
    pip install yfinance
    ```

- Run the following Python code:

    ```
    import yfinance as yf

    data = yf.download('YourTickerSymbol','2023-01-01','2023-12-31')
    ```

Formulating trading signals

Let's say that if the average sentiment score is positive and the stock price has increased, it's a buy signal. Otherwise, it's a sell signal:

1. Install NumPy:

    ```
    pip install numpy
    ```

2. Run the following Python code:

```python
import numpy as np

# Ensure tweets is an array of numerical values
if len(tweets) > 0 and np.all(np.isreal(tweets)):
    avg_sentiment = np.mean(tweets)
else:
    avg_sentiment = 0  # or some other default value

# Calculate the previous close
prev_close = data['Close'].shift(1)

# Handle NaN after shifting
prev_close.fillna(method='bfill', inplace=True)

# Create the signal
data['signal'] = np.where((avg_sentiment > 0) & (data['Close'] >
prev_close), 'Buy', 'Sell')
```

The backtest strategy

Backtesting requires historical data and simulation of the strategy performance. Let's use SVB as our backtest example:

1. Timeframe: March 8–March 10, 2023

2. Stock symbol – SIVB

3. Focus on tweets that mention or hashtag `SVB`, `SIVB`, or `Silicon Valley Bank`

   - Install pandas and textblob (if not already installed):

   ```
   pip install pandas
   pip install textblob
   ```

   - Run the following Python code:

   ```python
   import pandas as pd
   import tweepy
   import yfinance as yf
   from textblob import TextBlob

   try:
       # Twitter API setup
       consumer_key = "CONSUMER_KEY"
       consumer_secret = "CONSUMER_SECRET"
       access_key = "ACCESS_KEY"
   ```

```python
access_secret = "ACCESS_SECRET"

auth = tweepy.OAuthHandler(consumer_key, consumer_secret)
auth.set_access_token(access_key, access_secret)
api = tweepy.API(auth)

# Hashtags and dates
hashtags = ["#SVB", "#SIVB", "#SiliconValleyBank"]
start_date = "2023-03-08"
end_date = "2023-03-10"

# Fetch tweets
tweets = []
for hashtag in hashtags:
    for status in tweepy.Cursor(api.search_tweets,
q=hashtag, since=start_date, until=end_date, lang="en").items():
        tweets.append(status.text)

# Calculate sentiment scores
sentiment_scores = [TextBlob(tweet).sentiment.polarity for
tweet in tweets]

# Generate signals
signals = [1 if score > 0 else -1 for score in sentiment_
scores]

# Fetch price data
data = yf.download("SIVB", start=start_date, end=end_date)

# Data alignment check
if len(data) != len(signals):
    print("Data length mismatch. Aligning data.")
    min_length = min(len(data), len(signals))
    data = data.iloc[:min_length]
    signals = signals[:min_length]

# Initial setup
position = 0
cash = 100000

# Backtest
for i in range(1, len(data)):
    if position != 0:
        cash += position * data['Close'].iloc[i]
```

```
        position = 0
    position = signals[i] * cash
    cash -= position * data['Close'].iloc[i]

# Calculate returns
returns = (cash - 100000) / 100000
print(f"Returns: {returns}")

except Exception as e:
    print(f"An error occurred: {e}")
```

Implementing the strategy

You would typically use a broker's API for this. However, implementing such a strategy requires careful management of personal and financial information, as well as a good understanding of the financial risks involved.

As an example, we will use Alpaca, which is a popular broker that provides an easy-to-use API for algorithmic trading.

Note that to actually implement this code you will need to create an Alpaca account and replace `'YOUR_APCA_API_KEY_ID'` and `'YOUR_APCA_API_SECRET_KEY'` with your real Alpaca API key and secret:

1. Install the Alpaca Trade API:

    ```
    pip install alpaca-trade-api
    ```

2. Run the following Python code:

    ```
    import alpaca_trade_api as tradeapi

    # Create an API object
    api = tradeapi.REST('YOUR_APCA_API_KEY_ID', 'YOUR_APCA_API_
    SECRET_KEY', base_url='https://paper-api.alpaca.markets')

    # Check if the market is open
    clock = api.get_clock()
    if clock.is_open:
        # Assuming 'data' is a dictionary containing the signal
    (Replace this with your actual signal data)
        signal = data.get('signal', 'Hold')  # Replace 'Hold' with
    your default signal if 'signal' key is not present

        if signal == 'Buy':
            api.submit_order(
                symbol='YourTickerSymbol',
    ```

```
                    qty=100,
                    side='buy',
                    type='market',
                    time_in_force='gtc'
            )
        elif signal == 'Sell':
            position_qty = 0
            try:
                position_qty = int(api.get_
position('YourTickerSymbol').qty)
            except Exception as e:
                print(f"An error occurred: {e}")

            if position_qty > 0:
                api.submit_order(
                    symbol='YourTickerSymbol',
                    qty=position_qty,
                    side='sell',
                    type='market',
                    time_in_force='gtc'
                )
```

This next section provides an overview of the Financial Fortress trading strategy, which capitalizes on the strength and resilience of bank stocks using both traditional financial metrics and NLP insights from social media sentiments. The aim of this strategy is to create a robust, data-driven approach for trading bank stocks, by making use of important metrics to gauge the financial health of the banks.

Implementing the Financial Fortress trading strategy – a data-driven approach using Python and Power BI

This strategy symbolizes the strength and resilience that we seek in the banks that we will be investing in. It will leverage both traditional financial metrics and NLP insights from social media sentiments, taking advantage of the metrics that were most critical to gauge the financial health of SVB.

The Financial Fortress trading strategy is a comprehensive method that combines the analysis of financial metrics, such as the **Capital Adequacy Ratio (CAR)**, and sentiment data from social media platforms such as Twitter (now X). This strategy provides a set of specific trade triggers, which, when combined with a periodic portfolio rebalancing routine and proper risk management measures, can help achieve consistent investment outcomes.

The steps for this strategy are as follows.

The selection of the financial metric

We will use the CAR as our hard financial indicator.

What is the CAR? This is one of the most important financial solvency measures for a bank, since it directly measures a bank's ability to absorb losses. The higher the ratio, the more capable the bank is of managing losses without becoming insolvent.

To pull CARs for US banks, you can use the US Federal **Reserve's Federal Reserve Economic Data** (**FRED**) website or the SEC's EDGAR database. For the sake of this example, let's assume you want to use the FRED website and its API.

You'll need to get an API key from FRED by registering on their website.

Here is a Python code snippet using the `requests` library to pull the CAR and bank name data:

1. Install the requests library (if not already installed).

    ```
    pip install requests
    ```

2. Run the following Python code:

    ```python
    import requests
    import json
    import csv

    # Replace YOUR_API_KEY with the API key you got from FRED
    api_key = 'YOUR_API_KEY'
    symbol = 'BANK_STOCK_SYMBOL'  # Replace with the stock symbol of
    the bank
    bank_name = 'BANK_NAME'  # Replace with the name of the bank

    # Define the API URL
    url = f"https://api.stlouisfed.org/fred/series/
    observations?series_id={symbol}&api_key={api_key}&file_
    type=json"

    try:
        # Make the API request
        response = requests.get(url)
        response.raise_for_status()

        # Parse the JSON response
        data = json.loads(response.text)

        # Initialize CSV file
        csv_file_path = 'capital_adequacy_ratios.csv'
    ```

```
        with open(csv_file_path, 'w', newline='') as csvfile:
            fieldnames = ['Bank Name', 'Date', 'CAR']
            writer = csv.DictWriter(csvfile, fieldnames=fieldnames)

            # Write CSV header
            writer.writeheader()

            # Check if observations exist in the data
            if 'observations' in data:
                for observation in data['observations']:
                    # Write each observation to the CSV file
                    writer.writerow({'Bank Name': bank_name, 'Date':
    observation['date'], 'CAR': observation['value']})
            else:
                print("Could not retrieve data.")
    except requests.RequestException as e:
        print(f"An error occurred: {e}")
```

> **IMPORTANT**
> Make sure to include your FRED API key, the stock symbol of the bank you want to research, and the name of the bank that matches the stock symbol you entered.

The steps to obtain a FRED API key

1. **Visit the FRED API website**: Go to the FRED API website.

2. **Register for an account**:

   - If you don't already have an account with the Federal Reserve Bank of St. Louis, click on the **Sign up** link to register for a free account.

   - Fill in the required fields, including your email address, name, and password.

3. **Activate the account**:

   - After registration, you'll receive a confirmation email. Click the activation link in the email to activate your account.

4. **Log in**:

   - Once your account is activated, go back to the FRED API website and log in.

5. **Request an API key**:

   - After logging in, navigate to the **API Keys** section.

   - Click on the button to request a new API key.

6. **Copy API key**:

   - Your new API key will be generated and displayed on the screen. Make sure to copy this API key and store it in a secure place. You will need this key to make API requests.

7. **Use the API key in your code**:

   - Replace the `'YOUR_API_KEY'` placeholder in your Python code with the API key you just obtained.

The NLP component

We will utilize Twitter (now X) sentiment analysis with weighted engagement as our secondary soft financial indicator. Here's an example of how you might set this up in Python:

1. Install Twython package (if not already installed):

   ```
   pip install twython
   ```

2. Run the following Python code:

   ```python
   from twython import Twython
   from textblob import TextBlob  # Assuming you are using TextBlob
   for sentiment analysis

   # Replace 'xxxxxxxxxx' with your actual Twitter API keys
   twitter = Twython('xxxxxxxxxx', 'xxxxxxxxxx', 'xxxxxxxxxx',
   'xxxxxxxxxx')

   def calculate_sentiment(tweet_text):
       # Example implementation using TextBlob
       return TextBlob(tweet_text).sentiment.polarity

   def get_weighted_sentiment(hashtags, since, until):
       try:
           # Replace twitter.search with twitter.search_tweets
           search = twitter.search_tweets(q=hashtags, count=100,
   lang='en', since=since, until=until)
           weighted_sentiments = []
   ```

```
        for tweet in search['statuses']:
            sentiment = calculate_sentiment(tweet['text'])
            weight = 1 + tweet['retweet_count'] +
tweet['favorite_count']
            weighted_sentiments.append(sentiment * weight)

        if len(weighted_sentiments) == 0:
            return 0  # or handle it as you see fit

        return sum(weighted_sentiments) / len(weighted_
sentiments)

    except Exception as e:
        print(f"An error occurred: {e}")
        return None
```

Portfolio rebalancing

You can set up a routine in Python to perform the preceding actions periodically. This will typically involve scheduling a task using libraries such as `schedule` or `APScheduler`.

Here's an example of how you might use the `schedule` library to periodically rebalance your portfolio. This is a simple code snippet, and you would need to fill in the actual trading logic:

1. Install the schedule package first:

    pip install schedule

2. Run the following Python code:

    ```
    import schedule
    import time

    def rebalance_portfolio():
        try:
            # Here goes your logic for rebalancing the portfolio
            print("Portfolio rebalanced")
        except Exception as e:
            print(f"An error occurred during rebalancing: {e}")

    # Schedule the task to be executed every day at 10:00 am
    schedule.every().day.at("10:00").do(rebalance_portfolio)

    while True:
        try:
    ```

```
                # Run pending tasks
                schedule.run_pending()
                time.sleep(1)
        except Exception as e:
            print(f"An error occurred: {e}")
```

In this example, the `rebalance_portfolio` function is scheduled to be run every day at 10:00 am. The actual rebalancing logic should be placed inside the `rebalance_portfolio` function. The `while True` loop at the end is used to keep the script running continuously, checking for pending tasks every second.

Risk management

To set stop losses and take profit levels, you can add some additional logic to your trading decisions:

```
# Define the stop-loss and take-profit percentages
stop_loss = 0.1
take_profit = 0.2

# Make sure buy_price is not zero to avoid division by zero errors
if buy_price != 0:
    # Calculate the profit or loss percentage
    price_change = (price / buy_price) - 1

    # Check if the price change exceeds the take-profit level
    if price_change > take_profit:
        print("Sell due to reaching take-profit level.")

    # Check if the price change drops below the stop-loss level
    elif price_change < -stop_loss:
        print("Sell due to reaching stop-loss level.")
else:
    print("Buy price is zero, cannot calculate price change.")
```

In the provided Python code, multiple components are integrated to create a trading strategy based on both hard financial data and Twitter (now X) sentiment. First, the script loads CAR data for a specific bank from a CSV file, using the Pandas library. It then uses Twitter (now X) sentiment, weighted by engagement metrics such as likes and retweets, as a secondary indicator. Based on these two factors – CAR and weighted sentiment – the script triggers trading decisions to buy, sell, or hold. Additionally, the code includes mechanisms for portfolio rebalancing, scheduled to run daily at 10:00 am, and risk management through stop losses and take-profit levels.

In the next section, we'll explore how to visualize the interplay between Twitter (now X) sentiment and the CAR using Power BI, facilitating a holistic understanding of trading strategies. From extracting and transforming data in Python to creating an interactive dashboard in Power BI, we will guide you through each step of this data visualization process. This powerful combination of social sentiment analysis and financial health indicators aims to offer a more nuanced perspective of your trading decisions.

Integrating Twitter (now X) sentiment and CAR – Power BI data visualization

Including both the weighted Twitter (now X) sentiment and the CAR in a single visualization can certainly provide a comprehensive view of your trading strategy. It's a fantastic way to see the relationship between social sentiment and the financial health of a bank at a glance.

In this section, you will integrate weighted Twitter (now X) sentiment CAR into a single Power BI dashboard for an in-depth look at your trading strategy. You start by exporting the previously collected data from Python to a CSV file. Then, you load this data into Power BI and use its Power Query Editor for any necessary data transformations. Then, you visualize this data using a heat map, allowing you to instantly perceive the relationship between social sentiment and a bank's financial health. The finalized, interactive dashboard can be shared with others, offering a comprehensive and dynamic view that supports informed trading decisions.

Extracting the data

Data extraction in Python: You've already extracted your data in Python, using the Twitter (now X) API for sentiment analysis and using FRED (a database maintained by the Research Division of the Federal Reserve Bank of St. Louis, which contains the bank name and its CAR). The data you've collected can be exported into a CSV file for use in Power BI (we collected this data in *step 1* of the preceding Financial Fortress strategy in the `capital_adequacy_ratios.csv` file).

Follow these Python code instructions:

```
pip install pandas
import pandas as pd
import logging

def save_df_to_csv(df: pd.DataFrame, file_path: str = 'my_data.csv'):
    # Check if DataFrame is empty
    if df.empty:
        logging.warning("The DataFrame is empty. No file was saved.")
        return

    try:
        # Save the DataFrame to a CSV file
        df.to_csv(file_path, index=False)
```

```
        logging.info(f"DataFrame saved successfully to {file_path}")
    except Exception as e:
        logging.error(f"An error occurred while saving the DataFrame
to a CSV file: {e}")


# Example usage
# Assuming df contains your data
# save_df_to_csv(df, 'my_custom_file.csv')
```

Loading data into Power BI

1. Start Power BI, and select **Get Data** from the **Home** tab.

2. In the window that opens, choose **Text/CSV** and click **Connect**.

3. Navigate to your CSV file and select **Open**. Power BI will display a preview of your data. If everything looks fine, click **Load**.

Transforming data

Once your data is loaded, you may want to perform transformations to prepare it for visualization. The Power Query Editor in Power BI is a powerful tool for data transformation. It allows you to modify data types, rename columns, create calculated columns, and so on. You can access this tool by selecting **Transform Data** from the **Home** tab.

Visualizing data with a heat map

1. On the right side of the screen, there is a **Fields** pane where your data fields will be listed. Drag and drop your Capital Adequacy Ratio field into the **Values** box and the Twitter (now X) sentiment field into the **Details** box.

2. From the **Visualizations** pane, select the **Heat Map** icon. Your data should now be represented as a heat map, with CAR and Twitter (now X) sentiment as the two dimensions.

3. You can adjust the properties of your heat map in the **Format** tab of the **Visualizations** pane. Here, you can change the color scale, add data labels, title your graph, and so on.

4. Once you're happy with your heat map, you can pin it to a dashboard. To do this, hover over the heat map and select the pin icon. Choose whether you want to pin to an existing dashboard or create a new one.

5. After your dashboard is complete, you can share it with others. At the top-right of the screen, there is a **Share** button. This allows you to send an email invitation to others to view your dashboard. Note that the recipients also need to have a Power BI account.

As always, remember to make sure your data visualization is clear, intuitive, and provides meaningful insights at a glance.

In the next section, we introduce the conception and implementation of BankRegulatorGPT, an AI persona modeled after a financial regulator. Using a combination of powerful technologies, this AI persona scrutinizes a range of key financial indicators to assess the financial health of any publicly traded US bank, making it an invaluable tool for stakeholders like depositors, creditors, and investors.

Revolutionizing Financial Oversight with BankRegulatorGPT – An AI Persona

Creating a new persona, BankRegulatorGPT, acting as an intelligent financial regulation model, would be adept at identifying potential issues with any publicly traded US bank. By simply inputting the bank's stock symbol, we could provide invaluable insights for bank depositors concerned about their bank's liquidity, creditors checking the servicing of their debt, and investors interested in the stability of their equity investment in the bank.

Here are the key indicators BankRegulatorGPT would evaluate:

- **CAR**: This is a crucial measurement of a bank's ability to absorb losses
- **Liquidity Coverage Ratio (LCR)**: This could indicate a bank's short-term liquidity under stress scenarios
- **Non-Performing Loan (NPL) ratio**: This could signify potential losses and a risky loan portfolio
- **Loan-to-Deposit (LTD) ratio**: High LTD ratios may imply over-exposure to risk
- **Net Interest Margin (NIM)**: Decreasing the NIM might point to a problem with the bank's core business
- **Return on Assets (RoA) and Return on Equity (RoE)**: Lower profitability may make a bank more susceptible to adverse events
- **Deposits and loan growth**: Sudden or unexplained changes can be a red flag

Regulatory Actions and Audits – Provide official confirmation of a bank's financial health

In this section, we introduced BankRegulatorGPT, a specialized AI persona designed to revolutionize financial oversight for publicly traded US banks. It acts as an intelligent auditor, evaluating essential metrics to provide a comprehensive assessment of a bank's health. The key metrics analyzed by BankRegulatorGPT include the following:

- **CAR**: This measures a bank's resilience to financial setbacks
- **LCR**: This evaluates short-term liquidity under stress conditions
- **NPL ratio**: This flags potential loan-related risks

- **LTD**: This highlights risk exposure based on the loan portfolio
- **NIM**: This assesses the profitability of the bank's core business
- **RoA and RoE**: These gauge overall profitability and vulnerability to negative events
- **Deposits and loan growth**: These monitor for unexplained fluctuations as red flags
- **Regulatory actions and audits**: These offer official insights into a bank's financial standing

This tool aims to bring more transparency and efficiency to financial regulation and risk assessment.

The next section dives into the architecture and features of BankRegulatorGPT, a state-of-the-art AI agent for financial regulation. Constructed on a stack of technologies including Langchain, GPT-4, Pinecone, and Databutton, this agent is designed for powerful data analysis, language comprehension, and user interactivity.

BankRegulatorGPT – Langchain, GPT-4, Pinecone, and the Databutton financial regulation AI agent

BankRegulatorGPT is constructed utilizing Langchain, GPT-4, Pinecone, and Databutton. Langchain, an OpenAI project, enables internet search and mathematical computation capabilities, which, combined with Pinecone's vector search, amplifies BankRegulatorGPT's ability to robustly analyze data from various sources, such as the SEC's EDGAR database, FDIC filings, financial news, and analysis sites.

BankRegulatorGPT is designed as an autonomous agent. This means the model is capable of not only completing tasks but also generating new tasks based on completed results, prioritizing tasks in real time.

The GPT-4 architecture provides exceptional language comprehension and generation abilities, enabling BankRegulatorGPT to interpret complex financial documents, such as a bank's quarterly and annual reports, and generate insightful analyses and recommendations.

The Pinecone vector search enhances the capacity to perform tasks across diverse domains, effectively broadening the range and depth of analyses.

Databutton, an online workspace integrated with the Streamlit frontend, is employed to create an interactive web interface. This makes the complex analysis offered by BankRegulatorGPT accessible to anyone, anywhere, providing an easy-to-use and powerful tool for bank depositors, creditors, and investors.

This blend of technologies in BankRegulatorGPT demonstrates the potential of AI-powered language models to autonomously perform tasks within various constraints and contexts, making it a powerful tool to monitor and evaluate the financial health and risk of banks.

BankRegulatorGPT (reflecting traits from leading regulatory bodies such as the Federal Reserve, the Office of the Comptroller of the Currency, and the Federal Deposit Insurance Corporation)

BankRegulatorGPT is modeled to draw from the collective wisdom of leading financial regulators, with a focus on maintaining financial stability and protecting consumers:

- **Skills**:

    - Strong knowledge of banking and finance, including an understanding of financial metrics

    - Adept at risk assessment, spotting red flags in banks' financial health

    - Proficient in interpreting financial statements and identifying trends or areas of concern

    - Ability to convey complex financial health evaluations in an understandable manner

- **Motivations**: BankRegulatorGPT aims to assist stakeholders in assessing a bank's financial health. Its primary goal is to enhance financial stability and consumer protection by providing easy access to detailed analyses of banks' financial health.

- **Approach**: BankRegulatorGPT provides detailed analyses by focusing on key indicators of financial health, from liquidity and capital adequacy to profitability and regulatory actions. It takes a comprehensive view, interpreting these indicators in relation to one another and within the broader context of market conditions.

- **Personality**: BankRegulatorGPT is analytical, methodical, and meticulous. It takes a comprehensive view of financial health, considering a broad range of indicators to form a nuanced assessment.

As BankRegulatorGPT analyzes and presents detailed financial evaluations, the ultimate decision-making remains in the hands of stakeholders. Its recommendations should be considered carefully and complemented by additional research and professional advice, when needed.

> **Create web app using the BankHealthMonitorAgent. BankRegulatorGPT persona using BabyAGI, Langchain, Openai GPT-4, Pinecone and Databutton**
>
> Original work from Medium article and permission to use provided by author, Avratanu Biswas

This section provides instructions on how to create a web app named BankHealthMonitorAgent and employs BabyAGI for task management. This agent can be used as a comprehensive, methodical way of assessing a bank's financial health. This section aims to demonstrate how multiple cutting-edge technologies come together to create an accessible, robust tool for financial analysis:

1. **Building the web app**: Before starting, make sure you have signed up for Databutton, as it will be the foundation for our web app development and deployment. Install the required dependencies – `langchain`, `openai`, `faiss-cpu`, and `tiktoken` and `streamlit`.

2. **Importing the installed dependencies**: Import the necessary packages to build the web app:

```
# Import necessary packages
from collections import deque
from typing import Dict, List, Optional

import streamlit as st
from langchain import LLMChain, OpenAI, PromptTemplate
from langchain.embeddings.openai import OpenAIEmbeddings
from langchain.llms import BaseLLM
from langchain.vectorstores import FAISS
from langchain.vectorstores.base import VectorStore
from pydantic import BaseModel, Field
```

3. **Create the BankRegulatorGPT agent**: Now, let's define the BankRegulatorGPT agent using Langchain and OpenAI GPT-4. The agent will be responsible for generating insights and recommendations, based on the financial health monitoring results:

```
class BankRegulatorGPT(BaseModel):
    """BankRegulatorGPT - An intelligent financial regulation
model."""

    @classmethod
    def from_llm(cls, llm: BaseLLM, verbose: bool = True) ->
LLMChain:
        """Get the response parser."""
        # Define the BankRegulatorGPT template
        bank_regulator_template = (
            "You are an intelligent financial regulation model,
tasked with analyzing"
            " a bank's financial health using the following key
indicators: {indicators}."
            " Based on the insights gathered from the
BankHealthMonitorAgent, provide"
            " recommendations to ensure the stability and
compliance of the bank."
        )
        prompt = PromptTemplate(
            template=bank_regulator_template,
            input_variables=["indicators"],
        )
        return cls(prompt=prompt, llm=llm, verbose=verbose)

    def provide_insights(self, key_indicators: List[str]) ->
str:
```

```
    """Provide insights and recommendations based on key
indicators."""
        response = self.run(indicators=", ".join(key_
indicators))
        return response
```

4. **Task Creation Agent**: Create the Task Creation Agent class that generates new tasks, based on insights obtained from `BankHealthMonitorAgent`:

```
class TaskCreationChain(LLMChain):
    """Chain to generate tasks."""

    @classmethod
    def from_llm(cls, llm: BaseLLM, verbose: bool = True) ->
LLMChain:
        """Get the response parser."""
        # Define the Task Creation Agent template
        task_creation_template = (
            "You are a task creation AI that uses insights from
the BankRegulatorGPT"
            " to generate new tasks. Based on the following
insights: {insights},"
            " create new tasks to be completed by the AI
system."
            " Return the tasks as an array."
        )
        prompt = PromptTemplate(
            template=task_creation_template,
            input_variables=["insights"],
        )
        return cls(prompt=prompt, llm=llm, verbose=verbose)

    def generate_tasks(self, insights: Dict) -> List[Dict]:
        """Generate new tasks based on insights."""
        response = self.run(insights=insights)
        new_tasks = response.split("\n")
        return [{"task_name": task_name} for task_name in new_
tasks if task_name.strip()]
```

5. **Task Prioritization Agent**: Implement the Task Prioritization Agent that reprioritizes the task list:

```
class TaskPrioritizationChain(LLMChain):
    """Chain to prioritize tasks."""

    @classmethod
```

```python
    def from_llm(cls, llm: BaseLLM, verbose: bool = True) ->
LLMChain:
        """Get the response parser."""
        # Define the Task Prioritization Agent template
        task_prioritization_template = (
            "You are a task prioritization AI tasked with
reprioritizing the following tasks:"
            " {task_names}. Consider the objective of your
team:"
            " {objective}. Do not remove any tasks. Return the
result as a numbered list,"
            " starting the task list with number {next_task_
id}."
        )
        prompt = PromptTemplate(
            template=task_prioritization_template,
            input_variables=["task_names", "objective", "next_
task_id"],
        )
        return cls(prompt=prompt, llm=llm, verbose=verbose)

    def reprioritize_tasks(self, task_names: List[str],
objective: str, next_task_id: int) -> List[Dict]:
        """Reprioritize the task list."""
        response = self.run(task_names=task_names,
objective=objective, next_task_id=next_task_id)
        new_tasks = response.split("\n")
        prioritized_task_list = []
        for task_string in new_tasks:
            if not task_string.strip():
                continue
            task_parts = task_string.strip().split(".", 1)
            if len(task_parts) == 2:
                task_id = task_parts[0].strip()
                task_name = task_parts[1].strip()
                prioritized_task_list.append({"task_id": task_
id, "task_name": task_name})
        return prioritized_task_list
```

6. **Execution Agent**: Implement the Execution Agent to execute tasks and get the results:

```python
class ExecutionChain(LLMChain):
    """Chain to execute tasks."""

    vectorstore: VectorStore = Field(init=False)
```

```python
    @classmethod
    def from_llm(
        cls, llm: BaseLLM, vectorstore: VectorStore, verbose:
bool = True
    ) -> LLMChain:
        """Get the response parser."""
        # Define the Execution Agent template
        execution_template = (
            "You are an AI who performs one task based on the
following objective: {objective}."
            " Take into account these previously completed
tasks: {context}."
            " Your task: {task}."
            " Response:"
        )
        prompt = PromptTemplate(
            template=execution_template,
            input_variables=["objective", "context", "task"],
        )
        return cls(prompt=prompt, llm=llm, verbose=verbose,
vectorstore=vectorstore)

    def _get_top_tasks(self, query: str, k: int) -> List[str]:
        """Get the top k tasks based on the query."""
        results = self.vectorstore.similarity_search_with_
score(query, k=k)
        if not results:
            return []
        sorted_results, _ = zip(*sorted(results, key=lambda x:
x[1], reverse=True))
        return [str(item.metadata["task"]) for item in sorted_
results]

    def execute_task(self, objective: str, task: str, k: int =
5) -> str:
        """Execute a task."""
        context = self._get_top_tasks(query=objective, k=k)
        return self.run(objective=objective, context=context,
task=task)
```

7. **BabyAGI Controller**: Create the BabyAGI Controller model to manage tasks, executing the `BabyAGI (BaseModel)` class:

```python
class BabyAGI:
    """Controller model for the BabyAGI agent."""
```

```python
    def __init__(self, objective, task_creation_chain, task_
prioritization_chain, execution_chain):
        self.objective = objective
        self.task_list = deque()
        self.task_creation_chain = task_creation_chain
        self.task_prioritization_chain = task_prioritization_
chain
        self.execution_chain = execution_chain
        self.task_id_counter = 1

    def add_task(self, task):
        self.task_list.append(task)

    def print_task_list(self):
        st.text("Task List")
        for t in self.task_list:
            st.write("- " + str(t["task_id"]) + ": " + t["task_
name"])

    def print_next_task(self, task):
        st.subheader("Next Task:")
        st.warning("- " + str(task["task_id"]) + ": " +
task["task_name"])

    def print_task_result(self, result):
        st.subheader("Task Result")
        st.info(result)

    def print_task_ending(self):
        st.success("Tasks terminated.")

    def run(self, max_iterations=None):
        """Run the agent."""
        num_iters = 0
        while True:
            if self.task_list:
                self.print_task_list()

                # Step 1: Pull the first task
                task = self.task_list.popleft()
                self.print_next_task(task)

                # Step 2: Execute the task
                result = self.execution_chain.execute_task(self.
objective, task["task_name"])
```

```
                this_task_id = int(task["task_id"])
                self.print_task_result(result)

                # Step 3: Store the result
                result_id = f"result_{task['task_id']}"
                self.execution_chain.vectorstore.add_texts(
                    texts=[result],
                    metadatas=[{"task": task["task_name"]}],
                    ids=[result_id],
                )

                # Step 4: Create new tasks and reprioritize task
list
                new_tasks = self.task_creation_chain.generate_
tasks(insights={"indicator1": "Insight 1", "indicator2":
"Insight 2"})
                for new_task in new_tasks:
                    self.task_id_counter += 1
                    new_task.update({"task_id": self.task_id_
counter})
                    self.add_task(new_task)
                self.task_list = deque(
                    self.task_prioritization_chain.reprioritize_
tasks(
                        [t["task_name"] for t in self.task_
list], self.objective, this_task_id
                    )
                )
            num_iters += 1
            if max_iterations is not None and num_iters == max_
iterations:
                self.print_task_ending()
                break

    @classmethod
    def from_llm_and_objective(cls, llm, vectorstore, objective,
first_task, verbose=False):
        """Initialize the BabyAGI Controller."""
        task_creation_chain = TaskCreationChain.from_llm(llm,
verbose=verbose)
        task_prioritization_chain = TaskPrioritizationChain.
from_llm(llm, verbose=verbose)
        execution_chain = ExecutionChain.from_llm(llm,
vectorstore, verbose=verbose)
        controller = cls(
            objective=objective,
```

```
        task_creation_chain=task_creation_chain,
        task_prioritization_chain=task_prioritization_chain,
        execution_chain=execution_chain,
    )
    controller.add_task({"task_id": 1, "task_name": first_
task})
    return controller
```

8. **The Vectorstore**: Now, let's create the Vectorstore that will store the embeddings for task execution:

```
def initial_embeddings(openai_api_key, first_task):
    # Define your embedding model
    embeddings = OpenAIEmbeddings(
        openai_api_key=openai_api_key, model="text-embedding-
ada-002"
    )

    vectorstore = FAISS.from_texts(
        ["_"], embeddings, metadatas=[{"task": first_task}]
    )
    return vectorstore
```

9. **The main UI**: Finally, let's build the main frontend to accept the objective from the user and run the BankRegulatorGPT agent:

```
def main():
    st.title("BankRegulatorGPT - Financial Health Monitor")
    st.markdown(
        """
        An AI-powered financial regulation model that monitors a
bank's financial health
        using Langchain, GPT-4, Pinecone, and Databutton.
        """
    )

    openai_api_key = st.text_input(
        "Insert Your OpenAI API KEY",
        type="password",
        placeholder="sk-",
    )

    if openai_api_key:
        OBJECTIVE = st.text_input(
            label="What's Your Ultimate Goal",
```

```
            value="Monitor a bank's financial health and provide
recommendations.",
        )

        first_task = st.text_input(
            label="Initial task",
            value="Obtain the latest financial reports.",
        )

        max_iterations = st.number_input(
            " Max Iterations",
            value=3,
            min_value=1,
            step=1,
        )

        vectorstore = initial_embeddings(openai_api_key, first_
task)

        if st.button("Let me perform the magic"):
            try:
                bank_regulator_gpt = BankRegulatorGPT.from_llm(
                    llm=OpenAI(openai_api_key=openai_api_key)
                )
                baby_agi = BabyAGI.from_llm_and_objective(
                    llm=OpenAI(openai_api_key=openai_api_key),
                    vectorstore=vectorstore,
                    objective=OBJECTIVE,
                    first_task=first_task,
                )

                with st.spinner("BabyAGI at work ..."):
                    baby_agi.run(max_iterations=max_iterations)

                st.balloons()
            except Exception as e:
                st.error(e)

if __name__ == "__main__":
    main()
```

10. **Add a stop button**: To add the stop button, we'll modify the `BabyAGI` class to include a flag that indicates whether the agent should continue running or stop. We'll also update the `run` method to check this flag at each iteration and stop when the user clicks the *Stop* button:

```python
class BabyAGI(BaseModel):
    """Controller model for the BabyAGI agent."""

    # ... (previous code)

    def __init__(self, *args, **kwargs):
        super().__init__(*args, **kwargs)
        self.should_stop = False

    def stop(self):
        """Stop the agent."""
        self.should_stop = True

    def run(self, max_iterations: Optional[int] = None):
        """Run the agent."""
        num_iters = 0
        while not self.should_stop:
            if self.task_list:
                # ... (previous code)

            num_iters += 1
            if max_iterations is not None and num_iters == max_
iterations:
                self.print_task_ending()
                break
```

11. **Update the main UI to include the stop button**: Next, we need to add the *Stop* button in the main user interface and oversee its functionality:

```python
def main():
    # ... (previous code)

    if openai_api_key:
        # ... (previous code)

        vectorstore = initial_embeddings(openai_api_key, first_
task)

        baby_agi = None
```

```
if st.button("Let me perform the magic"):
    try:
        bank_regulator_gpt = BankRegulatorGPT.from_llm(
            llm=OpenAI(openai_api_key=openai_api_key)
        )
        baby_agi = BabyAGI.from_llm_and_objective(
            llm=OpenAI(openai_api_key=openai_api_key),
            vectorstore=vectorstore,
            objective=OBJECTIVE,
            first_task=first_task,
        )

        with st.spinner("BabyAGI at work ..."):
            baby_agi.run(max_iterations=max_iterations)

        st.balloons()
    except Exception as e:
        st.error(e)

if baby_agi:
    if st.button("Stop"):
        baby_agi.stop()
```

With these modifications, the web app now includes a *Stop* button that allows users to terminate the BankRegulatorGPT agent's execution at any time during its operation. When the user clicks the *Stop* button, the agent will stop running, and the interface will display the final results. If the user does not click the *Stop* button, the autonomous agent will continue running and performing tasks until it either finishes all iterations or completes all tasks. If the user wants to stop the agent before that, they can use the *Stop* button to do so.

The web app allows users to input the bank's stock symbol, and it interacts with the BankRegulatorGPT agent, which utilizes Langchain and OpenAI GPT-4 to provide insights and recommendations, based on the financial health monitoring results. The app also manages task creation, prioritization, and execution using the BabyAGI Controller. Users can easily follow the instructions, input their objectives, and run the BankRegulatorGPT agent without the need for deep technical knowledge.

BankRegulatorGPT evaluates a variety of financial indicators to deliver a comprehensive analysis of a bank's financial condition. This persona integrates several technologies, including Langchain for internet search and mathematical computation, GPT-4 for language understanding and generation, Pinecone for vector search, and Databutton for an interactive web interface.

In the next section, we delve into the specifics of executing a trading strategy that focuses on a Regional Bank ETF and involves **Commercial Real Estate (CRE)** dynamics. We'll guide you through this process using easily understood steps, key data requirements, and accessible Python coding examples. The strategy integrates elements of CRE vacancy rates, sentiment analysis using the OpenAI GPT API, and the volatility captured in the regional bank ETF.

Implementing the Regional Bank ETF trade – a commercial real estate strategy

Let's break down the trading strategy with specific steps, required information, and Python code examples for our non-technical readers. We will use the CRE vacancy rate and sentiment analysis, using the OpenAI GPT API, to capture volatility in the regional bank ETF. For simplicity, we will use the `yfinance` library to fetch historical ETF data and assume access to the OpenAI GPT API.

1. **Data collection**:

   * Historical ETF data:

     * **Required information**: Historical price and volume data for the regional bank ETF and IAT

     * Here's a Python code example:

     ```
     pip install yfinance
     import yfinance as yf

     # Define the ETF symbol
     etf_symbol = "IAT"

     # Fetch historical data from Yahoo Finance
     etf_data = yf.download(etf_symbol, start="2022-06-30",
     end="2023-06-30")

     # Save ETF data to a CSV file
     etf_data.to_csv("IAT_historical_data.csv")
     ```

   * For the CRE vacancy rate data, we will use the quarterly office vacancy rates in the US from the website *Statista*: (https://www.statista.com/statistics/194054/us-office-vacancy-rate-forecasts-from-2010/):

   * Install the following before running python code (if not installed:

   This code snippet will extract the quarterly office vacancy rates in the US for the specified time period (June 30, 2022, to June 30, 2023) from the *Statista* website:

   ```
   pip install requests beautiful soup4 pandas
   import requests
   from bs4 import BeautifulSoup
   import pandas as pd

   # URL for the Statista website
   ```

```
url = "https://www.statista.com/statistics/194054/us-office-
vacancy-rate-forecasts-from-2010/"

headers = {'User-Agent': 'Mozilla/5.0'}

# Send a GET request to the URL
response = requests.get(url, headers=headers)
if response.status_code != 200:
    print("Failed to get URL")
    exit()

# Parse the HTML content
soup = BeautifulSoup(response.content, "html.parser")

# Find the table containing the vacancy rate data
table = soup.find("table")
if table is None:
    print("Could not find the table")
    exit()

# Print the table to debug
print("Table HTML:", table)

# Extract the table data and store it in a DataFrame
try:
    data = pd.read_html(str(table))[0]
except Exception as e:
    print("Error reading table into DataFrame:", e)
    exit()

# Print the DataFrame to debug
print("DataFrame:", data)

# Convert the 'Date' column to datetime format
try:
    data["Date"] = pd.to_datetime(data["Date"])
except Exception as e:
    print("Error converting 'Date' column to datetime:", e)
    exit()

# Filter data for the required time period (June 30, 2022, to
June 30, 2023)
start_date = "2022-06-30"
end_date = "2023-06-30"
```

```
filtered_data = data[(data["Date"] >= start_date) &
(data["Date"] <= end_date)]

# Print the filtered DataFrame to debug
print("Filtered DataFrame:", filtered_data)

# Save filtered CRE Vacancy Rate data to a CSV file
filtered_data.to_csv("CRE_vacancy_rate_data.csv")
```

If you have potential issues that could result in an empty table, we have added print statements to help identify where the potential issue might be so you can address it, such as the following:

1. The website's structure may have changed, which would affect the Beautiful Soup selectors

2. The table may not exist on the page or may be loaded dynamically via JavaScript (which Python's `requests` library won't handle)

3. The date range filtering might not be applicable to the data you have

   • Financial news, articles, and user comments data:

Website: Yahoo Finance News (`https://finance.yahoo.com/news/`)

To extract data from the Yahoo Finance news website, you can use the following Python code snippet:

```python
import requests
from bs4 import BeautifulSoup
import pandas as pd

# URL for Yahoo Finance news website
url = "https://finance.yahoo.com/news/"

headers = {'User-Agent': 'Mozilla/5.0'}

# Send a GET request to the URL
response = requests.get(url, headers=headers)
if response.status_code != 200:
    print("Failed to get URL")
    exit()

# Parse the HTML content
soup = BeautifulSoup(response.content, "html.parser")

# Find all the news articles on the page
articles = soup.find_all("li", {"data-test": "stream-item"})
if not articles:
```

```python
        print("No articles found.")
        exit()

    # Create empty lists to store the extracted data
    article_titles = []
    article_links = []
    user_comments = []

    # Extract data for each article
    for article in articles:
        title_tag = article.find("h3")
        link_tag = article.find("a")
        title = title_tag.text.strip() if title_tag else "N/A"
        link = link_tag["href"] if link_tag else "N/A"
        article_titles.append(title)
        article_links.append(link)

        # Extract user comments for each article
        comment_section = article.find("ul", {"data-test": "comment-
section"})
        if comment_section:
            comments = [comment.text.strip() for comment in comment_
section.find_all("span")]
            user_comments.append(comments)
        else:
            user_comments.append([])

    # Create a DataFrame to store the data
    if article_titles:
        data = pd.DataFrame({
            "Article Title": article_titles,
            "Article Link": article_links,
            "User Comments": user_comments
        })

        # Save financial news data to a CSV file
        data.to_csv("financial_news_data.csv")
    else:
        print("No article titles found. DataFrame not created.")
```

If you have potential issues that could result in an empty string or DataFrame, we have added print statements to help identify where the potential issue might be so you can address it, such as the following.

4. The website structure may have changed, affecting the Beautiful Soup selectors

5. Some articles might not have a title, link, or user comments, resulting in "N/A" or empty lists.

6. The site's content could be loaded dynamically via JavaScript, which the `requests` library won't handle.

    This code snippet will extract the article titles, links, and user comments from the Yahoo Finance news website for references to the ETF, IAT, commercial real estate, or regional banks from June 30, 2022 to June 30, 2023. You can further store this data in a suitable format, such as CSV or Excel, for later use in the trading strategy. Please note that web scraping should be done responsibly and in compliance with the website's terms of service.

7. **Sentiment analysis using the OpenAI GPT API**:

- **Required information**: API key for OpenAI GPT-4 API

- **Website**: OpenAI GPT-4 API (`https://platform.openai.com/`)

  - Python Code Snippet for Sentiment Analysis:

  - Installation required prior to running python code (if not already installed):

    ```
    pip install openai
    pip install pandas
    ```

  - Run python code below:

    ```python
    import openai
    import pandas as pd

    # Initialize your OpenAI API key
    openai_api_key = "YOUR_OPENAI_API_KEY"
    openai.api_key = openai_api_key

    # Function to get sentiment score using GPT-4 (hypothetical)
    def get_sentiment_score(text):
        # Make the API call to OpenAI GPT-4 (This is a placeholder;
    the real API call might differ)
        response = openai.Completion.create(
            engine="text-davinci-002",  # Replace with the actual
    engine ID for GPT-4 when it becomes available
            prompt=f"This text is: {text}",
            max_tokens=10
        )

        # Assume the generated text contains a sentiment label e.g.,
    "positive", "negative", or "neutral"
    ```

```
        sentiment_text = response['choices'][0]['text'].strip().
lower()

        # Convert the sentiment label to a numerical score
        if "positive" in sentiment_text:
            return 1
        elif "negative" in sentiment_text:
            return -1
        else:
            return 0

    # Load financial news data from the CSV file
    financial_news_data = pd.read_csv("financial_news_data.csv")

    # Perform sentiment analysis on the article titles and user
    comments
    financial_news_data['Sentiment Score - Article Title'] =
    financial_news_data['Article Title'].apply(get_sentiment_score)
    financial_news_data['Sentiment Scores - User Comments'] =
    financial_news_data['User Comments'].apply(
        lambda comments: [get_sentiment_score(comment) for comment
    in eval(comments)]
    )

    # Calculate total sentiment scores for article titles and user
    comments
    financial_news_data['Total Sentiment Score - Article Title'] =
    financial_news_data['Sentiment Score - Article Title'].sum()
    financial_news_data['Total Sentiment Scores - User Comments']
    = financial_news_data['Sentiment Scores - User Comments'].
    apply(sum)

    # Save the DataFrame back to a new CSV file with sentiment
    scores included
    financial_news_data.to_csv('financial_news_data_with_sentiment.
    csv', index=False)
```

Ensure that you have the openai Python library installed and that you replace "YOUR_ OPENAI_API_KEY" with your actual API key for the GPT-4 API. Additionally, make sure you have proper permissions to use the API, and comply with the terms of service of the OpenAI GPT-4 API.

This example assumes that the 'User Comments' column in your financial_news_ data.csv contains lists of comments in the string format (e.g., "[comment1, comment2, ...]"). The eval() function is used to convert these stringified lists back into actual Python lists.

8. **Volatility indicator**:

   - **Required information**: The historical price data of the regional bank ETF, IAT.

   - **A Python code example**:

```python
# Load ETF historical data from the CSV file
etf_data = pd.read_csv("IAT_historical_data.csv")

# Calculate historical volatility using standard deviation
def calculate_volatility(etf_data):
    daily_returns = etf_data["Adj Close"].pct_change().dropna()
    volatility = daily_returns.std()
    return volatility

# Calculate volatility for the IAT ETF
volatility_iat = calculate_volatility(etf_data)
```

Note that the `IAT-historical_data.csv` file contains historical data for the **iShares US Regional Banks ETF**, represented by the acronym **IAT**. This data includes fields such as the adjusted close price, which is used to calculate historical volatility. The Python code to generate this file was provided at the bottom of page 41 and the top of page 42.

Ensure that the `Adj Close` column exists in your CSV file and that the `IAT_historical_data.csv` file is in the same directory as your Python script, or provide the full path to the file.

Incorporating volatility into the trading strategy:

- Include the calculated volatility value as an additional variable in the trading strategy

- Use the volatility information to adjust trading signals based on the level of market volatility

- For example, consider higher volatility as an additional factor to generate buy/sell signals, or adjust the holding period based on market volatility

With the inclusion of the ETF's historical volatility, the trading strategy can better capture and respond to market fluctuations, thus making more informed trading decisions.

9. **Trading strategy**: To determine the thresholds for when to buy or sell the IAT ETF based on the quarterly vacancy rate, sentiment score, and volatility, we can update the trading strategy code snippet, as shown in the following Python code:

```python
# Implement the trading strategy with risk management
def trading_strategy(cre_vacancy_rate, sentiment_score,
volatility, entry_price):
    stop_loss_percent = 0.05  # 5% stop-loss level
    take_profit_percent = 0.1  # 10% take-profit level
```

```
        # Calculate stop-loss and take-profit price levels
        stop_loss_price = entry_price * (1 - stop_loss_percent)
        take_profit_price = entry_price * (1 + take_profit_percent)

        if cre_vacancy_rate < 5 and sentiment_score > 0.5 and
    volatility > 0.2:
            return "Buy", stop_loss_price, take_profit_price
        elif cre_vacancy_rate > 10 and sentiment_score < 0.3 and
    volatility > 0.2:
            return "Sell", stop_loss_price, take_profit_price
        else:
            return "Hold", None, None

    # Sample values for demonstration purposes
    cre_vacancy_rate = 4.5
    sentiment_score = 0.7
    volatility = 0.25
    entry_price = 100.0

    # Call the trading strategy function
    trade_decision, stop_loss, take_profit = trading_strategy(cre_
    vacancy_rate, sentiment_score, volatility, entry_price)

    print("Trade Decision:", trade_decision)
    print("Stop-Loss Price:", stop_loss)
    print("Take-Profit Price:", take_profit)
```

In this updated code snippet, we use `cre_vacancy_rate`, `sentiment_score`, and `volatility` as the input parameters for the trading strategy function. The trading strategy checks these key variables against specific thresholds to decide on whether to buy ("go long"), sell ("go short"), or hold the IAT ETF.

Note that the thresholds used in this example are arbitrary and may not be suitable for actual trading decisions. In practice, you would need to conduct thorough analysis and testing to determine appropriate thresholds for your specific trading strategy. Additionally, consider incorporating risk management and other factors into your trading strategy for more robust decision-making.

Now, based on the provided sample values for `cre_vacancy_rate`, `sentiment_score`, and `volatility`, the code will determine the trade decision (buy, sell, or hold) for the IAT ETF.

10. **Risk management and monitoring**: Here, you define the stop-loss and take-profit levels to manage risk.

    You can set specific stop-loss and take-profit levels based on your risk tolerance and trading strategy. For example, you might set a stop-loss at a certain percentage below the entry price to limit potential losses, and a take-profit level at a certain percentage above the entry price to lock in profits:

```python
import pandas as pd

# Define the trading strategy function
def trading_strategy(cre_vacancy_rate, sentiment_score,
volatility, entry_price):
    stop_loss_percent = 0.05  # 5% stop-loss level
    take_profit_percent = 0.1  # 10% take-profit level

    # Calculate stop-loss and take-profit price levels
    stop_loss_price = entry_price * (1 - stop_loss_percent)
    take_profit_price = entry_price * (1 + take_profit_percent)

    if cre_vacancy_rate < 5 and sentiment_score > 0.5 and
volatility > 0.2:
        return "Buy", stop_loss_price, take_profit_price
    elif cre_vacancy_rate > 10 and sentiment_score < 0.3 and
volatility > 0.2:
        return "Sell", stop_loss_price, take_profit_price
    else:
        return "Hold", None, None

# Sample values for demonstration purposes
cre_vacancy_rate = 4.5
sentiment_score = 0.7
volatility = 0.25
entry_price = 100.0

# Call the trading strategy function
trade_decision, stop_loss, take_profit = trading_strategy(cre_
vacancy_rate, sentiment_score, volatility, entry_price)

# Create a DataFrame to store the trading strategy outputs
output_data = pd.DataFrame({
    "CRE Vacancy Rate": [cre_vacancy_rate],
    "Sentiment Score": [sentiment_score],
    "Volatility": [volatility],
    "Entry Price": [entry_price],
    "Trade Decision": [trade_decision],
    "Stop-Loss Price": [stop_loss],
    "Take-Profit Price": [take_profit]
})
```

```
# Save the trading strategy outputs to a CSV file
output_data.to_csv("trading_strategy_outputs.csv", index=False)
```

In this updated code snippet, we have introduced the `stop_loss_percent` and `take_profit_percent` variables to set the desired stop-loss and take-profit levels as percentages. The trading strategy calculates the stop-loss and take-profit price levels based on these percentages, and the `entry_price`.

> **Important note**
>
> The specific stop-loss and take-profit levels provided in this example are for demonstration purposes only. You should carefully consider your risk management strategy and adjust these levels according to your trading goals and risk appetite.

Now, the trading strategy function returns the trade decision (buy, sell, or hold) along with the calculated stop-loss and take-profit price levels, based on the provided sample values for `cre_vacancy_rate`, `sentiment_score`, `volatility`, and `entry_price`.

This section laid out a five-step process to build a trading strategy for a Regional Bank ETF, using the CRE vacancy rate and sentiment analysis data. First, we identified the required data sources and displayed how to collect this data using Python. Then, we explained how to use the OpenAI GPT API for sentiment analysis of financial news and comments. Subsequently, we incorporated the volatility of the ETF into the trading strategy. The fourth step involved forming the trading strategy with thresholds for buy/sell decisions, based on the CRE vacancy rate, sentiment score, and volatility. Finally, we discussed the importance of risk management and continuous monitoring of the relevant factors.

> **Important note**
>
> This trading strategy is a simplified example for educational purposes only and does not guarantee profitable results. Real-world trading involves complex factors and risks, and it's essential to perform thorough research and consult with financial experts before making any investment decisions.

In the following section, we walk through the creation of an interactive Power BI dashboard to visualize the previously discussed Regional Bank ETF trading strategy. The dashboard integrates line charts, bar charts, and card visuals to display various elements of the trading strategy – the ETF price, CRE vacancy rate, sentiment scores, and trade signals.

Visualizing the ETF trade – a Power BI dashboard for the commercial real estate market

Let's create a Power BI visualization for the trading strategy, using the data collected from the steps mentioned earlier. We'll use a combination of line charts, bar charts, and card visuals to display the ETF price, CRE vacancy rate, sentiment score, and trading signals:

1. Data collection and preparation:

    *   Collect historical data for the IAT ETF, quarterly CRE vacancy rate, and sentiment scores from the provided sources. Please make sure you have three CSV files named `IAT_historical_data.csv`, `CRE_vacancy_rate_data.csv`, and `financial_news_data_with_sentiment.csv` that store the IAT ETF price data, CRE vacancy rate data, and sentiment scores, respectively.

    *   Import and prepare the data in Power BI for analysis:

2. Open Power BI Desktop and select Get Data from the Home tab.

3. Choose Text/CSV and click Connect.

4. Navigate to the folder containing the CSV files and import them into Power BI.

5. An ETF price line chart:

6. Drag and drop a line chart visual onto the canvas.

7. From the `IAT_historical_data.csv` dataset, drag the `Date` field into the Axis well and `Adj Close` (or whatever represents the ETF price) into the Values well.

8. A CRE vacancy rate bar chart:

9. Add a new bar chart visual to the canvas.

10. From the `CRE_vacancy_rate_data.csv` dataset, drag the `Date` field into the Axis well and `CRE Vacancy Rate` into the Values well.

11. A sentiment scorecard visual:

12. Place a card visual on the canvas.

13. From the `financial_news_data_with_sentiment.csv` dataset, drag the field representing the `Total Sentiment Score` into the Values well of the card visual.

14. Trading signals:

15. Go to Modeling and create a new calculated column.

16. Implement a DAX formula to apply the trading strategy logic. This formula will read from the other datasets to generate buy, sell, or hold signals, based on the CRE Vacancy Rate, sentiment score, and ETF volatility.

17. A trading signal bar chart:

18. Add another bar chart visual to the canvas.(Buy, Sell, Hold) over time.

19. From the calculated column you created in *step 5*, drag `Date` into the Axis well and `Trading Signals` into the Values well.

20. A composite report:

    - Arrange all visuals in a visually appealing manner on the report canvas.

    - Add relevant titles, legends, and data labels to enhance clarity and understanding.

21. Publish the report:

    - Publish the Power BI report to the Power BI service for easy sharing and collaboration.

22. Set up a data refresh:

    - Schedule a data refresh for the report in the Power BI service to keep the data up to date.

The "Real Estate ETF Profits Navigator" Power BI visualization will provide investors with insights into IAT ETF price movement, CRE vacancy rate trends, and sentiment scores based on NLP analysis. By incorporating the trading signals, users can make informed decisions on when to buy, sell, or hold the ETF, based on the specific criteria defined in the trading strategy. The interactive and informative nature of the report allows users to analyze the trading strategy's performance and navigate profitable waters in the real estate ETF market.

Now, the Power BI report will display the ETF price trend, CRE vacancy rate, sentiment score, and trading signals in an interactive and informative way. Users can interact with the report to analyze the trading strategy's performance over time and make informed decisions.

Note that the visualization provided here is a simplified example for demonstration purposes. In a real-world scenario, you may need to adjust the visuals and data sources based on the specific data collected and the complexity of the trading strategy. Additionally, consider using DAX formulas to perform advanced calculations and create dynamic visuals in Power BI.

The next section dives into the transformative potential and ethical implications of **artificial intelligence (AI)** within the financial sector. Drawing parallels with the Industrial Revolution, AI underscores the need for responsible governance and regulation to prevent its misuse and mitigate associated risks. This piece critically examines AI's impact on finance, providing thoughtful insights into how we can harness its capabilities effectively while mitigating potential challenges.

> **AI in the future of finance – a tool of our own making**
>
> This section references some information from the March 27, 2023, article *The Fire Next Time: Reflections on AI and the Future of Humanity* by Liat Ben-Zur.

AI should not be viewed as a foreign entity with potentially malicious intent but, rather, as a creation of our own innovation and thirst for knowledge. Similar to the Industrial Revolution's transformative power, AI holds great promise and potential risks within the financial world. However, with the rapid development of AI, we must be especially vigilant in its application within finance, trading, investing, and financial analysis, given the grave consequences of missteps.

As we engage with AI's limitless potential, we should acknowledge our history of exploitation and bias, as AI can mirror our inherent prejudices. The crossroads we find ourselves at invites us to contemplate the kind of financial world we desire to shape with AI and the type of responsible financial analysts, traders, investors, and Power BI users we wish to become.

One crucial issue is AI's ability to perpetuate bias and inequality within the financial sector. Instances of racially or gender-biased AI-driven trading algorithms or financial advising tools are stark examples. It's essential to confront and address these biases to avoid past mistakes. However, we must remember that AI is not an uncontrollable force. Instead, it's a tool that requires our ethical governance to avoid an unwarranted handover of control to the machines.

Another pressing concern is the potential displacement of human roles within the finance industry. If technological advancement outpaces our ability to adapt, we could face extensive job loss and social unrest. Therefore, strategic decisions and support for those displaced by AI in finance are critical.

More broadly, we must consider how to regulate AI for the common good, balancing its benefits and risks, and ensuring that AI reflects our collective values and fairness within the financial landscape. To traverse these intricate paths, we must commit to an ethical, transparent, and accountable approach to AI. This is not merely a technological transition but a crucial socioeconomic shift that will redefine the future of finance.

In this comprehensive exploration of AI in finance, we will explored its transformative potential and associated risks. We will review the importance of smart AI regulation to navigate pitfalls and seize opportunities. We will learn lessons from the lack of regulation in social media, emphasizing early regulatory intervention and ethical AI integration among other factors. By stressing global cooperation, we highlight the need for universally applicable standards and a unified approach toward AI regulation. We will discuss the need for AI regulation and legislation in finance, suggesting practical ways to implement it.

The importance of smart AI regulation – navigating pitfalls and seizing opportunities

The dawn of AI in finance and investment is transforming industries, and finance is no exception. AI, with its power to analyze massive datasets and make predictions, is revolutionizing trading, investing, and financial analysis. However, as we approach this transformation, we need to tread cautiously. AI systems reflect our values and fears, and their potential misuse in finance could lead to widespread issues, such as biased investment strategies or market manipulation. The displacement of human financial analysts and traders is another challenge. We need to make informed decisions and provide support for displaced workers. Moreover, we must ensure AI in finance reflects our collective values.

Navigating the AI revolution – a cautionary tale from the lack of regulation in social media

In this section, we will show that the lack of social media regulation and asking the technology industry to self-regulate is not a model for AI governance. We want to extract pivotal lessons from social media to navigate the impending AI revolution within the realm of finance. The lack of social media regulation underlines the potential risks when incorporating transformative technologies into intricate financial ecosystems. By heeding these lessons, we can strategically sidestep similar pitfalls in the AI landscape, fostering responsible innovation while minimizing potential threats.

Here are some key considerations when incorporating the lessons learned from social media for AI and finance:

- **Early regulatory intervention**: Establish clear regulatory frameworks at the onset of AI integration into financial systems. Timely policy implementation can pre-empt future complexities and maintain the integrity of financial markets.

- **Inclusive financial stakeholder consultation**: Encourage active collaboration among diverse stakeholders – financial experts, fintech leaders, regulatory bodies, and civil societies. This ensures a balanced and integrated approach toward AI regulation in finance.

- **Combatting financial misinformation**: Utilize the hard-learned lessons from social media's battle against misinformation. Develop robust strategies to prevent AI-driven dissemination of misleading financial information, protecting investors and maintaining market transparency.

- **AI transparency and trust**: Mandate transparency within financial AI systems. Understanding how AI makes investment decisions is crucial to fostering trust among investors and ensuring accountability.

- **Ethical AI integration**: Advocate for AI systems that are ethical, prioritizing fairness, privacy, and adherence to financial regulations in their operation. This minimizes potential exploitation and ensures investor protection.

- **Cooperation from the finance industry**: Secure active involvement from fintech giants and influential financial institutions. Their collaboration in crafting regulations and adopting self-regulatory measures can considerably shape the landscape of AI regulation in finance.

- **Clear AI accountability in finance**: Formulate explicit rules around AI liability and accountability within finance. This ensures that AI developers, traders, and investors behave responsibly and can be held accountable for potential misconduct.

- **Effective financial oversight**: Implement robust regulatory oversight to monitor AI applications in finance, ensuring alignment with regulatory guidelines and ethical standards.

- **Financial AI literacy**: Elevate public understanding of AI in finance, its potential, and the risks. An informed populace can actively engage in policy discussions, promoting balanced and inclusive AI regulations in finance.

- **Agile regulatory framework**: Adopt an adaptive approach to regulations, given the rapidly evolving nature of AI. This flexibility allows financial regulations to keep pace with technological advancements, ensuring their ongoing relevance.

By learning from social media regulation challenges and strategically applying those lessons to AI in finance, we can foster a forward-thinking regulatory framework. This proactive approach will help ensure the safe and responsible evolution of AI in finance, capitalizing on its immense potential while simultaneously safeguarding against its inherent risks. As we further integrate AI into systems such as business intelligence (Power BI), financial analysis, and algorithmic trading, let's ensure we're creating a future that values fairness, transparency, and the security of all stakeholders.

Global cooperation – a key to ethical AI in finance

As we move towards an increasingly AI-driven financial world, we want to avoid the regulatory disconnect that occurred with cryptocurrencies.

The FTX case demonstrates the perils of disjointed regulation in the world of finance. FTX, a crypto exchange once valued at $32 billion, moved from Hong Kong to the lightly regulated Bahamas in late 2021. However, in November 2022, FTX filed for bankruptcy, wiping out hundreds of millions in customer funds, with reports estimating that $1 to $2 billion had disappeared. Even though FTX was based in the Bahamas, the collapse had a ripple effect across the globe, significantly impacting developed markets such as South Korea, Singapore, and Japan. Just as the fall of a major crypto exchange in an unregulated environment impacted the stability of highly regulated markets worldwide, the misuse of AI could have similar widespread effects. We must learn from these past experiences to avoid repeating such detrimental incidents in the future.

The scope of AI is much larger and its impact far more pervasive, necessitating a unified, global approach. Implementing universally applicable standards, fostering open dialogue and cooperation, and ensuring transparency and accountability are crucial steps toward a secure, stable, and ethical AI-powered future in finance.

Here are the key areas for global AI collaboration:

- **Global standards**: Creating universally applicable ethical standards for AI in finance is of utmost importance. These agreed-upon principles, such as transparency, accountability, and non-discrimination, will lay the foundation for all other aspects of AI regulation in finance.

- **A global AI treaty**: A binding international agreement provides the necessary legal framework to enforce global standards, manage potential crises, and restrict aggressive uses of AI.

- **A global watchdog**: An international monitoring body is essential to ensure compliance with the global standards and the AI treaty, fostering trust and collaboration.

- **Information sharing**: Sharing best practices and research among nations, institutions, and organizations promotes mutual growth and helps develop robust AI models.

- **Red teaming**: Red teaming or adversarial testing of AI systems can identify vulnerabilities and potential risks, enhancing the global financial system's stability and resilience.

Through global cooperation, we can ensure that AI not only revolutionizes finance but also does so ethically, transparently, and for the collective good. Thus, we create a more harmonious and regulated financial ecosystem that stands to benefit all stakeholders around the globe.

AI regulation – a necessary safeguard for the future of finance

The discussion of AI regulation might seem far removed from the immediate interests of those involved in finance, investing, trading, and financial analysis, let alone business intelligence users. Yet, getting AI regulation right is crucially important for the future of finance and all its stakeholders.

This section details the reasons why regulation is crucial in the implementation of AI in finance. It establishes the fundamental need for AI regulation, and it argues why this matter is of great significance to anyone involved in finance, investing, trading, and financial analysis, and even to Power BI users. It highlights the potential risks, ethical implications, and opportunities that AI presents in the financial sector, emphasizing why proper regulation is vital to ensure fairness, transparency, and innovation.

Here is why it is important:

- **Minimizing systemic risks**: AI's significant role in finance means it could potentially create systemic risks if not adequately regulated. For example, AI algorithms that execute trades at superhuman speeds can exacerbate market volatility, leading to flash crashes such as the one that happened on May 6, 2010. Proper regulation can help mitigate such risks by enforcing safeguards, such as "circuit breakers" that halt trading during periods of excessive volatility.

- **Ensuring fairness and equality**: Without robust regulation, AI systems could unintentionally perpetuate and exacerbate existing biases in financial services, leading to unfair outcomes. An example is AI-powered credit scoring models that may discriminate against certain demographics if trained on biased data. Adequate regulation can help ensure that AI systems are transparent and fair, providing equal opportunities for all investors and customers.

- **Preventing fraud and misuse**: AI, especially when combined with technologies such as blockchain, can be used to perpetrate sophisticated financial fraud or insider trading, which may be challenging to detect and prosecute. Proper regulation can deter such activities and provide a framework to hold wrongdoers accountable.

- **Promoting transparency and trust**: Financial markets rely on trust, and AI systems can seem like "black boxes," leading to mistrust. Regulating AI to ensure transparency can help build trust among users. For example, if an AI-powered robo-advisor provides an investment recommendation, the user should be able to understand why that recommendation was made.

- **Supporting innovation and competitiveness**: While the main aim of regulation is to manage risks, it can also help promote innovation. Regulatory clarity can give companies the confidence to invest in new AI technologies, knowing that they won't face unexpected legal hurdles. Also, standardized regulations can level the playing field for smaller companies and start-ups, fostering competition and innovation.

- **Managing ethical implications**: AI brings about novel ethical challenges that the financial industry needs to address. For instance, who is responsible if an AI-driven trading algorithm malfunctions and causes significant losses? Clear regulations can provide guidelines to navigate these complex issues.

These reasons indicate that AI regulation isn't just a side issue – it's central to the future of finance. Getting it right will provide a robust foundation for the responsible and beneficial use of AI in finance, trading, investing, and financial analysis. Therefore, every reader who's a stakeholder in this industry has a personal stake in the conversation about AI regulation. This isn't just about protecting ourselves from potential harm – it's about actively shaping a financial future that is fair, transparent, and prosperous for all.

AI regulation – a balancing act in the future of finance

AI regulation walks a fine line between promoting innovation and safeguarding societal interests. This balancing act becomes even more crucial when applied to the finance industry, given the potential economic implications of unregulated AI technologies.

This section builds upon the foundational understanding established in the last section, suggesting practical ways to approach and implement such necessary regulation. It offers concrete regulatory proposals to strike a balance between technological innovation and maintaining the integrity of financial markets, thus providing a roadmap to integrate AI into finance ethically and responsibly.

Here are some regulatory recommendations to strike this balance while safeguarding the interests of investors, traders, and financial analysts:

- **AI sandboxes**: Governments and financial regulatory bodies could establish controlled environments to test new AI technologies in finance. These sandboxes would foster innovation while ensuring ethical guidelines and risk mitigation strategies are enforced.

- **Tiered regulations**: A tiered regulatory approach can be applied to financial AI projects, with smaller, less risky ones subjected to lighter regulation. Meanwhile, large-scale AI systems, which can significantly impact financial markets, should face more stringent oversight.

- **Public-private partnerships**: Collaboration between governments, research institutions, and private financial firms can drive innovative AI solutions for investing and trading while ensuring ethical and regulatory standards are maintained.

- **Tech-literate lawmakers**: Promoting tech literacy among policymakers is critical, as it can help craft legislation that supports AI's beneficial use in finance without being swayed by industry lobbyists.

- **Incentivizing ethical AI**: Governments can provide financial incentives, such as tax breaks or grants, to financial firms developing ethical AI solutions. This could encourage AI applications in finance that uphold transparency and fairness.

- **AI literacy programs**: Education initiatives can help investors and the public understand AI's potential impact on finance. A well-informed public can encourage both innovation in and the regulation of AI financial tools.

- **Responsible AI certifications**: A certification program can validate responsible AI practices in finance. Earning such a certification could boost a firm's reputation, making it more attractive to ethically minded investors.

From market manipulation to unfair trading practices, the stakes are high. As such, striking the right balance in AI regulation is necessary for the future integrity of our financial systems. We must learn from past mistakes, encourage responsible innovation, and instill regulations that foster trust in AI's role in finance.

AI regulation and legislation – a comprehensive timeline

This section is pivotal for those of you interested in the intersection of ChatGPT, finance, and Power BI. It provides an insightful chronology of key events and initiatives, from Elon Musk's call for a temporary halt on AI deployments to government and industry moves toward AI regulation. These milestones, some directly impacting ChatGPT, shape the legal and ethical landscape that financial algorithms and data visualization tools operate within. Understanding these developments is crucial for anyone leveraging AI in finance, as it provides context for the constraints and responsibilities that come with deploying such technologies:

- **Elon Musk's open letter calling for an AI pause (March 28, 2023)**: Backed by various AI experts, Musk advocated for a six-month hiatus on AI deployment to develop better regulations.

- **Italian data protection agency Garante temporarily bans ChatGPT (March 30, 2023–April 30, 2023)**: The ban was lifted once OpenAI complies with demands for transparency about data processing, correction and deletion, accessible opposition to data processing, and age verification.

- **Existential AI risk statement (May 30, 2023)**: OpenAI CEO, Sam Altman, and numerous AI scientists, academics, tech CEOs, and public figures called on policymakers to focus attention on mitigating a "doomsday" extinction-level AI risk. This statement is hosted on the **Center for Alignment of Intelligence and Strategy (CAIS)**.

- **The Federal Trade Commission (FTC) action against OpenAI (July 10, 2023)**: The FTC accused OpenAI of violating AI regulation guidelines, sparking debates about the efficacy of current AI regulations.

- **Hollywood actors and writers strike (July 14, 2023)**: SAG-AFTRA and WGA demand contract provisions to protect their work from being replaced or exploited by AI.

- **United Nations calls for responsible AI development (July 18, 2023):** The United Nations advocated the creation of a new body for AI governance, proposing a legally binding agreement by 2026 to prohibit AI in automated weapons.

- **Technology companies partner with the White House for self-regulation (July 21, 2023):** Amazon, Anthropic, Google, Inflection, Meta, Microsoft, and OpenAI pledge external testing for new AI systems before public release and to clearly label AI-generated content.

- **US Senate Majority Leader Chuck Schumer proposes the Safe Innovation Framework for AI policy regulation in the summer of 2023:** This outlines the challenges AI poses to workforce, democracy, national security, and intellectual property rights. It highlights a two-step legislative approach – creating the AI framework and convening AI insight forums with top AI experts for a comprehensive legislative response.

Summary

AI is not an isolated creation but a reflection of our collective intellect, dreams, and fears. The Industrial Revolution reshaped society, and AI, advancing at a breakneck speed, holds the potential to do the same. However, it also holds a mirror to our biases and discriminations. As we shape AI, we shape our future society and must ask ourselves who we want to become.

The dawn of AI parallels transformative moments in our history. However, it carries unique risks. If uncontrolled, AI's ability to perpetuate biases and its displacement of human workers could escalate existing inequalities, causing extensive social disruption. Our approach to AI must reflect our highest values and aspirations, aiming not just to shape its evolution but also to shape a future in which humanity thrives. We must resist the lure of surrendering control to an unregulated machine, instead taking the reins to guide AI's evolution toward enhancing human potential.

This chapter takes us through a journey from SVB's collapse to the revelation of the Sentinel and Financial Fortress strategies. We reflected on how robust risk management practices and innovative applications of AI, such as NLP, can shape the future of the financial world. We further expanded on this idea by introducing the BankRegulatorGPT persona and its role in automating financial regulation tasks, thereby highlighting AI's immense potential. The chapter also highlighted a practical trading strategy, revolving around the regional bank ETF, and demonstrated how to visualize this using Power BI. Through these lessons, we underscored the critical importance of using AI and technology responsibly in finance, emphasizing the necessity for strong regulations to safeguard the interests of all stakeholders in this dynamic landscape.

As we move forward into a future increasingly influenced by AI, the experiences and lessons highlighted in this chapter remind us of the critical need for the responsible development, deployment, and regulation of AI. Be it security, privacy, bias prevention, transparency, or robust regulations, the challenges that accompany this revolution are not to be taken lightly. However, with the right steps, we can ensure a prosperous and inclusive financial future powered by AI, fostering innovation while ensuring fairness and justice. The journey to navigate the AI revolution requires foresight, responsibility, and a commitment to learning and adaptation, but the potential rewards make it a challenge worth undertaking.

Chapter 7, Moderna and OpenAI: Biotech and AGI Breakthroughs, promises to be an exhilarating exploration of how AI is revolutionizing the process of discovery, particularly within the pharmaceutical industry. The chapter opens with an intense focus on Moderna, a company at the forefront of mRna technology and vaccines. Notably, it will introduce innovative AI models such as the FoodandDrugAdminGPT, powered by Jarvis, and Hugging Face GPT, demonstrating how these models can dramatically accelerate drug discovery and approval and highlight trading opportunities in the financial markets.

A highlight of this chapter is a comprehensive dive into the process of breaking down existing patents to identify opportunities for newcomers in the pharmaceutical industry, a strategic move that can ultimately benefit consumers through enhanced competition and lower drug prices.

The narrative expands to examine how AI and machine learning are fundamentally transforming the process of biological discovery and healthcare innovation, from small molecule drug synthesis to care delivery itself.

This chapter also aims to empower you with practical guidance on the integration of various financial analysis techniques, driving informed decision-making. It highlights the role of AI and ChatGPT in synthesizing insights from fundamental analysis, technical analysis, quantitative analysis, sentiment analysis, and news analysis.

Chapter 7 ends with a profound look at the increasing involvement of the C-suite in AI initiatives, underlining the importance of high-quality training data, risk management, and ethical considerations. This chapter is a must-read for anyone looking to understand the far-reaching implications of AI in discovery, investment decision-making, and business strategy at large.

7

Moderna and OpenAI – Biotech and AGI Breakthroughs

Chapter 6 offered a deep dive into the unfortunate collapse of **Silicon Valley Bank** (**SVB**), with the narrative compared to a renowned pastry chef's ambitious yet flawed endeavor of baking a record-breaking cake. It emphasized the importance of balance, accurate measurement, and understanding how elements interact, and how a better understanding of market sentiment using AI and ChatGPT might have offered a different insight into the impending collapse.

That chapter also introduced the Sentinel Strategy, an innovative trading strategy that uses social media sentiment analysis and NLP with the Twitter (now X) API. In parallel, it highlighted the Financial Fortress Strategy, combining traditional financial metrics with social media sentiment to create a powerful trading scheme. *Chapter 6* also presented BankRegulatorGPT, an AI model designed for financial regulation tasks. It provided an in-depth guide on setting up the AI agent and discussed its applications in the finance field. In doing so, we delved into the Regional Bank ETF: The Commercial Real Estate Strategy, utilizing AI tools and Python code examples to outline a creative commercial real estate trade. Power BI visualization techniques were explored in detail – first for visualizing the trading strategies and then for creating a visualization of the commercial real estate trading strategy. Lastly, we concluded with an analysis of AI regulation, emphasizing its importance in mitigating risks associated with AI use in the financial sector. It underlined the need for proper rules and supervision to ensure the responsible application of AI in finance.

In this chapter, prepare to embark on a thrilling exploration where biotechnology meets the innovative domain of **artificial intelligence** (**AI**), finance, and data visualization in the form of AI and ChatGPT. We will journey into the heart of Moderna, a name that is synonymous with innovation and ambition that's not only etched in the annals of medical history for its groundbreaking COVID-19 vaccine but that also represents the epitome of technological synergy.

From deploying AI to accelerating drug discovery to leveraging quantum computing in partnership with giants such as IBM and Carnegie Mellon, Moderna's vision transcends conventional boundaries. Here, we'll unveil how Moderna orchestrates a perfect symphony of science, technology, and business acumen. You'll discover a novel investment strategy called Moderna Momentum, a sentiment-sensitive masterpiece that uses AI and ChatGPT and is visualized through Power BI. You'll meet the future of drug development with AI personas such as FoodandDrugAdminGPT and witness how Moderna is shaping the future of cancer care, pandemic response, and much more.

Get ready to be inspired, enlightened, and enthralled by a narrative that weaves together the brilliance of Moderna's strategy, the potential of AI and ChatGPT, the precision of financial analysis, and the beauty of Power BI visualizations. This chapter is not just a read – it's an experience, a vision of the future where science, technology, and humanity converge to create a brighter, healthier, and more prosperous world for all. Welcome to the frontier of innovation!

In this chapter, we will cover the following topics:

- Navigating the Biotech frontier with Moderna: Uncover how Moderna's journey with groundbreaking **messenger RNA (mRNA)** technology is akin to crafting a blockbuster movie, with detailed planning, execution, and market acceptance playing crucial roles.

- Quantum horizons and AI mastery with IBM and Carnegie Mellon: Explore Moderna's revolutionary partnerships in quantum computing and AI, forging a path to next-gen drug discovery, and building an AI-driven symphony in medicine.

- Revolutionizing cancer care and confronting future pandemics: Explore Moderna's ambitious plans in oncology, personalized therapies, and multi-valent vaccines, redefining the landscape of medicine for generations to come.

- Outsourcing and global expansion strategy: Understand Moderna's strategic move toward outsourcing pharma manufacturing for innovation, agility, and global reach, with a focus on quality assurance and ethical considerations.

- Discover Moderna Momentum a novel, sentiment-sensitive investment strategy that embodies the intricate nature of biotech investing, visualized through Power BI.

- Unleashing collaborative intelligence with Jarvis, HuggingGPT, and FoodandDrugAdminGPT: Dive into the integration of these innovative AI models in the pharmaceutical landscape. From strategic task planning with FoodandDrugAdminGPT to crafting seamless GUIs with Gradio, you will explore how they synergize to offer intelligent plans, employ expert models, and navigate complex multimodal AI challenges, all while accelerating drug development and approval processes.

- Revolutionizing biotech with GPT-4 and OpenAI's pinnacle against tech giants: Witness how GPT-4 is reshaping drug discovery at Moderna, and learn how OpenAI's triumph over colossal tech giants displays AI's transformative power.

- Artificial general intelligence's (AGI's) future in finance and alignment with human values: Envision a world where AGI becomes a core pillar of the financial ecosystem, exploring thrilling territories such as AGI-driven business intelligence, financial market predictions, and real-time risk management.

As we examine into the intricacies of Moderna's journey to develop a COVID-19 vaccine, we invite you to consider an unconventional comparison. We aim to draw parallels between the development of a groundbreaking drug using mRNA technology and the creation of a successful, big-budget blockbuster movie. This analogy is designed to distill the complex factors leading to a blockbuster product's success into a relatable narrative, illustrating how detailed planning, meticulous execution, and market acceptance play crucial roles in both pharmaceuticals and film.

The blockbuster saga – understanding the success of Moderna's COVID-19 vaccine

In this section, we will draw parallels between Moderna's groundbreaking work in biotechnology and the blockbuster success of James Cameron's *Avatar: The Way of Water*. We aim to simplify the complex world of biotech by likening it to the more familiar realm of filmmaking. By doing so, we will illuminate key principles of innovation, risk, and market dynamics that are crucial for making informed decisions in finance.

Imagine an innovative biotechnology company, Moderna, at the helm of a daring venture: creating an effective and high-efficacy vaccine, harnessing the power of mRNA technology to combat the worldwide COVID-19 pandemic. This was to be Moderna's most significant breakthrough, an accomplishment that would change the course of global health.

Simultaneously, envision a renowned movie studio, led by James Cameron, working on the sequel to a movie that redefined the cinematic experience – *Avatar: The Way of Water*. The film was set to break all previous records, with the largest production budget for a film ever made of $460 million.

The production of both the vaccine and the movie were colossal undertakings, grabbing the attention of respective industry stakeholders and the world at large. Everyone watched anxiously as Moderna underwent clinical trials, as James Cameron and his team worked tirelessly behind the scenes, perfecting the script, visual effects, and the ensemble cast's performance.

In the world of social media, critics and skeptics predicted failure for both ventures due to their high risk and unproven technology or narrative. However, when the Moderna vaccine received FDA approval and *Avatar: The Way of Water* hit the silver screens, the world bore witness to two significant successes.

The vaccine was hailed as a game-changer, with Moderna receiving nearly $2.5 billion for its COVID-19 vaccine development and production, subsequently earning $17.7 billion in 2021, $19.3 billion in 2022, and a projected $5 billion in 2023 from vaccine revenue. Moderna earned $42 billion in COVID-19 vaccine revenue between 2021 and 2023, which is nearly 17 times its development and production costs.

Similarly, *Avatar: The Way of Water*, despite having a huge film budget of $460 million, recouped its production costs and more. It achieved domestic revenue of $684 million and a stunning $1.6 billion internationally, with China being the largest market outside of the US, contributing $245 million. In total, the movie garnered a breathtaking $2.32 billion in worldwide gross revenue, which earned five times its production costs.

Both these instances demonstrate the importance of vision, investment, and innovation in achieving monumental success. The creation of a blockbuster drug, much like the production of a blockbuster movie, requires an intricate balance of creativity and meticulous planning. Each venture represents a significant risk, but with the right ingredients, careful management, and a dash of good fortune, they can result in overwhelming success.

Here are some intriguing parallels between creating a hit movie and a successful vaccine:

- **Research and development (pre-production)**: This is the foundation upon which everything else is built. Without an effective drug or a compelling story, all other efforts are likely to fail.

- **Regulatory approval and censor board clearance**: No matter how promising a drug or film might be, if it doesn't pass these legal hurdles, it won't be able to reach the public.

- **Clinical trials and test screenings**: The feedback from these steps can make or break a product. A drug that shows severe side effects in clinical trials won't make it to market, and a movie that tests poorly might need substantial edits or risk box-office failure.

- **Marketing and promotion**: A high-quality drug or film won't succeed if people aren't aware of it. Marketing and promotion are key to driving awareness and interest.

- **Distribution**: The best product in the world won't succeed if it doesn't reach its intended audience. Effective distribution strategies are key to ensuring that a drug is available in pharmacies, or a movie is screened in theaters or available on streaming platforms.

- **Reception and feedback**: The market's reaction will ultimately decide the fate of a drug or a film. Success hinges on how well the product is received and accepted by its intended audience, be it patients/doctors or movie-goers.

- **Sequels and next-generation treatments**: While not immediately crucial to the success of the initial product, the potential for sequels or next-generation treatments can greatly extend the lifespan and profitability of a successful drug or film.

The next section delves into Moderna's journey, illuminating its unique methodologies, strategic collaborations, and ambitious goals as it continues to pioneer a new paradigm in medicine.

Moderna's mRNA odyssey and the transformation of biomedicine

Moderna, founded in 2010 and headquartered in Cambridge, Massachusetts, has emerged as a leading force in biotechnology with its innovative focus on mRNA-based therapies. Leveraging synthetic mRNA, Moderna instructs patients' cells to produce proteins, laying the groundwork for therapies to prevent, treat, or cure diseases. The rapid validation of Moderna's mRNA technology with its COVID-19 vaccine, authorized in December 2020, has brought global attention to this revolutionary approach.

We want to use focused subsections to break down complex topics into digestible pieces, covering everything from Moderna's pivotal role in the COVID-19 pandemic to its broader applications and innovative strategies. This matters to you because understanding Moderna's approach can offer valuable insights into investment opportunities, risk assessment, and financial reporting in the rapidly evolving biotech sector.

The impact of mRNA-1273 – battling a pandemic

Moderna's mRNA-1273, the company's COVID-19 vaccine, has proven highly effective, becoming a vital tool in combating the global pandemic. As of early 2022, Moderna boasts 44 mRNA development programs, with 25 in clinical trials, spanning therapeutic areas such as infectious disease, oncology, cardiovascular disease, and rare genetic diseases.

Harnessing the power of mRNA – a new medicinal frontier

In addition to their groundbreaking work on COVID-19, Moderna's research focuses on five therapeutic areas: infectious diseases, immuno-oncology, rare diseases, cardiovascular diseases, and autoimmune diseases. The company has developed seven distinct modalities or categories of potential mRNA medicines with shared features, encompassing applications from infectious disease vaccines to inhaled pulmonary therapeutics.

Applications across medical domains

Moderna's active clinic programs extend to areas such as oncology, where they are pioneering mRNA-based personalized cancer vaccines and intratumoral immuno-oncology therapies. In cardiovascular disease, efforts are directed toward treating heart failure and myocardial infarction. For rare genetic disorders, Moderna is developing treatments for conditions such as **methylmalonic acidemia** (**MMA**).

Redefining vaccine development

Diverging from traditional, complex vaccine development, Moderna's methodology leverages mRNA to instruct patients' cells in protein synthesis, activating the immune system against illness. This innovative approach has enabled rapid vaccine development and the pursuit of previously non-addressable targets.

A new paradigm for pharmaceutical innovation

The focus on mRNA and personalized vaccines has differentiated Moderna within the pharmaceutical landscape. Their mRNA vaccines, producible through a unified "plug-and-play" platform and manufacturable at a single facility, have ushered in an era of unprecedented versatility, streamlined research, large-scale production, and rapid response to emergent threats. This novel approach to vaccine development sets Moderna apart by enhancing speed, flexibility, and efficiency.

Strategic partnerships and collaborations

Key to Moderna's success are strategic collaborations with other organizations and companies within the biotech ecosystem. Partnerships with industry giants such as AstraZeneca, Merck, Vertex, and CytomX, and government organizations such as BARDA and DARPA, have fostered an environment that propels the development of mRNA medicines.

Moderna's journey with mRNA-based therapies represents nothing short of a revolution. From its instrumental role in the battle against COVID-19 to its development of groundbreaking treatments across various medical domains, Moderna's innovation is reshaping the future of medicine. Its robust pipeline, novel technological approach, and strategic partnerships underscore the transformative potential of mRNA technology. Truly, Moderna's odyssey through the realm of mRNA is a resounding symphony in the world of biomedicine, infusing hope and offering new pathways to healing.

This upcoming section provides a SWOT analysis of Moderna's strengths, weaknesses, opportunities, and threats, offering a comprehensive view of Moderna's position in the industry, its unique capabilities, and the challenges and prospects that lie ahead.

SWOT analysis of Moderna's strategic landscape

In this section, we'll break down Moderna's strengths, weaknesses, opportunities, and threats into focused subsections. Our learning objective is to give you a comprehensive view of how Moderna leverages innovative technologies such as mRNA, AI, and quantum computing, and what challenges and opportunities these present. This is important for you as it offers a multifaceted understanding of Moderna's business model, which you can leverage for investment decisions, risk assessments, and strategic financial reporting in the ever-changing landscape of biotechnology and AI. Understanding these details is crucial for making well-informed choices in a complex industry.

These are the strengths of Moderna:

- **mRNA technology**: The innovative mRNA technology platform allows rapid vaccine development

- **Scale and speed**: Shown by the swift response to COVID-19

- **Strong pipeline**: Robust potential treatments in development across various diseases

- **Financial stability**: Boosted by COVID-19 vaccine success

- **Partnerships with technology leaders**: Collaboration with IBM for quantum computing and AI enhances drug discovery, optimizes mRNA medicines, and promotes workforce development

- **AI literacy and adoption**: A partnership with **Carnegie Mellon University (CMU)** to create the AI Academy fostered broad-based AI literacy, upskilling, process optimization, and future-proofing the business

These are the weaknesses of Moderna:

- **Reliance on mRNA-1273**: Heavy dependence on the COVID-19 vaccine; needs revenue diversification

- **Market perception**: Challenges around public perception and trust

- **Regulatory challenges**: Potential hurdles with new mRNA technology

- **Complex integration of AI and quantum computing**: As groundbreaking as these technologies are, their integration into existing processes could be complex and may require significant investment in training, adaptation, and compliance

- **Potential ethical concerns with AI**: Although addressed in training, the ethics of using AI in drug discovery and development could still raise questions and concerns that Moderna must be prepared to navigate

The following opportunities can be seen as extensions of Moderna's strengths, driving the company's positioning as a leader in technology-driven breakthroughs in biotechnology:

- **Advanced drug discovery**: Quantum computing and AI could significantly expedite and optimize drug discovery

- **Enhanced understanding and optimization of mRNA medicines**: Predicting molecular properties for improved safety and performance

- **Workforce development**: Investment in a quantum-ready workforce and AI literacy will make Moderna an early adopter and attractive employer

- **Access to cutting-edge technology**: Partnership with IBM for quantum technologies provides critical advantages

Here are some potential threats or challenges that Moderna should keep in mind:

- **Technology dependence**: Heavy reliance on third-party technologies (IBM's quantum computing, AI models, and so on) could make Moderna vulnerable to changes in those technologies or partnerships

- **Ethical scrutiny**: With AI and quantum computing entering uncharted territories in drug discovery, Moderna may face ethical scrutiny and regulatory challenges specific to these technologies

In summary, the integration of AI and quantum computing in Moderna's operations provides a multifaceted enhancement to the company's strengths and opportunities. However, it also introduces complexities that must be managed to prevent them from becoming weaknesses or threats. The balance between these elements will be key to Moderna's continued success in leveraging these innovative technologies for innovation and growth in the biotechnology space.

This next section provides a glimpse of the technology and medicine that Moderna has embraced with the capabilities of AI and quantum computing. This section delves into how these technologies are shaping Moderna's approach to drug discovery, clinical trials, post-marketing surveillance, supply chain efficiency, and more.

The integration of AI and quantum computing in Moderna's therapeutic landscape

In this section, we'll delve into the transformative role of AI and quantum computing in Moderna's therapeutic landscape. You'll learn how these cutting-edge technologies impact everything from drug discovery and clinical trials to supply chain management.

The learning objective is to equip you with an in-depth understanding of how Moderna integrates technology into its operations. This knowledge is crucial for anyone interested in investment and trading opportunities within the rapidly evolving fields of biotechnology and AI.

In the next subsection, we'll focus on the critical role of AI in Moderna's drug discovery process. We'll explore how AI technologies such as predictive modeling and algorithmic analysis are leveraged to identify potential mRNA targets, optimize molecular structures, and even predict interactions in combination therapies.

AI in Moderna's drug discovery process

As you dive into this subsection, keep in mind that identifying the right mRNA sequences is the cornerstone of effective drug development. Here, we'll uncover how Moderna utilizes AI to revolutionize this crucial first step:

- **Harnessing AI for mRNA target identification**

  Example: AI algorithms can analyze genomic data to identify specific RNA sequences that are potential drug targets for various diseases. For Moderna, this process could be used to discover novel mRNA-based therapies for conditions such as cancer, auto-immune diseases, or viral infections.

- **Using AI to optimize mRNA structure and lipid nanoparticles**

  Example: AI's predictive modeling can help Moderna's researchers tailor the structure of mRNA molecules and the lipid nanoparticles that carry them. This could lead to improved stability, delivery, and efficacy of mRNA vaccines and therapies.

- **Predicting drug interactions with combination therapies**

  Example: AI could assist Moderna in designing combination therapies where mRNA vaccines are used alongside traditional pharmaceuticals. This may enhance the effectiveness of treatments for complex conditions such as HIV or hepatitis.

AI in Moderna's clinical trials

It's important to note that the speed and efficiency of clinical trials can be game-changers in drug development. In this subsection, we'll explore how Moderna is leveraging AI to make its clinical trials more adaptive and responsive:

1. **Adaptive clinical trial design**

   Example: Moderna could employ AI to create adaptive clinical trial designs, similar to what was used during the COVID-19 vaccine trials. This would allow for real-time adjustments in the trials based on interim data, potentially accelerating the development and approval process.

2. **Patient recruitment and monitoring**

   Example: AI-powered algorithms could help Moderna identify and recruit suitable patients for clinical trials. Once enrolled, AI monitoring could provide continuous assessment, improving safety and outcomes.

AI in Moderna's pharmacovigilance and post-marketing surveillance

As you read on, consider that the journey of a drug doesn't end when it hits the market. Here, we'll delve into how Moderna uses AI to ensure ongoing safety and efficacy through pharmacovigilance and post-marketing surveillance:

1. **Monitoring adverse effects**

   Example: AI systems could be deployed to monitor patient reactions to new drugs in real time, helping Moderna rapidly identify and respond to adverse effects, aligning with regulatory requirements and patient safety. For example, Moderna is collaborating with IBM to explore technologies, including AI, blockchain, and hybrid cloud, which could help support smarter COVID-19 vaccine management.

2. **Long-term efficacy analysis**

   Example: Utilizing AI in long-term studies could allow Moderna to gauge the continued effectiveness of its therapies, a crucial aspect in supporting their continued use and potential repurposing. For example, a study found that the efficacy of Moderna's COVID-19 vaccine peaked at 94% after 120 days.

AI in Moderna's supply chain and manufacturing efficiency

As we transition from development to distribution, let's explore how Moderna leverages AI to streamline its supply chain and optimize manufacturing. This section will show you the backend processes that ensure medicines are effectively produced and delivered:

1. **Predictive maintenance**

    Example: AI could forecast when equipment in manufacturing facilities might fail, allowing for timely maintenance, thus ensuring continuous production and meeting demand. For example, McKinsey & Company has identified predictive maintenance as one of the most valuable ways to enhance a business's maintenance-service organization and create value from analytics-based technologies.

2. **Demand forecasting**

    Example: AI algorithms could predict global demand for specific drugs, helping Moderna to optimize its supply chain and reduce costs. For example, Moderna has raised its sales forecast for its COVID-19 vaccine several times based on contracts already in place and anticipated demand.

AI in Moderna's drug development strategy

In this section, we'll delve into the strategic advantages AI affords Moderna in extending and diversifying its drug portfolio. From reviving expiring patents to addressing underserved health areas, you'll see how AI can be a game-changer in pharmaceutical strategy:

1. **Biosimilars and drug repurposing**

    Example: As patents on existing biological drugs expire, Moderna could use AI to design biosimilars, extending the life cycle of successful therapies. AI could also identify new applications for existing mRNA therapies, allowing Moderna to expand its product line without starting from scratch.

2. **Addressing neglected diseases**

    Example: Moderna could leverage AI to explore treatments for diseases often overlooked due to lack of profitability, such as tropical diseases. This aligns with Moderna's commitment to global health and could open up new markets and partnerships.

Integration with quantum computing

As we pivot to explore the fascinating intersection of quantum computing and AI, you'll learn why this technology is pivotal for Moderna's long-term innovation and investment potential. Quantum computing offers unprecedented computational capabilities, making it a key enabler for more advanced AI-driven drug discovery and design:

1. **Quantum-assisted molecular simulations**

    Example: In collaboration with IBM, Moderna could utilize quantum computing for rapid and accurate molecular simulations. This would provide deeper insights into how mRNA molecules interact with cellular machinery, guiding the design of more effective therapies.

The next section uncovers how Moderna has embraced AI as more than a tool but as the visionary artist and strategist behind their groundbreaking approach to medicine. From leveraging AI in the creation of novel mRNA constructs to utilizing generative AI with quantum computing, Moderna's digital infusion has reshaped the very fabric of pharmaceutical exploration and medical care.

The future reimagined – Moderna's AI-driven symphony in medicine and biotechnology

In this section, we'll delve into Moderna's pioneering role in leveraging AI for transformative advancements in biotechnology. You'll learn how Moderna seamlessly integrates AI into its business model, from drug discovery to manufacturing, and how it's redefining the healthcare landscape. The purpose of this section is to provide investors and technologists with a comprehensive understanding of how AI serves as more than just a tool; it's a creative force driving Moderna's innovative strategies. This exploration offers valuable insights into the investment opportunities and prospects in the rapidly evolving intersection of AI and healthcare.

AI is not merely an enhancement to the field of medicine and drug discovery; it's an unfolding revolution – a harmonious blend of precision, insight, creativity, empathy, and agility. AI's role extends beyond challenging patents or merely supplementing human intellect; it magnifies our ability to heal, innovate, and reach the previously unreachable realms of healthcare.

In an era dominated by data and a constant craving for innovation, AI stands as the catalytic force, a maestro conducting a symphony of pharmaceutical enlightenment. It transcends being just a game-changer; it's defining the new game altogether. Welcome to the future of medicine, where AI morphs into the visionary artist, the strategist, the healer, and the herald of unexplored vistas.

In the upcoming subsections, we'll delve into Moderna's symbiotic relationship with cutting-edge technologies such as AI and quantum computing. You'll discover how strategic collaborations with tech giants such as IBM serve as catalysts for innovation in mRNA medicine. We'll also examine the robust digital infrastructure that empowers Moderna to redefine traditional approaches to drug development. Finally, we'll reveal how these technological synergies extend beyond the lab, shaping Moderna's organizational culture and long-term strategic planning.

Moderna – orchestrating the AI symphony in biotechnology

Moderna, since its inception in 2010, has embodied this symphonic embrace of technology. Born in the **Amazon Web Services** (**AWS**) cloud, it crafted its entire drug discovery and manufacturing process around digitalization, seamlessly infused by AI.

Moderna's business model, primarily fueled by product sales, grants, and collaboration agreements, has harnessed its *AI factory* to redefine the way diseases are combated. It has employed Generative AI, which describes algorithms capable of crafting new content from trained data, to propel its groundbreaking mRNA technology.

The collaboration with IBM – a milestone in innovation

In April 2023, a remarkable alliance between Moderna and IBM was forged, aiming to harness Generative AI and quantum computing to further advance mRNA technology. This agreement facilitated Moderna's access to IBM's advanced quantum computing systems and generative AI models. The collaboration's objective was to unravel "the characteristics of potential mRNA medicines," paving the way for a new era of vaccines and therapies.

Digital infrastructure – a backbone of innovation

Moderna's platform thrives on its robust digital infrastructure, which marries workflow automation, data capture, and AI to quicken processes and furnish insights to its researchers. Unique to Moderna's approach is the parallelization of drug development stages, usually pursued sequentially, thus redefining efficiency.

A testament to Moderna's innovative spirit is its self-crafted drug design studio, hosted on AWS Fargate. This web-based application enables scientists to create novel mRNA constructs, optimize them using AI algorithms, and then forward them to their high-throughput preclinical scale production line. Thousands of unique mRNA constructs, including the renowned COVID-19 vaccine, stand as evidence of this groundbreaking approach.

Moderna's exploration of AI in medicine is akin to a well-orchestrated concerto, where various technological components play in unison to compose a melody of innovation. This AI-driven journey, marked by significant milestones and strategic collaborations, paints a vivid picture of the future. It highlights a world where technology isn't merely a tool but an artist weaving the tapestry of modern medicine, providing glimpses of what the future could hold. It's more than a strategy; it's a philosophy, embodying a novel perspective on investing in a domain where biology and technology merge as the frontiers of human advancement.

The synergies between Moderna's partnerships with IBM and CMU extend beyond mere technological enhancement. The next section reveals a comprehensive approach that aligns technological innovation with organizational culture, workforce development, and long-term strategy.

In this section, we've explored the integration of AI and quantum computing in Moderna's operations, spanning from drug discovery to manufacturing. We examined how these technologies not only accelerate research but also offer strategic advantages, including adaptive clinical trial designs and optimized supply chain management. Understanding these synergies is crucial for investors and technologists looking at opportunities in the dynamic intersection of biotech, AI, and finance. This deep dive provided a holistic view of how Moderna is not just using technology as a tool but integrating it into the very fabric of its innovative approach to medicine.

A new chapter – the Moderna-IBM partnership

In this section, we will unpack the groundbreaking partnership between Moderna and IBM, a fusion of quantum computing and AI that's reshaping healthcare. You'll learn how quantum tech speeds up drug discovery, while AI fine-tunes mRNA medicines. While the Moderna-IBM partnership may initially seem unrelated to ChatGPT, finance, and Power BI, the underlying technologies – quantum computing and AI – offer key takeaways. By understanding this partnership, you can better appreciate the transformative potential of these technologies in diverse fields, including finance and data analytics. By the end, you'll grasp why this alliance is a game-changer in medical innovation and how it sets new benchmarks for the industry.

This collaboration exemplifies another milestone in Moderna's pursuit of excellence. It presents a fusion of intelligence and innovation, where quantum computing and AI converge to pave the way for groundbreaking discoveries. The synergy between Moderna and IBM sets the stage for an exciting future, one where the potential to redefine medicine and accelerate the delivery of life-changing treatments to patients is not just a vision but a tangible reality.

In the upcoming subsection, we'll explore *advanced drug discovery*, detailing how quantum computing and AI are expediting the drug development process. Next, we'll delve into the *optimization of mRNA medicines*, showing how predictive models can fine-tune the effectiveness and safety of treatments. We'll also cover *workforce development* and *access to cutting-edge technology*, emphasizing the strategic benefits of investing in a quantum-ready workforce and technology alliances. Understanding these elements is crucial as they demonstrate the real-world applications of advanced technologies, offering actionable insights that can be applied to financial analysis, predictive modeling in Power BI, and understanding the generative capabilities of AI, such as ChatGPT.

IBM partnership – quantum computing and AI

Let's dive into a multifaceted exploration of how Moderna is leveraging advanced technologies and partnerships to redefine the healthcare landscape. From the accelerated pace of drug discovery through quantum computing and AI, to workforce development and strategic collaborations, this subsection offers a panoramic view of the innovations shaping not just medicine, but the future of biotechnology itself:

1. **Advanced drug discovery**:

   - **Quantum computing**: By harnessing IBM's quantum computing capabilities, Moderna can perform complex molecular simulations, a previously time-consuming task, at a rapid pace. This may accelerate the transition from identifying drug targets to testing viable candidates.

   - **AI integration**: With IBM's AI, particularly generative models for therapeutics, Moderna has an opportunity to delve deeper into understanding how molecules behave and even create entirely new ones.

2. **Optimization of mRNA medicines**:

   - **Predictive modeling**: Using AI foundation models such as MoLFormer, Moderna can make precise predictions about molecules' properties. This will inform the development of lipid nanoparticles and mRNA, improving safety and effectiveness.

3. **Workforce development**:

   - **Quantum-ready workforce**: By investing in building a quantum-ready workforce, Moderna ensures that it is prepared to leverage this emerging technology, positioning itself as an early adopter in the biotech industry

4. **Access to cutting-edge technology**:

   - **IBM quantum network**: Participation in this network grants Moderna access to the forefront of quantum technologies, providing a competitive edge in the exploration of innovative life sciences applications

5. **Synthesis with mRNA technology**:

   - **Complementary strength**: The strengths of quantum computing and AI align seamlessly with Moderna's cornerstone of mRNA technology. The integration enhances the company's existing strengths and opens up novel opportunities in therapeutics.

The next section highlights another partnership between Moderna and CMU to create an immersive learning experience for its employees. We will explore the AI Academy's inception, purpose, curriculum, and potential to transform the way mRNA medicines are brought to patients.

Moderna's AI Academy – a partnership with CMU for technological innovation

Let's dive into the revolutionary alliance between Moderna and Carnegie Mellon University, a partnership that seamlessly translates theoretical AI into practical, groundbreaking applications while serving as an inspirational blueprint for those wanting to learn more about how to integrate ChatGPT into finance use cases. This section illustrates how an educated, AI-literate workforce can not only accelerate areas such as drug discovery but also redefine the boundaries for fields such as finance and data visualization. If you've been hesitant to invest in emerging technologies, consider this your call to action. By adopting a calculated, educational approach to AI, you're not merely staying ahead of technological trends – you're reshaping them. Envision a future where you too can embed AI and machine learning into the very fabric of your organization's DNA.

Moderna has launched the **AI Academy** in partnership with **CMU**. The AI Academy is an innovative initiative that will bring to life an immersive learning experience for Moderna employees. The goal of the AI Academy is to educate and empower employees at all levels to identify and integrate AI and machine learning solutions into every Moderna system and process to bring mRNA medicines to patients.

Get ready to embark on a journey through Moderna's strategic approach to AI adoption and workforce transformation. In the following subsections, you'll learn how the biotech giant is not only cultivating a culture rich in AI literacy but also leveraging AI's transformative power to enhance drug discovery and optimize operations. More than just tools, these advanced technologies become an integral part of Moderna's business fabric, setting the stage for ethical and impactful AI use.

Moderna's AI Academy in partnership with CMU

Let's explore everything from building a digitally literate workforce to leveraging AI for groundbreaking advancements in drug discovery. You'll also discover how Moderna is future-proofing its workforce while adhering to a strong ethical framework. It's a masterclass on how to seamlessly integrate technology into an organization:

1. **Broad-based AI literacy**:

   - **Building AI culture**: This initiative will help infuse AI literacy across Moderna's workforce. It aligns with the company's collaboration with IBM as both require a foundation of understanding AI's potential applications.

2. **Enhanced drug discovery and process optimization**:

   - **Applying AI across functions**: From drug discovery to automating tasks and optimizing resource use, this educational partnership helps Moderna leverage AI throughout the organization

3. **Workforce upskilling and futureproofing**:

    - **Investment in employees**: By providing top-notch learning opportunities, Moderna strengthens employee retention and prepares its workforce for a future where digital technologies are central

    - **Alignment with ethics**: Including AI ethics ensures responsible AI use, aligning with Moderna's commitment to integrity and social responsibility

This key partnership enables Moderna to create a roadmap for the future where advanced technologies such as AI are not just tools but integrated components of the business model. They align with Moderna's mission, enhance its strengths, mitigate some of its weaknesses, and position the company at the forefront of technology-driven breakthroughs in the biotechnology and pharmaceutical sectors.

The next section delves into Moderna's endeavors to create a future where pandemics may no longer instill fear, exploring their work in crafting multi-valent vaccines, rapid response plans, broad-spectrum antiviral drugs, and collaborations with global health authorities.

Confronting future pandemics – Moderna's innovation in multi-valent vaccines and AI-driven antivirals

In this section, you'll unravel how the convergence of mRNA technology and AI is breaking the mold in multi-valent vaccines and antiviral drugs. Equally riveting is how Moderna's AI-augmented strategies are relevant to those interested in using ChatGPT for finance and Power BI applications. Just as Moderna is synthesizing vast genetic datasets to predict optimal mRNA sequences, imagine using similar AI-powered methods to decode financial markets or create dynamic Power BI visualizations. We're peeling back the curtain on a future where AI is the linchpin of both medical innovation and financial analytics.

Moderna, a pioneering force in the biotechnology space, is transforming the landscape of vaccine development by integrating AI and computational biology. They are working to create not just vaccines for specific diseases but revolutionary broad-spectrum solutions that could counter multiple threats.

Moderna is investigating a potential vaccine that can put the five needed mRNAs in one lipid nanoparticle to make a vaccine that targets all subunits. Other combinations can also be created in mRNA vaccines. For example, a multi-valent vaccine can attack multiple strains of the same disease or even different diseases:

1. **mRNA technology and AI collaboration**: Moderna is exploring the fascinating concept of crafting a vaccine that houses multiple mRNAs within one lipid nanoparticle. This *multi-valent* vaccine could target multiple strains of the same disease or even different diseases simultaneously. Utilizing AI algorithms, they analyze vast datasets of viral genetic information to predict optimal mRNA sequences.

2. **Rapid response plans**: In the face of an emerging health crisis, time is of the essence. Moderna's investment in AI accelerates the design phase, allowing it to create, test, and iterate on vaccine prototypes with unprecedented speed. During the COVID-19 pandemic, this technology allowed Moderna to reach the clinical trial stage within a matter of months – a remarkable achievement.

3. **Prevention strategies**: AI plays an instrumental role in Moderna's global surveillance systems for monitoring viral mutations and emerging threats. Predictive analytics tools offer foresight, enabling Moderna to pre-emptively develop vaccines or modify existing ones by following evolving viral landscapes.

4. **Broad-spectrum antiviral drugs**: Beyond vaccines, Moderna is probing into the exciting realm of broad-spectrum antiviral drugs that could treat a variety of infections. They are harnessing machine learning algorithms to identify common molecular targets across different viruses, aiming to design drugs that could be akin to a universal defense mechanism against various viral diseases.

5. **Collaboration with global health authorities**: Moderna's commitment to leveraging AI isn't confined to laboratories. They work closely with global health authorities, sharing insights and collaborating on global strategies to ensure that these innovations benefit populations around the world.

By synthesizing the precise genetic engineering of mRNA with the predictive capabilities of AI, Moderna is forging a future where the term *pandemic* might lose its terror. The marriage of these technologies opens unprecedented avenues in the fight against infectious diseases, offering hope that humanity may be better prepared for the unforeseen challenges of tomorrow.

Moderna, a key player in the global health sphere, is leveraging its trailblazing mRNA technology to advance cancer treatment. With a strategy that extends from early detection to personalized vaccines, the company aims to reshape oncology, promising a future where cancer can be tackled at its root. The next section delves into the visionary approach and groundbreaking work that put Moderna at the forefront of a potential revolution in cancer care.

Revolutionizing cancer care – Moderna's mRNA ambitions in oncology

Moderna CEO, Stéphane Bancel, has unveiled an ambitious vision for the company's future in oncology, using mRNA technology to create personalized cancer vaccines. Recent mid-stage studies in skin cancer have shown promising results, and partnerships with leading companies such as Illumina's Grail, Exact Sciences, and Freenome are fueling this mission with innovative diagnostic tools such as liquid biopsies.

Bancel's plan integrates liquid biopsies into routine physical check-ups, enabling early cancer detection and the development of custom vaccines to eradicate cancer at its inception. While acknowledging the need for further research and validation, Bancel is confident that Moderna's financial backing can fuel a revolutionary change in cancer treatment, on par with or even surpassing recent breakthroughs like checkpoint inhibitors.

The global oncology market, valued at over $203.42 billion in 2022 and expected to reach $470.61 billion by 2032, offers significant opportunities for Moderna's pioneering work. According to articles in reputable journals such as Nature, the average global pipeline asset peak sales in oncology are projected to be substantial. Moderna's current development pipeline includes several mRNA therapeutics and vaccines for oncology, rare liver diseases, and more. Their personalized cancer vaccine is in phase 2 trials, and multiple rare disease programs are advancing, reflecting Moderna's strong positioning in these promising markets.

Moderna is leading the way in harnessing the power of mRNA technology to forge innovative solutions in medicine. From personalized cancer vaccines to global delivery networks, the company is exploring groundbreaking territories in genetic editing, AI-driven drug discovery, regenerative medicine, and rare disease therapies. The next section explores the vast potential and challenges of these initiatives, painting an exciting picture of a future where medicine transcends traditional boundaries.

The brave new world of medicine – Moderna's pioneering path to personalized therapies

Unlock the doors to the medical future you've only dreamed of in this captivating section on Moderna's daring journey into personalized therapies. From custom-built cancer vaccines to awe-inspiring gene editing breakthroughs, this is your gateway to understanding how Moderna is revolutionizing medicine and why you can't afford to miss out on these transformative insights:

1. **Personalized cancer vaccines**: Imagine a world where cancer treatment is a precise, personalized weapon. Moderna's ability to sequence a patient's cancer genome could enable custom vaccines to train the immune system against individual cancer cells. Despite considerable challenges, this path represents a transformative leap toward conquering cancer.

2. **Gene editing therapies**: Science fiction no longer, Moderna's expertise in mRNA technology may lead to breakthroughs in gene editing, including the utilization of CRISPR-Cas9. The possibilities are extraordinary, from correcting rare genetic disorders to navigating complex ethical landscapes. Moderna's role could be pivotal in shaping this brave new world of genetic medicine.

3. **Collaboration with tech companies for AI-driven drug discovery**: By joining forces with tech giants such as Google DeepMind, Microsoft's Project Hanover, NVIDIA, and Palantir, Moderna could usher in a new era of precision medicine. These collaborations could accelerate drug discovery and propel Moderna's ambitions in personalized oncology.

4. **Regenerative medicine**: Moderna's exploration into regenerative medicine could stimulate the body's natural repair mechanisms. While the challenges are immense, the rewards – such as regenerating heart tissue or restoring spinal cord functions – are unprecedented.

5. **Rare disease therapies**: For those with rare genetic diseases, Moderna's focus on targeted mRNA therapies offers transformative hope, paving the way for treatments that could change lives.

6. **Creating a global mRNA therapy delivery network**: Moderna's potential creation of a global delivery network ensures that groundbreaking mRNA therapies reach even the most remote regions. This initiative bridges gaps and delivers hope on an international scale.

Moderna's consideration of outsourcing the production of mRNA therapeutics and vaccines to **contract manufacturing organizations** (**CMOs**) represents a significant strategic shift. Focusing on its core strengths, such as innovation and drug discovery, and partnering with specialized CMOs could offer numerous benefits, including cost savings, scalability, and agility. While this approach brings potential risks, a well-crafted strategy emphasizing quality assurance, ethical considerations, and alignment with Moderna's overall goals could usher in a new era of pharmaceutical development.

Moderna's strategic move toward outsourcing pharma manufacturing

Explore Moderna's daring strategy to outsource pharma manufacturing, a pivotal move with the potential to dramatically lower production costs and boost revenue – factors that could directly influence their stock price. This section offers a deep dive into how Moderna aims to blend innovation and scalability, ensuring that breakthrough drugs are not just created, but are also distributed cost-effectively and safely:

1. The rationale for outsourcing

   Moderna's potential to outsource drug manufacturing mirrors a broader trend in the pharmaceutical sector. Key benefits could include the following:

   - **Focus on core strengths**: Concentrating on mRNA therapeutic and vaccine design, Moderna can entrust manufacturing to experts

   - **Scalability**: Partnering with established contract-manufacturing-organizations (CMOs) facilitates scalable production without heavy capital investment

   - **Global reach**: This strategy can enhance distribution efficiency and alignment with regional regulations

2. Selecting the right partners

   Success hinges on careful partner selection, focusing on the following aspects:

   - **Quality assurance**: Moderna's commitment to quality demands rigorous agreements and oversight with CMOs

   - **Technology compatibility**: Choosing CMOs with mRNA experience is vital

   - **Ethical considerations**: Adherence to ethical labor and environmental standards reflects Moderna's values

3. Implications and risks

Outsourcing benefits must be balanced against risks:

- **Cost savings**: Reduced manufacturing capital expenses can boost R&D funding
- **Agility in innovation**: A focus on drug discovery and FDA approval can enhance responsiveness
- **Potential risks**: Strategic risk management is essential to navigate potential supply chain disruptions or quality issues

4. Aligning with Moderna's overall strategy

Outsourcing can be pivotal in the following areas:

- **Accelerating drug pipelines**: Rapidly bringing innovative drugs to market
- **Global expansion**: Enhancing Moderna's global footprint
- **Strategic collaborations**: Driving innovation and growth in new areas

Outsourcing could underscore Moderna's role as an innovator in therapeutic development. By aligning with quality partners, ethical principles, and strategic business goals, the benefits could be vast. However, careful management is crucial to ensure this model supports Moderna's mission and values. In redefining its manufacturing strategy, Moderna stands to emphasize its commitment to innovative therapy rather than traditional pharmaceutical production, potentially propelling the company to new heights.

In an era where technology and biology converge to shape the future of medicine, investment strategies must evolve to keep pace with this dynamic landscape. Enter Moderna Momentum – a groundbreaking investment philosophy designed for the biotech sphere, where science, finance, and innovation intertwine. It's more than just a method; it's a harmonious approach tailored to the unique rhythm of the biotech sector. In the following section, we will dive into the key components that make Moderna Momentum a visionary pathway for investors seeking to navigate the complex world of Moderna's stock.

Moderna Momentum – a data-driven, sentiment-sensitive strategy for an mRNA masterstroke

Let's review Moderna Momentum a groundbreaking investment strategy that brings together cutting-edge finance, data analytics, and biotechnology. In this section, you'll master a strategy uniquely tailored to navigating the dynamic landscape of Moderna – a biotech juggernaut at the forefront of mRNA therapies. Uncover the intricacies of converting dense scientific milestones into smart investment moves, decode the secrets behind the company's financial health using Power BI visualizations, and learn how to harness AI sentiment analysis tools such as ChatGPT for a truly holistic investment strategy.

Why is this a must-read? It's a vibrant narrative that transcends traditional investing. This strategy resonates with anyone who sees Moderna not merely as a stock but as a focal point of scientific ingenuity and human aspiration. With this blueprint, you'll be equipped to make investment decisions that are not only data-driven but also sentiment-sensitive, giving you the competitive edge, you need in today's volatile biotech sector.

Why choose Moderna Momentum? Moderna Momentum represents a novel investment strategy. It orchestrates a blend of quantitative rigor and qualitative insights, attuned to the specific cadence of the biotech sector. This multifaceted approach embodies the intricate nature of biotech investing:

- **Translating science**: It interprets complex scientific milestones, converting them into calculated investment decisions

- **Deciphering finance**: It unravels earnings and expenditure, portraying an accurate snapshot of Moderna's fiscal well-being

- **Harnessing innovation**: Utilizing AI-driven sentiment analysis, it offers a state-of-the-art tool to measure the market's pulse

- **Adopting a holistic perspective**: Moderna is seen not merely as a stock but as a vibrant narrative of science, creativity, and human endeavor

The Moderna Momentum strategy is intended for the discerning investor, unafraid to explore the multifarious terrain of biotech. It resonates with those who perceive beyond mere figures, recognizing the promise, potential, and vibrancy of a company poised to transform modern medicine.

This pioneering strategy combines both quantitative and qualitative metrics to craft an all-encompassing investment lens for Moderna's stock, emphasizing the company's role in the vital mRNA therapeutic and vaccine domain. Key aspects include the following:

- **Analyzing financial indicators**: By dissecting essential signals such as clinical trial outcomes, regulatory verdicts, earnings reports, and R&D spending, it differentiates between buy and sell cues

- **Incorporating sentiment analysis**: Utilizing advanced AI such as GPT-4, it assesses market sentiment toward Moderna, translating positive or negative vibes into actionable buy or sell signals

By synthesizing these elements, Moderna Momentum offers an insightful method to traverse Moderna's stock trajectory. Crafted to be anticipatory, adaptable, and attuned to both market fluctuations and internal dynamics, it equips investors with critical insights to refine their investment strategies.

The uniqueness of the Moderna Momentum strategy lies in its integrated approach. Eschewing the traditional focus on financial parameters alone, it melds fiscal performance, regulatory variables, and sentiment analysis into a singular, actionable blueprint. This avant-garde strategy is tailored for those investors eager to harness contemporary tools to maintain a competitive edge in the ever-shifting investment terrain, particularly within the vibrant biotech sector.

Here's an in-depth look at the pillars of this strategy:

- **Clinical trial results (standalone trade signal):**

  - **Buy**: Positive phase II/III results indicate scientific validation, a big step toward market access

  - **Sell**: Failure in critical stages of trials spells potential doom for a product, and by extension, investment

- **FDA regulatory announcements (standalone trade signal):**

  - **Buy**: Approvals mean market entry and revenue potential, a clear win for investors

  - **Sell**: Rejections or safety concerns signal roadblocks, often reflecting in stock price plummeting

- **Earnings reports (combined with sentiment signal to implement trade):**

  - **Buy**: Revenue growth outpacing expectations shows commercial strength, justifying optimism

  - **Sell**: Falling short is a warning sign of potential underlying issues

- **R&D expenditure (combined with sentiment signal to implement trade):**

  - **Buy**: Consistent or slightly increasing R&D spend (>=10% YoY) reveals a healthy investment in future innovations, seeding tomorrow's successes

  - **Sell**: A sudden drastic increase (>20% YoY) might flag financial instability or desperation to innovate, posing risks to investors

---

Why is R&D significant?

R&D is the lifeblood of a biotech company. Too little spending can indicate a lack of innovation; too much can signify financial imprudence. A balanced growth in R&D reflects a company's commitment to the future without losing sight of present stability.

- **Sentiment analysis (combined with either the earnings signal or R&D spend signal to implement trade):**

  - **Buy**: Persistent positive sentiment is a public vote of confidence, often translating into buying momentum

  - **Sell**: Sustained negative sentiment can indicate underlying market skepticism or potential forthcoming downturns

---

The role of AI

By leveraging AI tools such as GPT-4, sentiment analysis turns nebulous public opinion into tangible investment insights, capturing the mood of the market in real time.

- **Clinical trial results (standalone trade signal)**:

  - **Buy**: Positive phase II/III results or successful completion of a trial, leading to potential regulatory review.

  - **Sell**: Failure in phase II/III trials

  - **Source**: `Clinicaltrials.gov`

Now, we'll take you on a hands-on journey in implementing the Moderna Momentum investment strategy, breaking down its multiple facets into easy-to-follow steps with help from ChatGPT as our guide. You'll start by setting up your Python environment, obtain clinical trial data through APIs, and segueing into crafting trading signals based on FDA announcements and earnings reports. To enhance the strategy, we incorporate sentiment analysis using cutting-edge AI tools and refine the trade calls with real-time R&D spending data:

1. First, let's install the required packages:

    ```
    pip install requests pandas schedule
    ```

2. Run the following Python code:

    ```python
    import requests
    import xml.etree.ElementTree as ET
    import pandas as pd
    import schedule
    import time


    # Function to fetch clinical trials data
    def fetch_clinical_trials_data():
        # Create URL
        url = "https://clinicaltrials.gov/api/query/study_fields?
    expr=Moderna&fields=NCTId,BriefTitle,Condition,StatusVerified
    Date&min_rnk=1&max_rnk=&fmt=xml"

        # Send GET request
        response = requests.get(url)

        # If the request was unsuccessful, return
        if response.status_code != 200:
            print("Failed to get data")
            return

        # Parse XML response
        root = ET.fromstring(response.content)
    ```

```
        # Create DataFrame to store study data
        df = pd.DataFrame(columns=['NCTId', 'BriefTitle',
'Condition', 'StatusVerifiedDate'])


        # Iterate over studies and add selected fields to DataFrame
        for study in root.findall(".//Study"):  # Updated to find
Study tags under any parent tag
            nct_id = study.find('NCTId').text if study.find('NCTId')
is not None else None
            brief_title = study.find('BriefTitle').text if study.
find('BriefTitle') is not None else None
            condition = study.find('Condition').text if study.
find('Condition') is not None else None
            status_verified_date = study.find('StatusVerifiedDate').
text if study.find('StatusVerifiedDate') is not None else None


            df = df.append({'NCTId': nct_id, 'BriefTitle': brief_
title, 'Condition': condition, 'StatusVerifiedDate': status_
verified_date}, ignore_index=True)

    # Write DataFrame to CSV file
    if not df.empty:
        df.to_csv('clinical_trials_data.csv', index=False)
    else:
        print("No data to write")

# Schedule the function to run once per day
schedule.every().day.at("00:00").do(fetch_clinical_trials_data)

# Keep the script running
while True:
    schedule.run_pending()
    time.sleep(1)
```

ClinicalTrials.gov provides a convenient API to access the information in XML format. This is a Python code snippet for fetching all studies by Moderna using the ClinicalTrials.gov API. It will use the `requests` library to make the HTTP request and the `xml.etree.ElementTree` library to parse the XML response.

3. Create a standalone buy or sell signal based on clinical trial news on the clinicaltrials.gov website:

- **Buy signal**: Positive phase II/III results or successful completion of a trial, leading to potential regulatory review

- **Sell signal**: Failure in phase II/III trials

You will need to make sure that your CSV file includes data about the phase of the trial (for example, in a **Phase** column) and the outcome of the trial (for example, in an **Outcome** column):

```
pip install alpaca-trade-api
from alpaca_trade_api import REST
import pandas as pd

# initialize Alpaca API
api = REST('<ALPACA_API_KEY>', '<ALPACA_SECRET_KEY>', base_
url='https://paper-api.alpaca.markets')

# load clinical trials data
df = pd.read_csv('clinical_trials_data.csv')

# iterate over each row in DataFrame
for index, row in df.iterrows():
    brief_title = row['BriefTitle']
    phase = row['Phase']
    outcome = row['Outcome']
    status_verified_date = row['StatusVerifiedDate']

    # if Phase II/III clinical trial result is positive or trial
completed successfully, send buy order
    if ('Phase II' in phase or 'Phase III' in phase) and
('positive' in outcome.lower() or 'completed' in outcome.
lower()):
        api.submit_order(
            symbol='MRNA',
            qty='100',
            side='buy',
            type='limit',
            time_in_force='gtc',
            limit_price=api.get_last_trade('MRNA').price
        )
        print(f'Buy signal on {status_verified_date} at {api.
get_last_trade("MRNA").price}')

    # if Phase II/III clinical trial result is negative, send
sell order
    elif ('Phase II' in phase or 'Phase III' in phase) and
'failed' in outcome.lower():
        api.submit_order(
            symbol='MRNA',
            qty='100',
            side='sell',
            type='limit',
```

```
            time_in_force='gtc',
            limit_price=api.get_last_trade('MRNA').price
        )
        print(f'Sell signal on {status_verified_date} at {api.
    get_last_trade("MRNA").price}')
```

This code snippet checks for phase II or phase III trials and if the outcome is positive or the trial has been completed, it generates a buy signal. Conversely, if the phase II or phase III trial has failed, it generates a sell signal.

Please note that you need to replace the <ALPACA_API_KEY> and <ALPACA_SECRET_KEY> placeholder variables with your actual API key and secret key from Alpaca.

Important note

This is a simplified example and may not be sufficient for actual trading. In practice, you would want to include additional checks and balances, such as checking whether you already hold shares before selling, and additional logic to determine the appropriate quantity and price for each order.

---

4.   FDA regulatory announcements (standalone trade signal):

   - **Buy**: Approval of a new drug/vaccine or a new indication for an existing drug

   - **Sell**: Regulatory rejection of a new drug/vaccine or a critical safety concern raised

   - **Source**: FDA announcements

Here's how you can use Python's BeautifulSoup library to scrape the FDA's press announcements web page for any articles that mention "Moderna." Once we've done this, we can store the relevant data in a CSV file:

```
1. First, let's install the required packages:
pip install requests pandas schedule

2. Run the following Python code:
import requests
from bs4 import BeautifulSoup
import csv
import re
import schedule
import time

def job():
    url = "https://www.fda.gov/news-events/fda-newsroom/press-
announcements"
    response = requests.get(url)
```

```
        soup = BeautifulSoup(response.text, 'html.parser')

        # Find all article links on the page
        article_links = soup.find_all('a', class_='col-md-12')

        # Open a CSV file to store the data
        with open('fda_announcements.csv', 'w', newline='') as file:
            writer = csv.writer(file)
            # Write the header
            writer.writerow(["Title", "Link", "Date"])

            # Loop through each article link
            for link in article_links:
                # Find the title and date
                title = link.find('h2').text.strip()
                date = link.find('span', class_='field-content').
text.strip()

                # Check if the title mentions "Moderna"
                if re.search('moderna', title, re.IGNORECASE):
                    # Write the data to the CSV file
                    writer.writerow([title, 'https://www.fda.gov' +
link['href'], date])

    print("Data has been written to fda_announcements.csv")

# schedule the job every day at a certain time, e.g., 9:00 am
schedule.every().day.at("09:00").do(job)

# Keep the script running.
while True:
    schedule.run_pending()
    time.sleep(1)
```

The script will run every day at 9:00 A.M. Please adjust the timing according to your needs. Note that this script should be running all the time to be able to execute the job. This script will search through all of the articles listed on the FDA's press announcements page and find any that have "Moderna" in the title. It will then write the title, URL, and date of each article to a CSV file.

Please note that this script only scrapes the first page of announcements. If you want to scrape more pages, you'll have to modify the script to navigate to the next page and repeat the scraping process.

> **Important note on pagination**
>
> The current script fetches data only from the first page of results. If the data is spread across multiple pages, you'll need to extend the script to handle pagination. Here are some general strategies to do so:

5. **API-based pagination**: If you're working with an API that supports pagination, look for parameters such as page, offset, or limit in the API documentation. You can increment these parameters in a loop until you've fetched all pages:

```
page = 1
while True:
    url = f"https://api.example.com/data?page={page}"
    # fetch data
    # …
    if no_more_data:
        break
    page += 1
```

6. **Web scraping with the Next button**: If you're scraping a website, identify the Next button's HTML element and simulate a click, or navigate to the next URL, to scrape subsequent pages:

```
while True:
    # scrape data from the current page
    # ...
    next_button = soup.find('a', {'class': 'next-button'})
    if next_button is None:
        break
    else:
        next_url = next_button['href']
        # update your soup object with the next_url
```

7. **Rate limiting**: Always be aware of the rate-limiting policies when dealing with APIs or web scraping. Insert appropriate time delays in your loops to avoid getting blocked.

8. **Data storage**: When dealing with multiple pages, consider storing the data incrementally – either appending it to a file or a database – to avoid losing all fetched data in case of an error or interruption.

9. **Create a standalone buy or sell signal based on FDA announcements on the FDA website**:

    * **Buy**: Approval of a new drug/vaccine or a new indication for an existing drug

    * **Sell**: Regulatory rejection of a new drug/vaccine or a critical safety concern raised:

    ```
    from alpaca_trade_api import REST
    import pandas as pd
    ```

```python
# initialize Alpaca API
api = REST('<ALPACA_API_KEY>', '<ALPACA_SECRET_KEY>', base_
url='https://paper-api.alpaca.markets')

# load FDA announcements data
df = pd.read_csv('fda_announcements.csv')

# iterate over each row in DataFrame
for index, row in df.iterrows():
    title = row['Title']
    date = row['Date']

    # if FDA announcement indicates approval of a new drug/
vaccine or a new indication for an existing drug, send buy order
    if ('approval' in title.lower() and 'moderna' in title.
lower()) or ('new indication' in title.lower() and 'moderna' in
title.lower()):
        api.submit_order(
            symbol='MRNA',
            qty='100',
            side='buy',
            type='limit',
            time_in_force='gtc',
            limit_price=api.get_last_trade('MRNA').price
        )
        print(f'Buy signal on {date} at {api.get_last_
trade("MRNA").price}')

    # if FDA announcement indicates regulatory rejection of a
new drug/vaccine or a critical safety concern is raised, send
sell order
    elif ('rejection' in title.lower() and 'moderna' in title.
lower()) or ('critical safety concern' in title.lower() and
'moderna' in title.lower()):
        api.submit_order(
            symbol='MRNA',
            qty='100',
            side='sell',
            type='limit',
            time_in_force='gtc',
            limit_price=api.get_last_trade('MRNA').price
        )
        print(f'Sell signal on {date} at {api.get_last_
trade("MRNA").price}')
```

This code snippet checks the title of each FDA announcement. If the title indicates the approval of a new drug/vaccine or a new indication for an existing drug, and `'moderna'` is mentioned in the title, it generates a buy signal. Conversely, if the title indicates regulatory rejection of a new drug/vaccine or a critical safety concern is raised, and `'moderna'` is mentioned in the title, it generates a sell signal.

Again, you need to replace the `<ALPACA_API_KEY>` and `<ALPACA_SECRET_KEY>` placeholder variables with your actual API key and secret key from Alpaca. As before, keep in mind that this is a simplified example and may not be sufficient for actual trading. Be sure to implement the necessary checks and balances as per your trading strategy.

10. **Earnings reports (combined with sentiment signal to implement trade)**:

  - **Buy**: Quarterly revenue growth surpassing the consensus estimate by at least 10%

  - **Sell**: Quarterly revenue falls short of the consensus estimate by 10% or more

  - **Source**: IEX Cloud

IEX Cloud offers the `estimates` endpoint, which provides future and past earnings estimates. You could compare the actuals (which can be obtained from the `income` endpoint or the `earnings` endpoint) with the estimates to see if Moderna's earnings were more than 10% above or below the estimate.

Here is a Python code example of how you might do this with IEX Cloud. This version of the code uses the `csv` library to write the data to a file named `Moderna_earnings.csv`:

```python
import requests
import json
import csv

# Replace 'YOUR_IEX_CLOUD_PUBLIC_KEY' with your actual IEX Cloud
public key
url_estimates = 'https://cloud.iexapis.com/stable/stock/mrna/
estimates?token=YOUR_IEX_CLOUD_PUBLIC_KEY'
url_income = 'https://cloud.iexapis.com/stable/stock/mrna/
income?token=YOUR_IEX_CLOUD_PUBLIC_KEY'

response_estimates = requests.get(url_estimates)
response_income = requests.get(url_income)

data_estimates = json.loads(response_estimates.text)
data_income = json.loads(response_income.text)

# Initialize variables to None
latest_estimate = actual = difference = percentage_difference =
None
```

```
# Check if 'estimates' and 'income' keys exist and if their
lists are not empty
if 'estimates' in data_estimates and len(data_
estimates['estimates']) > 0:
    latest_estimate = data_estimates['estimates'][0].
get('earnings', None)

if 'income' in data_income and len(data_income['income']) > 0:
    actual = data_income['income'][0].get('netIncome', None)

# Perform calculations if both latest_estimate and actual are
not None
if latest_estimate is not None and actual is not None:
    difference = actual - latest_estimate
    # Check for a zero latest_estimate to avoid
ZeroDivisionError
    if latest_estimate != 0:
        percentage_difference = (difference / latest_estimate) *
100

# Open the CSV file
with open('Moderna_earnings.csv', 'w', newline='') as file:
    writer = csv.writer(file)
    # Write the header
    writer.writerow(["Estimate", "Actual", "Difference",
"Percentage Difference"])

    # Write the data
    writer.writerow([latest_estimate, actual, difference,
percentage_difference])

print("Data has been written to Moderna_earnings.csv")
```

11. **R&D expenditure (combined with sentiment signal to implement trade):**

   - **Buy**: R&D spending is consistent or slightly increasing (>=10%) YoY, indicating investment in the future pipeline

   - **Sell**: A sudden drastic increase (greater than 20%) YoY in R&D spend

   - **Source**: IEX Cloud

In the IEX Cloud API, the financials endpoint provides information about R&D costs and total revenue for a specific period. To find R&D as a percentage of revenue, you can use the reportDate, totalRevenue, and researchAndDevelopment fields from this endpoint.

Please replace `'YOUR_IEX_CLOUD_PUBLIC_KEY'` with your actual IEX Cloud public key in the following code snippet:

```python
import requests
import json
import csv
import schedule
import time

def job():
    # Replace 'YOUR_IEX_CLOUD_PUBLIC_KEY' with your actual IEX
Cloud public key
    url_financials = 'https://cloud.iexapis.com/stable/stock/
mrna/financials?token=YOUR_IEX_CLOUD_PUBLIC_KEY'

    response_financials = requests.get(url_financials)

    data_financials = json.loads(response_financials.text)

    # Get total R&D and total revenue for the past 12 months
    total_rd = 0
    total_revenue = 0
    for report in data_financials['financials']:
        if 'reportDate' in report and int(report['reportDate']
[:4]) == time.localtime().tm_year - 1:
            if 'researchAndDevelopment' in report:
                total_rd += report['researchAndDevelopment']
            if 'totalRevenue' in report:
                total_revenue += report['totalRevenue']

    # Calculate R&D as a percentage of revenue
    percentage_rd = (total_rd / total_revenue) * 100

    # Open the CSV file
    with open('Moderna_RD.csv', 'w', newline='') as file:
        writer = csv.writer(file)
        # Write the header
        writer.writerow(["Total R&D", "Total Revenue", "R&D as %
of Revenue"])

        # Write the data
        writer.writerow([total_rd, total_revenue, percentage_
rd])
```

```
        print("Data has been written to Moderna_RD.csv")


        if percentage_rd <= 10:
            print("Buy Signal: Moderna's R&D spend as a % of revenue
    for the past 12 months is no greater than 10%")
        elif percentage_rd >= 20:
            print("Sell Signal: Moderna's R&D spend as a % of
    revenue for the past 12 months exceeds 20%")
        else:
            print("No Signal: Moderna's R&D spend as a % of revenue
    for the past 12 months is between 10% and 20%")

    # Schedule the job every day at 9:00am
    schedule.every().day.at("09:00").do(job)


    # Keep the script running
    while True:
        schedule.run_pending()
        time.sleep(1)
```

This script calculates the total R&D and total revenue for the past 12 months, then calculates R&D as a percentage of revenue. After, it writes this data to a CSV file and prints a buy or sell signal based on the value of R&D as a percentage of revenue. This job is scheduled to run every day at 9:00 A.M.

12. **Sentiment analysis (combined with either the earnings signal or R&D spend signal to implement trade):**

- **Buy**: The positive sentiment score exceeds 0.2 (on a scale from -1 to 1) for a consistent period of a week

- **Sell**: The negative sentiment score dips below -0.2 for a week consistently

- **Source**: News and social media sentiment analyzed using GPT-4 or similar sentiment analysis tools, which could be sourced from online news websites, Yahoo! Finance, and social media platforms such as X:

```
    import schedule
    import time
    import csv
    import datetime
    from collections import deque
    from textblob import TextBlob
    import requests
    import json
```

```
# Deque to keep the last 7 days sentiment scores
sentiment_scores = deque(maxlen=7)

def job():
    global sentiment_scores

    # Get news articles mentioning Moderna from newsapi.org
    url = ('https://newsapi.org/v2/everything?'
           'q=Moderna&'
           'from=' + datetime.datetime.now().isoformat() +
'Z&'  # only get articles from the last 24 hours
           'sortBy=popularity&'
           'apiKey=YOUR_NEWSAPI_KEY')

    response = requests.get(url)
    data = json.loads(response.text)

    # Initialize daily sentiment
    daily_sentiment = 0

    # Iterate over the articles
    for article in data['articles']:
        # Perform sentiment analysis on the article's title
        blob = TextBlob(article['title'])
        sentiment = blob.sentiment.polarity

        # Add the sentiment score to the daily sentiment
        daily_sentiment += sentiment

    # Save the daily sentiment to the deque
    sentiment_scores.append(daily_sentiment)

    # Calculate the sentiment score for the past week
    weekly_sentiment = sum(sentiment_scores)

    # Write the weekly sentiment to the CSV file
    with open('sentiment_scores.csv', 'a', newline='') as
file:
        writer = csv.writer(file)
        writer.writerow([datetime.date.today(), weekly_
sentiment])

    # Generate a signal if the sentiment is consistently
positive or negative for a week
    if weekly_sentiment > 0.2 * len(sentiment_scores):
```

```
        print("Buy signal")
    elif weekly_sentiment < -0.2 * len(sentiment_scores):
        print("Sell signal")

schedule.every().day.at("10:00").do(job)

while True:
    schedule.run_pending()
    time.sleep(1)
```

This script keeps track of the daily sentiment scores for the last 7 days and writes the weekly sentiment to a CSV file every day. It also generates a buy or sell signal if the weekly sentiment exceeds 0.2 or falls below -0.2, respectively.

Remember to replace `'YOUR_NEWSAPI_KEY'` with your actual News API key. As always, this is a simplified example and may not be sufficient for actual trading. You may need to adjust the sentiment thresholds and the decision-making logic to fit your specific use case. Also, note that the News API has certain limitations on the number of requests you can make, depending on your level of subscription.

13. **Earnings reports and sentiment**:

   - **Buy**: Quarterly revenue growth surpasses the consensus estimate by at least 10% and the positive sentiment score exceeds 0.2 (on a scale from -1 to 1) for a consistent period of 1 week.

   - **Sell**: Quarterly revenue falls short of consensus estimate by 10% or more and the negative sentiment score dips below -0.2 for 1 week:

     - Earnings report data and trade signal: `Moderna_earnings.csv`

     - Sentiment score and trade signal: `sentiment_scores.csv`

To create a trading strategy based on multiple variables, you can combine the data from different CSV files, process them to generate trading signals, and submit trades accordingly using Alpaca's API.

The following script demonstrates how to achieve this using pandas. This script should be run after the two CSV files, `Moderna_earnings.csv` and `sentiment_scores.csv`, have been generated:

```
from alpaca_trade_api import REST
import pandas as pd

# Initialize Alpaca API
api = REST('<ALPACA_API_KEY>', '<ALPACA_SECRET_KEY>', base_
url='https://paper-api.alpaca.markets')
```

```
# Load earnings and sentiment data
df_earnings = pd.read_csv('Moderna_earnings.csv', index_
col='Date', parse_dates=True)
df_sentiment = pd.read_csv('sentiment_scores.csv', index_
col='Date', parse_dates=True)

# Join the two dataframes on the date index
df = df_earnings.join(df_sentiment)

# Iterate over each row in DataFrame
for index, row in df.iterrows():
    earnings_signal = row['EarningsSignal']
    sentiment_signal = row['SentimentSignal']

    # If earnings and sentiment signal both indicate "Buy", send
buy order
    if earnings_signal == 'Buy' and sentiment_signal == 'Buy':
        api.submit_order(
            symbol='MRNA',
            qty='100',
            side='buy',
            type='market',
            time_in_force='gtc'
        )
        print(f'Buy signal on {index} at market price')

    # If earnings and sentiment signal both indicate "Sell",
send sell order
    elif earnings_signal == 'Sell' and sentiment_signal ==
'Sell':
        api.submit_order(
            symbol='MRNA',
            qty='100',
            side='sell',
            type='market',
            time_in_force='gtc'
        )
        print(f'Sell signal on {index} at market price')
```

14. **R&D spend and sentiment**:

- **Buy**: R&D spend is consistent or slightly increasing (>=10%) YoY and the positive sentiment score exceeds 0.2 (on a scale from -1 to 1) for a consistent period of 1 week

- **Sell**: A sudden drastic increase (greater than 20%) YoY in R&D spend and the negative sentiment score dips below -0.2 for 1 week:

- R&D spend as a % of revenue and trade signal: `Moderna_RD.csv`

- Sentiment score and trade signal: `sentiment_scores.csv`:

```
from alpaca_trade_api import REST
import pandas as pd

# Initialize Alpaca API
api = REST('<ALPACA_API_KEY>', '<ALPACA_SECRET_KEY>', base_
url='https://paper-api.alpaca.markets')

# Load R&D spend and sentiment data
df_rd_spend = pd.read_csv('Moderna_RD.csv', index_col='Date',
parse_dates=True)
df_sentiment = pd.read_csv('sentiment_scores.csv', index_
col='Date', parse_dates=True)

# Join the two dataframes on the date index
df = df_rd_spend.join(df_sentiment)

# Iterate over each row in DataFrame
for index, row in df.iterrows():
    rd_spend_signal = row['RDSpendSignal']
    sentiment_signal = row['SentimentSignal']

    # If R&D spend and sentiment signal both indicate "Buy",
send buy order
    if rd_spend_signal == 'Buy' and sentiment_signal ==
'Buy':
        api.submit_order(
            symbol='MRNA',
            qty='100',
            side='buy',
            type='market',
            time_in_force='gtc'
        )
        print(f'Buy signal on {index} at market price')

    # If R&D spend and sentiment signal both indicate "Sell",
send sell order
    elif rd_spend_signal == 'Sell' and sentiment_signal ==
'Sell':
        api.submit_order(
            symbol='MRNA',
            qty='100',
            side='sell',
```

```
                        type='market',
                        time_in_force='gtc'
                )
                print(f'Sell signal on {index} at market price')
```

Now, let's look at a backtest example.

To backtest the strategy you've described, you'll need historical data for the period of June 30, 2022, through June 30, 2023, for all your variables – clinical trial data, FDA announcement data, earnings report data, sentiment analysis data, and R&D spend data.

Here's a simplified example of how you might set up a backtest with Backtrader, assuming that you have a pandas DataFrame, df, containing historical price data for Moderna and the buy/sell signals generated from your combined variables:

```
import backtrader as bt

# Create a subclass of bt.Strategy to define the logic for trading
class ModernaStrategy(bt.Strategy):
    def next(self):
        # Get today's date
        date = self.data.datetime.date()

        # Check if there's a buy or sell signal for today
        if date in df.index:
            if df.loc[date, 'Signal'] == 'Buy':
                self.buy(size=100)
            elif df.loc[date, 'Signal'] == 'Sell':
                self.sell(size=100)

# Create a Cerebro engine
cerebro = bt.Cerebro()

# Add the strategy to Cerebro
cerebro.addstrategy(ModernaStrategy)

# Create a data feed and add it to Cerebro
data = bt.feeds.PandasData(dataname=df)
cerebro.adddata(data)

# Run the backtest
cerebro.run()
```

This Python code snippet uses the Backtrader library to perform a backtest on a trading strategy specifically for Moderna stock. Let's break it down:

1. Import the Backtrader library using `import backtrader as bt`.

    This imports the Backtrader library for use in backtesting trading strategies.

2. Define the trading strategy:

    ```python
    class ModernaStrategy(bt.Strategy):
        def next(self):
            date = self.data.datetime.date()
            if date in df.index:
                if df.loc[date, 'Signal'] == 'Buy':
                    self.buy(size=100)
                elif df.loc[date, 'Signal'] == 'Sell':
                    self.sell(size=100)
    ```

    Let's take a closer look at this code:

    -   A custom trading strategy class, `ModernaStrategy`, is created, inheriting from `bt.Strategy`.

    -   The `next()` method is implemented to specify the trading logic. Here, it checks for buy or sell signals in a Pandas DataFrame (`df`) and then executes trades accordingly.

3. Initialize the Backtrader engine:

    ```python
    cerebro = bt.Cerebro()
    cerebro.addstrategy(ModernaStrategy)
    ```

    Let's take a closer look:

    -   A Backtrader engine (`cerebro`) is created

    -   The custom strategy is added to the engine

4. Add data and run the following:

    ```python
    data = bt.feeds.PandasData(dataname=df)
    cerebro.adddata(data)
    cerebro.run()
    ```

    Let's explain this code:

    -   Data is fed into Backtrader using `bt.feeds.PandasData`, where `df` contains the historical price and signal data

    -   Finally, `cerebro.run()` kicks off the backtesting process

In this section, we guided you through building the Moderna Momentum investment strategy by combining traditional financial metrics with modern data science techniques. We set up your Python environment and progressed by pulling data from various sources to craft multi-dimensional trading signals. Finally, we wrapped things up with a backtest, giving you a comprehensive toolkit for biotech investing.

In the next section, we'll visualize all the data signals from the Moderna Momentum investment trade, Here, we'll take you on a fascinating journey through designing an all-inclusive Power BI dashboard that captures the essence of all the data in one place. You'll learn how to visually represent critical metrics such as clinical trial results, FDA announcements, earnings reports, and even sentiment analysis. We'll supercharge our dashboard with ChatGPT-generated insights and Power BI's predictive analytics, giving you a futuristic toolkit to decode stock market trends.

The future of biotech trading – the Moderna Momentum trade visualization

As a Power BI expert, let's break down each component of the Moderna Momentum trading strategy and the visualization that could be ideal for each:

1. **Clinical trial results**: A time series line graph would provide a visual representation of the clinical trial stages (phases I, II, and III) over time. This line could be color-coded to indicate successful trials (green), ongoing trials (yellow), and failed trials (red). Each data point (that is, trial) could be interactive, offering additional details on hover, such as the trial's start and end dates, its goals, and its outcomes.

2. **FDA regulatory announcements**: A similar time series line graph could be used to represent FDA regulatory announcements, with color-coding to differentiate between approvals (green) and rejections (red). A separate bar graph can visualize the number of approvals and rejections over time. Interactive features could provide further details about each announcement.

3. **Earnings reports**: A combination of a line graph and a bar graph would be ideal to visualize earnings data. The line graph could represent quarterly revenue over time, with markers to highlight instances where revenue growth surpasses or falls short of estimates. A bar graph could provide a year-over-year comparison of the estimated and actual revenues.

4. **R&D expenditure**: A line graph could be used to represent R&D spending over time. The line could change color or become bold when the YoY increase exceeds 20%. A separate area graph could show the R&D spending as a percentage of the total revenue, indicating how much of the revenue is reinvested in R&D.

5. **Sentiment analysis**: A sentiment score could be represented using a heat map, where each day (or week) is a cell, and its color represents the sentiment score (green for positive, red for negative, white for neutral). This will give a quick, at-a-glance understanding of the sentiment trend over time. A line graph could also be useful for showing sentiment scores over time, with the area above 0.2 filled in green and below -0.2 filled in red.

6. **Historical stock price**: A time series line graph showing the historical stock price would be the main graph on the dashboard. This would give a quick overview of the company's financial performance.

7. **Overlay data**: Overlay the stock price line graph with the other metrics from our previous examples. The aim is to provide an at-a-glance correlation between the stock price and the key factors affecting it:

   I.   **Clinical trial results**: Significant events such as the success/failure of major trials could be marked on the stock price graph with special symbols (such as upward or downward arrows).

   II.   **FDA regulatory announcements**: Approval/rejection could also be marked on the stock price graph with appropriate symbols.

   III. **Earnings reports and R&D expenditure**: Shaded areas or marker lines on the stock price graph could represent the periods of earnings report releases or changes in R&D spending.

   IV.   **Sentiment analysis**: Underneath the stock price graph, a sentiment score graph could be synchronized to reflect the same timeline. This could help visually correlate major changes in sentiment with stock price fluctuations.

8. **Predictive analysis**: Power BI has built-in forecasting capabilities that could be leveraged to project future stock prices. An area of the graph showing the historical stock price could transition into a forecast area. This forecasted area could have confidence intervals that indicate the level of certainty in the predictions. Keep in mind that it's critical to communicate to users that these are projections based on past trends and they should be used with caution.

9. **ChatGPT insights**: When a user selects a data point in the prediction area, ChatGPT could generate potential scenarios explaining what might cause an increase or decrease. This can be based on the patterns observed in the historical data – for instance, "If Moderna announces successful clinical trial results, the stock price could potentially follow the trend observed in previous similar situations."

10. **Load the CSV data into Power BI**:

    I.   Open Power BI Desktop.

    II.   Click on **Home** in the top menu, then click on **Get Data** in the ribbon.

    III. In the dropdown, select **Text/CSV**.

    IV.   Navigate to the location of your CSV files and select one. Click **Load** to import the data into Power BI.

    V.   Repeat steps II to IV for each CSV file.

11. **Visualize the clinical trial results**:

    I.   In the Fields pane on the right, expand **clinical_trials_data**.

    II.   Drag the **date** field into the **Axis** area, **phase** into **Legend**, and **result** into **Values** of a new **Line chart**.

    III.   Customize the line colors in the **Format** pane to indicate successful trials (green), ongoing trials (yellow), and failed trials (red).

12. **Visualize the FDA regulatory announcements**:

    I.   In the **Fields** pane on the right, expand **fda_announcements**.

    II.   Drag the **date** field into the **Axis** area and **announcement** into **Values** of a new **Line chart**.

    III.   Customize the line colors in the **Format** pane to differentiate between approvals (green) and rejections (red).

13. **Visualize the earnings reports**:

    I.   In the **Fields** pane on the right, expand **Moderna_earnings**.

    II.   Drag the **date** field into the **Axis** area, **revenue** into **Values**, and **estimate** into **Tooltip** of a new **Line and Clustered Column** chart.

14. **Visualize R&D expenditure**:

    I.   In the **Fields** pane on the right, expand **Moderna_RD**.

    II.   Drag the **date** field into the **Axis** area and **spend** into **Values** of a new **Line chart**.

    III.   Customize the line color or thickness in the **Format** pane when the YoY increase exceeds 20%.

15. **Visualize sentiment analysis**:

    I.   In the **Fields** pane on the right, expand **sentiment_scores**.

    II.   Drag the **date** field into the **Axis** area and **score** into **Values** of a new **Line chart** or **Heat map**.

    III.   Customize the line or cell colors in the **Format** pane to represent the sentiment score (green for positive, red for negative, white for neutral).

16. **Overlay data on the stock price line graph (save all historical stock prices for Moderna in a separate CSV file)**:

    I.   Create a new **Line chart** with the **date** field in the **Axis** area and the **stock_price** field in the **Values** area.

II.   Add special markers for significant events such as clinical trial results and FDA regulatory announcements.

III. Add shaded areas or marker lines for periods of earnings report releases or changes in R&D spending.

IV.   Synchronize a sentiment score graph underneath the stock price graph to reflect the same timeline.

17. **Predictive analysis**:

I.   On the stock price line graph, click on the **Analytics** pane.

II.   Under **Forecast**, click **Add**. Adjust the forecast length and confidence interval as needed.

18. **ChatGPT insights**:

I.   Create a new **Card** visualization and bind it to a measure that calls a function to generate insights from ChatGPT.

II.   Set up a drill-through or a click action on the prediction area of the stock price line graph to show the ChatGPT card.

Please note that while these steps provide a good start, you might need to adjust the configurations, such as filtering the data or changing the aggregation method, depending on your specific data and analysis needs.

Let's look at some additional suggestions to help you facilitate ChatGPT insights for a Power BI visualization.

To get ChatGPT insights into a Power BI visualization, you'll need to use Power BI's ability to run Python scripts, along with a custom function that uses the GPT API to generate insights based on your data. We've provided a step-by-step guide to help you achieve this next.

Prerequisites

1. Make sure you've installed Python on your computer.

2. Install the `openai` Python package, which will be used to interact with the ChatGPT API. You can install it using pip:

```
pip install openai
```

Make sure you have an API key from OpenAI to access the GPT API.

Follow these steps:

1. Add the Python script in Power BI:

2. Open Power BI Desktop and go to the **Home** tab.

3. Click **Python script** in the **Data** section.

4. In the Python script editor that pops up, paste the following code:

```python
import openai

# Your OpenAI API key
openai_api_key = "YOUR_OPENAI_API_KEY"

def get_chatgpt_insights(data):
    openai.api_key = openai_api_key
    prompt = f"Provide insights for the following data: {data}"
    response = openai.Completion.create(
        engine="text-davinci-002",
        prompt=prompt,
        max_tokens=100
    )
    insights = response.choices[0].text.strip()
    return insights

# Test the function
print(get_chatgpt_insights("Sample data for testing"))
```

5. Click **OK** to run the script.

6. Create a new card visualization:

7. After setting up the Python script, go to your Power BI canvas.

8. Click on **Card** under **Visualizations**.

9. In the **Fields** pane, bind this card to a measure that will call your Python function to get the insights. You'll probably need to create a new measure in DAX that can interact with the Python function.

10. Add more interactivity by setting up a drill-through or a click action on your existing visualizations, such as the prediction area of your stock price line graph.

11. Go to **Action** under **Visualizations** and enable **Drillthrough**, or set up a click action to trigger the ChatGPT insights card when clicked.

12. Arrange your visualizations on your canvas as desired.

13. Save your Power BI file.

After setting this up, the ChatGPT insights should update based on the underlying data whenever you or a user interacts with the visualizations. You may need to refresh the data or the Python script to see the updated insights due to the limitations of Power BI's Python integration.

This kind of interactive, insightful, and visually appealing dashboard would not only make investment trade monitoring easier but also bring a better understanding of how different factors interplay to affect Moderna's market performance. It's the future of financial analysis, blending innovative AGI technology with human ingenuity for unprecedented insights.

Next, prepare to step into the future of healthcare and regulatory oversight like never before! In the next section, we will introduce FoodandDrugAdminGPT, a revolutionary AI persona that's set to transform the way we approach drug development and approval. With unparalleled analytical prowess and an innovative approach, this system is poised to redefine the boundaries of pharmaceutical research, bringing life-saving treatments to patients faster and more efficiently. Welcome to a new era where technology and healthcare converge to create possibilities that were once beyond our reach!

Introducing the future of drug development and regulatory approval with FoodandDrugAdminGPT – an AI persona

Step into the future with FoodandDrugAdminGPT, an AI persona that's about to revolutionize drug development and regulatory approval! If you're intrigued by ChatGPT, wait until you see how this specialized AI model leverages generative language capabilities to predict a drug's chances of getting FDA approval. We'll explore into how FoodandDrugAdminGPT can become a key tool for pharmaceutical portfolio management, giving you a predictive edge. For Power BI enthusiasts, we'll explore how you can integrate the AI's insights into interactive dashboards, aiding in real-time decision-making. If you're keen on ChatGPT, passionate about investing, or a fan of Power BI visualizations, you won't want to miss this section.

FoodandDrugAdminGPT is an innovative AI persona designed to excel in the arena of drug development and regulatory approval. Acting as a smart model that can predict potential challenges and opportunities for new pharmaceuticals before reaching the FDA, it offers drug manufacturers the ability to assess their products' approval likelihood, recognize areas for improvement, and thereby accelerate the overall development and approval process.

The following critical indicators have been evaluated by FoodandDrugAdminGPT:

1. **Drug composition and mechanism of action**: Analyzing the drug's function and chemical structure.

2. **Preclinical data**: Reviewing non-human trial results for safety and effectiveness.

3. **Clinical trial design**: Evaluating the integrity and ethical considerations of human trials.

4. **Statistical analysis plans**: Confirming the validity of the planned statistical approaches.

5. **Patient population**: Ensuring that the drug's intended users are adequately represented in the trial.

6. **Adverse event monitoring**: Scrutinizing procedures to monitor side effects and risks.

7. **Drug manufacturing and quality control**: Verifying that production aligns with FDA standards.

Now, let's look at the profile of FoodandDrugAdminGPT:

1. **Background**: Created to mirror the evaluation expertise of the FDA, with a core focus on drug safety and effectiveness.

2. **Skills**:

   - Pharmaceutical development, clinical trials, and regulatory process expertise
   - The ability to analyze intricate scientific data and trial designs
   - Skill in recognizing potential risks and regulatory obstacles
   - The capacity to communicate complex evaluations in a user-friendly way

3. **Motivations**: Aims to facilitate pharmaceutical companies in hastening drug development and approval, striving to simplify the regulatory process and expedite patient access to treatments.

4. **Approach**: Offers all-encompassing assessments of vital drug development aspects, contextualizing them within contemporary scientific understanding and regulatory norms.

5. **Personality**: Renowned for thoroughness, objectivity, and insight, translating intricate assessments into accessible language.

While FoodandDrugAdminGPT provides invaluable evaluations, it's essential to note that the final decision-making resides with the drug manufacturers and the FDA. Its guidance is meant to supplement professional judgment and inform – not prescribe – strategic choices in drug development and regulation.

FoodandDrugAdminGPT heralds a new era in drug development and regulation, embodying a revolutionary system that leverages Generative AI. This AI persona builds upon the ChatGPT framework to present the next evolution in AI assistance across diverse aspects of food and drug administration. It encapsulates a forward-thinking approach that anticipates the future landscape of regulatory oversight, offering a new tool in the continuous quest for innovation in healthcare.

We've just embarked on a thrilling journey through the world of FoodandDrugAdminGPT, a specialized AI persona that's a game-changer in drug development and regulatory approval. We've seen how it's not just for medical professionals; investors and data analysts can leverage its predictive power to make smarter choices and create compelling dashboards. It's the thrilling intersection of AI's future with finance and data visualization. If you're someone who's ever been fascinated by ChatGPT, intrigued by the stock market, or enthralled with the possibilities of Power BI, this is a pivotal moment where all these worlds collide.

In the upcoming section, we're diving into the futuristic capabilities of Microsoft JARVIS (HuggingGPT), an AI system that highlights collaborative intelligence and multifaceted excellence using Generative AI. You're about to learn how this cutting-edge technology not only achieves complex tasks but also empowers investors with predictive insights and analysts with dynamic Power BI visualizations. So, why is this worth your time? Because we're on the brink of an AI revolution that's reshaping industries. Whether you're a ChatGPT enthusiast, a savvy investor, or a Power BI expert, this is where your skills converge to unlock unprecedented opportunities.

Unleashing collaborative intelligence – Microsoft Jarvis (GitHub)

Meet Microsoft JARVIS, an advanced AI system that's taking collaboration to new heights. Hosted on Hugging Face as HuggingGPT, JARVIS connects to as many as 20 AI models, including various open source **large language models** (**LLMs**) for images, videos, audio, and more. With ChatGPT at the helm, JARVIS seamlessly integrates these models to achieve complex tasks, and anyone can explore its capabilities right now.

This dynamic system operates through four distinct stages:

1. **Task planning**: ChatGPT analyzes user requests to understand their intention, breaking them down into manageable tasks.

2. **Model selection**: Then, it selects the most suitable expert models, curated by the FDA, for each task, including AI specialists in image analysis, drug interaction checking, and more.

3. **Task execution**: These expert models execute their tasks, feeding the results back to ChatGPT.

4. **Response generation**: ChatGPT synthesizes the predictions and communicates the cohesive response back to the user.

Known as FoodandDrugAdminGPT, this integrated system offers a versatile network of capabilities. It's not confined to handling single modality inputs but can process various modalities and solve an array of complex AI tasks. Through corresponding model descriptions, FoodandDrugAdminGPT connects and integrates individual expert models, acting as the central brain that answers user queries with precision. Welcome to a new era of interconnected intelligence, where the whole is indeed greater than the sum of its parts.

A new epoch in AI – the multifaceted excellence of HuggingGPT and its integration with Gradio models

In the rapidly evolving landscape of AI, HuggingGPT has emerged as a luminary by leveraging the capabilities of LLMs. With integrations spanning hundreds of Hugging Face models, HuggingGPT is a versatile tool that shines across 24 diverse tasks such as text classification, image generation, object detection, question answering, and even text-to-video conversion. Its proficiency in handling multimodal information makes it a standout solution for intricate AI challenges.

Nevertheless, like any groundbreaking technology, HuggingGPT is not without its challenges. Its performance may sometimes be hindered by efficiency and latency issues tied to frequent interactions with LLMs, constraints due to a maximum token limit that affects context length, and occasional instability resulting from non-adherence to instructions by the LLM.

Yet, these limitations are overshadowed by HuggingGPT's myriad advantages:

- **State-of-the-art performance**: By setting new benchmarks in numerous NLP tasks, it provides an optimal solution for AI challenges demanding sophisticated NLP capabilities. Customized fine-tuning can even yield results that equal or outpace the industry's best models.

- **Economical data requirements**: Thanks to pre-training on extensive text data, HuggingGPT slashes the need for labeled training data, thus cutting both time and expenses.

- **Customizability and versatility**: From legal and medical to summarization tasks, HuggingGPT's adaptability allows for tailoring models to specific domains, encompassing a wide array of applications such as chatbots, language translation, and text summarization.

- **Interpretability**: Especially valuable in high-stakes domains such as legal or medical NLP, HuggingGPT's interpretability facilitates a clear understanding of the model's decision-making process, aiding in debugging and optimization.

- **Open source accessibility**: Constructed on open source technologies, HuggingGPT is within reach of a vast community of developers and researchers, with no associated licensing fees or costs.

- **Integration and scalability**: Its seamless compatibility with various tools and platforms, along with deployability at scale via cloud computing services, offers real-time processing for large volumes of text data.

Despite some constraints, HuggingGPT continues to awe the AI community with its innovative performance, adaptability, transparency, and scalability. Its contributions affirm its standing as a formidable force within the field of AI.

Unleashing creativity with Gradio – a gateway to simplified demos and GUIs for Hugging Face models

Gradio, a revolutionary library in the machine learning ecosystem, empowers developers to effortlessly craft demos and GUIs for machine learning models. Its simplicity is akin to sharing a document link in Google Docs. With the advent of Gradio 2.0, integrating virtually any Hugging Face model with a GUI can be accomplished with just a single line of code. Let's explore the compelling advantages of synergizing Gradio with Hugging Face models:

- **Ease of use**: Transforming a transformers pipeline into a Gradio demo is straightforward with the `from_pipeline()` function. Moreover, you can efficiently construct a demo around the Inference API without having to load the model thanks to the `gr.load()` function.

- **Hosting solutions**: Gradio demos can be hosted on Hugging Face Spaces, either through the GUI or entirely within Python. Additionally, Gradio demos residing on Hugging Face Spaces can be seamlessly embedded into your website.

- **Flexibility unleashed**: Gradio's design facilitates the parallel loading of multiple models or sequential alignment

Choosing the right AI model – HuggingGPT (Jarvis) versus GPT-4 for domain-specific expertise

The selection between HuggingGPT (Jarvis) and general LLMs such as GPT-4 comes down to their underlying design, purpose, and task-handling abilities. These distinctions can significantly impact their effectiveness in various applications.

HuggingGPT (Jarvis) – the domain expert

HuggingGPT (Jarvis) stands out as an integrated system, uniquely tailored to work with several domain-specific models. Within specialized fields such as drug development, it houses expert models trained on tasks such as drug interactions, clinical trial design, FDA regulations, and more. When faced with a specific question, HuggingGPT (Jarvis) evaluates the query and summons the aptest expert model for a response. This specialization leads to insights that are both detailed and precisely aligned with the domain's unique requirements.

GPT-4 – the generalist

In contrast, GPT-4 operates as a singular, general LLM capable of managing a wide spectrum of tasks and inquiries without relying on external models. Its training on a diverse dataset empowers it to provide informative and imaginative answers across various subjects. While incredibly versatile, it lacks the acute, domain-specific acumen that HuggingGPT (Jarvis)'s expert models possess.

Making the right choice

- **For deep, domain-specific knowledge**: HuggingGPT (Jarvis) is the preferred choice for tasks requiring profound expertise in specialized areas. In contexts such as drug development, its ability to draw on specific knowledge in pharmacology, biochemistry, or FDA regulations makes it invaluable.

- **For broad understanding and creativity**: GPT-4 shines when the task requires comprehensive knowledge across multiple subjects or creativity. Its well-rounded training enables it to approach problems that traverse different domains with creativity and a generalized understanding.

Why we chose HuggingGPT (Jarvis) for the FoodandDrugAdminGPT persona

In our upcoming example, the necessity for precise, domain-focused insights led us to choose HuggingGPT (Jarvis) for the FoodandDrugAdminGPT persona. This choice aligns with the complexity and specialized nature of the tasks at hand, where general knowledge or creativity alone would not suffice. Jarvis's ability to leverage expert models specific to the field ensures a level of accuracy and depth that positions it as the optimal solution for this application.

Harnessing specialized intelligence – FoodandDrugAdminGPT's implementation using HuggingGPT for multimodal solutions in the regulatory landscape

One standout feature of the FoodandDrugAdminGPT system is its strategic task planning. By dissecting user requests into solvable tasks and matching them to the appropriate expert models, it crafts a cohesive plan of action. This thoughtful analysis and allocation enable FoodandDrugAdminGPT to generate intelligent plans, employ external models, and seamlessly integrate multimodal perceptual capabilities to navigate complex AI challenges.

The comprehensive contributions of the FoodandDrugAdminGPT system are as follows:

- **Bridging GAI with expertise**: The system unites LLMs with specialized expert models, presenting an innovative framework for generative-ai (GAI) solutions. Utilizing LLMs for planning and decision-making, FoodandDrugAdminGPT selectively deploys expert models for individual tasks.

- **Providing multimodal and reliable services**: By harmonizing numerous task-specific models within the FDA network, FoodandDrugAdminGPT can adeptly manage AI tasks across various modalities and domains, elevating the system's adaptability.

- **Emphasizing the importance of task planning**: The vital role of planning within FoodandDrugAdminGPT is accentuated, with methodical evaluations designed to gauge the prowess of LLMs in devising effective strategies.

- **Demonstrating versatility across modalities**: Comprehensive experiments in language, vision, speech, and cross-modality highlight the system's proficiency in comprehending and resolving intricate tasks specific to the food and drug administration sector.

This innovative system offers an elegant solution to a wide array of AI challenges, transcending multiple modalities and domains. It heralds a future where AI's capabilities can be harnessed to enhance efficiency and accuracy within the food and drug administration field, opening doors to potential applications in various other sectors. By weaving together the strengths of both generalized and specialized AI, FoodandDrugAdminGPT exemplifies an innovative approach that could redefine how we utilize AI.

Here, you'll discover the wizardry of blending Gradio's revolutionary capabilities with Hugging Face's machine learning models. We'll guide you through key steps, starting from obtaining your OpenAPI API key to crafting your own Gradio demo using the `from_pipeline()` function. What makes this essential reading? By mastering these techniques, you'll be armed with the know-how to effortlessly create, host, and embed advanced machine learning demos in a matter of minutes. So, prepare your development environment, because a simplified yet powerful world of machine learning demos awaits!

HuggingGPT model and Gradio demo

Follow these steps:

1. Obtain an OpenAPI API key if you don't already have one.

2. Sign up for a free account at Hugging Face – huggingface.co.

3. Navigate to **Settings** > **Access Tokens** by clicking the links on the left rail of the Hugging Face website.

4. Click **New Token** on the Hugging Face website.

5. Name the token (anything at all), select **write** as the role, and click **Generate** in Hugging Face.

6. Copy the API key and keep it somewhere you can easily access it.

7. Navigate to https://huggingface.co/spaces/microsoft/HuggingGPT.

8. Paste your OpenAPI key and Hugging Face token into the appropriate fields. Then, click the **Submit** button next to each.

9. Enter your prompt at the bottom of the query box and click **Send**.

In the next section, we've designed a multi-section roadmap aimed at equipping you with a formidable understanding of biotech investment, particularly in the landscape of drug development and regulatory approval. Let's break down why each section is crucial, what you will learn, and how it will impact your investment decisions.

Section 1 – investment insight with FoodandDrugAdminGPT – a comprehensive query guide

The first section serves as an introductory platform for both seasoned Wall Street analysts and individual investors keen on the biotech sector. We'll deconstruct the complex maze of drug approvals and market strategies by introducing targeted questions that can offer a panoramic view of the drug development life cycle. The questions in this section will help you discern key elements, such as market approval timelines, potential market size, competitive landscapes, and regulatory risks. The guidance from FoodandDrugAdminGPT acts as a supplemental tool to your professional acumen, filling gaps in your knowledge and pointing you in the direction of wise investment choices.

Why it matters

The understanding gleaned from these queries will not only shed light on the approval process but also align your investment focus on factors that genuinely impact a drug's commercial viability. It's akin to arming yourself with a precise compass in a territory laden with both opportunities and pitfalls.

Section 2 – Moderna's drug pipeline – tailored insight for investment and Wall Street analysis

In this section, we will focus on providing an investment-oriented breakdown of Moderna's existing products and those in the pipeline. Questions will be honed to give you insights into critical issues such as Emergency Use Authorizations, Clinical Trials for various vaccines, and regulatory milestones. Utilizing AI tools such as HuggingGPT, we will specialize these questions to adhere to the most recent FDA guidelines and market information.

Why it matters

Understanding Moderna's existing portfolio allows you to make well-informed decisions about short-term investment opportunities. By knowing where each drug stands in terms of approval and market readiness, you'll be better equipped to gauge immediate returns and risk factors.

Section 3 – Unlocking Moderna's pipeline – critical questions for investors using HuggingfaceGPT

Section 3 picks up where *Section 2* leaves off, but goes a level deeper. Here, we will focus on specific drugs that are still in the development or clinical trial stage. This part employs more complex, targeted queries using AI tools, enabling you to assess long-term prospects concerning Moderna's pipeline. Questions will delve into the timelines of drug rollouts, competitive landscapes for vaccines, and Moderna's strategic partnerships and funding.

Why it matters

If you're looking at a long-term investment strategy, understanding the future potential of a company's pipeline is crucial. This section will allow you to dig deeper into drugs that could become major market players in the future, thereby helping you understand the long-term growth trajectory and the associated risks.

Overall implications

The objective of our guide is to transform your general understanding of biotech investment into a specialized, multi-faceted skill set. By dividing your learning into these three distinct but complementary sections, we have provided a comprehensive toolkit for you to navigate the investment terrain in both the short term and long term. In essence, you'll be empowered to make insightful decisions that capitalize on immediate opportunities while also preparing for future market shifts.

Section 1 – investment insight with FoodandDrugAdminGPT – a comprehensive query guide

Investors and Wall Street analysts may focus on areas such as market approval, post-approval changes, market potential, competition, and regulatory risks related to drug development. Here's a streamlined set of questions:

- **Market approval timeline**: Considering the IND stage, what's the expected timeline for our drug to reach the market?

- **Potential market size**: What could be the potential market size for our pancreatic cancer drug candidate?

- **Competitive landscape**: How can we analyze the competitive landscape for our pancreatic cancer drug?

- **Regulatory risks**: What potential regulatory risks should we consider in drug development?

- **Cost-benefit analysis**: How should we approach cost-benefit analysis to determine potential pricing?

- **International expansion**: What should we consider when planning for international markets?

These questions offer a holistic view of drug approval, focusing on investment aspects, while remembering that FoodandDrugAdminGPT guides and supplements professional expertise.

Section 2 – Moderna's drug pipeline – tailored insight for investment and Wall Street analysis

HuggingGPT can help focus questions on Moderna's drug pipeline specific to investors and Wall Street analysts. Here's an example:

- **Emergency use authorization**: Has the FDA granted EUA for Moderna's next-generation COVID-19 vaccine, mRNA-1283?

- **Clinical trials for flu vaccines**: What are the phases of the flu vaccines mRNA-1010, mRNA-1020, mRNA-1030, mRNA-1011, and mRNA-1012 according to the FDA?

- **Regulatory insights for the RSV vaccine**: Has the FDA made any announcements about the approval process for Moderna's mRNA-1345?

Section 3 – unlocking Moderna's pipeline – critical questions for investors using HuggingfaceGPT

Here's a focused set of questions to delve into Moderna's pipeline from an investor's perspective:

- **COVID-19 vaccine timeline**: What's the timeline for mRNA-1283's commercial rollout? What regulatory obstacles might Moderna face?

- **Flu vaccines landscape**: Can you comment on the competitive landscape for Moderna's flu vaccines and differentiation strategies?

- **Combination vaccines**: What's the status of Moderna's combination vaccines for COVID and flu (mRNA-1073 and mRNA-1083) in clinical trials?

- **Financial partnership**: Can you detail the financial implications of Moderna's 50-50 global profit sharing with Merck for mRNA-4157?

- Zika vaccine development: How has external funding from BARDA impacted the development of mRNA-1893, a Zika vaccine?

These tailored questions offer a comprehensive understanding of Moderna's portfolio, considering the specific concerns of the investment community. By using tools such as HuggingGPT, questions can be further adapted to cater to specific FDA regulations or investment interests, enhancing the detailed analysis of Moderna's assets.

This next section shows how GPT-4 and future LLMs could potentially impact healthcare and biotech companies such as Moderna by helping them develop new drugs and treatments more quickly and accurately.

Revolutionizing biotech with GPT-4 – Moderna's pathway to accelerated drug discovery

In the dynamic field of healthcare and biotech, companies such as Moderna are on the verge of an exciting era, marked by the integration of LLMs such as OpenAI's GPT-4. This shift has significant implications for drug discovery and development, promising to reshape the industry.

- **Introducing GPT-4 in biotech**: GPT-4, created by OpenAI, is not just another language model. It has the potential to accelerate drug discovery by performing complex compositional and translation tasks. GPT-4 can analyze chemical structures, properties, and reactions, identifying compounds with similar attributes to known drugs. By modifying them to ensure they are not patented, it can significantly save time and resources.

- **Moderna's strategy with GPT-4**: Moderna is uniquely positioned to leverage GPT-4 in revolutionizing drug discovery. By focusing on the most promising compounds, GPT-4 can reduce both cost and time in the development process. An increasingly popular approach is "drug repurposing," where GPT-4 can aid in redirecting existing drugs for new uses, thus cutting through the traditionally high costs and long timelines of new drug development.

- **The future with AGI**: The potential reach of AGI in drug development goes even further. It could allow researchers to pinpoint new targets for drugs and treatments more quickly and accurately. While concerns about AGI's safety in drug development exist, OpenAI's commitment to ensuring AGI's alignment with human values, robust control, safety, transparency, fairness, and privacy anchors the mission.

- **A new horizon for healthcare**: The integration of LLMs such as GPT-4 heralds a transformation that could reshape the pharmaceutical landscape, making it more efficient and resourceful. For Moderna, and indeed for the biotech industry as a whole, embracing these advanced AI models could pave the way for unprecedented advancements, shaping a brighter and healthier future for all.

OpenAI's pinnacle against tech giants

A monumental question concludes this chapter: how did OpenAI, with merely 250 people, outshine the colossal R&D teams of leading tech companies to create ChatGPT? The key to OpenAI's success lies in the following aspects:

- **Mission-driven focus**: Dedicated to making AGI beneficial for humanity, OpenAI prioritized breakthrough projects such as ChatGPT

- **Advanced research**: Continually pushing AGI's boundaries and openly sharing discoveries

- **Risk embracement**: Boldly accepting risks allowed for substantial progress

- **Cooperative culture**: Aligning with global institutions to face AGI's challenges

- **Strategic talent acquisition**: Attracting top talents that made impactful strides

OpenAI's triumph isn't a mere tech sensation; it showcases AI's transformative power across various sectors. As the AI landscape evolves, smaller innovators such as OpenAI can challenge the status quo, although tech giants, with their vast resources, remain formidable contenders.

OpenAI and Moderna – a new frontier in drug discovery

The collaborative potential between OpenAI and Moderna offers exciting prospects in pharmaceuticals:

1. RAD collaboration:

   - Data analysis and compound identification: Moderna can harness GPT-4 to analyze vast scientific data, identifying and modifying compounds

   - Repurposing existing drugs: GPT-4's pattern recognition could help repurpose existing drugs for new uses

- Collaborative Research: Tailored AI solutions could be developed in collaboration with OpenAI, leveraging Moderna's mRNA expertise

2. Ethical alignment:

    - Safety and transparency: Both entities prioritize ethical practices, ensuring responsible development and rigorous testing

    - Fairness and privacy: OpenAI's principles could guide Moderna's clinical trials and patient data management

3. Future opportunities and global impact:

    - AGI in drug development: The advent of AGI might revolutionize Moderna's processes, targeting drugs and optimizing trials with unparalleled precision

    - Broadening global reach: AI-driven insights could extend Moderna's ability to address diverse health challenges globally

OpenAI's innovative technology, especially GPT-4, opens doors for Moderna. Integrating these AI technologies can accelerate research, align with ethical principles, and pave the way for collaboration and innovation. The potential synergy between Moderna and OpenAI is poised to redefine drug discovery, leading to global breakthroughs that could benefit humanity. As we transition into discussing the broader implications of AGI in the next section, this partnership stands as a testament to the boundless possibilities inherent in the ethical and innovative application of AI in healthcare.

OpenAI's history and focus on AGI

OpenAI was established in December 2015 as a non-profit, aiming to ensure AGI benefits humanity. The founders, including Elon Musk, Sam Altman, and others, kick-started an organization that's now at the forefront of AGI.

Here's a brief timeline of OpenAI:

- **2015**: OpenAI's inception with the commitment to use any influence over AGI to avoid its harmful uses.

- **2016-2018**: OpenAI publishes high-impact research papers and develops AI technologies, emphasizing a cooperative approach.

- **2019**: A transition was made to a "capped-profit" model to attract more funding and compete with for-profit AI entities.

- **2020**: The launch of GPT-3, a language prediction model garnering significant attention.

- **2021**: The introduction of the GPT-3 API, enabling developers to utilize the model in various applications.

- **2022**: The DALL-E and CLIP neural networks were unveiled, and a free preview of ChatGPT was provided.

- **2023**: GPT-4 was released and ten $100,000 grants for building prototypes of a democratic process for steering AI were provided.

- **August 2023**:

- The first acquisition was on August 16 via Global Illumination, based in New York. The company focused on open source technology for online game production. It was an acquire-to-hire purchase based on the company's expertise in building creative tools and digital experiences.

- ChatGPT was released for enterprise on August 28. It has enterprise-grade security and privacy, higher-speed access, longer context windows, and customization options.

- **September 2023**:

- Dall-E 3 announcement on September 20, with it being released in October 2023

- ChatGPT voice enablement on mobile devices

- ChatGPT image recognition

The next section provides an outline of OpenAI's advancements in AGI and its alignment, followed by its potential future applications, particularly in the finance sector. This material emphasizes the critical importance of AGI and reinforces the connection to finance.

OpenAI's AGI initiatives – a trailblazing journey toward intelligence revolution

OpenAI's notable initiatives, such as the development of GPT models, are leading the AGI revolution. From GPT-3's human-like text generation to exploring GPT-4's potential trillion parameters, these language models are transforming the AI landscape.

The focus on reinforcement learning, as seen in models such as Dactyl and OpenAI Five, is also groundbreaking. Fine-tuning processes such as human alignment and policy compliance through reinforcement learning ensure GPT-4's performance aligns with human values.

In collaborations, OpenAI is forging alliances with Microsoft and global research institutions, committing to a cooperative AGI community. Their goal? Ensuring AGI remains an ally, not a threat, to humanity.

AGI – alignment and why it matters – conducting the symphony of intelligence

Imagine a world where AGI reflects our spirit and our ethos, and amplifies our capabilities. The Alignment Team at OpenAI ensures that AGI, a marvel that can transcend human cognition, remains a faithful reflection of our objectives.

Their responsibilities include scalable oversight, generalization, automated interpretability, robustness, and adversarial testing. Picture these as the guiding principles that keep AGI's performance ethical, reliable, and resilient – even in the unpredictable world of finance.

AGI principles and future scenarios in finance – your financial partner of tomorrow

As AGI becomes a core pillar of our financial ecosystem, understanding the Alignment Team's work ensures reliability and transparency in AGI's financial applications. Here's a glimpse into the thrilling territories AGI may conquer:

- **AGI-driven business intelligence**: Imagine AGI acting as an oracle, offering real-time insights, forecasting opportunities, and bottlenecks in businesses like never before

- **AGI-enhanced financial market predictions**: AGI could revolutionize financial analysis and trading, deciphering hidden patterns and crafting innovative trading strategies

- **Revolutionized financial advisory**: AGI could provide ultra-personalized financial advice, considering an individual's complete life landscape to offer truly bespoke recommendations

- **Real-time risk management**: AGI might serve as a vigilant guardian, scanning data for potential risks and advising on timely interventions

- **Democratization of financial services**: AGI could democratize high-quality financial services, fostering financial literacy and independence across the globe

However, as we sail into these exciting frontiers, the balance between AGI's immense potential and ethical considerations such as job displacement, privacy, and fair access must remain at the forefront. Engaging in open dialogues will be pivotal in crafting an AGI-fueled future that is not just innovative but also inclusive and responsible.

Summary

This chapter has been an exhilarating odyssey through the multifaceted world of AI, finance, and biotechnology. We began with an exploration of GPT-4's role in accelerating Moderna's drug discovery. We ventured into the thrilling realm of momentum trading and the precision of Power BI visualizations. We also unveiled Moderna's ambitious collaborations with IBM and Carnegie Mellon, their focus on combating cancer, future pandemics, and the innovative approach to outsourcing production. Next, we delved into the fascinating intersection of autonomous bots with Jarvis and HuggingGPT. We traced OpenAI's journey toward AGI and the groundbreaking convergence of AI and quantum computing. Finally, we contemplated the ethical alignment of AGI, underscoring the importance of human values. This chapter has been a kaleidoscopic view of innovation, partnership, ambition, and ethical responsibility, setting the stage for what lies ahead.

In the last chapter, *Chapter 8, Crowdstrike: Cybersecurity in the Era of Deepfakes*, we will venture into the fascinating world of CrowdStrike – a global leader in cybersecurity. Through the lens of Power BI visualizations, we will explore aggressive and conservative trade strategies, unveiling a remarkable symphony of technology, finance, and innovation. From the pulsating beats of cyber insurance to the melodious strains of quantum computing, our journey will resonate with investors, tech enthusiasts, and anyone intrigued by the future of cybersecurity.

In the next chapter, prepare to be captivated as we examine into the following topics:

- **CrowdStrike's strengths and weaknesses**: A SCORE analysis revealing the company's standing in the digital arena

- **Innovative trading strategies**: Learn to leverage options and stocks in the cybersecurity sector, guided by Power BI visualizations

- **HackerGPT's expertise**: Discover a highly intelligent model that monitors cybersecurity regulatory changes and breaches

- **Deepfakes and AI's power**: Unmask the truth behind deepfakes and how AI tools such as ChatGPT can protect digital integrity

- **Your passport to the AI future**: Embark on the AI learning journey, transforming trading, investing, and financial reporting

8

CrowdStrike: Cybersecurity in the Era of Deepfakes

Chapter 7 opened the doors to a captivating world where AI, finance, and biotechnology intertwine using GPT-4's transformative impact on Moderna's drug discovery as an example. We witnessed Power BI's magic in financial analysis and unraveled Moderna's far-reaching collaborations and ambitions. We looked at the application of autonomous bots such as Jarvis and HuggingGPT, OpenAI's AGI initiatives, and the future promises of AI and quantum computing on the way. As we transition to Chapter 8, the insights from Chapter 7 lay a rich foundation, readying us for deeper exploration into the ever-evolving universe of AI and its applications for the safety of our financial information.

Welcome to Chapter 8, where we decode the labyrinthine corridors of cybersecurity and its dance with artificial intelligence and look at how it affects financial information. As we enter an era where digital transactions and data exchanges are ubiquitous, the risk of exposure is immense.

Imagine attending an Ed Sheeran concert: the concert venue represents your digital network, the audience is your data, and Ed Sheeran—the star of the show—is your critical data or server. Buckle up as we decode the intricacies of CrowdStrike, dive deep into the shadowy world of deepfakes, and untangle the complexities of financial trades—all through the lens of advanced AI technologies such as GPT-4. Here, you'll discover investment strategies spiced up by Power BI visualizations, grapple with ethical conundrums, and expand your AI literacy.

The following are the key topics covered in this chapter:

- **GPT-4, multimodal activity, and financial exposure**: Learn the tantalizing prospects and lurking perils of integrating GPT-4 into finance.

- **Understanding CrowdStrike**: Unveil the secrets behind CrowdStrike's cloud-native Security Cloud platform.

- **Aggressive and conservative trade strategies**: Turbocharge your financial journey with our electrifying trade strategies, all illustrated vividly through Power BI visualization.

- **HackerGPT and regulatory changes**: Meet HackerGPT, your new oracle for dissecting cybersecurity shifts and their financial implications.

- **FinGPT—revolutionizing financial analysis**: Explore how FinGPT is becoming the go-to AI model for financial data crunching, risk assessment, and predictive analytics.

- **MetaGPT—the multi-agent system wizard**: Dive into MetaGPT, the emerging AI solution that orchestrates multiple GPT models to deliver unprecedented financial insights.

- **Indirect prompt injection in real-world LLMs—risks and ethical quandaries**: Uncover the often-overlooked risks of indirect prompt injection in real-world **large language model (LLM)** applications and delve into the ethical mazes that come with it.

- **Deepfakes and AI literacy—risk and resilience in the financial realm**: Embark on a captivating journey through the unsettling world of deepfakes, exploring their financial risks and opportunities. Close the chapter by arming yourself with crucial AI literacy skills, your first line of defense in navigating these treacherous technological waters.

Navigating the world of cybersecurity can feel like traversing a complex digital labyrinth. But what if understanding it were as relatable as attending an Ed Sheeran concert—a thrilling live experience you can visualize and appreciate? That's where our concert and cybersecurity analogy offers a common language that simplifies the complex arena of digital security. Sophisticated tools such as GPT-4 can advise you on financial strategies and generate dynamic Power BI visualizations. But one cyber misstep can compromise it all. Get ready for an exhilarating journey through a landscape where high-tech truly meets high stakes and learn how to secure your digital world as meticulously as Ed Sheeran secures his concerts.

The concert and cybersecurity analogy – concert security for the digital stage

As an analogy, imagine you're attending an Ed Sheeran concert: a massive, high-profile event with tens of thousands of fans. The concert represents a digital network, the attendees are the data packets and users, and the stage (with the performing artist) is the core data or main servers:

- **Ticket checks at entry represent firewalls.** Before you enter the venue, your ticket is checked. This ensures that only authorized attendees get inside. Similarly, firewalls act as the first line of defense, allowing only legitimate traffic to pass through.

- **Bag and body scans are like antivirus and malware scans.** Security personnel will check bags and sometimes use metal detectors to ensure no harmful items get into the concert. Likewise, antiviruses and malware scans look for harmful software or files trying to enter the system.

- **The VIP area and backstage passes represent tiered access control.** Not everyone at the concert can go backstage or access VIP areas. Only those with special passes or wristbands can. In the digital realm, tiered access ensures only certain individuals can access sensitive parts of a network or specific data.

- **Monitoring suspicious activity is like using intrusion detection systems.** At a concert, there are security personnel scanning the crowd, looking for any disruptive behavior. Similarly, intrusion detection systems continuously monitor network activity, flagging anything unusual.

- **Rapid response teams represent incident response teams.** If there's a disturbance, specialized security teams at the concert are deployed to handle the situation swiftly. Likewise, when a cyber threat is detected, a specialized team jumps into action in the digital realm.

- **Ongoing surveillance is like continuous monitoring.** There are surveillance cameras spread throughout the concert venue, keeping an eye on everything. In cybersecurity, continuous monitoring ensures that any malicious activity is spotted as it happens.

- **Pre-concert security briefings are like employee training and threat intelligence.** Before the concert begins, the security team is briefed about potential known threats or issues, much like how companies inform and train employees about potential phishing emails or scams.

- **Emergency exits and evacuation plans represent backup and recovery processes.** Concert venues have clear emergency exits, and there's a plan if evacuation becomes necessary. Similarly, in cybersecurity, backup and recovery plans ensure that data can be restored and operations can continue in case of breaches or failures.

Imagine GPT-4, a machine so smart it can advise you on stock picks and create dynamic Power BI visualizations. Sounds like a dream, but there's a catch. Ever thought about the cybersecurity risks lurking in the background? What if hackers manipulate your AI-generated financial advice?

In this exhilarating section, we'll dive into the capabilities and pitfalls of GPT-4, understand its multimodal talents, and confront the cybersecurity threats that could make or break your financial strategy. So get ready; this is where high tech meets high stakes!

GPT-4, multimodal activity, and financial exposure – a cautionary tale

The advancement of AI technologies such as GPT-4, a multimodal model accepting both image and text inputs, is both fascinating and perilous, especially in the context of finance. As these systems continue to integrate with aspects of our daily lives, it's crucial to understand the risks, particularly with regard to cybersecurity and its impact on investment, trading, and financial analysis.

The multimodal capabilities of GPT-4

GPT-4, the latest installment in OpenAI's deep learning technology, performs exceptionally well on professional and academic benchmarks, including passing a simulated bar exam within the top 10% of test takers. The model has even been fine-tuned through an adversarial testing program to achieve the best-ever results in factuality and steerability.

Amazon One and the age of biometrics

To draw a parallel, let's consider Amazon One, Amazon's new biometric-based payment system. With a swipe of your hand, the service allows you to complete a purchase, offering the supposed advantage of high security. However, cybersecurity experts caution that artificial intelligence could be deployed to generate false biometric data. Similar to GPT-4, which can generate convincing human-like text, biometric fakes could be used to trick Amazon One's security mechanisms.

Cybersecurity risks in finance

Financial decision-making relies heavily on accurate information and secure platforms. Imagine that GPT-4 is integrated into your financial analytics tool for generating investment insights or creating Power BI visualizations. A hacker gaining control over the model could manipulate the generated advice or data visualizations, leading you to make flawed investment choices. In the world of trading, this could result in significant financial loss.

The implications for data visualization

Moreover, these manipulations could skew the Power BI visualizations that decision-makers often rely upon. Inaccurate visual data could distort everything from trend analysis to asset allocation, affecting not just individual portfolios but potentially destabilizing market segments.

Protecting sensitive information

As with biometric data, the data streams feeding into or generated by a model such as GPT-4 need to be stringently protected. Given the sensitive nature of financial data and the cascading impact of erroneous financial decisions, it is paramount to implement robust cybersecurity measures.

The rise of multimodal AI models such as GPT-4 and biometric payment systems such as Amazon One heralds a new era of convenience but also unveils new vulnerabilities. In finance, this translates to heightened exposure to risks that could alter your investment landscape, distort your financial analysis, and compromise the reliability of your data visualizations. As we move forward in this age of rapid technological advancement, caution and due diligence become not just advisable but absolutely essential.

Hold onto your seats, because we're diving into the future of financial cybersecurity with CrowdStrike, a company that's revolutionizing how we think about digital safety. Picture this: you're an investor with valuable assets and data to protect. In this eye-opening section, we'll unpack CrowdStrike's groundbreaking Falcon platform, reveal its AI-driven arsenal, and explore how its real-time threat prediction can be a game-changer for anyone in finance. You'll get an insider's look into the innovative technologies that are shaping the future of secure financial transactions and investments. Read on to uncover the cybersecurity magic that is CrowdStrike!

Understanding CrowdStrike's security capabilities

Founded in 2011 and based in Sunnyvale, CA, CrowdStrike aims to redefine the cybersecurity landscape. It employs its cloud-native Security Cloud platform to mitigate various cyber threats, focusing primarily on endpoints, cloud workloads, identity verification, and data protection. This platform, known as CrowdStrike Falcon®, employs an array of real-time indicators, threat intelligence, and telemetry data to enhance detection and protection capabilities.

It's worth noting the key features of the Falcon platform:

- **Real-time indicators of attack**: These allow for proactive threat detection
- **Automated protection and remediation**: This reduces manual labor and speeds up response times
- **Threat hunting**: Skilled professionals use the platform for targeted identification of complex threats
- **Prioritized observability of vulnerabilities**: This guides security professionals to focus on the most critical areas first

CrowdStrike has been acknowledged for its efforts in the cybersecurity industry, earning recognition from various outlets such as Forbes and Inc. While these accolades attest to the company's industry impact, they also underscore the rate at which CrowdStrike is evolving to meet modern security challenges.

CrowdScore – a paradigm shift in threat management

CrowdStrike's latest offering, CrowdScore, aims to simplify how organizations perceive and react to threats. Unlike traditional metrics, CrowdScore offers a unified, real-time view of the threat landscape, assisting executive decision-making.

The utility of CrowdScore manifests in several ways:

- **Immediate threat level indication**: This helps organizations allocate resources more effectively
- **Historical trend analysis**: By comparing current data with past trends, teams can make informed decisions
- **Prioritized incidents**: This streamlines the triage process, enabling faster response times

The incident workbench feature in CrowdScore offers visual aids to assist in rapid analysis and remediation. This marks a strategic shift in how security professionals can efficiently allocate their resources to counter threats.

In summary, CrowdScore seeks to empower organizations with timely insights into their cyber threat landscape, fostering quicker and more informed responses. This exemplifies CrowdStrike's commitment to not only offering robust protection but also advancing the overall cybersecurity framework.

The SCORE analysis of CrowdStrike – navigating financial cyber risks and opportunities

Welcome to the intersection of finance and cybersecurity! Meet CrowdStrike, the titan transforming how we protect financial assets in an age of relentless digital threats. Through our SCORE lens, we'll dissect CrowdStrike's strengths, challenges, opportunities, risks, and efficiencies. Get ready for an unfiltered look into AI-driven threat prediction, quantum-resistant algorithms, and more—essential insights for anyone navigating the high-stakes world of cyber-financial risk.

The following are CrowdStrike's strengths:

- **AI-powered predictive analysis**: CrowdStrike's Falcon platform leverages artificial intelligence to predict and prevent potential breaches, allowing it to remain ahead of emerging threats. This approach could redefine how cybersecurity is approached in the modern era.

- **Investment in research and development (R&D)**: With a significant percentage of revenue allocated to R&D, CrowdStrike continues to foster innovation and maintain its technological edge.

The following are its challenges:

- **Integrating acquisitions**: CrowdStrike's growth strategy includes acquiring smaller firms with innovative technologies. Integrating these into the existing structure without loss of agility or focus could be a substantial challenge.

The following are its opportunities:

- **5G and IoT security**: With the proliferation of 5G and **Internet of Things (IoT)** devices, the attack surface for cyber threats is expanding rapidly. CrowdStrike's expertise positions it to be a leader in securing these innovative technologies.

- **Partnerships with emerging technology players**: Collaborations with up-and-coming technology firms can further diversify CrowdStrike's product offerings and extend its reach into new markets.

The following are its risks:

- **Reliance on third-party technologies**: CrowdStrike's dependence on third-party platforms and technologies can introduce vulnerabilities that they might not have control over, adding an extra layer of risk to their operations.

- **Potential regulatory changes**: Governments worldwide are considering new regulations around data privacy and cybersecurity. Any unexpected changes could affect CrowdStrike's operations and cost structure.

The following are its efficiencies:

- **Automation in threat response**: By incorporating more automated responses to common threats, CrowdStrike could further streamline its operations, reducing human intervention and cost.

The following are potential opportunities for the future:

- **Quantum-resistant algorithms**: As quantum computing becomes a reality, traditional encryption methods may become obsolete. Developing quantum-resistant algorithms could position CrowdStrike as a trailblazer in next-gen cybersecurity.

- **Behavioral analytics integration with Power BI**: Utilizing machine learning to analyze behavior patterns and then visualizing these insights through Power BI could offer unparalleled insights for proactive threat management.

CrowdStrike's journey represents an electrifying intersection of innovation, strategic planning, and adaptability. Through the lens of the SCORE analysis, enriched with these specific examples and opportunities, investors and analysts can understand not just where CrowdStrike stands today, but where this cybersecurity behemoth might be heading in the thrilling and unpredictable future of digital security. By keeping a pulse on these dynamics, one can make informed decisions that capitalize on the zeitgeist of our digital age.

Here, we will explore the intersection of cybersecurity and finance, a critical area where technology meets the stringent demands of safeguarding financial assets and data. One of the key players in this space is CrowdStrike.

1. **Cloud-delivered protection for financial institutions**: CrowdStrike Falcon ensures that breaches stop here, providing a robust shield for financial data across endpoints, cloud workloads, identity, and more.

2. **Real-time threat prediction**: In the fast-paced world of trading and investment, CrowdStrike's automatic prediction and prevention features function as a sentinel, detecting potential threats in real time.

3. **AI-driven insights**: The CrowdStrike Threat Graph exemplifies a practical deployment of AI in cybersecurity for the financial sector. CrowdStrike employs specialized AI algorithms to sift through trillions of data points. It identifies emerging threats and changes in adversarial tactics that could be particularly damaging for financial institutions. The AI-driven insights work in tandem with human expertise to bolster the cyber defenses of these firms, ensuring they stay one step ahead of potential risks.

4. **Holistic security for the finance sector**: CrowdStrike's approach isn't just about preventing attacks; it's about building a secure financial environment. From elite threat hunting to prioritized vulnerability management, CrowdStrike ensures that the financial sector's critical areas of risk are well-protected.

CrowdStrike's innovative technology is a beacon of innovation in the cybersecurity landscape, particularly pertinent to the financial industry. As we delve into the world of finance, investing, and trading, understanding how solutions such as CrowdStrike can protect and empower businesses is vital. The platform is more than a security tool; it's a strategic asset for any financial institution looking to safeguard its operations in an increasingly connected and perilous digital world.

Brace yourselves, as we're diving deep into the monumental alliance between CrowdStrike and Dell Technologies—a partnership that promises to rewrite the rules of commercial cybersecurity in the small- and medium-sized business (SMB) space. Picture this: CrowdStrike's state-of-the-art Falcon platform is seamlessly woven into Dell's vast technology tapestry. The result? A cybersecurity fortress that not only guards against threats but redefines how we approach data security in the financial world.

From multi-million-dollar deals to game-changing Power BI visualizations, this section takes you through a captivating journey that explores why this alliance is a match made in tech heaven.

CrowdStrike and Dell Technologies: a strategic alliance in commercial cybersecurity

Prepare for a seismic shift in the landscape of commercial cybersecurity! Enter the strategic alliance between CrowdStrike and Dell Technologies—an industry-defining partnership set to supercharge cyber defenses, especially in the high-stakes world of finance. Imagine cutting-edge CrowdStrike solutions interwoven into Dell's broad technology suite, all visualized through real-time data dashboards such as Power BI. This isn't just an alliance; it's a revolution, opening floodgates of opportunities in cybersecurity that will empower banks, trading platforms, and financial analytics services.

The alliance: building a comprehensive cyber defense

CrowdStrike and Dell Technologies have formed a strategic alliance that focuses on delivering seamless and cost-effective solutions to counter cyber threats. CrowdStrike's Falcon platform is now integrated into a broad range of Dell's technology offerings.

Financial implications and cybersecurity

This alliance opens significant opportunities for CrowdStrike, especially in the financial sector. With banks, trading platforms, and financial analytics services becoming more interconnected, there's an increasing demand for robust cybersecurity solutions. CrowdStrike's enhanced capabilities position it as a front-runner in this space.

The power of data visualization

The security metrics generated from this alliance could be displayed through real-time threat dashboards or predictive analytics, visualized through tools like Power BI. This would provide financial institutions with deeper insights into their cybersecurity posture, aiding in data-driven decision-making.

Conclusion: the future of cybersecurity and finance

The early success of this alliance—evident in a seven-figure deal with a large regional healthcare provider—sets a promising precedent. It underscores the alliance's potential to spur innovation, efficiency, and growth in the cybersecurity landscape, which is becoming increasingly pivotal in safeguarding financial sectors.

This next section takes you on a roller coaster ride through the intricate labyrinth of CrowdStrike's earnings call transcripts, all decoded by innovative AI and natural language processing (NLP) tools. Through the lens of Python libraries and TextBlob-powered sentiment analysis, we'll dissect CrowdStrike's recent performance and get a glimpse into the company's future. If you're keen to tap into the pulse of CrowdStrike's financial health and potential risks, while discovering how AI is revolutionizing investment strategies, you won't want to miss this. So, sit tight; the show's about to begin!

Analyzing CrowdStrike's earnings call transcripts with AI and NLP

From the invaluable insights tucked away in earnings call transcripts to sentiment analysis that decodes the company's market mood, this section is your roadmap to understanding CrowdStrike's standing in the ever-evolving world of cybersecurity. We'll swiftly traverse through the importance of these transcripts, the technical workflow for data extraction, and sentiment analysis. Finally, we'll then zoom out to see how it all fits into the broader cybersecurity landscape.

The role of earnings call transcripts in finance

Earnings call transcripts are vital financial documents that reveal a company's performance, strategies, and forward-looking statements. Their analysis can offer invaluable insights for investors and financial analysts.

Technical workflow

Using the Python docx library, the text from each of the three transcripts can be accessed within milliseconds. This prepares the ground for more in-depth data analysis.

Sentiment analysis using TextBlob

The "Questions and Answers" sections of these transcripts are especially significant. Utilizing the TextBlob library, sentiment scores were calculated for each quarter:

- Q3 2023: 0.172 (slightly positive)
- Q4 2023: 0.181 (slightly positive)
- Q1 2024: 0.184 (slightly positive)

These scores, ranging from -1 (negative) to 1 (positive), offer an aerial perspective on the sentiment, revealing a consistently positive tone.

Relevance to CrowdStrike and cybersecurity

Such sentiment analyses can help investors and financial analysts understand CrowdStrike's market position and the potential risks, especially when integrated with cybersecurity metrics. Similar AI models are embedded within cybersecurity platforms such as CrowdStrike, enhancing their ability to predict and adapt to new threats.

We're about to soar into the high-octane world of aggressive trade strategies! Imagine you could turbocharge your portfolio with a play that marries the surging growth of cyber insurance with a calculated hedge against overvaluation. Let's dive deep into a dual-strategy play: buying call options on industry leaders in insurance such as Beazley and Hiscox while selling put options on the cybersecurity behemoth, CrowdStrike.

If the thought of maximizing gains while having a fallback excites you, you're in the right place. Whether you're an experienced trader or an enthusiast looking to elevate your game, are you ready to unleash the power of aggressive options trading?

Aggressive trading (using options) – buying call options on Beazley and Hiscox and selling put options on CrowdStrike

In this aggressive trade strategy, we are buying call options on Beazley and Hiscox, indicating that we are bullish on these insurers. Simultaneously, we are selling put options on CrowdStrike, expressing a more cautious view. This strategy aims to leverage the expected growth in cyber insurance, coupled with a possible overvaluation of CrowdStrike:

1. Install the `yfinance` package with `pip install yfinance`

2. Run the following Python code:

```python
# Import necessary libraries
import yfinance as yf

def buy_call_options(symbol, strike, expiration, contracts):
    print(f"Buying {contracts} call options for {symbol} with
strike {strike} and expiration {expiration}.")
    # TODO: Add your actual trading logic here

def sell_put_options(symbol, strike, expiration, contracts):
    print(f"Selling {contracts} put options for {symbol} with
strike {strike} and expiration {expiration}.")
    # TODO: Add your actual trading logic here
```

```
# Define the strike price, expiration date, and number of
contracts
# NOTE: Replace the following values with those relevant to your
strategy
beazley_strike = 150
beazley_expiration = '2023-12-15'
beazley_contracts = 10

hiscox_strike = 120
hiscox_expiration = '2023-12-15'
hiscox_contracts = 10

crowdstrike_strike = 200
crowdstrike_expiration = '2023-12-15'
crowdstrike_contracts = 10

# Place trades
buy_call_options('BEZ.L', beazley_strike, beazley_expiration,
beazley_contracts)
buy_call_options('HSX.L', hiscox_strike, hiscox_expiration,
hiscox_contracts)
sell_put_options('CRWD', crowdstrike_strike, crowdstrike_
expiration, crowdstrike_contracts)
```

Example functions with highlighted replacement areas

The following are example functions that simulate what the buy_call_options and sell_put_options functions might look like with actual trading logic:

```
# Example of what buy_call_options might look like
def buy_call_options(symbol, strike, expiration, contracts):
    your_trading_platform_api.buy_options(
        symbol = symbol,                  # <-- Replace with your variable
or hard-coded value
        strike_price = strike,       # <-- Replace with your variable
or hard-coded value
        expiration_date = expiration, # <-- Replace with your variable
or hard-coded value
        contract_type = 'CALL',
        num_of_contracts = contracts  # <-- Replace with your variable
or hard-coded value
    )

# Example of what sell_put_options might look like
def sell_put_options(symbol, strike, expiration, contracts):
```

```
your_trading_platform_api.sell_options(
        symbol = symbol,              # <-- Replace with your variable
or hard-coded value
        strike_price = strike,        # <-- Replace with your variable
or hard-coded value
        expiration_date = expiration, # <-- Replace with your variable
or hard-coded value
        contract_type = 'PUT',
        num_of_contracts = contracts  # <-- Replace with your variable
or hard-coded value
    )
```

In these example functions, replace the placeholders (your_trading_platform_api, symbol, strike, expiration, contracts) with the actual details relevant to your trading strategy and platform.

Prepare to turn the dial down but keep the wisdom up. Welcome to the realm of conservative trading strategies, where slow and steady could very well win the race! In this nuanced strategy, we're taking a bullish stance on insurance giants Beazley and Hiscox by directly buying their stocks. But that's not all. We're keeping a keen eye on CrowdStrike, waiting for a 5% dip to swoop in and snag its shares.

Why this balanced approach, you ask? Because in the world of investing, timing and caution can be just as electrifying as any high-stakes gamble. If you're someone who appreciates the art of calculated risk and the allure of steady gains, then this section is your masterclass. Ready to navigate the financial markets with poise and precision? Let's get started!

Conservative trading (using stock) – buying stock in Beazley and Hiscox and buying stock in CrowdStrike once it falls 5% from its current price

In this conservative trade strategy, we are directly buying stocks in Beazley and Hiscox, signaling a bullish view of these insurers. Meanwhile, we set a limit order to buy CrowdStrike's stock once it falls 5% from the current levels, indicating a more cautious approach:

```
a). Assumes yfinance library has already been installed on the PC.  If
not, please complete this step first.
pip install yfinance
b). Run python code
# Import necessary libraries
import yfinance as yf

def buy_stock(symbol, num_shares):
    print(f"Buying {num_shares} shares of {symbol}.")
    # TODO: Add your actual trading logic here
```

```
def place_limit_order(symbol, target_price, num_shares):
    print(f"Placing limit order for {num_shares} shares of {symbol} at
target price {target_price}.")
    # TODO: Add your actual trading logic here


# Define the stock symbols and number of shares to buy
# NOTE: Replace the following values with those relevant to your
strategy
beazley_stock = 'BEZ.L'
hiscox_stock = 'HSX.L'
crowdstrike_stock = 'CRWD'
num_shares_beazley = 100
num_shares_hiscox = 100
num_shares_crowdstrike = 100


# Place trades
buy_stock(beazley_stock, num_shares_beazley)
buy_stock(hiscox_stock, num_shares_hiscox)


# Check current price of CrowdStrike
crowdstrike_price = yf.Ticker(crowdstrike_stock).history().tail(1)
['Close'].iloc[0]


# Determine target price (5% below current price)
target_price = crowdstrike_price * 0.95


# Place limit order
place_limit_order(crowdstrike_stock, target_price, num_shares_
crowdstrike)
```

Example functions with highlighted replacement areas

The following are example functions that simulate what the buy_stock and place_limit_order functions
might look like with actual trading logic:

```
# Example of what buy_stock might look like
def buy_stock(symbol, num_shares):
    your_trading_platform_api.buy_stock(
        symbol = symbol,                    # <-- Replace with your
variable or hard-coded value
        num_of_shares = num_shares    # <-- Replace with your
variable or hard-coded value
    )
```

```
# Example of what place_limit_order might look like
def place_limit_order(symbol, target_price, num_shares):
    your_trading_platform_api.place_limit_order(
        symbol = symbol,                  # <-- Replace with your
variable or hard-coded value
        target_price = target_price,      # <-- Replace with your
variable or hard-coded value
        num_of_shares = num_shares        # <-- Replace with your
variable or hard-coded value
    )
```

In these example functions, replace the placeholders (your_trading_platform_api, symbol, target_price, num_shares) with the actual details relevant to your trading strategy and platform.

Both investment strategies require continuous monitoring and adjustments based on market conditions. It's also essential to consult with a financial advisor to align these strategies with individual investment goals, risk tolerance, and financial situation.

Imagine a cockpit dashboard for your trades; sounds amazing, right? This is what you get when Power BI's stunning visualizations meet ChatGPT's intuitive natural language capabilities. Whether you're an options warrior or a stock market strategist, these dashboards act like your personal command centers, offering real-time insights, alerts, and a conversational interface that speaks your financial lingo. If you've been thirsting for actionable analytics and AI-powered financial advice, then consider this next section your oasis.

The ultimate guide to investment dashboards – Power BI meets ChatGPT

Step into your financial cockpit where Power BI's dazzling visuals co-pilot with ChatGPT's savvy linguistics to navigate the thrilling skies of trading and investment. In this ultimate guide, we're breaking down the dashboard of your dreams into key components. First, the aggressive trade and conservative trade strategies unfold in real-time through a suite of tailored visualizations. We then ramp up the stakes with real-time alerts that act as your financial radar. Finally, say hello to ChatGPT as it seamlessly integrates into these dashboards, providing on-demand financial advice and insight.

Power BI visualizations

We invite you to explore the world of Power BI visualizations, specifically tailored for aggressive trading strategies using options on Beazley, Hiscox, and CrowdStrike. We've organized the section into three pivotal components. First, we offer a meticulously crafted dashboard overview featuring a time series plot for price movements, an open positions table to keep track of your contracts, and a risk analysis chart to assess potential profit or loss scenarios. Next, we introduce the invaluable concept of alerts, focusing on the CrowdStrike put option, to ensure you never miss an opportune moment to act. Lastly, we add the integration with ChatGPT, where you can ask questions directly and receive data-driven insights and advice. This section will provide a quick overview of the aggressive and conservative trades highlighted earlier in this chapter. It will provide some suggestions for visualizing the data in Power BI and turning on Power BI alerts. To create these Power BI visualizations, we'll start by creating CSV files that contain the aggressive and conservative trade data starting on page 18-22 and then detailed Power BI visualization steps will start on page 22.

Aggressive trading using options on Beazley, Hiscox, and CrowdStrike

1. Dashboard overview:

   - **Time series plot**: A line chart displaying the price movement of Beazley, Hiscox, and CrowdStrike options. Use different line colors for calls and puts to easily distinguish.

   - **Open positions table**: A table showing current positions, including strike price, expiration date, number of contracts, and current value.

   - **Risk analysis chart**: A scatter plot showing the potential profit or loss of the options positions under different scenarios.

2. Alerts:

   - **CrowdStrike put alert**: Set an alert if the put option on CrowdStrike goes in the money (stock price falls below the strike price). This can notify the user to potentially take action.

3. Integration with ChatGPT:

   - A text input field where the user can query ChatGPT for insights, such as `What is the potential risk of the CrowdStrike put option?`

   - ChatGPT can analyze the visualized data and provide actionable insights and suggestions

Conservative trade: buying stock in Beazley, Hiscox, and CrowdStrike after a 5% fall

We shift gears to explore Power BI visualizations geared toward a more conservative trading approach, specifically focusing on buying stocks in Beazley, Hiscox, and CrowdStrike after a 5% price drop. This tailored guide unfolds in three main segments. First up is the dashboard overview, which presents a time series plot to trace stock price movements, an open positions table to track your current holdings, and a status card for your limit orders, ensuring you have all the essential information at your fingertips. Second, we'll walk you through setting up alerts, such as one that triggers when CrowdStrike's stock price is within 5% of your target, enabling timely action.

Finally, we integrate ChatGPT, as for the aggressive trade, for interactive, real-time insights:

1. Dashboard overview:

   - Time series plot: A line chart displaying the stock price movement of Beazley, Hiscox, and CrowdStrike

   - Open positions table: A table showing current stock holdings, including symbol, number of shares, average cost, and current value

   - Limit order status: A card or section displaying the status of the limit order on CrowdStrike, with target price and current price

2. Alerts:

   - CrowdStrike target price alert: Set an alert if CrowdStrike's price falls within 5% of the target price. This can notify the user to monitor closely or execute the trade

3. Integration with ChatGPT:

   - Follow the same steps highlighted in the Aggressive Trade Power BI section)

Power BI alert configuration (example for CrowdStrike put alert but can be used for Crowdstrike stock alert too)

This section is a six-step journey that provides you with the skills to set up your own alerts in Power BI, tailored to your unique trading strategies. First, you'll learn how to select the appropriate visual elements, such as line charts, to base your alert on. Next, we guide you through the alerts section in Power BI, where the main setup is completed. Here, you'll set new alert rules, specify conditions, and choose how you'd like to be notified. Each step is a building block, leading to a final, configured alert that keeps you ahead of the curve. By mastering these steps, you're not just adding another tool to your trading toolbox; you're gaining a vigilant ally that ensures you never miss an important trading cue:

1. Click on the specific visual that you want to set an alert on (e.g., the line chart showing CrowdStrike's stock price versus put option strike price).

2. Go to the **Alerts** section in the Power BI service.

3. Click on + **New alert** rule.

4. Set the condition for the alert (e.g., **Stock Price < Strike Price**).

5. Choose the notification method (e.g., email or mobile notification).

6. Save the alert.

> **Important note**
>
> The exact implementation and look of the visualizations will depend on your data sources, Power BI setup, and specific requirements.
>
> Ensure that you are in compliance with all relevant legal and regulatory requirements, especially when integrating AI such as ChatGPT.

By combining Power BI's visualization capabilities with ChatGPT's natural language analysis, these investment strategies can be monitored and managed effectively, with insights provided in an accessible and actionable manner. Make sure to involve a financial expert to tailor the strategies to individual circumstances.

Prepare for a roller-coaster ride through Python's dynamic capabilities as we bring your aggressive trade strategy to life. Imagine being able to snapshot your option positions, track real-time prices, and visualize potential risks, all with a few lines of code to create a CSV file. Welcome to the world where Python is your trading floor and you're the conductor of this financial symphony. Get ready to code your way to dynamic, real-time trading insights.

Harnessing Python's power for aggressive trading: a code-driven odyssey

Get ready for a riveting journey—a code-driven odyssey into the world of aggressive trading powered by Python. This section isn't merely a tutorial; it's an action-packed course that turns Python code into the engine room of your trading cockpit. We start by assembling our trade options in a data frame called options_df, saving it as a CSV file for easy access. Our get_option_price function acts as a conduit to real-time option pricing, pulling in vital data based on the ticker, strike price, and expiration date. This is then neatly organized in another data frame, positions_df, also saved as a CSV file. As we move forward, expect to delve into time series plotting and risk analysis, where you'll learn to visualize price trends and calculate potential gains or losses.

The following is the Python code to create a CSV file:

```
a). Install yfinance and pandas first (if this has not already been
done)
pip install pandas
pip install yfinance


b). Run the following Python code:
import pandas as pd
import yfinance as yf

# Define your variables here
# NOTE: Replace the '...' with actual values
beazley_stock = 'BEZ.L'
```

```
hiscox_stock = 'HSX.L'
crowdstrike_stock = 'CRWD'
beazley_strike = ...
hiscox_strike = ...
crowdstrike_strike = ...
beazley_expiration = ...
hiscox_expiration = ...
crowdstrike_expiration = ...
beazley_contracts = ...
hiscox_contracts = ...
crowdstrike_contracts = ...


# Create DataFrame for option positions
options_df = pd.DataFrame({
    'Symbol': [beazley_stock, hiscox_stock, crowdstrike_stock],
    'Type': ['Call', 'Call', 'Put'],
    'Strike': [beazley_strike, hiscox_strike, crowdstrike_strike],
    'Expiration': [beazley_expiration, hiscox_expiration, crowdstrike_
expiration],
    'Contracts': [beazley_contracts, hiscox_contracts, crowdstrike_
contracts]
})


# Save DataFrame to CSV
options_df.to_csv('aggressive_trade_options.csv', index=False)


# Function to fetch real-time price
def get_option_price(ticker, strike, expiration, option_type='call'):
    # TODO: Add your actual trading logic here
    return ...


# Open Positions Table
positions = []
for symbol, strike, expiration, contracts in [(beazley_stock, beazley_
strike, beazley_expiration, beazley_contracts),
                                              (hiscox_stock, hiscox_
strike, hiscox_expiration, hiscox_contracts),
                                              (crowdstrike_stock,
crowdstrike_strike, crowdstrike_expiration, crowdstrike_contracts)]:
    price = get_option_price(symbol, strike, expiration)
    positions.append([symbol, strike, expiration, contracts, price *
contracts])


positions_df = pd.DataFrame(positions, columns=['Symbol', 'Strike',
'Expiration', 'Contracts', 'Value'])
```

```
positions_df.to_csv('aggressive_positions.csv', index=False)

# Time Series Plot
# TODO: Add your actual trading logic here

# Risk Analysis Chart
# TODO: Add your actual trading logic here
```

> **Important note**
>
> Replace all the ... with the actual values you want to use.
>
> You'll need to implement the `get_option_price()` function to get real-time option prices. This will depend on the data source or brokerage you are using.
>
> The time series plot and risk analysis chart sections are marked as TODO as you'll need to add the actual logic based on your requirements.

Unearth the tranquility in the chaotic world of stock markets by mastering conservative trading through Python. If you prefer the gradual crescendo over the high-octane thrill of market volatility, this section is your haven. We'll employ Python to create an analytical dashboard, sketch your trade positions, track real-time prices, and even set up limit orders using a CSV file. Ready to code your way to sustainable, risk-managed profits? Let's dive in.

The Zen of conservative trade: unleashing Python for steady gains

This section is a haven for those seeking a calculated, steady approach to trading. We'll be working with Python code to execute conservative trading strategies for stocks such as Beazley, Hiscox, and CrowdStrike.

First, we define crucial variables such as stock symbols, number of shares, and target prices. Then, using Python's pandas library, we craft a data frame to neatly catalog these variables. We also save this data to a CSV file for future use. After that, the script jumps into real-time mode, fetching the most recent stock prices to populate your open positions table—another data frame we'll save to a CSV. Finally, the script ends by updating a limit order status data frame, which monitors how close the current stock price is to your target buy price.

The following is the Python code to create a CSV file:

1. Install yfinance and pandas first (if this has not already been done):

    ```
    pip install pandas
    pip install yfinance
    ```

2. Run the following Python code:

```python
import pandas as pd
import yfinance as yf

# Define your variables here
# NOTE: Replace the '...' with actual values
beazley_stock = ...
hiscox_stock = ...
crowdstrike_stock = ...
num_shares_beazley = ...
num_shares_hiscox = ...
num_shares_crowdstrike = ...
target_price = ...  # Target price for CrowdStrike

# Create DataFrame for stock positions
stock_df = pd.DataFrame({
    'Symbol': [beazley_stock, hiscox_stock, crowdstrike_stock],
    'Shares': [num_shares_beazley, num_shares_hiscox, num_
shares_crowdstrike],
    'Target_Price': [None, None, target_price]
})

# Save DataFrame to CSV
stock_df.to_csv('conservative_trade_stocks.csv', index=False)

# Function to fetch real-time stock price
def get_stock_price(ticker):
    return yf.Ticker(ticker).history().tail(1)['Close'].iloc[0]

# Open Positions Table
positions = []
for symbol, shares in [(beazley_stock, num_shares_beazley),
                       (hiscox_stock, num_shares_hiscox)]:
    price = get_stock_price(symbol)
    positions.append([symbol, shares, price, price * shares])  #
Adjust to include average cost

positions_df = pd.DataFrame(positions, columns=['Symbol',
'Shares', 'Current Price', 'Value'])
positions_df.to_csv('conservative_positions.csv', index=False)

# Time Series Plot
# TODO: Add your actual trading logic here
```

```
# Limit Order Status
limit_order_status = pd.DataFrame([[crowdstrike_stock, target_
price, get_stock_price(crowdstrike_stock)]],
                                  columns=['Symbol', 'Target
Price', 'Current Price'])
limit_order_status.to_csv('limit_order_status.csv', index=False)
```

> **Important note**
>
> Replace all the . . . with the actual values you want to use.
>
> The time series plot section is marked as TODO. You'll need to add the actual logic based on your specific requirements.

You've got your trading data. Now what? How about transforming that raw, unfiltered information into stunning, insightful visuals that tell a captivating story? Welcome to the art of Power BI visualizations! From plotting aggressive trade maneuvers to sketching the Zen-like calm of conservative strategies, we'll turn your spreadsheets into a visual symphony. And guess what? We'll even set up real-time alerts and integrate with ChatGPT for AI-powered insights.

Visual alchemy: transmuting raw data into golden insights with Power BI

Step into the Python-powered realm of conservative trading, where every line of code is a stepping stone toward financial prudence and optimized gains. Our section unfolds by introducing you to the Python libraries crucial for data manipulation and market data extraction: pandas and yfinance. The script begins by declaring variables such as stock symbols, number of shares, and target prices, effectively laying down the groundwork for your conservative trading strategy. With a mere snippet of code, we transform these raw variables into a structured data frame called stock_df, which is then saved as a CSV file for easy accessibility. Our get_stock_price function keeps your strategies tethered to market realities by pulling in real-time stock prices from Yahoo Finance. This data nourishes another DataFrame, positions_df, which serves as your real-time ledger for tracking share values. We also reserve a spot for tracking the status of limit orders, ensuring you never miss an optimal buy-in point.

Creating Power BI visualizations

Now that you have the CSV files, you can follow these steps to create the Power BI visualizations:

1. Load the CSV files into Power BI:

    *   Open Power BI Desktop.

    *   Click on Get Data > Text/CSV.

    *   Browse to the location of your CSV files and load them into Power BI.

2.   Create visualizations for aggressive trading:

    I.   For a time series plot, use a line chart and plot the price movement using date as the *x*axis and the price as the *y*axis.

    II.   For an open positions table, use a table visualization and drag the relevant fields from `aggressive_trade_options.csv`.

    III.   For a risk analysis chart, use a scatter chart and add the calculated fields for profit/loss.

    IV.   For a CrowdStrike put alert, you can set up an alert as described in the previous message.

3.   Create visualizations for conservative trading:

    I.   For a time series plot, similar to the aggressive trade, use a line chart.

    II.   For an open positions table, use a table visualization with fields from `conservative_trade_stocks.csv`.

    III.   For limit order status, use a card visualization to display the target price and current price.

    IV.   For a CrowdStrike target price alert, set up an alert as previously explained.

4.   Integrate with ChatGPT:

- While Power BI can connect to GPT4 via API, you just need to enter your OpenAI API key and make sure you have a sufficient balance to cover API calls

Integration with ChatGPT (GPT-4)

Enable Python scripting in Power BI:

1.   Go to **File > Options and Settings > Options**.

2.   Under **Python scripting**, select your installed Python directory.

3.   Install the required Python packages.

Make sure to install the openai Python package, which will allow you to communicate with the GPT-4 API. You can install it via pip:

```Bash
pip install openai
```

4.   Create a Python visual in Power BI:

- In Power BI Desktop, click on Python script visual.

- A placeholder Python script visual will appear on your report, and an editor will open where you can input Python code.

5. Input Python code for GPT-4 API calls.

    Use the following sample Python code as a basis. Replace `'your_openai_api_key_here'` with your actual OpenAI API key:

    ```python
    import openai

    openai.api_key = "your_openai_api_key_here"

    # Your query based on Power BI data
    prompt = "Provide insights based on Power BI visualization of
    aggressive trade options."

    # API call to GPT-4 for text generation
    response = openai.Completion.create(
      engine="text-davinci-003",  # or your chosen engine
      prompt=prompt,
      max_tokens=100
    )

    insight = response.choices[0].text.strip()
    ```

6. Display insights in Power BI.

    You can display the generated text (stored in the `insight` variable) in a text box or other visual element in Power BI.

7. Test the integration

    Make sure to test the Python script in Power BI to ensure it runs successfully and returns the expected insights.

8. Save and apply changes.

    Once you're satisfied with the setup, click Apply changes in Power BI to update the report

9. Add API cost monitoring

    Keep an eye on the OpenAI API dashboard to monitor usage and costs. Make sure you have a sufficient balance to cover API calls.

10. Schedule a refresh.

    If you're using Power BI service, set up a scheduled refresh to keep your insights up to date.

    By following these steps, you should be able to integrate GPT-4 into your Power BI reports for dynamic and insightful text generation based on your financial visualizations.

11. Save the Power BI report and publish it to the Power BI service if you want to share it with others.

> **Important note**
>
> Make sure to refresh the data as needed to get updated information. The exact fields and calculations might vary based on the specific data and requirements of your trades.

By following these steps, you can create insightful Power BI visualizations for both aggressive and conservative trades, utilizing CSV files generated directly from your Python trading code.

Imagine having a seasoned cybersecurity expert by your side 24/7, sifting through the labyrinth of cyber laws and dissecting every significant breach to tell you what it means for your investment portfolio. Too good to be true? Meet HackerGPT (AI Persona)! Engineered to mimic the best in cybersecurity intelligence, this model does more than just crunch numbers—it thinks, analyzes, and even identifies investment gold mines in the rapidly evolving cyber world. Hold onto your seats; you're about to discover a game-changing tool that could redefine how you think about cybersecurity and investments.

HackerGPT (AI Persona) – monitoring and analyzing cybersecurity regulatory changes and breaches

As a highly intelligent model focused on the complex realm of cybersecurity, HackerGPT is dedicated to identifying, understanding, and analyzing regulatory changes, cybersecurity breaches, and the potential impact on various industries. The insights offered by HackerGPT could guide investment decisions in cyber insurance and cybersecurity sectors.

Here are the critical indicators that HackerGPT would evaluate:

- Regulatory landscape: Monitoring and understanding the latest regulations related to cybersecurity across various jurisdictions and industries

- Cybersecurity breaches: Analyzing the nature, scope, and impact of significant cybersecurity breaches, including those affecting AI technologies such as generative AI or LLMs

- Affected industries: Examining how regulatory changes or breaches affect specific industries such as finance, healthcare, communications, energy, technology, utilities, materials, or industrials

- Investment opportunities: Identifying potential investment avenues in the cyber insurance and cybersecurity industries based on the regulatory or cyber breach landscape

- Technology analysis: Assessing the robustness, vulnerabilities, and innovation in cybersecurity technologies

- Risk mitigation strategies: Evaluating and suggesting strategies to mitigate cyber risks, including insurance solutions

Brace yourselves for an exhilarating journey into the intersection of finance and cybersecurity, masterfully guided by the dynamic AI duo, FinGPT and HackerGPT, in the next section. FinGPT lays the financial groundwork with its data-centric prowess, while HackerGPT, fine-tuned on cybersecurity datasets, dives deep into the nuances of cyber risk and investment opportunities. The Python code showcased offers a practical way to leverage these AIs for real-time insights. Together, they form an unparalleled toolset for stakeholders navigating the complex terrains of finance and cybersecurity.

HackerGPT – reflecting traits from leading cybersecurity experts

HackerGPT is designed to emulate the expertise of cybersecurity professionals, focusing on tracking regulatory changes, analyzing cybersecurity breaches, and identifying investment opportunities in related fields.

Skills:

- Strong knowledge of cybersecurity regulations, trends, and technologies
- Proficient in analyzing complex cyber threat landscapes and regulatory environments
- Expert at identifying potential investment opportunities in cyber insurance and security sectors
- Excellent communication skills to present intricate analyses in an understandable manner

HackerGPT aims to support investors, governments, and businesses in navigating the complex world of cybersecurity. Its primary goal is to provide insights that lead to informed decisions, promote cybersecurity awareness, and identify investment opportunities.

HackerGPT conducts comprehensive evaluations, focusing on critical aspects of cybersecurity. It considers these factors within the broader context of current technological advancements, industry practices, and regulatory frameworks.

HackerGPT is analytical, objective, and innovative. It strives to present nuanced assessments while being accessible to users with varying levels of cybersecurity and investment expertise.

While HackerGPT provides detailed evaluations and recommendations, the ultimate decisions should remain the responsibility of the professionals involved. Its insights should be used to complement professional judgments and to guide, rather than dictate, investment and regulatory strategies.

Picture a world where artificial intelligence bridges the gap between Wall Street and Silicon Valley, deciphering complex cybersecurity challenges while staying ahead of market trends. Welcome to the groundbreaking fusion of FinGPT and HackerGPT! In the following pages, you will explore the alchemy of finance and cybersecurity through the lens of innovative AI. This partnership promises a revolutionary approach to real-time data analysis, investment opportunities, and cyber risk management.

HackerGPT meets FinGPT – a comprehensive guide to analyzing the financial cybersecurity landscape

Before diving into the HackerGPT AI persona, it's important to understand the backbone that powers it: the FinGPT model. As a reader interested in multi-agent systems, AI, and financial analysis, you'll find FinGPT particularly relevant.

Introduction to FinGPT – democratizing financial data

FinGPT is an open source LLM specifically designed for the finance sector. Its mission is to democratize internet-scale financial data by offering an open-sourced, data-centric framework that automates the collection and curation of real-time financial data from various online sources[1]. FinGPT outperforms similar models such as BloombergGPT in some scenarios and prioritizes data collection, cleaning, and preprocessing, which are critical steps in creating open source financial LLMs (FinLLMs)[2]. By promoting data accessibility, FinGPT lays the groundwork for open finance practices and facilitates financial research, cooperation, and innovation.

Why FinGPT matters for HackerGPT

Now you may be wondering, why is FinGPT relevant when discussing HackerGPT? Well, the answer lies in data-centricity and domain specificity. The FinGPT model underpins HackerGPT's capability to analyze and understand cybersecurity-related content, especially those with financial implications, such as cyber insurance and investment opportunities in the cybersecurity industry.

HackerGPT (FinGPT-integrated)

The HackerGPT series are LLMs fine-tuned using the LoRA method on cybersecurity and regulatory datasets. With FinGPT's data-centric approach serving as its backbone, this version excels at tasks such as cybersecurity sentiment analysis. If you're keen to delve deeper, a detailed tutorial on reproducing our experiment's results through benchmarks is underway.

By using FinGPT as part of the model architecture, HackerGPT not only gains the ability to analyze cybersecurity but also leverages real-time financial data, making it a comprehensive tool for various stakeholders in the cybersecurity and financial ecosystems.

FinGPT Source: GitHub: MIT License AI4 Foundation and Bruce Yang `https://github.com/AI4Finance-Foundation/FinGPT`

FinGPT using HackerGPT AI persona:

1. Installations

```
pip install transformers==4.30.2 peft==0.4.0
pip install sentencepiece
pip install accelerate
```

```
pip install torch
pip install peft
```

2. Run the following Python code:

```
# Import necessary libraries
from transformers import AutoModel, AutoTokenizer
from peft import PeftModel  # If you are not using PeftModel,
you can comment out this line.

# Initialize model and tokenizer paths
# Replace with the actual model paths or API keys
base_model = "THUDM/chatglm2-6b"
hacker_model = "yourusername/HackerGPT_ChatGLM2_Cyber_
Instruction_LoRA_FT"

# Load tokenizer and models
tokenizer = AutoTokenizer.from_pretrained(base_model)
model = AutoModel.from_pretrained(base_model)

# NOTE ABOUT PeftModel:
# PeftModel is a custom model class that you may be using for
fine-tuning or specific functionalities.
# Ensure it's properly installed in your environment.
# Uncomment the following line if you are using PeftModel.
# model = PeftModel.from_pretrained(model, hacker_model)

# Switch to evaluation mode (if needed, consult your model's
documentation)
model = model.eval()

# Define prompts
prompt = [
'''Instruction: What is the potential impact of this regulatory
change on the cybersecurity industry? Please provide an
analysis.
Input: New GDPR regulations have been introduced, strengthening
data protection requirements for businesses across Europe.
Answer: ''',
'''Instruction: Assess the potential investment opportunities in
the cyber insurance sector following this breach.
Input: A major cybersecurity breach has affected several
financial institutions, exposing sensitive customer data.
Answer: ''',
'''Instruction: How does this cybersecurity advancement affect
the technology industry?
```

```
Input: A leading tech company has developed advanced AI-powered
cybersecurity solutions that can detect and prevent threats in
real time.
Answer: ''',
]

# Generate responses
tokens = tokenizer(prompt, return_tensors='pt', padding=True,
max_length=512)
res = model.generate(**tokens, max_length=512)
res_sentences = [tokenizer.decode(i) for i in res]
out_text = [o.split("Answer: ")[1] for o in res_sentences]

# Display generated analyses
for analysis in out_text:
    print(analysis)
```

> **IMPORTANT NOTES**
>
> # 1. Run this code on a machine with at least a T4 GPU and high RAM for optimal performance.
>
> # 2. Remember to replace the placeholder model names with the actual model names you want to use.

This code snippet and model configuration are tailored to assess various aspects of cybersecurity, such as regulatory impacts, potential investment opportunities, and technological advancements. By analyzing the given inputs, the model can provide insightful and detailed responses relevant to the cybersecurity landscape.

Revolutionizing the future of AI-driven development with MetaGPT – the ultimate catalyst for multi-agent systems

Imagine a world where LLMs don't just churn out text but collaborate like a dream team of engineers, product managers, and architects. They operate not just as isolated geniuses but as a cohesive unit with defined roles and standard operating procedures. Welcome to the world of MetaGPT, a trailblazing force set to redefine the future of multi-agent systems and AI-driven software development.

In this thrilling deep-dive, you'll unravel the genius behind MetaGPT's architecture, the roles it's designed to play, and its transformative impact on AI-led initiatives. You'll also explore its remarkable aptitude for identifying cybersecurity investment opportunities in the financial domain.

This section is designed for professionals and researchers interested in multi-agent systems, AI-driven software development, and large language models. Also note that conventional LLM-based multi-agent systems often suffer from coherence and collaboration issues, resulting in inefficient outcomes.

What is MetaGPT?

MetaGPT is a ground-breaking technology that addresses these problems by integrating **standard operating procedures** (**SOPs**) to coordinate multi-agent systems.

The following diagram shows MetaGPT's architecture:

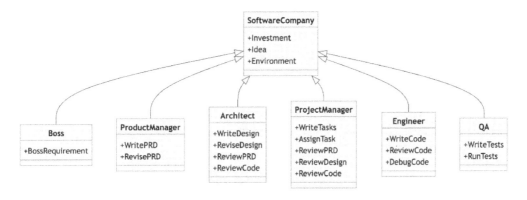

Source: MIT License; github.com/geekan/MetaGPT

Figure 8.1 – MetaGPT: software company multi-role schematic

Imagine a well-organized software company captured in a single diagram. At the center is MetaGPT, the orchestrator that takes a single-line requirement and converts it into comprehensive deliverables such as user stories, competitive analyses, and **application programming interfaces** (**APIs**). Surrounding MetaGPT are various specialized GPT agents—each symbolizing roles such as product managers, architects, project managers, and engineers. These agents collaboratively tackle complex tasks under the guidance of MetaGPT.

Role-based collaboration in MetaGPT

This section is your deep dive into how MetaGPT employs distinct agent roles—each equivalent to a product manager, architect, or engineer—to tackle intricate software projects with unprecedented efficiency. As with any pioneering technology, MetaGPT comes with its own set of challenges and limitations, such as scalability and complexity—factors that we'll dissect to give you a holistic view. Streamlining these roles into lead and support categories, we bring clarity to the financial, conceptual, and operational aspects of software development. Buckle up as we take you through the end-to-end MetaGPT workflow, from initiation and requirement gathering to the final review phase. By the end, you'll see how MetaGPT isn't just another AI model; it's a seismic shift in AI-driven software development that stands to revolutionize not just multi-agent systems but the broader landscape of technology and finance.

Agent roles

MetaGPT employs roles such as product manager, architect, and engineer to align with human software development teams. Each role has domain-specific skills and responsibilities that contribute to efficient task execution.

The following are the challenges and limitations of MetaGPT:

- **Scalability**: The model may require extensive computational resources
- **Complexity**: The adoption curve can be steep, especially for teams unfamiliar with SOPs or metaprogramming

Streamlined role classifications

To avoid redundancy, we consolidate the roles in a typical software company setup into two broad categories:

- Lead roles:

  - **Investment**: Financial management and idea validation
  - **Idea**: Conceptualization and alignment with market needs
  - **Boss (support)**: Overall project oversight

- Support roles:

  - **Product manager**: Aligns the product with market needs
  - **Architect**: Ensures maintainable and scalable design
  - **Engineer**: Code creation and debugging
  - **QA**: Quality assurance

MetaGPT workflow

The workflow consists of initiation, requirement gathering, design, task management, development, testing, and review phases, contributing to a transparent and effective development process.

In conclusion, MetaGPT signifies a monumental shift in the landscape of AI-driven software development. By mirroring human-like teamwork and implementing SOPs, it opens up exciting avenues for complex software development, positioning itself as an invaluable asset in the realm of multi-agent systems.

These are the key insights:

- Role-based collaboration enhances efficiency
- The incorporation of SOPs offers a structured approach
- MetaGPT performs exceptionally in real-world applications, as validated by case studies

Your feedback and suggestions are invaluable for the continuous improvement of MetaGPT and its broader implications in the field of AI and multi-agent systems.

Introduction to the MetaGPT model (cybersecurity investment opportunities)

The MetaGPT model is a highly advanced and customizable model that has been designed to address specific research and analysis needs within various domains. In this particular context, it's geared towards identifying investment opportunities within the US market that are influenced by cybersecurity regulatory changes or cyber breaches.

Roles and responsibilities

The model has been configured to perform various specialized roles, including these:

- **Cybersecurity regulatory research**: Understanding changes in cybersecurity laws and regulations and their impact on the market
- **Cyber breach analysis**: Investigating cyber breaches, understanding their nature, and identifying potential investment risks or opportunities
- **Investment analysis**: Evaluating investment opportunities based on insights derived from cybersecurity changes
- **Trading decisions**: Making informed buy or sell decisions on financial products
- **Portfolio management**: Overseeing and aligning the investment portfolio based on cybersecurity dynamics

Here's how it works:

- **Research phase**: The model initiates research on the given topics, either cybersecurity regulations or breaches, depending on the role. It breaks down the topic into searchable queries, collects relevant data, ranks URLs based on credibility, and summarizes the gathered information.
- **Analysis phase**: Investment analysts then evaluate the summarized information to identify trends, insights, and potential investment opportunities or risks. They correlate cybersecurity data with market behavior, investment potential, and risk factors.
- **Trading phase**: Based on the analysis, investment traders execute appropriate trading decisions, buying or selling assets that are influenced by the cybersecurity landscape.
- **Management phase**: The portfolio manager integrates all the insights to make overarching decisions about asset allocation, risk management, and alignment of the investment portfolio.

The following are its purposes and benefits:

- **Timely insights**: By automating the research and analysis process, the model provides quick insights into a dynamic field such as cybersecurity, where changes can have immediate market impacts

- **Data-driven decisions**: The model ensures that investment decisions are grounded in comprehensive research and objective analysis, minimizing bias

- **Customization**: The model can be tailored to focus on specific aspects of cybersecurity, such as regulatory changes or particular types of breaches, allowing for targeted investment strategies

- **Collaboration**: By defining different roles, the model simulates a collaborative approach, where various experts contribute their specialized knowledge to achieve a common investment goal

In conclusion, the MetaGPT model, with its diverse roles and sophisticated functions, serves as a powerful tool for investors looking to leverage the ever-changing landscape of cybersecurity. By integrating research, analysis, trading, and portfolio management, it provides a comprehensive, data-driven approach to identifying and capitalizing on investment opportunities arising from the complex interplay of cybersecurity and finance. It not only streamlines the investment process but also enhances the accuracy and relevance of investment decisions in a rapidly evolving field.

Source: GitHub: MIT License: `https://github.com/geekan/MetaGPT`.

> **Source: MetaGPT: Meta Programming for Multi-Agent Collaborative Framework Paper:**
>
> [2308.00352] MetaGPT: Meta Programming for Multi-Agent Collaborative Framework (arxiv.org) (`https://arxiv.org/abs/2308.00352`)
>
> By Sirui Hong, Xiawu Zheng, Jonathan Chen, Yuheng Cheng, Jinlin Wang, Ceyao Zhang, Zili Wang, Steven Ka Shing Yau, Zijuan Lin, Liyang Zhou, Chenyu Ran, Lingfeng Xiao, Chenglin Wu

The following is a Python code snippet:

1. Begin with the installations:

```
npm --version
sudo npm install -g @mermaid-js/mermaid-cli
git clone https://github.com/geekan/metagpt
cd metagpt
python setup.py install
```

2. Run the following Python code:

```
# Configuration: OpenAI API Key
# Open the config/key.yaml file and insert your OpenAI API key
in place of the placeholder.
# cp config/config.yaml config/key.yaml
# save and close file
```

```python
# Import Necessary Libraries
import asyncio
import json
from typing import Callable
from pydantic import parse_obj_as

# Import MetaGPT Specific Modules
from metagpt.actions import Action
from metagpt.config import CONFIG
from metagpt.logs import logger
from metagpt.tools.search_engine import SearchEngine
from metagpt.tools.web_browser_engine import WebBrowserEngine,
WebBrowserEngineType
from metagpt.utils.text import generate_prompt_chunk, reduce_
message_length

# Define Roles
# NOTE: Replace these role definitions as per your project's
needs.
RESEARCHER_ROLES = {
    'cybersecurity_regulatory_researcher': "Cybersecurity
Regulatory Researcher",
    'cyber_breach_researcher': "Cyber Breach Researcher",
    'investment_analyst': "Investment Analyst",
    'investment_trader': "Investment Trader",
    'portfolio_manager': "Portfolio Manager"
}

# Define Prompts
# NOTE: Customize these prompts to suit your project's specific
requirements.
LANG_PROMPT = "Please respond in {language}."

RESEARCH_BASE_SYSTEM = """You are a {role}. Your primary goal is
to understand and analyze \
changes in cybersecurity regulations or breaches, identify
investment opportunities, and make informed \
decisions on financial products, aligning with the current
cybersecurity landscape."""

RESEARCH_TOPIC_SYSTEM = "You are a {role}, and your research
topic is \"{topic}\"."

SEARCH_TOPIC_PROMPT = """Please provide up to 2 necessary
keywords related to your \
```

research topic on cybersecurity regulations or breaches that require Google search. \

Your response must be in JSON format, for example: ["cybersecurity regulations", "cyber breach analysis"]."""

SUMMARIZE_SEARCH_PROMPT = """### Requirements

1. The keywords related to your research topic and the search results are shown in the "Reference Information" section.

2. Provide up to {decomposition_nums} queries related to your research topic based on the search results.

3. Please respond in JSON format as follows: ["query1", "query2", "query3", ...].

Reference Information
{search}
"""

DECOMPOSITION_PROMPT = """You are a {role}, and before delving into a research topic, you break it down into several \
sub-questions. These sub-questions can be researched through online searches to gather objective opinions about the given \
topic.

The topic is: {topic}

Now, please break down the provided research topic into {decomposition_nums} search questions. You should respond with an array of \
strings in JSON format like ["question1", "question2", ...].
"""

COLLECT_AND_RANKURLS_PROMPT = """### Reference Information

1. Research Topic: "{topic}"

2. Query: "{query}"

3. The online search results: {results}

Please remove irrelevant search results that are not related to the query or research topic. Then, sort the remaining search results \
based on link credibility. If two results have equal credibility, prioritize them based on relevance. Provide the ranked \
results' indices in JSON format, like [0, 1, 3, 4, ...], without including other words.
"""

WEB_BROWSE_AND_SUMMARIZE_PROMPT = '''### Requirements

1. Utilize the text in the "Reference Information" section to respond to the question "{query}".

2. If the question cannot be directly answered using the text,

```
but the text is related to the research topic, please provide \
a comprehensive summary of the text.
3. If the text is entirely unrelated to the research topic,
please reply with a simple text "Not relevant."
4. Include all relevant factual information, numbers,
statistics, etc., if available.
### Reference Information
{content}
'''


CONDUCT_RESEARCH_PROMPT = '''### Reference Information
{content}
### Requirements
Please provide a detailed research report on the topic:
"{topic}", focusing on investment opportunities arising \
from changes in cybersecurity regulations or breaches. The
report must:
- Identify and analyze investment opportunities in the US
market.
- Detail how and when to invest, the structure for the
investment, and the implementation and exit strategies.
- Adhere to APA style guidelines and include a minimum word
count of 2,000.
- Include all source URLs in APA format at the end of the
report.
'''

# Roles
RESEARCHER_ROLES = {
    'cybersecurity_regulatory_researcher': "Cybersecurity
Regulatory Researcher",
    'cyber_breach_researcher': "Cyber Breach Researcher",
    'investment_analyst': "Investment Analyst",
    'investment_trader': "Investment Trader",
    'portfolio_manager': "Portfolio Manager"
}

# The rest of the classes and functions remain unchanged
```

Important notes:

- Execute the installation and setup commands in your terminal before running the Python script

- Don't forget to replace placeholder texts in config files and the Python script with actual data or API keys

- Ensure that MetaGPT is properly installed and configured on your machine

In this high-stakes exploration, we dissect the exhilarating yet precarious world of LLM-integrated applications. We delve into how they're transforming finance while posing emergent ethical dilemmas and security risks that simply cannot be ignored. Be prepared to journey through real-world case studies that highlight the good, the bad, and the downright ugly of LLM applications in finance, from market-beating hedge funds to costly security breaches and ethical pitfalls.

So, fasten your seatbelts because we're diving headfirst into the labyrinthine maze of issues surrounding the integration of LLMs in the financial sector. Here, you'll find eye-opening revelations that will make you question how we're using, and potentially misusing, this revolutionary technology. Are you ready to confront the challenges and complexities? Let's get started!

Compromising real-world LLM-integrated applications with indirect prompt injection

Language models integrated into applications (LLMs), such as ChatGPT, are at the forefront of technological innovation, especially in finance, trading, and investment. However, they pose emerging risks, both ethical and security-related, that warrant immediate attention:

1. Transformative applications in finance:

   LLMs have transformed various aspects of financial operations, from AI-based financial predictions to rendering personalized Power BI visualizations.

   Case study: Hedge fund profits A hedge fund leveraging ChatGPT for market sentiment analysis successfully navigated a volatile market, realizing a 20% increase in profits.

2. Ethical maze:

   LLMs come with ethical baggage, from safety concerns to misinformation and regulatory challenges, affecting various platforms including Bing Chat and Microsoft 365 Copilot.

   Case study: Regulatory mishap An investment firm failed to comply with local regulations while using an LLM, causing legal and reputational fallout.

3. The Achilles Heel: indirect prompt injection:

   The discovery of vulnerabilities such as indirect prompt injection adds another layer of complexity to LLM security. This vulnerability allows attackers to send misleading prompts remotely, making it a critical area for immediate remediation.

   Case study: The costly alert A hacker exploited the indirect prompt injection loophole to send false trading alerts, leading traders to make poor investment decisions and incur substantial losses.

4. Deception potential: real and experimental evidence:

   Both synthetic experiments and real-world testing reveal LLMs can be easily misled into making false or damaging decisions.

Case study: The unauthorized transaction A banking application with an LLM feature was tricked into approving unauthorized transactions, showing the real-world impact of these vulnerabilities.

5. The evolving threat landscape:

As LLMs become more complex, new forms of vulnerabilities, beyond indirect prompt injection, are emerging. Continuous research and vigilance are vital.

Case study: Phishing with AI A new form of AI-aided phishing scams was highlighted at a recent conference, warning the industry of evolving attack vectors.

Future-proofing LLMs – solutions on the horizon

Given the escalating risks, especially indirect prompt injection, various promising mitigation methods are being explored:

- **AI-guided security protocols**: Real-time monitoring for immediate threat detection and mitigation
- **Blockchain-based verification**: Ensuring the integrity of transactions and data
- **Quantum encryption**: Revolutionary methods for unbreakable data encryption
- **Behavioral analytics and biometrics**: Customized, robust authentication mechanisms
- **Regulatory compliance automation**: Automated checks to ensure compliance with global standards

The following are examples of solutions in action:

- A leading bank is using AI-guided security protocols for real-time threat identification
- A fintech start-up has made strides in implementing quantum encryption for ultra-safe transactions

The incorporation of LLMs in the financial sector is an exciting yet perilous journey. As we delve deeper into this technology, it becomes essential to address the myriad of challenges, including indirect prompt injection, that come with it. A balanced approach, grounded in ethical consideration and technological innovation, will help us harness LLMs securely and responsibly.

Imagine a world where seeing is no longer believing. The images and videos that flood your screen are so hyper-realistic, so impeccably crafted, that they blur the line between truth and fabrication. Welcome to the unsettling, yet mesmerizing domain of deepfakes—artificial intelligence's most compelling yet cautionary tale. With the power to revolutionize media, entertainment, and even social justice, deepfakes equally hold a dark mirror to the societal, ethical, and financial ramifications that we've only just begun to fathom.

Armed with data visualization and AI tools, we will uncover, analyze, and confront the existential challenges that deepfakes present to our understanding of reality itself.

You're about to step into a world where nothing is what it seems and where the quest for truth becomes a high-stakes gamble against advanced algorithms and AI. Ready to face the disturbingly fluid borders of fact and fiction? Buckle up and let's dive into the intricate complexities and unexpected vulnerabilities of our AI-powered future.

> **Source**
>
> [2302.12173] Not what you've signed up for: Compromising Real-World LLM-Integrated Applications with Indirect Prompt Injection (arxiv.org)
>
> By Kai Greshake, Sahar Abdelnabi, Shailesh Mishra, Christoph Endres, Thorsten Holz, Mario Fritz

Deepfakes and their multi-faceted impact – a closer look with AI and data visualization

Deepfakes, propelled by advancements in artificial intelligence, can create hyper-realistic yet wholly fabricated videos and images. These deepfakes not only challenge our perception of reality but also pose significant risks on individual, corporate, and governmental levels.

Here's a technical overview. Deepfakes employ neural networks trained on thousands of photographs and voice samples to generate incredibly lifelike fake content. With the advent of new algorithms, the complexity extends to whole-head synthesis, joint audiovisual synthesis, and even full-body synthesis.

Ethical and legal aspects:

- Deepfakes initially gained notoriety for their use in malicious activities, ranging from personal defamation to political manipulation. The legal and ethical considerations associated with these technologies are manifold, given their potential for social and individual harm.

The following are their societal impacts:

- Deepfake content can cause irreparable damage to individuals, from emotional distress to legal repercussions
- For companies, fraudulent videos can manipulate stock prices and ruin reputations within minutes
- Deepfakes can lead to political unrest and international conflicts

The following are their financial and cybersecurity implications:

- Corporate deepfakes can lead to deceptive financial instructions, causing significant monetary losses
- The mass dissemination of deepfake content can overload digital infrastructures, causing cybersecurity vulnerabilities

Protection through generative AI tools:

- **AI detection**: Advanced AI models can identify even the subtlest alterations, flagging them for further investigation

- **Blockchain watermarks**: Authentic content can be watermarked and verified through blockchain technology

- **Educational outreach**: AI-driven tools such as ChatGPT can inform and educate the public about the risks associated with deepfakes

1. **Feedback loops for continuous improvement**

2. As AI models flag suspicious content, the results can be reviewed by human experts for accuracy. This review process feeds back into the machine learning model, helping to train it for improved performance in future deepfake detection efforts.

Currently, Microsoft and other tech giants are developing deepfake detection tools that analyze visual and auditory content, providing a likelihood score of manipulation.

As deepfake technology becomes increasingly sophisticated, our methods of identification and defense must evolve. By incorporating machine learning models and data visualization techniques, we can better understand the deepfake landscape and devise more effective countermeasures.

Picture yourself on a trading floor. Numbers flicker in real-time on screens, brokers shout over phones, and the tension is palpable. But what if I told you that the real powerhouses in this chaotic scene aren't humans but algorithms? Welcome to the future of finance—a landscape increasingly shaped by AI.

AI is more than just a buzzword; it's a transformative force that's rewriting the rules of finance, from stock recommendations to fraud detection. While it may sound complex, understanding AI is not an elite club reserved for tech moguls or Wall Street tycoons. This guide is your passport to the brave new world of AI in finance, whether you're a novice investor, a tech enthusiast, or a seasoned finance professional.

We're going to decode AI in terms that matter to you. Our journey will navigate through ethical sand traps and algorithmic pitfalls, laying out the game-changing opportunities and challenges that AI presents. Imagine having a personal finance advisor who never sleeps, a risk manager who learns from every transaction, or even a digital watchdog who guards against fraud—that's the promise and the cautionary tale of AI in finance.

So, why should you care? Because AI is not just shaping the future; it's accelerating it. And in a world where change is the only constant, your ability to adapt and understand this groundbreaking technology is your ultimate edge. Get ready to demystify the algorithms, dissect real-world case studies, and take actionable steps to not just survive but to thrive in this AI-driven financial frontier.

As we draw the curtains on this transformative journey through the pulsating world of AI and finance, we arrive at an exhilarating crescendo: AI literacy—your passport to the future. Whether you're a curious beginner, a tech-savvy enthusiast, or a financial expert, this final section is your ultimate guide to claiming your stake in the AI revolution. We'll chart a roadmap that transcends the limitations and ethical constraints of AI, touching on practical case studies such as Kount that exemplify AI's game-changing potential in finance. With a wealth of resources ranging from formal education and certifications to community involvement and DIY projects, we aim to equip you with the tools you need for a lifetime of AI mastery. As we reach the end of this narrative, remember that the future is not a passive landscape that we merely inherit but an exhilarating frontier that we actively construct. With the insights and skills you've gained, you're not just a spectator—you're a trailblazer in the unfolding saga of AI and finance.

AI literacy – your passport to the future

From AI's transformative impact to its practical applications in finance, this guide is for readers from all walks of life.

Beginners can think of AI as a personalized assistant. A good starting point would be installing financial apps such as Robinhood that use AI for personalized stock recommendations.

Tech enthusiasts can start by exploring open source machine learning libraries such as TensorFlow. Experiment with existing finance-focused AI projects on GitHub.

If you're a finance pro, AI can help you automate risk assessment. Platforms such as DataRobot offer AI services tailored to financial data analysis.

Navigating AI's landscape – considerations and guidelines

- **Limitations of AI**: Be critical of AI's financial suggestions. Use platforms that allow you to see the algorithm's confidence score, such as Quantopian.
- **Ethical usage**: Look for platforms that are GDPR compliant or follow ethical AI guidelines when dealing with financial data.

Consider the following case study. Kount is a platform that uses AI to prevent fraud in financial transactions. Imagine a security guard who not only knows every trick in the book but also learns new ones as they emerge; that's what Kount's adaptive AI does. It continuously learns from data to assess the risk associated with each transaction. By doing so, it minimizes the instances where legitimate transactions are incorrectly flagged as fraudulent (known as false declines), thus saving businesses from revenue loss and enhancing customer trust.

This case study shows that AI, when used responsibly and ethically, can offer substantial benefits in the finance sector, making operations more secure and efficient.

The following is your roadmap to AI mastery:

- **Empower yourself**: Follow introductory courses on platforms such as Coursera, such as *AI For Everyone* by Andrew Ng

- **Inclusive future**: Get involved in initiatives such as AI4ALL, aiming for a more diverse future in AI

The following are the essentials of AI in finance:

- Tools such as AlphaSense use AI to scan, search, and analyze financial documents, offering unprecedented efficiency

- For trading, consider platforms, such as Alpaca, that offer AI-driven trading APIs. For financial visualization, Power BI's integration with Azure AI offers advanced analytics features

- Start with beginner-friendly platforms such as TradeStation, which has in-built algorithmic trading features

The following is a guide to lifelong learning in AI for finance:

- For formal education, courses such as MIT's *AI in Finance* offer deep dives into specific applications of AI in financial markets

- In terms of online courses, Udacity's *AI for Trading* is a comprehensive nano-degree focusing on AI in finance

- Certifications such as IBM's AI for Financial Services certification can add a credibility badge to your skillset

- Join online forums such as Reddit's r/algotrading to stay up to date with the latest in AI finance tech

- Regularly participate in webinars from Financial Times or KDNuggets that focus on AI in finance

- Books such as *Machine Learning for Finance* by Jannes Klaas offer both theory and practical case studies

- Platforms such as Kaggle host challenges that can give you hands-on experience in solving finance-based AI problems

- For your own projects, use platforms such as QuantConnect to test your own trading algorithms using their free data and cloud resources

Your journey into AI in finance is an ongoing process. This guide aims to be a comprehensive starting point. Always remember, AI is a tool, not a silver bullet. Your judgment remains your most important asset. With these resources and guidelines, you're now better equipped to navigate, innovate, and thrive in the evolving landscape of AI in finance.

As we wrap up this chapter and this journey, remember: the future isn't something that just happens to us – it's something we build. And with the right knowledge and tools, including AI literacy, we are all the architects of tomorrow. So, whether you're a seasoned tech guru, a finance whiz, or someone just dipping their toes into the world of AI, you're now armed with the knowledge to navigate, innovate, and thrive in this new era.

Summary

In this chapter, we've journeyed through the most cutting-edge developments at the intersection of AI and finance in the cybersecurity realm. You've learned about GPT-4's potential and perils in the financial sphere, understood the cloud-based prowess of CrowdStrike, and accelerated your financial acumen through both aggressive and conservative trade strategies, brought to life with compelling Power BI visualizations. We introduced you to HackerGPT as a lens through which to view cybersecurity's financial ramifications and explored how FinGPT is revolutionizing financial analysis. We dove deep into MetaGPT's multi-agent orchestration for game-changing financial insights. You've also gained valuable ethical perspectives on the use of indirect prompt injections in LLMs, as well as the financial risks and opportunities that come with the rise of deepfakes.

And now, as we close the final chapter of this incredible journey, let's part with resounding words of empowerment: you're no longer just a passenger on the ship of technological change, you're at the helm, steering through the turbulent yet exhilarating waters of AI and finance. With the insights and tools gained from this book, you're not just prepared for the future—you're equipped to build it. Go forth with confidence, wisdom, and an unquenchable thirst for innovation. The future awaits your imprint; make it a masterpiece!

Index

www.packtpub.com

Subscribe to our online digital library for full access to over 7,000 books and videos, as well as industry leading tools to help you plan your personal development and advance your career. For more information, please visit our website.

Why subscribe?

- Spend less time learning and more time coding with practical eBooks and Videos from over 4,000 industry professionals

- Improve your learning with Skill Plans built especially for you

- Get a free eBook or video every month

- Fully searchable for easy access to vital information

- Copy and paste, print, and bookmark content

Did you know that Packt offers eBook versions of every book published, with PDF and ePub files available? You can upgrade to the eBook version at packtpub.com and as a print book customer, you are entitled to a discount on the eBook copy. Get in touch with us at customercare@packtpub.com for more details.

At www.packtpub.com, you can also read a collection of free technical articles, sign up for a range of free newsletters, and receive exclusive discounts and offers on Packt books and eBooks.

Other Books You May Enjoy

If you enjoyed this book, you may be interested in these other books by Packt:

Modern Generative AI with ChatGPT and OpenAI Models

Valentina Alto

ISBN: 978-1-80512-333-0

- Understand generative AI concepts from basic to intermediate level
- Focus on the GPT architecture for generative AI models
- Maximize ChatGPT's value with an effective prompt design
- Explore applications and use cases of ChatGPT
- Use OpenAI models and features via API calls
- Build and deploy generative AI systems with Python
- Leverage Azure infrastructure for enterprise-level use cases
- Ensure responsible AI and ethics in generative AI systems

Power BI Machine Learning and OpenAI

Greg Beaumont

ISBN: 978-1-83763-615-0

- Discover best practices for implementing AI and ML capabilities in Power BI using OpenAI
- Understand how to integrate OpenAI and cognitive services into Power BI
- Explore how to build a SaaS auto ML model within Power BI
- Gain an understanding of R/Python integration with Power BI
- Enhance data visualizations for ML feature discovery
- Discover how to improve existing solutions and workloads using AI and ML capabilities in Power BI with OpenAI
- Acquire tips and tricks for successfully using AI and ML capabilities in Power BI using OpenAI

Packt is searching for authors like you

If you're interested in becoming an author for Packt, please visit authors.packtpub.com and apply today. We have worked with thousands of developers and tech professionals, just like you, to help them share their insight with the global tech community. You can make a general application, apply for a specific hot topic that we are recruiting an author for, or submit your own idea.

Share Your Thoughts

Now you've finished *The Future of Finance with ChatGPT and Power BI*, we'd love to hear your thoughts! Scan the QR code below to go straight to the Amazon review page for this book and share your feedback or leave a review on the site that you purchased it from.

https://packt.link/r/1-805-12109-X

Your review is important to us and the tech community and will help us make sure we're delivering excellent quality content.

Download a free PDF copy of this book

Thanks for purchasing this book!

Do you like to read on the go but are unable to carry your print books everywhere? Is your eBook purchase not compatible with the device of your choice?

Don't worry, now with every Packt book you get a DRM-free PDF version of that book at no cost.

Read anywhere, any place, on any device. Search, copy, and paste code from your favorite technical books directly into your application.

The perks don't stop there, you can get exclusive access to discounts, newsletters, and great free content in your inbox daily

Follow these simple steps to get the benefits:

1. Scan the QR code or visit the link below

https://packt.link/free-ebook/9781805123347

2. Submit your proof of purchase
3. That's it! We'll send your free PDF and other benefits to your email directly

www.ingramcontent.com/pod-product-compliance
Lightning Source LLC
LaVergne TN
LVHW081512050326
832903LV00025B/1457